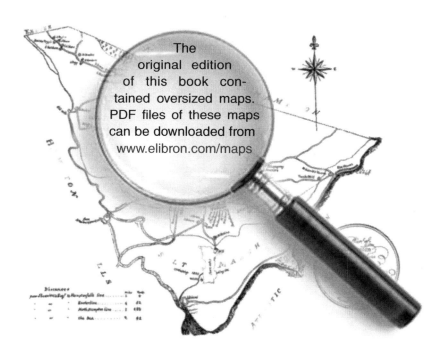

BEHÂ ED-DÎN

THE LIFE

OF

SALADIN

Elibron Classics
www.elibron.com

THE LIFE

OF

SALADIN.

BY

BEHÂ ED-DÎN

(1137—1193 A.D.).

PUBLISHED BY THE
COMMITTEE OF THE PALESTINE EXPLORATION FUND,
24, HANOVER SQUARE, LONDON.
1897.

'SALADIN';

OR,

WHAT BEFELL SULTAN YÛSUF

(*SALÂH ED-DÎN*).

(1137—1193 A.D.)

COMPOSED BY THE LEARNED

IMÂM, GRAND KÂDI OF THE MOSLEMS,

BEHÂ ED-DÎN ABU EL-MEHÂSAN YÛSUF,

IBN RÂFI, IBN TEMÎM, GENERALLY KNOWN BY THE SURNAME OF IBN SHEDDÂD,
KÂDI OF THE FORTIFIED CITY OF ALEPPO.

WITH THE PERMISSION OF

The (Khalif) Commander of the Faithful.

May God hear his prayers, and award him Paradise for his resting-place and abode!

CONTENTS.

PART I.

BIRTH OF SALÂH ED-DÎN, HIS GOOD QUALITIES, HIS CHARACTER,
AND NATURAL DISPOSITION.

PART II.

IN WHICH ARE SET FORTH THE CHANGES OF FORTUNE EXPERI-
ENCED BY THE SULTAN, AND THE HISTORY OF HIS CON-
QUESTS.

MAPS, ETC.

PREFACE.

THE present volume closes the series of translations issued by the Palestine Pilgrims' Text Society, and I am glad to take this opportunity of conveying the thanks of the Committee to those gentlemen who have so kindly and readily given their assistance in translating, annotating, and editing the works. Without the cordial assistance of those gentlemen it would not have been possible to carry out the original programme of the Society, and place within the reach of English readers the more important of the records which the early and mediæval pilgrims have left of their pilgrimages to Jerusalem and the Holy Land.

The Committee and the Society are also deeply indebted to the Hon. Secretary and Treasurer, who has done so much to further the interests of the work.

C. W. WILSON.

May, 1897.

INTRODUCTION.

THE author of the Life of Salâh ed-Dîn (Saladin), Abû el-Mehâsan Yûsuf ibn-Râfî ibn-Temîm el-Asadi, is better known by his surname, Behâ ed-Dîn (Bohadin), 'lustre of religion.' He was brought up by his maternal uncles, the Beni Sheddâd, whence he is often called Ibn Sheddâd, and he became a legist of the Shâfite sect, a noted traditionist, and the Kâdi of Aleppo. He was born on March 5, 1145, at Mosul, and there learnt the Kurân under the celebrated *hâfiz* (traditionist) Abû Bekr Yahya Ibn S'adûn of Cordova. Towards the end of 1170 he went to Baghdad and acted as assistant master in the Nizâmiya College. In 1174 he returned to Mosul and became professor in the college founded by Kemal ed-Dîn Abû el-Fadl Muhammad.

In 1188 Behâ ed-Dîn made the pilgrimage to Mecca, and afterwards that to Jerusalem and Hebron. He then went to Damascus, and whilst he was staying there Salâh ed-Dîn, who had heard of his arrival, sent for him. He visited the Sultan, who was then besieging Kaukab, and was offered, but refused, the chief professorship at the College of Menâzil el-Izz at Old Cairo. Afterwards, when the Sultan was encamped on the plain before Hisn el-Akrad (Castle of the Kurds), he paid him another visit, and on this occasion presented him with a book on the merit of waging war against the infidels. Later he entered the service of Salâh ed-Dîn, and was appointed *Kâdi el-Askar* (Kâdi of the Army), and *hâkim* (magistrate with full executive power) of Jerusalem. He accompanied Salâh ed-Dîn during his later campaigns, and, on the Sultan's death, went to Aleppo to establish harmony amongst his sons. Ez-Zâher, the Prince of Aleppo, sent him to his brother el-Azîz, who ruled at Cairo, and on his return made him Kâdi of Aleppo.

Behâ ed-Dîn was also adminstrator of the Wakfs, Vizir, and privy counsellor to ez-Zâher. He reorganized the colleges at Aleppo, and provided them with good teachers ; and, out of the *ikta* (State revenue) granted to him, he founded a college and mosque near the Irak Gate, opposite the College of Nûr ed-Dîn. Close to the college he also founded a school for teaching the 'Traditions' of the Prophet. When ez-Zâher died he was succeeded by his son el-Melek el-Azîz Abu el-Muzaffer Muhammad, who, being still a child, remained under the care of the eunuch Shibâb ed-Dîn Abû Saîd Toghrul, an Armenian by birth, who acted as his *atabeg* (guardian) and administered the Principality under Behâ ed-Dîn.

The fame of Behâ ed-Dîn attracted many visitors to Aleppo, and legists especially were always warmly welcomed. In his old age the learned Kâdi taught the ' Traditions ' in his own house, to which he had added a sheltered alcove where he sat winter and summer. After the Friday prayers people went to his house to hear him repeat the ' Traditions,' and to enjoy his conversation, which was agreeable, and chiefly turned on literature. Ibn Khallikân gives a touching picture of his failing strength in his later years. As he frequently had a bad cough he rarely left his alcove, and in winter he always had beside him a large brasier of charcoal. He constantly wore a coat lined with furs of Bortâs (north of the Caspian) and a number of tunics, and sat on a very soft cushion placed on a pile of carpets. Old age had made him 'as weak as a little bird just hatched,' and his legs ' had so little flesh on them that they were like thin sticks.' It was with the greatest pain and difficulty that he was able to move in order to say his prayers. Except in the height of summer he never prayed in the mosque, and even then, when with extreme difficulty he stood up to pray, he was always ready to fall.

In November, 1231, at the advanced age of eighty-six, he was sent to Egypt to bring back the daughter of el-Melek el-Kâmil, who had been betrothed to el-Azîz. He returned in June, 1232, to find that Toghrul had been dismissed, and that el-Azîz had taken the management of affairs into his own hands. A younger generation had grown up, and Behâ ed-Dîn was no longer consulted on questions of state. The old Kâdi gradually became so feeble that he could not recognise his friends, and, on November 8, 1234, he died, in his ninetieth year, leaving his house as a *Khangâh* (monastery) to the Sûfis.

Salâh ed-Dîn (Saladin) was the son of Ayûb, and grandson of Shâdi, a Rawâdiya Kurd of the great Hadâniya tribe. He was thus of Kurd descent. Several of his bravest warriors and most trusted counsellors were Kurds, and during his reign, and that of his brother el-'Âdel, Kurds ruled in Armenia, Mesopotamia, Syria, Palestine, Egypt, and Arabia.

Shâdi lived near Tovin, apparently at the village of Ajdânakân, where Ayûb is said to have been born. After the birth of his two sons, Ayûb and Shîrkûh, he left the Armenian plateau, and proceeded first to Baghdad and then to Tekrît, where he settled, and afterwards died.

His sons entered the service of Mujâhid ed-Dîn Bihrûz, a Greek slave, who governed the province of Irak for the Seljûk Sultan Masûd, and had been granted Tekrît as an appanage. Bihrûz appointed Ayûb Governor of Tekrît, and here Salâh ed-Dîn was born. The action of Ayûb in assisting Zenghi to cross the Tigris, when he was marching on Baghdad, greatly displeased Bihrûz, and some time afterwards the two brothers were expelled from the city. They at once entered the service of Zenghi, then Lord of Mosul, and, on the capture of Ba'albek, Ayûb was appointed Governor of that place.

After the murder of Zenghi, Ayûb was attacked by the Seljûk, Mujîr ed-Dîn Abek, who then ruled at Damascus, and not receiving any support from Mosul, surrendered, and became one of the chief Emirs of Damascus. On Zenghi's death Shîrkûh entered the service of his son, Nûr ed-Dîn, then Lord of Aleppo, who made him commander of the army, and gave him Emessa and other cities as an appanage. When Nûr ed-Dîn took Damascus he attached Ayûb and Salâh ed-Dîn to his person, and the latter remained in attendance, learning much from his over-lord, until he accompanied his uncle, Shîrkûh, on his first expedition to Egypt. The further history of Salâh ed-Dîn is fully related by his biographer, and the accompanying genealogical tables will explain the relationship of the most important personages mentioned in the narrative.

The translation, originally made from the French edition published in the ' Recueil des histor. d. Croisades, auteurs Arabes, iii., 1-393,' has been carefully revised and compared with the edition of Schultens by Lieut.-Colonel Conder, R.E., and in several passages, especially those relating to the death of Salâh ed-Dîn, the rendering has been very materially altered. The notes with the initial W are by the Editor ; all other notes are by Lieut.-Colonel Conder, R.E., who has very kindly revised all the proofs, and thrown light on many doubtful points.

The biographical notices in the notes are principally from Ibn Khallikân's Biographical Dictionary, translated by Baron MacGuckin de Slane for the Oriental Translation Fund.

C. W. W.

No. I.

SHÁDI.

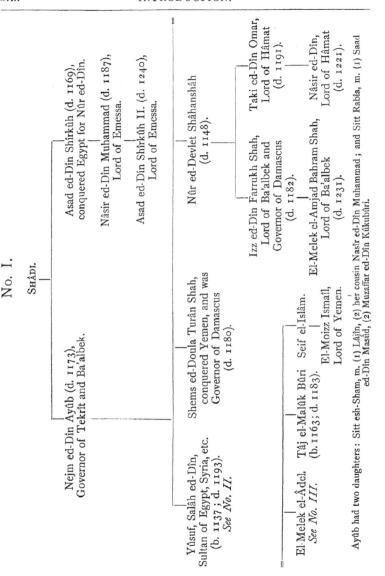

Nejm ed-Dín Ayúb (d. 1173), Governor of Tekrít and Ba'albek.

Yúsuf, Saláh ed-Dín, Sultan of Egypt, Syria, etc. (b. 1137; d. 1193). *See No. II.*

El-Melek el-Ádel. *See No. III.*

Táj el-Malúk Búri (b. 1163; d. 1183).

Seif el-Islám.

El-Moïzz Ismaíl, Lord of Yemen.

Shems ed-Doula Turán Shah, conquered Yemen, and was Governor of Damascus (d. 1180).

Asad ed-Dín Shírkúh (d. 1169), conquered Egypt for Núr ed-Dín.

Násir ed-Dín Muhammad (d. 1187), Lord of Emessa.

Asad ed-Dín Shírkúh II. (d. 1240), Lord of Emessa.

Núr ed-Devlet Sháhansháh (d. 1148).

Izz ed-Dín Farrukh Shah, Lord of Ba'albek and Governor of Damascus (d. 1182).

El-Melek el-Amjad Bahram Shah, Lord of Ba'albek (d. 1231).

Taki ed-Dín Omar, Lord of Hámat (d. 1191).

Násir ed-Dín, Lord of Hámat (d. 1221).

Ayúb had two daughters: Sitt esh-Sham, m. (1) Lájín, (2) her cousin Nasír ed-Dín Muhammad; and Sitt Rabía, m. (1) Saad ed-Dín Masúd, (2) Muzaffar ed-Dín Kúkubúri.

No. II.

SULTAN YÚSUF SALÂH ED-DÍN
(b. 1137; d. 1193).

El-Melek el-Afdal, Lord of Damascus (b. 1171; d. 1225).

El-Melek el-Azíz, Sultan of Egypt (b. 1172; d. 1198).

El-Melek el-Mansûr, Sultan of Egypt.

El-Melek ez-Zâher, Lord of Aleppo (b. 1173; d. 1216).

El-Melek el-Azíz, Lord of Aleppo (b. 1214; d. 1236).

El-Melek es-Sâlih, Lord of 'Ain Tâb (b. 1203; d. 1253).

El-Melek ez-Zafir (b. 1173; d. 1230).

No. III.

EL-MELEK EL-ÂDEL,
Governor of Egypt, Aleppo, etc.,
Later Sultan of Egypt, Arabia, Syria, Mesopotamia, etc.
(b. 1145; d. 1218).

El-Melek el-Kâmil, Sultan of Egypt (b. 1180; d. 1238.)

El-Melek el-Moazzem, Lord of Damascus.

El-Melek en-Nâsir, Salâh ed-Dín.

El-Fâiz (d. 1219).

El-Ashraf, Lord of Mesopotamia (b. 1182; d. 1237).

El-Auhad, Lord of Armenia (d. 1212).

No. IV.

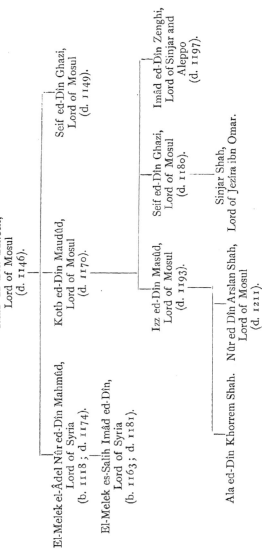

IMÁD ED-DÍN ZENGHI,
Lord of Mosul
(d. 1146).

El-Melek el-Ádel Núr ed-Dín Mahmúd,
Lord of Syria
(b. 1118 ; d. 1174).

El-Melek es-Salih Imád ed-Dín,
Lord of Syria
(b. 1163; d. 1181).

Kotb ed-Dín Maudúd,
Lord of Mosul
(d. 1170).

Seif ed-Dín Ghazi,
Lord of Mosul
(d. 1149).

Izz ed-Dín Masúd,
Lord of Mosul
(d. 1193).

Ala ed-Dín Khorrem Shah.   Núr ed Dín Arslan Shah,
Lord of Mosul
(d. 1211).

Seif ed-Dín Ghazi,
Lord of Mosul
(d. 1180).

Sinjar Shah,
Lord of Jezíra ibn Omar.

Imád ed-Dín Zenghi,
Lord of Sinjar and
Aleppo
(d. 1197).

WHAT BEFELL SULTAN YÛSUF

PREFACE.

In the name of God, the merciful, the compassionate !

PRAISE be to God, who has given us Islâm, who has led us to a faith so exalted, and who, in His mercy, has granted us our Prophet (Muhammad) to intercede for us. Praise be to Him, who has ordered the lives of past generations for the instruction of thinking men, and has allowed the vicissitudes of this life to be a sure proof of the instability of all created things. By this means He desires to prevent the favourite of fortune from suffering himself to be led astray by prosperity, and to preserve from despair the man who has become a plaything in the hands of adversity.

I bear witness that there is but one God, and there is none like Him. This is a faith which heals souls perishing with thirst (for the truth). I also testify that Muhammad is His servant and messenger, he who has opened the doors of right living to those who use the keys of submission and resignation. May God shed blessings unending upon him and his family, as long as this world endures.

Let us pass to our subject, and write of that Prince strong to aid (*el-Melek en-Nâsr*), who re-established the doctrine of the true faith, struck to earth the worshippers of the Cross,

and raised the standard of justice and benevolence ; he
who was the prosperity (*Salâh*) of the world and of the
faith (*ed-Dîn*), the Sultan of Islâm and of the Moslems, the
warrior who delivered the Holy City from the hands of the
polytheists, the servant (*Khâdim*) of the two Sanctuaries
(Mecca and Jerusalem), Abu el-Mozaffer Yûsuf, son of
Ayûb, and grandson of Shâdhi. May God shed on his tomb
the dew of His approval, and allow him to taste, in the
abode of mercy, all the sweetness of the faith.   Having
seen the goodly days of the reign of our Lord the Sultan,
it was possible for me to believe certain traditions of the
men of olden time that are commonly considered im-
probable and fictitious, and to accept as true, anecdotes
of noble and benevolent men.   I was able to credit what
is told us of the lives of brave warriors, because I had
witnessed the noble deeds of certain Memlûks, deeds of
which the truth has been called in question.   With my
own eyes I had seen men who fought in God's cause display a hardihood in the midst of danger which would
surpass belief.   I myself had seen wonderful deeds which
heart and brain could hardly conceive ; actions so marvellous that the tongue would be powerless to picture them,
and the hand to describe them on paper.   Nevertheless,
these deeds are of such a nature that he who knows them
cannot keep them concealed, and he who has witnessed
them feels compelled to pass on to others a narrative of the
wonders he has seen.

Overwhelmed by the favours of Salâh ed-Din, honoured
by his friendship and attached to his service, I felt obliged,
both by gratitude and duty, to relate to the world all that
I knew and all that I had learnt of his noble character and
his heroic actions.   But I have thought it right to confine
myself to those things which I have seen with my own
eyes, and to such information from others as appeared to

be of indisputable authority. Although this be but a part of the whole, a little gathered from much, this part will be sufficient to enable all to judge of the rest, just as after the appearance of dawn the rays of light announce the approach of the sun.

I have called this work 'What befell Sultan Yûsuf,' and have divided it into two parts. The first deals with his birth and youth, his noble character, his sweet disposition, and those natural qualities which so distinguished him, and which are so acceptable in the sight of God's law. In the second part I shall describe, in chronological order, the vicissitudes of his life, his wars, and his conquests, to the hour of his death. May God have mercy on him!

I pray that God may preserve me from the errors to which tongue and pen are liable, and hinder my spirit from taking a path wherein my foot must stumble. God will suffice me : He is the best of all guardians.

PART I.

Birth of Salâh ed-Dîn, his Good Qualities, his Character, and Natural Disposition.

I learn from the lips of certain persons worthy of credence, who had made inquiries concerning the date of the birth of Salâh ed-Dîn, in order to construct the horoscope of this prince according to the rules of astrology, that he was born in the course of the year 532 (A.D. 1137-1138), in the citadel of Tekrît, where his father, Ayûb, son of Shâdhi, discharged his duties as Governor. Ayûb was an honourable, generous, and good man. He was born at Dovîn.[1] Circumstances afterwards obliged him to leave Tekrît,[2] and he betook himself to Mosul, taking his son with him. Here he remained until his son had grown up. Ayûb and his brother, Asad ed-Dîn Shîrkûh, were held in high esteem by the Atabeg Zenghi (Prince of Mosul). Proceeding afterwards into Syria, Ayûb obtained the government of B'albek, and dwelt for some time in that place. His son, who had accompanied him, entered upon his first service under his direction. Brought up in his

[1] *Dovîn* (*Tovin*, Armenian *Devin*) near Erivan in Trans-Caucasia.

[2] *Tekrît*, the ancient *Birtha*, is situated on the right bank of the Tigris, between Mosul and Baghdad. The events to which our author here alludes are related by Ibn el-Athîr in his 'History of the Atabegs of Mosul.'

father's bosom, and nourished on the lofty principles which
his father set before him, he soon showed signs of the good
fortune which was always to accompany him, and gave
evidence of a spirit born to command. El-Melek el-'Adel
Nûr ed-Dîn Mahmûd, son of Zenghî, bestowed upon him
advancement, and, as a mark of his confidence and high
esteem, attached him to his service, and admitted him to the
number of his friends. The higher Salâh ed-Dîn rose in
degree, the more apparent became qualities which entitled
him to a still more exalted rank. This state of things
continued until his uncle, Asad ed-Dîn Shîrkûh, started
upon the Egyptian expedition. Later, in a more suitable
place, we will give a detailed account of this expedition,
with all particulars.

CHAPTER I.

WHAT I HAVE OBSERVED OF SALÂH ED-DÎN'S ATTACH-
MENT TO THE PRINCIPLES OF RELIGION, AND HIS
RESPECT FOR EVERY PART OF THE HOLY LAW.

IN our collection of authentic traditions stands the following saying of the Holy Prophet : 'Islâm is built upon five
columns : confession of the unity of God, the regular performance of prayer, payment of the tenth (tithe) in charity,
the fast of the month Ramadân, and pilgrimage to the
Holy House of God (Mecca).'

Salâh ed-Dîn—may God be merciful to him !—truly
believed in the doctrines of the faith, and often recited
prayers in praise of God. He had accepted the dogmas
of religion upon demonstrable proofs, the result of his
conversations with the most learned doctors and the most
eminent jurisconsults. In these arguments he acquired

knowledge that enabled him to speak to the purpose when a discussion took place in his presence, although he did not employ the technical language of the lawyers. These conversations confirmed him in a true faith, which remained undisturbed by any doubt, and, in his case, prevented the arrow of speculation from overshooting the mark, and striking at last on doubt and infidelity.

The learned doctor Kotb ed-Dîn[1] en-Nisabûri[2] had composed an exposition of Islâm (*akîda*) for the benefit of this prince, containing all that was necessary for him to know. As he was much pleased with this treatise, he made his younger sons learn it by heart, so that good doctrine might be established in their souls from their tenderest years. I have myself seen him take this book and read it aloud to his children, after they had committed its contents to memory.

As to prayer, he was always regular in his attendance at the public service (on Fridays), and he said one day that for several years he had never failed in this duty. When he was ill, he used to send for the Imâm alone, and forcing himself to keep on his feet, would recite the Friday

[1] Abu el Ma'ali Mas'ûd Ibn Muhammad, surnamed Kotb ed-Dîn, 'pivot of the faith,' was born in the district of *Nishapûr*. He studied law at Nishapûr and Merv, and was a professor in the college founded by Nûr ed-Dîn at Aleppo. He prepared for Salâh ed-Dîn an *akîda*, or exposition of Islâm, which contained all necessary information on religious matters. He died at Damascus in A.D. 1183 (Ibn Khallikan, III. 351).—W.

[2] *Nisabûr* (*Nishapûr*) was, according to tradition, founded by Shahpûr (Sapor); and, under the Sassanians, one of the three holiest fire-temples stood near it. Under the Moslems it contained a large Arab element, and became the capital and most important town of Khora'sân. Its gardens and fruits were famous, and it was called the 'Little Damascus.' Many students were attracted by its colleges, which had a high reputation. It was the birthplace of Omar Khayyâm, the celebrated astronomer-poet of Persia, who died in A.D. 1123.—W.

prayers.[1] He recited the usual prayers regularly, and, if he woke during the night, said a prayer. If he did not wake, he used to pray before the morning prayer. As long as consciousness lasted, he never failed to say his prayers. I saw him perform this duty regularly during his last illness, and he discontinued it only during the three days in which his mind was wandering. When he was travelling, he used to get down from his horse at the appointed hours[2] to pray.

Let us speak of his tenth in charity. The sum of money he left at his death was not large enough to be submitted to this tax ; his private charities had absorbed everything. He who had possessed such abundant wealth left in his treasury, when he died, but seven-and-forty Nâsri dirhems, and a single Tyrian gold piece.[3] He left neither goods, nor house, nor real estate, neither garden, nor village, nor cultivated land, nor any other species of property.

Let us pass to the fast of the month Ramadân. Several

---

[1] Attendance at the Friday prayers (*Salât el-Jum'a*) is regarded by Moslems as a *farz* duty, that is, as one commanded from God in the Kurân. The prayers take the place of the ordinary mid-day service, and differ from it only in the omission of four *rak'as*, and the addition of a *Khutba*, or sermon, preached by the *Khâtib*, who is generally the *Imâm*. The usual prayers, recited by Salâh ed-Dîn, were the five daily services, and perhaps also the three voluntary services. The prayer during the night was probably a service of two *rak'as*. Each service consists of a certain number of obligatory and voluntary *rak'as ;* it may be said in public or in private, but when said in a mosque it must be preceded by the *azân*, or call to prayers, and the *ikâma*, a repetition of the azân, concluding with the words ' Prayer has commenced.' The *rak'a* is an act of worship, consisting of the recitation of verses from the Kurân, sentences of praise offered to God, and acts of ritual, including the prostrations.—W.

[2] The appointed hours are (1) from dawn to sunrise ; (2) when the sun has begun to decline ; (3) midway between 2 and 4 ; (4) a few minutes after sunset ; and (5) when the night has closed in.—W.

[3] The Tyrian *dinar* (Greek *denarion*) was so called because it was struck at Tyre. The Nâsri *dirhem* (Greek *drachme*) was a silver coin, probably inscribed with the name of el-Melek en-Nâsr Salâh ed-Dîn.

of these fasts remained to be fulfilled, as he had not observed them in consequence of his frequent illnesses. It was the duty of el-Kâdi el-Fâdel[1] to keep an account of the number of these days. The prince—may God have mercy on him!—was in the last year of his life, and was dwelling at Jerusalem, when he began to make reparation for the fasts he had omitted. He then fasted for a period exceeding the ordinary month, for he had still a fast of two Ramadâns to keep, which he had been prevented from observing by constant disorders of the body, and the continual cares of the Holy War. Fasting did not suit his health; but thus, by the inspiration of God, he undertook to repair his omissions during that year. It fell to me to keep account of the days, for the Kâdi was absent. It was useless for his physician to disapprove of what he was doing. The prince would not listen to him, and said, ' I do not know what may happen.' It seems as though God had inspired Salâh ed-Dîn to save his responsibility by paying his debt, and so he continued to fast until the days were wholly accomplished.

Let us now speak of the pilgrimage. He always intended to perform it, and, above all, in the last year of his life. He had made up his mind, and given orders for the necessary preparations to be made. We had collected provisions for the journey, and all was ready for the start, when he decided to postpone the pilgrimage till the following year on account of want of time and

---

[1] Abu 'Ali Abd er-Rahîm el-Lakhmi el-'Askalâni, generally known as el-Kâdi el-Fâdel, ' the talented Kâdi,' was vizir of Salâh ed-Dîn, by whom he was treated with the highest favour. He was surnamed el-Misri, because he lived in Egypt, and el-Beisâni because his father was Kâdi of *Beisân*. He was famous as a letter-writer, and was also a poet. Born at Ascalon (A.D. 1135), he died in Egypt (A.D. 1200), after having been vizir to Salâh ed-Dîn, el-Melek el-'Azîz, and el-Melek el-Mansûr (Ibn Khallikan, ii. 111).—W.

lack of money sufficient for one of his high rank. But God decreed as He did decree. What I have related on that subject is a thing known to all the world.

Salâh ed-Dîn was very fond of hearing the Kurân read, and he used to argue with the Imâm. This man had to be master of all knowledge connected with the text of the Kurân, and to know the book by heart. When the prince passed the night in the alcove[1] (of his tent), he used to charge the man on guard to read him two, three, or four sections.[2] When he gave public audiences, he would have from one to twenty verses, and sometimes more, read by men accustomed to do so. One day he passed a little boy who was reading the Kurân very well at his father's side, and was so pleased that he had the boy called, and gave him some of the food set aside for his own special use. Also he granted to him and his father part of the produce of a certain field. His heart was humble, and full of compassion; tears came readily into his eyes. When he was listening to the reading of the Kurân, his heart melted, and tears generally flowed down his cheeks. He was very fond of listening to the recital of traditions[3] when the narrator could trace each tradition that he related to its source, and when he was learned in such lore. If one of the doctors visited the court, he received him personally, and made those of his sons who happened to be present as well as the

---

[1] The word *burj*, rendered 'alcove,' usually signifies 'a tower.' Here it appears to mean a small room, built of wood, which contained a bed, and opened into the tent.

[2] The text of the Kurân is divided into thirty sections (*jûz*, or *sîfâra*), so that a pious man, taking one section a day, can recite the whole Kurân in the month of Ramadan.

[3] The Traditions (*Hadîth*) contain the record of all that Muhammad did and said. They form an important part of Moslem theology, and occupy a place second only to the Kurân.—W.

memlûks on duty, listen to the traditions recited. He
would order all those who were present to be seated
during the narration, as a sign of respect. If any of the
doctors of traditionary lore were such characters as do
not frequent the gates of Sultans, and are unwilling to
present themselves in such places, Salâh ed-Dîn would go
himself to seek them out and listen to them. When he
was at Alexandria, he often visited Hâfiz el-Isfahâni,[1] and
learnt from him a great number of traditions. He himself
was fond of reading traditions, so he used to make me
come into his private chamber, and there, surrounded by
books of traditions which he had had collected, he would
begin to read; and whenever he came to a tradition
containing an instructive passage, he was so touched that
the tears came into his eyes.

He showed the greatest zeal in his observance of the
precepts of religion, openly maintaining his belief in the
resurrection of the bodies of the just in Paradise, and of
the wicked in Hell. He believed steadfastly in all the
teaching of the Divine Law, accepting its doctrines with
an open heart. He detested philosophers, heretics,[2]
materialists, and all adversaries of orthodox religion. He
even ordered his son el-Melek ez-Zâher, Prince of Aleppo—
may God exalt his supporters !—to put to death a young
man named Suhraverdi.[3] He had been accused of not

---

[1] This Hâfiz el-Isfahâni does not appear to be otherwise known.—W.

[2] The Arabic text has *el-Mu'attila* (*Mu'tazila*, 'the Separatists').
This word, in scholastic theology, is applied to a sect who rejected
the idea of eternal attributes, saying that eternity was the formal
attribute of the essence of God. The Mu'attilites were the free-
thinkers of Islâm, and were regarded by the orthodox as heretics,
and tainted with atheism.

[3] Abu el-Futûh Yahya Ibn Habash es-Suhraverdi was born at
Suhraverdi, a village in Persian Irak, and was one of the most
learned men of his age. He had studied at Marâgha in Azerbijan,
and was said by some to be a fire-worshipper (*zendîk*), and by others

recognising the ordinances of the law, and of paying no regard to the doctrines of the faith. Ez-Zâher,[1] having sent this man to prison, reported what had passed to his father, and at Salâh ed-Dîn's command had him executed, and his body hung upon a cross for several days.

Having perfect trust in God, he looked upon Him as his great support, and turned ever to Him. I will give an instance of this which I myself witnessed. The Franks — may God confound them!—had pitched their camp at Beit-Nûba,[2] a place situated about a day's journey from Jerusalem. The Sultan occupied this city, after having surrounded the enemy with out-posts, and sent out men to spy and watch all their movements. He received constant news of the Franks, and of their fixed determination to come up to the Holy City and lay siege to it. As this struck great terror among the Moslems, he called his emirs together, informed them of the calamity which threatened the faithful, and submitted to them whether it was right to remain in the city. They appeared, one and all, of good courage, but their real sentiments were very different from those which they expressed. They declared unanimously that the Sultan's presence in Jerusalem would be of no advantage, and might, indeed, endanger Islâm ; that they themselves would remain there, while he went out with a body of men to surround the Franks, as had

---

to be an infidel and acquainted with magic. He was really a very advanced Sûfî, and so an abomination to Salâh ed-Dîn. He was strangled in the castle at Aleppo, in A.D. 1191, at the early age of thirty-eight.(Ibn Khallikân, iv. 153).—W.

[1] Abû el-Fath Ghâzi Abû Mansûr el-Melek ez-Zâher Ghiâth ed-Dîn was fond of learning and generous to poets. He was resolute, animated by a lofty spirit, skilled in the administration of affairs, and intent on the diffusion of justice. He was born in 1173, made Governor of Aleppo in 1187, and died in 1216 (Ibn Khallikan, ii. 443).—W.

[2] *Beit Nûba*, called by the Franks Betenoble, 12 miles N.W. of Jerusalem, immediately N. of Ajalon, at the foot of the mountains.

been done at Acre. At the head of this army, he was to
keep the enemy narrowly hemmed in, and cut off their
supplies of provisions ; meanwhile, they would hold the
city and repel attacks. The council having broken up,
the Sultan forthwith determined to hold the city, knowing full well that otherwise no one would remain there.
After the emirs had left to return to their houses, a
messenger came from them to the Sultan to inform him
that they would not remain in Jerusalem, unless he left
at their head either his brother el-Melek el-'Âdel, or one
of his own sons. He felt that this communication meant
that they did not intend to remain in the city, and
his heart was sorely oppressed, and he knew not what to
decide. On this same night, which was the eve of Friday,
I was on duty in his chamber, having to stay there from
evening until dawn. It was in the rainy season, and with
us two there was no third but God. We made plans, and
discussed the consequences of each plan ; but at last I grew
concerned for him, seeing him so overwhelmed with despair,
and I began to fear for his health. So I begged him to lie
down on his bed, and sleep a little if possible. He replied :
'You must be sleepy, too,' then he rose (to withdraw).
Passing into my house, I busied myself with some private
affairs until dawn, when the summons to prayer sounded.
As I usually said the morning-prayer with him, I went into
his chamber, where I found him washing. 'I have not
slept a single moment,' he said. I replied that I knew it.
' How ?' he asked. I answered, ' Because I have not slept
myself, not having had the time.' We then said our
prayers, after which we sat down to what we had to do.
At last I said : ' I have an idea that, I believe, is a good
one, please God !' ' What is it ?' he asked. I replied :

'And what shall we do?' he inquired. I answered : ' To-day is Friday; your Highness will perform a ceremonial ablution before going this afternoon to the Aksa ; you will say your prayer as usual in the holy place[1] of the Prophet's night journey. You will charge a confidential servant to give alms in secret ; then you will say a prayer of two rak'a after the azân and before the ikâma,[2] and whilst you remain prostrate, you will call upon God for help. We have a credible tradition on this subject. Your Highness will say within yourself : *Oh God ! all earthly means that I have employed, for the defence of religion, now fail me. There remains for me no resource but to seek support in Thee, to put myself in Thy hand, and to trust myself to Thy goodness. Upon Thee alone do I count, Thou art the best of guardians.* Rest assured that God is too generous to reject your appeal.' He did exactly as I had advised, and I prayed by his side as usual. Whilst he said the two rak'a between the azân and the ikâma, his body prostrate, I saw the tears fall on to his grizzling beard, and then on to the prayer-carpet; but I did not hear what he had said. Before we had reached the end of the day a dispatch arrived in which 'Izz ed-Dîn Jurdîk,[3] who was then in command of the advanced guard, informed us that a great disturbance reigned amongst the Franks ; that their men had this day mounted their horses and be-

[1] The Prophet is traditionally supposed to have ascended from the Cave in the *Sakhrah*, or holy 'rock' in the Kubbet es-Sakhrah. The word *Aksa* stands for the whole enclosure of the Haram esh-Sherîf.

[2] The *azân*, or 'call to prayer,' is given by the Mu'ezzin at the time of public prayer. When the prayers are said in a mosque they commence with the *ikâma*, a repetition of the azân, with the addition of the words, ' Prayer has commenced.' For *rak'a*, see p. 7.—W.

[3] 'Izz ed-Dîn Jurdîk was a freedman of Nûr ed-Dîn, who accompanied Shîrkûh to Egypt. He and Salâh ed-Dîn killed Shâwar, the vizir of the Fatimite Khalif of Egypt ; and he was afterwards one of Salâh-ed-Dîn's emirs.—W.

taken themselves to the plain;[1] that they had halted
there until noon, and then all at once returned to their
camp. Early on Saturday a second dispatch arrived with
the same news. During the day a spy came in and reported
that discord was rampant amongst the Franks, the king
of France having declared that they must absolutely lay
siege to Jerusalem, whilst the king of England and his
supporters were unwilling to risk the Christian cause by
throwing their troops into a mountainous country, where
their water-supply would be entirely cut off, for the Sultan
had destroyed all the wells round the city. Also that their
chiefs had gone out (from the camp) to hold a council in
their usual manner, for it is their custom, when it is a
question of war, to take counsel together on horseback.
Also that they had agreed to refer the point to the consideration of ten persons whom they had chosen from
amongst themselves, and to abide by their decision. On
Monday morning a messenger came to announce that the
enemy had struck their camp, and were marching towards
Ramla.[2] This was an instance of the Sultan's great trust
in God. I myself was a witness of it.

CHAPTER II.

HIS LOVE OF JUSTICE.

ABU BEKR[3]—God be gracious to him!—records that the
Holy Prophet said : ' A just governor is the shadow of God
upon earth. He who serves God faithfully himself and for
others, God will place under the shadow of His throne on

---

[1] The plain of Ajalon.
[2] See p. 295.
[3] The first Khalífa, or successor of Muhammad.

that day when no other will remain except that shadow ; but he who seeks to deceive God in matters which concern himself or other men, God will deprive of all hope on the day of resurrection. To the just governor, for the good work he has done day by day, He will assign a reward equal to that of sixty true-hearted men who each have worked for their own salvation.' Our Sultan—may the mercy of God rest upon him !—was just, merciful, compassionate, and ready to aid the weak against the strong. Every Monday and Thursday he sat in public to administer justice, and on these occasions jurisconsults, kâdis, and men learned in the law were present. Every one who had a grievance was admitted—great and small, aged women and feeble men. He sat thus, not only when he was in the city, but even when he was travelling ; and he always received with his own hand the petitions that were presented to him, and did his utmost to put an end to every form of oppression that was reported. Every day he made a packet of these documents, and opened the doors of justice (to the complainants) ; he never sent away those who came to complain of their wrongs or to demand redress. Every day, either during the daytime or in the night, he spent an hour with his secretary, and wrote on each petition, in the terms which God suggested to him, an answer to its prayer.

Whenever a petitioner applied to him, he would stop to listen, to receive his complaint, and to inquire into the rights of the matter. I myself saw a man of Damascus, named Ibn-Zoheir, deliver a complaint against Taki ed-Dîn, the Sultan's nephew, demanding justice. Although Taki ed-Dîn was high in the affection and esteem of his uncle, the Sultan would not spare him in a matter where justice was at stake, and caused him to appear before the tribunal.

Here is an anecdote still more remarkable than the fore-
going, which likewise shows his great sense of justice.   I
was one day presiding in the tribunal in the Holy City of
Jerusalem, when I saw a fine old man enter who usually
went by the name of 'Omar el-Khelâti. He was a merchant
and native of Khelât.[1] This man placed in my hands a
certified memorandum, and begged me to read its contents.
I asked him who was his adversary, and he replied : 'My
affair is with the Sultan ; this is the seat of justice, and I
have heard that here you make no distinction of persons.'
'Why,' I said, 'do you bring a suit against him ?' He
replied : 'I had a memlûk named Sonkor el-Khelâti, who
remained in my possession until his death. At that time
he had several large sums of money in hand, all of which
belonged to me. He died, leaving these sums : the Sultan
took possession of them, and I lay claim to them as my
property.' I then asked him why he had delayed so long
before making his claim, and he replied : 'One does not
forfeit one's rights by delaying to claim them, and here I
have a certified document proving that the slave remained
in my possession until his death.' I took the paper, and
having read it through, saw it contained a description of
Sonkor el-Khelâti, with a note that his master had bought
him of such an one, a merchant of Arjîsh[2] (in Armenia), on
a certain day of a certain month in a certain year ; I found
also that the memlûk had remained in his master's
possession until a certain year, when he had escaped by
flight, and that the witnesses named in the document had
never understood that the man had ceased to be the

---

[1] *Akhlat*, on the shore of Lake Van. See p. 84.

[2] *Arjîsh*, the Byzantine *Arses*, was taken by the Seljûks in 1071,
and by a prince of the house of Salâh ed-Dîn in 1207. It was on the
north shore of Lake Van, and was submerged by a sudden rise of the
waters of the lake about fifty years ago.— W.

property of his master in any manner whatever. The instrument was in legal form — nothing was wanting. Wondering very much at this affair, I said to the man : ' It is not meet to adjudge a claim in the absence of the party sued ; I will inform the Sultan, and will let you know what he says in this matter.' The man appreciated my remark, and withdrew. On the same day, having occasion to present myself before the Sultan, I acquainted him with the business. He thought the claim utterly absurd, and asked if I had examined the written document. I replied that it had been taken to Damascus, and laid before the kâdi there, who had examined it officially, and appended a certificate to that effect, which was witnessed by the signatures of various well-known persons. ' Very well,' he cried, ' we will let the man appear, and I will defend myself against him, and conform to all the regulations prescribed by law.' Some time afterwards, sitting with him in private, I told him that this man came constantly to speak to me, and that it was absolutely necessary to give him a hearing. He replied : ' Appoint an attorney to act in my name, and then receive the depositions of witnesses ; do not open the document until the man appears here.' I did according to his command, then, when the plaintiff appeared, the Sultan ordered him to draw near and to be seated in front of him. I was by the side of the prince. He then left the couch on which he was sitting, and placing himself by the side of the man, called upon him to state his case. He accordingly set forth his claim in the manner related above, and the Sultan replied in these words : ' This Sonkor was a memlûk of mine ; he never ceased to be my property till the time when I gave him his freedom ; he is dead, and his heirs have entered upon the inheritance he left.' Then the man answered and said : ' I hold in my hand an instrument that will prove the truth of what I state. Please to

open it, that its contents may be known.' I opened the
document, and found that it bore out the statements of the
complainant. The Sultan, having informed himself of the
date of the paper, replied : ' I have witnesses to prove that
at the said date Sonkor was in my possession and at
Cairo; the year previous I had bought him with eight
others, and he remained in my possession till he received
his freedom.' He then summoned several of his chief
military officers, who bore witness that the facts were in
accordance with the statements of the Sultan, and declared
that the date he had given was exact. The plaintiff was
confounded, and I said to the Sultan : ' My lord ! the man
has done this only that he may obtain mercy at my·lord's
hands, being in your presence ; and it will not be meet to
let him depart disappointed.' ' Ah !' said the Sultan,
' that is quite another matter.' He then ordered a robe of
honour to be given to the man, and a sum of money, of
which I have forgotten the amount, but which was ample
to cover his expenses. Observe the rare and admirable
qualities shown by the Sultan in this matter, his conde-
scension, his submission to the regulations prescribed by
law, the putting aside of his pride, and the generosity he
displayed at a time when he might justly have inflicted a
punishment.

CHAPTER III.

SOME INSTANCES OF HIS GENEROSITY.

OUR Holy Prophet says : ' When the generous man
stumbles, God takes him by the hand.' Among our
traditions (Hadîth) are several which relate to generosity.
This quality of the Sultan's character—may God hallow
his soul!—is too well known to need setting forth in

writing, and too patent to require notice. Nevertheless, I
will just allude to it, and mention that he who had possessed such abundance of riches, left in his treasury, at his
death, but forty-seven Nâṣri dirhems, and one Tyrian gold
piece, the weight of which I do not know. Yet he had
given away whole provinces. When he took the city of
Amid,[1] he bestowed it upon the son of Kara Arslân,[2] who
had asked him for it. I was present on one occasion at
Jerusalem, when he received a great number of deputa-
tions, just as he was departing for Damascus, and had
not sufficient money in the treasury to make presents to
the delegates. I continually reminded him of this, until
at last he sold one of his farms to the public treasury (*beit
el-mâl*), in order that he might distribute the price of it
among them. This was done with our help, and in the
end there remained not a single dirhem. He gave just as
liberally when he was in straits as when he was in the
enjoyment of plenty. His treasurers were always careful
to conceal from him certain sums of money, as a provision
for unforeseen contingencies ; for they knew that if he saw
them he would spend them at once. I once heard him
say, in the course of conversation about one of the traditions : ' It may be that there is someone in the world who
esteems money of as little value as the dust of the earth.'
He was apparently alluding to himself. He always gave
more than they expected to those who asked. I never
heard him say : ' We have already given to him.' He
made numerous presents ; to those who had already received gifts he gave again, and with as much pleasure as
though he had not given them anything before. He

---

[1] *Diarbekr.* See p. 85.

[2] This was Nûr ed-Dîn Mahmûd Jebu, the Ortokid prince of *Hisn
Keifa* (1167-1185). He was the son of Fakhr ed-Dîn Kara Arslân, and
great-grandson of Sokmân, son of Ortok.—W.

always acted with great generosity, giving more on a second occasion than the recipient had obtained before. This was so well known that people were always trying to make opportunities for getting money from him. I never once heard him say : ' I have already given to you several times; how often shall I have to give to you again?' Most of the replies to these requests were written at my dictation, and sometimes with my own hand. I was often ashamed at the greed shown by those who asked ; but I never hesitated to approach the Sultan in their behalf, knowing how generous and kind-hearted he was. No one ever entered his service without receiving from him such gifts as rendered it unnecessary for him ever to court another's generosity. To enumerate his gifts, and to describe their varied forms, would be a task impossible to fulfil in any satisfactory way. In a conversation on this subject, I once heard the chief of the Diwân declare : ' We kept an account of the number of horses he gave away in the plain of Acre alone, and it mounted up to ten thousand.'[1] Those who have witnessed the multitude of his gifts will think but little of this. Great God, Thou it was who didst inspire his generosity, Thou, the most generous among the generous ! Shower upon him Thy mercy and Thy favour, oh, Thou most merciful of those who show mercy !

CHAPTER IV.

HIS VALOUR AND INTREPIDITY—MAY GOD HALLOW HIS SOUL !

THE Holy Prophet is reported to have said : ' God loves bravery, even (if displayed) only in killing a serpent.' The

---

[1] He gave horses to the horsemen of his army who had lost their own.

Sultan was bravest among the brave; he was distinguished by his energy of soul, his vigour of character, and his intrepidity. I have seen him take up his position immediately in front of a large body of Franks, who were every moment being increased and relieved, and the sight (of this danger) only strengthened his courage and nerve. One evening there came up more than seventy of the enemy's ships; it took me the whole of the time between the 'Asr prayer[1] and the prayer at sunset to count them; but their appearance only served to inspirit him anew. On another occasion, at the commencement of the rainy season, he gave leave to his troops, and remained himself, attended by very few men, in the face of a strong force of the enemy. On the day when peace was concluded, Bâliân, son of Bârizân,[2] one of the chief princes of the coast, was seated before the Sultan, and I inquired of him what was the number of their troops. I received this answer through the interpreter: 'When the Lord of Sidon' (another of their chiefs, and one of the most intelligent among them) 'and I left Tyre to join our army (at the siege of Acre), and when we sighted them from the top of the hill, we tried to guess as nearly as we could the number of those engaged. The Lord of Sidon said there were five hundred thousand; I said six hundred thousand.' I then asked him how many they had lost, and he replied: 'Nearly a hundred thousand on the field of battle; but God alone knows the number of those who have died from sickness, or who have been drowned.' And of all this multitude but a very small number ever returned to their native land.

---

[1] According to tradition, the *'Asr* prayers can be said from the time when the shadow of a person is the length of his own stature, till the sun assumes a yellow appearance. The *Maghrib* prayers commence a few moments after sunset.

[2] Balian I. of Ibelin (*Yebnah*), on the coast.

When we were close upon the enemy, the Sultan insisted on making a reconnaissance round their army once or twice every day. In the height of the fighting he used to pass between the two lines of battle, accompanied by a young page, who led his horse. He would make his way in front of his own troops from the right wing to the left, intent on the marshalling of his battalions, calling them up to the front, and stationing them in positions which he deemed advantageous to command the enemy or to approach them. On one occasion, whilst standing between the two armies, he ordered that some traditions should· be read to him. It is a fact. I told him that traditions could be read in all important places, but that there was no instance of its having been done between two armies. I added that if his Highness would like such a thing told of him, it would be fine. He listened to this. A volume was brought, and someone who was present, and had studied the book, read to him from it. Meanwhile, we remained on horseback, sometimes walking up and down, sometimes standing still, but all the while on the ground between the two armies.

I never heard him express any anxiety as to the numbers or force of the enemy. Whilst occupied with his own thoughts and with the affairs of government, he would listen to all sorts of plans, and discuss their (probable) results without any excitement, and without losing his composure. When the Moslem army was routed in the great battle in the plain of Acre, and even the troops in the centre had taken to flight after throwing away their drums and standards, he maintained the position he had taken up, having only a handful of men to support him. At last he managed to reach some rising ground, and there rallied his men. His reproaches made them so deeply ashamed that they returned with him to the fight. The victory eventually lay with the Moslems, and the enemy had more than seven thousand men killed, both horse and foot. The Sultan continued to fight, but at last, seeing the strength of the enemy and the weakness of the Moslems, he listened to the proposals of his adversaries, and consented to a truce. The fact was, that they were very much exhausted, and had suffered greater loss than we. But they expected the arrival of reinforcements, while we had none to hope for. Thus it was for our advantage to conclude an armistice. This was recognised when Fate revealed what she had in her bosom for us. At this period the Sultan was very frequently ill, and suffered terrible pain ; but he, nevertheless, kept the field throughout. Each army could see the fires of the other ; we heard the sound of their bells[1] (Nâkûs), and they heard our call to prayer. This state of things lasted for some time, and all ended for the best. May God hallow the soul of this prince and shed light upon his tomb !

CHAPTER V.

OF HIS ZEAL IN FIGHTING IN GOD'S CAUSE.

GOD ALMIGHTY said (Kurân xxix. 69) : ' Those who fight strenuously for Us we will surely guide in Our way, for, verily, God is with those who do well.' There are numerous texts in the Book exhorting us to fight for the faith. And, of a truth, the Sultan entertained an ardent passion for the Holy War ; his mind was always filled with it. Therefore one might swear, in absolute security and

[1] The *Nâkûs* is a thin oblong piece of wood, which is beaten by a flexible rod. It is still used by the Christians in many places in Asiatic Turkey to summon the people to worship.—W.

without risk of perjury, that from the time when he first issued forth to fight the infidel, he spent not a single piece of gold or silver except for the carrying on of the Holy War[1] or for distribution among his troops. With him to wage war in God's name was a veritable passion ; his whole heart was filled with it, and he gave body and soul to the cause. He spoke of nothing else ; all his thoughts were of instruments of war ; his soldiers monopolised every idea. He showed all deference to those who talked of the Holy War and who encouraged the people to take part in it. His desire to fight in God's cause forced him to leave his family, his children, his native land, the place of his abode, and all else in his land. Leaving all these earthly enjoyments, he contented himself with dwelling beneath the shadow of a tent, shaken to the right hand and to the left by the breath of every wind. One night, when he was in the plain of Acre, it happened, in a very high wind, that his tent fell upon him, and had he not been in the alcove,[2] he would have lost his life. But this tended only to increase his passion, to strengthen his purpose, and con-firm his resolution. Anyone anxious to ingratiate himself with the Sultan had only to encourage him in his passion for the Holy War and to narrate to him stories connected with it. Therefore, a number of treatises upon this subject were composed for his use, and I myself wrote a work, on his account, on the Holy War, and the rules and precepts to be observed therein. I incorporated in this work all the verses of the Kurân bearing upon the subject, all the tradi-tions which refer to it, and an explanation of all the rare words. His Highness valued this treatise so highly, that

---

[1] The *Jihâd*, or religious war with unbelievers, is an incumbent religious duty, established in the Kurân, and in the Traditions as a Divine institution.—Hughes, ' Dictionary of Islâm.'

[2] See p. 9.

he taught the whole of its contents to his son, el-Melek el-Afdel.

Whilst on this subject, I will relate what I heard told. In the month of Zu el-K'ada, in the year 584 (December, 1188-January, 1189), he took the fortress of Kaukab,[1] and gave his troops permission to return home immediately. El-Melek el-'Âdel[2] set out upon his return to Egypt at the head of the contingent furnished by that country, and his brother, the Sultan, accompanied him as far as Jerusalem, so that he might bid him good-bye in that city, and be present at 'the Feast of Sacrifice.'[3] We travelled with him. After having attended the prayers at this festival, he conceived the idea of going to Ascalon with the Egyptian troops, and, after parting with them, of returning by the coast road, so as to inspect the coast lands as far as Acre, and restore order as he passed. We tried to make him give up this project, representing that after the departure of the troops he would have but a very small number of men with him, whilst the Franks were assembled at Tyre, and that he would thus be running great risk. The

[1] *Kaukab el-Hawa* (Belvoir), 6½ miles S. of Tiberias ; a fortress of the Knights' Hospitallers, built in 1182.

[2] Abu Bekr Muhammad el-Melek el-'Âdel Seif ed-Dîn was brother of Salâh ed-Dîn, and went with him, under his uncle Shirkûh, to Egypt. Under Salâh ed-Dîn he was Viceroy of Egypt, Governor of Aleppo (1183-1186), of Kerak, and of other provinces. In 1200 he deposed el-Mansûr, the grandson of Salâh ed-Dîn, and made himself master of Egypt. In 1202 he obtained possession of Aleppo and Syria and, later, of Mesopotamia, Khelat (1207-1208), and Yemen (1215-1216). He was born at Damascus in 1145, and died near the same town in 1218, after dividing his great empire amongst his sons (Ibn Khallikan, iii. 235).—W.

[3] The *'Id el-Azha*, 'feast of sacrifice,' known in Turkey and Egypt as *Bairâm*, is celebrated on the tenth day of Zu el-Hijja, the last month of the Moslem year. It was instituted by Muhammad in the second year of the Hijra, and is the great central festival of Islâm. The sacrifice forms part of the rites of the pilgrimage to Mecca.—W.

Sultan paid no attention to our remonstrances, but proceeded to Ascalon, where he took leave of his brother and
the Egyptian army. We departed with him to the coast,
being at that time on duty about his person, and took the
road towards Acre. The rain fell, the sea was tossed to
and fro, and the *waves were like mountains*, as the Most
High has said (in the Kurân, xi. 44). This was the
first time that I had ever seen the sea, and such was
the impression it made upon me that if anyone had said,
'Go but one mile upon the sea, and I will make you
master of the world,' I should have refused to go. I
looked upon those who go to sea to earn a few pieces of
gold or silver as mad, and I endorsed the opinion of the
doctors who have declared that one cannot accept the
evidence of a man who is travelling on the ocean. Such
were the thoughts that came into my mind at the sight of
the terrible restlessness of the sea and the size of its waves.
While I gave myself up to these reflections, the Sultan
turned to me and said : 'Would you like me to tell you
something ?' 'Very much,' I replied. 'Well,' he said,
'when by God's help not a Frank is left on this coast,
I mean to divide my territories, and to charge (my
successors) with my last commands ; then, having taken
leave of them, I will sail on this sea to its islands in
pursuit of them, until there shall not remain upon the face
of this earth one unbeliever in God, or I will die in the
attempt.' These words made all the deeper impression
upon me because they were so utterly opposed to what I
myself had just been feeling, and I said : 'My lord, there
is no man in this world braver than you, nor any man more
firmly resolved to maintain the true Faith.' 'Why do you
say that ?' he said. I answered : 'As to bravery, I see
that your Highness is not infected with the dread which
the sea inspires in others ; and as to your zeal for the true

Faith, I see that your Highness is not content with driving
the enemies of God from one particular place, but that you
would purify the whole earth from the presence of the
infidel. Will you now allow me to tell you what was
passing through my own mind?' He commanded me to
do so, and I described to him the feelings I had experienced.
Then I added : ' The intention of your Highness is excellent indeed. Embark your troops, and let them depart ;
but you, who are the pillar and the bulwark of Islâm, must
not thus expose yourself and risk your life.' He replied :
' What, I ask you, is the most glorious of deaths?' ' To
die,' I answered, ' in the way of God.' ' Then,' he replied,
' I strive for the door of the most glorious of deaths.'
What noble sentiments ! How pure, how brave, how full
of courage was his soul ! Great God ! Thou knowest he
lavished his strength in defence of Thy Faith, and that he
did all to deserve Thy mercy. Then be merciful unto
him, Thou who art merciful above all others !

CHAPTER VI.

OF HIS PATIENCE, AND OF HIS TRUST IN THE MERCY
OF GOD.

GOD ALMIGHTY has said : ' To those who then fought
strenuously (to maintain the cause of God), and were
patient, verily, thy Lord after that will be forgiving and
merciful ' (Kurân xvi. 111). I have seen our Sultan, in
the plain of Acre, in great suffering from a sickness that
had come upon him ; an eruption of pustules appeared
all over his body, from his waist to his knees, and this
prevented him from sitting up. He was obliged to sit
leaning on one side when he was in his tent, and he could

not sit at table. Therefore he had all the dishes which
had been prepared for him distributed among the people
who were there. In spite of that, he repaired to his war-
tent close to the enemy. After having drawn up his army,
in order of battle, on the right wing, on the left, and in
the centre, he remained on horseback from early morning
until after mid-day prayer,[1] engaged in surveying the
battalions, and again from the third hour of the afternoon
until sunset. During the whole time he bore most patiently
the great pain caused by the throbbing of the tumours. I
was astounded at this, but he kept on saying, 'The pain
leaves me when I am on horseback, and only returns when
I dismount.' What a proof of God's favour !

Whilst we were at el-Kharrûba,[2] after the Sultan had
been obliged to leave Tell el-Hajl (the hill of partridges)
on account of illness, the Franks received news of his
departure, and sallied (from their camp) in the hope of
striking a blow at the Moslems. It was the day on which
they usually took their horses to the watering-place. They
marched on as far as the wells (*el-Abár*), which lay a day's
journey away, and at the foot of Tell (el-Hajl). The Sultan
sent his baggage back in the direction of Nazareth, and
allowed 'Imâd ed-Dîn,[3] Lord of Sinjâr, to accompany it,
for this prince also was ill. The Sultan himself maintained
his position. The next day, seeing that the enemy were

---

[1] The mid-day prayer, *Salât ez-Zuhr*, is said when the sun has
begun to decline.—W.

[2] *Kharrûba* or *Kharnûba* (' carob-trees ') was apparently on the road
from Nazareth at the mouth of *Wâdy el-Melek*. *Tell el-Hajl* seems
to be near the *Tell el-'Ajjûl* noticed later (p. 176), about 10 miles N.
of Kharrûba, and 2 or 3 miles E. of Acre.

[3] 'Imâd ed-Dîn, son of Kotb ed-Dîn, Lord of Mosul, was made
Lord of *Sinjar*, the ancient *Singara*, by his uncle, the celebrated
Nûr ed-Dîn, about 1170, and died there in 1197. He was in posses-
sion of Aleppo when it was taken by Salâh ed-Dîn.—W.

marching upon us, he mounted his horse, sick as he was, and drew up his men to await the attack. To el-Melek el-'Âdel he gave the command of the right wing; to (his nephew) Taki ed-Dîn[1] he entrusted the left; and he placed his sons, el-Melek ez-Zâher and el-Melek el-Afdal,[2] in the centre. He himself took up a position threatening the enemy's rear. Directly he came down from the hill, a Frank was brought up who had just been made prisoner, and, as the unhappy man refused to embrace Islâm, he had him beheaded in his presence. The enemy continued their march to the river head, and, as they advanced, the Sultan made a flank movement so as to get in their rear, and cut them off from their camp. From time to time he halted to dismount, and rest under the shadow of a piece of cloth that was held over his head. Although the heat of the sun was excessive, he would not suffer a tent to be pitched, for fear that the enemy might learn that he was ill. The Franks, having reached the river head,[3] halted, and the Sultan took up a commanding position on rising ground opposite to them. When day was closing, he ordered his men to return to the posts they had at first

[1] Abû S'aîd 'Omar el-Melek el-Muzaffer Taki ed-Dîn, was son of Shâhanshâh, the elder brother of Salâh ed-Dîn. He was brave, and successful in war, and particularly distinguished himself at the battle of Hattîn. He was Lord of *Hamât* (Hamath, now *Hamah*), Viceroy of Egypt (1183), and Governor of Mesopotamia. He died (1191) whilst besieging *Manazgerd* (now *Melasgerd*), one of the ancient cities of Armenia (Ibn Khallikan, ii. 391).—W.

[2] Abû el-Hasan 'Ali el-Melek el-Afdal Nûr ed-Dîn was the eldest son of Salâh ed-Dîn. When his father died (1193) he took posses- sion of Damascus, but was driven out by his brother (el-Melek el-'Azîz, who had seized Egypt), and his uncle, el-Melek el-'Âdel. On his . brother's death (1198) he became *Atabeg*, 'guardian' to his nephew, el-Melek el-Mansûr; but when el-'Âdel took possession of Egypt, he was given Sumeisât (Samosata), where he died in 1225, aged 54 years (Ibn Khallikan, ii. 353).—W.

[3] The Belus River, S. of Acre.

occupied, and to remain all night under arms. He himself withdrew to the rear with us, who were on duty, and had his tent pitched on the summit of the hill. His physician and I passed the night in ministering to him. His sleep, which was often broken, lasted till daybreak. At the sound of the trumpet he mounted his horse, and drew up his troops with a view of surrounding the enemy. Their army then commenced to retire, towards the camp, from the west bank of the river, and the Moslems pressed close upon them during the whole of that day. The Sultan sent forward those of his sons who were with him, putting his trust (in God)—namely, el-Melek el-Afdal and el-Melek ez-Zâher. One after another he sent all the members of his suite to the fight, until at last he had no one with him but his physician, myself, the inspector of military stores and equipment, and the young pages who bore the banners and standards—not a soul beside. Anyone seeing these standards from afar would have thought that a great number of people were drawn up beneath them. The enemy continued their march in spite of their losses. Every time a man was killed, they buried him at once, and they carried off their wounded so that no one might know the extent of their loss. We watched every movement of their retreat, and perceived that they were sorely harassed before they reached the bridge[1] and made a stand. Each time they halted the Moslems drew off, for as soon as the Franks formed line, and stood shoulder to shoulder, they were able to resist all attacks with vigour and effect. Until the evening, and as long as his troops were engaged with the enemy, the Sultan kept the saddle. He gave orders that this night should be passed like the last. We again took up our former positions, and occupied them until morning. This day our troops began to annoy the enemy as they

---

[1] The bridge over the Belus, 3½ miles S.E. of Acre, north of *D'aûk.*

had done on the previous day, and forced them to continue their march, much harassed by fighting, and the loss of men. On nearing the camp, they received reinforcements that enabled them to reach it in safety.

What patience we here see displayed! what self-control this man exerted, trusting the mercy of God! O God, it was Thou who didst arouse in him this patience and this trust! Do not refuse him his reward, Thou who art merciful above all!

I was present on the day when he received the news of the death of his son Ism'aîl, a young man just in the flower of his youth. He read the contents of the letter, but said nothing about it to anyone. We learnt the loss he had sustained through another channel. His face had given no sign whilst he read the despatch, but we had seen the tears in his eyes.

One night, whilst we were under the walls of Safed,[1] a fortified city to which he was laying siege, I heard him say : 'We will not sleep to-night until they have planted five mangonels,' and at each mangonel he stationed workmen sufficient to put it together. We spent the night with him most pleasantly, enjoying a charming conversation, whilst all the time messengers kept arriving, one after another, to report the progress made in the construction of these engines. By morning the work was finished, and nothing remained but to lay the ' Khanâzîr.'[2] Throughout

[1] *Sâfed*, in Upper Galilee, above the Sea of Galilee ; a fortress of the Knights' Hospitallers. It was considered impregnable.

[2] This word, the plural of *Khanzîr*, 'pig,' apparently applies to some part of the mangonel—possibly the lever. ' Mangonel ' was a generic term applied to all the smaller machines for throwing darts (quarrels) or stones. These machines acted by means of a great weight fastened to the short arm of a lever, which, being let fall, raised the end of the long arm with a great velocity. Other parts of the mangonel were the wheel (*luleb*) for winding the rope attached to the

the night, which was very long, the cold and the rain were grievous.

I was present when he received the news of the death of his nephew, Taki ed-Dîn. We were encamped at the time with a detachment of light cavalry in the neighbourhood of Ramleh, opposite to the Franks. Their troops were stationed at Yazûr,[1] and so near to us that they could have reached us by a short gallop. He summoned el-Melek el-'Âdel, 'Âlim ed-Dîn Suleimân Ibn Jinder, Sâbek ed-Dîn Ibn ed-Daya, and 'Izz ed-Dîn Ibn el-Mokaddem : then he commanded all the people in his tent to withdraw a bow-shot off. He then drew out the letter and read it, weeping so much that those who were present wept with him, without knowing the cause of his sorrow. Then, his voice choked with tears, he announced to them that Taki ed-Dîn was dead. His lamentations, and those of all around, had commenced afresh when I recovered my presence of mind, and uttered these words : ' Ask God's forgiveness for allowing yourselves thus to give way ; behold where you are, and in what you are engaged. Cease your weeping, and turn your thoughts to something else.' The Sultan replied by begging forgiveness of God again and again. He then enjoined us to say nothing on this subject to any person. Then, having called for a little rose-water, he bathed his eyes, and ordered a meal to be served, of which we were all to partake. No one knew anything of what had occurred until the enemy had withdrawn in the direction of Jaffa. We subsequently retired again to Natrûn,[2] where we had left our baggage.

---

long end of the lever to raise the weight ; the pulley (*bekra*) through which the rope passed ; and the trigger (*keffu*) for releasing the long end of the lever. It has been proposed to read *jenâzîr*, the popular form of *zenâjîr*, ' chains,' for *khanâzîr*.—W.

[1] *Yazûr* is 3½ miles S.E. of Jaffa, 8 miles N.W. of Ramleh.

[2] *Natrûn*, now *Latrûn*, 9 miles S.E. of Ramleh, on the Jerusalem road, called by the Franks ' Toron of the Knights.'

The Sultan was tenderly attached to his young children, yet he deliberately left them, and was content to lead a hard, painful life, although it was in his power to act otherwise. He trusted in God to maintain the war against the infidels. Great God! he forsook all to please Thee! Oh, deign to grant him Thy grace and Thy mercy!

CHAPTER VII.

INSTANCES OF HIS KINDNESS AND TOLERANCE.

GOD MOST HIGH has said: ' And as for those who pardon men, God loves the kind' (Kurân iii. 128). Our Sultan was most indulgent to all who were at fault, and very rarely did he show anger. I was on duty, in the presence, at Merj 'Ayûn[1] some time before the Franks attacked Acre—may God enable us to conquer it! It was his custom to ride out each day at the hour appointed for mounting on horseback; afterwards, when he dismounted, he had dinner served, and ate with all his suite. Then he retired to a specially-reserved tent, where he took a siesta. On awaking, he used to say his prayers, and remain alone with me for some time. He then read some passages from a collection of traditions, or a treatise on law. With my assistance he even read a work by Soleim er-Râzi,[2] wherein the doctor epitomises the four component

---

[1] *Merj 'Ayûn*, ' meadow of springs.' A plain 9 miles N.W. of Baniâs, E. of Shakîf Arnûn (Belfort).

[2] Abû el-Fath Soleim er-Râzi was born at *Rai* (*Rhey*, ancient *Rhagae*), near Tehran, the birthplace of Harûn er-Rashîd, and one of the great cities of the Seljûk sovereigns. He was noted for his learning and piety, and, besides works on Moslem law, wrote an explanation of obscure terms in the traditions. He settled at Tyre, and was drowned in the Red Sea whilst returning from the pilgrimage (1055), when he was over 80 years of age (Ibn Khallikan, i. 584).—W.

3

sections of the science of jurisprudence. One day, having returned at the usual hour, he presided at the meal which he had ordered to be prepared, and was about to retire when he was informed that the hour of prayer was at hand. He returned to his seat, saying : 'We will say the prayer, and lie down afterwards.' Then he entered into conversation, although he looked very weary. He had already dismissed all those who were not on duty. Shortly afterwards an old memlûk, for whom he entertained great esteem, entered the tent, and presented a petition on behalf of the volunteers who were fighting for the faith. The Sultan replied : 'I am tired ; let me have it later.' Instead of obeying, the man opened the petition for the Sultan to read, holding it so close to him that it almost touched his face. His master, seeing the name which stood at the head of the petition, remarked that this man was justly entitled to a favourable hearing. The memlûk said : 'Then let my master write his approval on the petition.' The Sultan answered : 'There is no inkstand here.' The prince was sitting just at the entrance to the tent, which was a large one. No one, therefore, could pass in, but we could see the inkstand inside. 'It is there, within the tent,' replied the memlûk, as though requesting his master to fetch the inkstand himself. The Sultan turned, and, seeing the object he sought, cried : 'By God! he is right.' Then, leaning upon his left arm, he stretched out his right, reached the inkstand, and put it in front of him. Whilst he was notifying his approval on the petition, I remarked to him : 'God said to His Holy Prophet : *Thou art of a grand nature* (Kurân lxviii. 4), and I cannot but think your Highness is possessed of the same nature as the Prophet.' He answered : 'It is not worth speaking of; I have satisfied a petitioner, and that is ample reward.' If such a thing had occurred to the best of common folk, it would have angered him. Where is there another man who would answer one under his authority with such gentleness? Here, indeed, were kindness and gentleness carried to their utmost limits, *and God wastes not the hire of those who do well* (Kurân ix. 121).

It sometimes happened that the cushion on which he was seated would be trampled under foot, so great was the crowd of suppliants presenting their petitions ; but he was never disturbed by it. One day, when I was on duty, the mule I rode started off, terrified at some camels, and he forced me against the Sultan with such violence that I hurt his thigh ; but he only smiled—may God be merciful to him ! On another occasion—on a rainy, windy day—I rode into Jerusalem before him on my mule, and it was so muddy that, as she splashed along, the mud was spattered even over him, and his clothes were quite spoilt. But he only laughed, and seeing that I wanted to get behind him, he would not suffer me to do so.

The people who came to implore his help or to complain to him of injustice sometimes addressed him in the most unseemly manner, but he always listened smiling, and attended to their requests. Here is an instance, the like of which it would be difficult to find on record : The brother of the king of the Franks[1] was marching on Jaffa, for our troops had withdrawn from the vicinity of the enemy and returned to en-Natrûn. From this place to

---

[1] Probably Henry of Champagne is here intended. He marched from Acre to relieve Jaffa in 1192. He married Isabel, half-sister of Sibyl, wife of King Guy, and was in this sense his brother. He had, however, been then made King of Jerusalem, Guy of Lusignan having been given Cyprus. King Richard had left Jaffa when Salâh ed-Din attacked it, but returned from Haifa by sea, and, landing August 1, 1192, defeated Salâh ed-Dîn's forces outside the walls. Henry of Champagne arrived later. See chap. clxvi., Part II.

Jaffa is two long or three ordinary marches for an army.[1] The Sultan ordered his troops to march in the direction of Cæsarea, hoping to fall in with reinforcements expected by the Franks, and to take any advantage possible. The Franks in Jaffa had notice of this manœuvre, and the king of England, who was there with a large force, embarked the greater portion of it, and sent it by sea to Cæsarea, fearing lest some mischance should befall the reinforcements. He himself remained at Jaffa, knowing that the Sultan and his army had withdrawn. When the Sultan reached the neighbourhood of Cæsarea, he found that the reinforcements had entered that place and were safe, so that he could do nothing. He therefore resumed his march the same evening just as night began to close in, pushed on until daybreak, and appeared unexpectedly before Jaffa. The king of England was encamped outside the walls of the city, and had only seventeen knights with him and about three hundred foot-soldiers. At the first alarm this accursed man mounted his horse, for he was brave and fearless, and possessed excellent judgment in all military matters. Instead of retiring into the city, he maintained his position in face of the Moslem troops (who surrounded him on all sides except towards the sea), and drew up his own men in order of battle. The Sultan, anxious to make the most of the opportunity, gave the order to charge; but one of the emirs,[2] a Kurd by birth, addressed him at that moment with the greatest rudeness, in anger at the smallness of his share of booty. The Sultan turned his rein and hastened away like a man in

---

[1] *Latrûn* is only 20 miles from Jaffa, but as Salâh ed-Dîn advanced to the 'Auja to intercept Henry of Champagne, his total march, from Latrûn to Jaffa, was 30 miles.   Boha ed-Dîn seems to reckon 10 miles a long march.

[2] This was el-Jenâh. See p. 375.

wrath, for he saw very clearly that his troops would do no good that day. Leaving them there, he ordered the tent which had been pitched for him to be struck, and his soldiers were withdrawn from their position. They felt certain that the Sultan that same day would crucify a great number. His son, el-Melek ez-Zâher, told me that he was so afraid on this occasion that he did not dare to come into his father's sight, although he had charged the enemy and pushed forward until he had received the countermanding order. The Sultan, he said, continued his retreat, and did not halt until he reached Yâzûr,[1] having been marching almost the whole of the day. Here a small tent was pitched for him, in which he rested. The troops also encamped in the places where they had halted before, and bivouacked under slight shelter,[2] as is usual in such cases. There was not one of the emirs but trembled for himself, expecting to suffer a severe punishment or reprimand at the hands of the Sultan. The prince added : ' I had not the courage to enter his tent until he called for me. When I went in, I saw that he had just received a quantity of fruit that had been sent to him from Damascus. " Send for the emirs," he said, " let them come and taste." These words removed my anxiety, and I went to summon the emirs. They entered trembling, but he received them with smiles and so graciously that they were reassured and set at their ease. And when they left his presence they were ready to march as though nothing had happened. What true gentleness of heart ! There is nothing like it in these days, and the history of former kings does not afford us any similar instance.

---

[1] He only retreated 3½ miles.
[2] *Sawâiwiniat*, plural from *Sawâni*, ' a cloth.'

CHAPTER VIII.

HIS CARE TO BE POLITE.

THE Holy Prophet said : ' I have been sent to make mani-
fest in all their beauty the noble qualities of the soul.'
When any man gave his hand to the Prophet he clasped
it until the other withdrew it. And so, too, our Sultan
was very noble of heart ; his face expressed kindliness, his
modesty was great, and his politeness perfect. No visitor
ever came to him without being given to eat, and receiving
what he desired. He greeted everyone, even infidels, politely.
For instance, after the conclusion of peace in the month of
Shawâl, in the year 588 (October to November, A.D. 1192),
he left Jerusalem to journey to Damascus, and whilst he
was on his way he saw the Prince of Antioch, who had
come up unexpectedly, and was standing at the entrance
of his tent. This prince had come to ask something from
him, and the Sultan gave him back el-'Amk,[1] which territory he had acquired in the year 584 (A.D. 1188-1189), at
the time of the conquest of the coast-lands. So, too, I was
present at Nazareth when the Sultan received the visit of
the Lord of Sidon ; he showed him every mark of respect,
treated him with honour, and admitted him to his own
table. He even proposed to him that he should embrace
Islâm, set before him some of the beauties of our religion,
and urged him to adopt it.

He always gave a kind reception to sheikhs, to all
learned and gifted men, and to the various influential

---

[1] The great plain of *el-'Amk* was known in ancient times as the
Plain of Antioch. It lies N.E. of the city, and is the widening out of
the valley of the *Kara Su.* It was the scene of Aurelian's victory over
Zenobia (A.D. 273), and within its limits is the Lake of Antioch.—W.

persons who came to see him. He enjoined us to present to him every notable sheikh passing through the camp, so that he might exercise his generosity. In the year 584 (A.D. 1188-1189) there came a man, who united to great learning the practices of a Sûfî.[1] He was an important personage, whose father was Lord of Tôrîz.[2] He had renounced his father's rank to give himself up to study and the practice of good works. He had just performed the pilgrimage (*Hâj*) and visited Jerusalem; then, having inspected that city, and having seen there works of the Sultan, he conceived the wish to see him. He arrived in the camp, and entered my tent unannounced. I made haste to bid him welcome, and asked what motive had brought him thither. He answered that the sight of the wonderful and beautiful works of the Sultan had inspired him with the desire to see him. I reported this to the Sultan the same night, and he ordered the man to be presented to him. He learnt from his lips a tradition concerning the Prophet, and listened to a discourse pronounced by his visitor, who exhorted him to practice good works. This man passed the night with me in my tent, and after morning prayer took his leave. I remarked to him that it would be very unseemly to depart without bidding the

---

[1] A Sûfî is a man who professes the mystic principles of the *Tasawwuf*, or Sûfiism. The principal occupation of a Sûfî, whilst in the body, is meditation on the Unity of God, the remembrance of God's names, and progressive advancement in the journey of life, so as to attain unification with God. Human life is likened to a journey, and the seeker after God to a traveller. The first stage of the 'traveller' is 'service,' that is, to serve God as the first step towards a knowledge of Him. The last stage is death, which is regarded as 'extinction,' or total absorption into the Deity. The great object of the Sûfî mystic is to lose his own identity. Having effected this, perfection is attained.—Hughes, 'Dictionary of Islâm.'

[2] *Tôrîz*, or *Tavrîz*, the modern *Tabrîz*, the capital of Azerbijan in Persia.—W.

Sultan farewell, but he would not yield to my remonstrances, and carried out his original purpose. 'I have
accomplished my desire,' said he, 'with regard to the
prince ; my only object in coming here was to visit
and see him ;' and he departed forthwith. Some days
afterwards the Sultan inquired after him, and I told him
what had occurred. He was much vexed that I had not
informed him of the visitor's departure. ' What !' cried he,
' am I to receive the visit of a man like that and let him
depart with no experience of my liberality ?' He expressed
such strong disapproval of my conduct, that I wrote to
Mohi ed-Dîn,[1] Kâdi of Damascus, charging him to seek the
man out and give him a letter I enclosed, which was written
with my own hand. In this note I informed the holy man
of the Sultan's displeasure on learning that he had left
without seeing him again, and I begged him, in the name
of our friendship, to return. He arrived when I was least
thinking of him, and I conducted him at once to the
Sultan, who received him graciously, kept him for several
days, and sent him away laden with gifts—a robe of
honour, a suitable riding-animal, and a great number of
garments for distribution amongst the members of his
family, and his disciples and neighbours. He gave him
also money for the expenses of his journey. Ever afterwards the man displayed the keenest gratitude to the
Sultan, and offered up the most sincere prayers for the
preservation of his life.

I was present one day when a Frank prisoner was

---

[1] Abû el-Maâli Muhammad Mohi ed-Dîn, generally known as Ibn
ez-Zaki, was a descendant of the Khalif Othman, and a member of the
tribe of the Koreish. He was well versed in law, literature, and the
sciences, and was highly esteemed by Salâh ed-Dîn. He was selected
to pronounce the *Khutba* at the first Friday prayer after the capture
of Jerusalem. He died in 1202. His father, surnamed Zaki ed-Dîn,
was also Kâdi of Damascus (Ibn Khallikan, ii. 633).—W.

brought before him. This man was in such a state of excitement that his terror was visible in every feature. The interpreter asked him the cause of his fear, and God put the following answer in the mouth of the unfortunate fellow : ' Before I saw his face I was greatly afraid, but now that I am in the presence (of the prince) and can see him, I am certain that he will do me no harm.' The Sultan, moved by these words, gave him his life, and sent him away free.

I was attending the prince on one of the expeditions he used to make on the flanks of the enemy, when one of the scouts brought up a woman, rending her garments, weeping and beating her breast without ceasing. ' This woman,' the soldier said, ' came out from among the Franks, and asked to be taken to the Sultan ; so I brought her here.' The Sultan asked her, through his interpreter, what was the matter, and she replied : ' Some Moslem thieves got into my tent last night and carried off my child, a little girl. All night long I have never ceased begging for help, and our princes advised me to appeal to the King of the Moslems. "He is very merciful," they said. "We will allow you to go out to seek him and ask for your daughter." Therefore they permitted me to pass through the lines, and in you lies my only hope of finding my child.' The Sultan was moved by her distress ; tears came into his eyes, and, acting from the generosity of his heart, he sent a messenger to the market-place of the camp, to seek her little one and bring her away, after repaying her purchaser the price he had given. It was early morning when her case was heard, and in less than an hour the horseman returned, bearing the little girl on his shoulder. As soon as the mother caught sight of her, she threw herself on the ground, rolling her face in the dust, and weeping so violently that it drew tears from all who saw her. She raised her eyes to heaven, and uttered words which we did not understand. We gave her back her daughter, and she was mounted to return to the enemy's army.

The Sultan was very averse to the infliction of corporal punishment on his servants, even when they cheated him beyond endurance. On one occasion two purses filled with Egyptian gold-pieces had been lodged in the treasury ; these were stolen, and two purses full of copper coins left in their place. All he did was to dismiss the people employed in that department from his service.

In the year 583 (A.D. 1187), at the battle of Haṭṭîn—a famous day's fight of which, please God, we shall speak in its proper place—Prince Arnâṭ (Renaud de Chatillon), Lord of el-Kerak,[1] and the king of the Franks of the seacoast, were both taken prisoners, and the Sultan commanded them to be brought before him. This accursed Arnâṭ was a great infidel, and a very strong man. On one occasion, when there was a truce between the Moslems and the Franks, he treacherously attacked and carried off a caravan that passed through his territory, coming from Egypt. He seized these people, put them to torture, and put some of them in grain-pits (*metamîr*), and imprisoned some in narrow cells. When they objected that there was a truce between the two peoples, he replied : 'Ask your

---

[1] Rénaud de Chatillon came to Palestine in 1148 with Louis VII. of France. He became ruler of Antioch next year, having married Constance, the heiress of Bohemund II., and widow of Raymond of Poitou. He was taken prisoner by Manuel Comnenos at Malmistra, November 23, 1160, and by Nûr ed-Dîn, on August 12, 1163. He remained prisoner fourteen years at Aleppo, and on his release married the widow of Humphrey of Toron, and so acquired the great fief of Oultre Jourdan, including the castles of Kerak and Shôbek (Montreal), commanding the Hâj Road to Mecca. He was a bitter enemy of the Moslems, and marched on Medina in 1182-1183, escaping with difficulty back to Kerak. He seized a Moslem caravan from Mecca, near Shôbek, in 1187, during a truce with Salâh ed-Dîn.—See ' Jacques de Vitry,' p. 99.

Muhammad to deliver you.' The Sultan, to whom these words were reported, took an oath to slay the infidel with his own hand, if God should ever place him in his power. The day of the battle of Haṭṭin God delivered this man into the hands of the Sultan, and he resolved at once to slay him, that he might fulfil his oath. He commanded him to be brought before him, together with the king. The latter complained of thirst, and the Sultan ordered a cup of sherbet to be given him. The king, having drunk some of it, handed the cup to Arnât, whereupon the Sultan said to the interpreter : ' Say to the king, " It is you who give him drink, but I give him neither to drink nor to eat." ' By these words he wished it to be understood that honour forbade him to harm any man who had tasted his hospitality. He then struck him on the neck[1] with his own hand, to fulfil the vow he had made. After this, when he had taken Acre, he delivered all the prisoners, to the number of about four thousand, from their wretched durance, and sent them back to their own country and their homes, giving each of them a sum of money for the expenses of his journey. This is what I have been told by many persons, for I was not present myself when it took place.

The Sultan was of a sociable disposition, of a sweet temper, and delightful to talk with. He was well acquainted with the pedigrees of the old Arabs, and with the details of their battles ; he knew all their adventures ; he had the pedigrees of their horses at his fingers' ends, and was master of all curious and strange lore. Thus in conversation with him people always heard things which they could never have learned from others. In company, he put everyone at their ease. He comforted those who were in trouble, questioned those who were ill on the nature of their malady, on the treatment they had adopted, on

---

[1] He was then beheaded by the slaves. See p. 115.

their diet, and on the changes they experienced in their system. He insisted strictly upon due seemliness in conversation, never suffering anyone to be spoken of except with respect ; he would talk with none but persons of good conversation, lest his ears should be offended ; having his tongue under perfect control, he never gave way to abusive language ; he could also control his pen, and never made use of cutting words in writing to a Moslem. He was most strict in the fulfilment of his promises.

When an orphan was brought before him, he always exclaimed : ' May the mercy of God be upon the two (parents) who have left this child behind them !' Then he would lavish comfort upon him, and allow him the same emoluments that his father had enjoyed. If the orphan had an experienced and trustworthy person amongst his relations he would charge him with the care of the boy ; if not, he would deduct, from the father's emoluments, sufficient for the orphan's maintenance, and then place him with some person who superintended his education and bringing-up. He never saw an old man without showing him the kindest marks of respect and good-will, and making him some present. And all these noble qualities remained undimmed in his heart until God recalled him to Himself, and removed him to the throne of His mercy, to the abode of His grace.

This is but a meagre sketch of his lofty disposition and of his noble character. My aim has been to be concise, and to avoid prolixity lest I should weary my readers. I have mentioned nothing that I have not witnessed, adding thereto information obtained from credible authorities which I have myself tested. What I have here told is but a part of that which I was able to observe whilst in the Sultan's service, and is little indeed in comparison with all that could be told by his life-long friends, and those who have grown old in his service. But what I have given will convince an intelligent reader of the grandeur and purity of the prince's character and feelings.

Now, having brought to a close the first part of my work, I will pass to the second, in which I shall treat of the changes of fortune experienced by the Sultan, and of his battles and conquests. May God hallow his soul and shed the light of His mercy upon his tomb!

PART II.

IN WHICH ARE SET FORTH THE CHANGES OF FORTUNE
EXPERIENCED BY THE SULTAN, AND THE HISTORY
OF HIS CONQUESTS.

CHAPTER I.

HIS FIRST CAMPAIGN IN EGYPT, IN WHICH HE SERVED
UNDER HIS UNCLE, ASAD ED-DÎN (SHÎRKÛH).

A CERTAIN man, named ed-Darghâm, rebelled against
Shâwer,[1] Vizier of the Egyptians, with the view of
depriving him of the viziership. Shâwer collected a great
number of men to oppose him, but could not overcome
him, even with the support of this army. He was driven
out of Cairo by his adversary, and his eldest son, Tai,
perished in the revolution. Darghâm then assumed the

---

[1] Abû Shujâ Shâwer es-S'âdi, the Arab Governor of Upper Egypt,
killed the vizier of el-'Âdid the Fatimite Khalif of Egypt, and took
possession of the vizierate. He was driven from office by Abû
el-Ashbâl Darghâm, the prefect of the palace, and fled for protection
to Nûr ed-Dîn, the Lord of Syria. He returned to Egypt with Shîrkûh
and his troops, and in the battle that ensued, Darghâm was killed
(1164). Shâwer then became vizier, but on the occasion of Shîrkûh's
third expedition to Egypt, he was killed (1168) by Salâh ed-Dîn and
'Izz ed-Dîn Jurdîk (Ibn Khallikan, i. 608).—W.

viziership. It was the custom when anyone successfully raised the standard of revolt against a vizier (of the Fatimite khalifs) to submit to the victor, and establish him with full authority in the office for which he had fought. Indeed, the whole power of the government lay in the vizier's army, and the vizier had the title of Sultan. They (the Khalifs) took care not to look into matters too closely, and had followed this policy from the first establishment of their dominion. Shâwer, thus defeated and driven from Cairo, set out at once for Syria, and presenting himself at the court of Nûr ed-Dîn,[1] ibn Zenghi, asked for troops to fight his enemies. Nûr ed-Dîn ordered Asad ed-Dîn[2] to proceed to the strong city of Misr,[3] and when there to maintain the rights of the man who had asked his assistance, and to inquire into the condition and

---

[1] Abû el-Kâsim Mahmûd el-Melek el-'Âdel Nûr ed-Dîn was son of Imâd ed-Dîn Zenghi. On the death of his father (1146) he took possession of Aleppo, whilst his brother occupied Mosul. In 1154 he took Damascus, Hamath, Baalbek, and Membij ; and by 1164 he had gained possession of Hârim, 'Azâz, and Bâniâs. In 1173 he took Mar'ash and Behesne. He sent Shîrkûh and Salâh ed-Dîn to Egypt three times, and his name was struck on coins and pronounced in the *Khutba* (Friday sermon) in Egypt when Salâh ed-Dîn was his Viceroy in that country. He was an enlightened prince, and was respected by both Christians and Moslems. He died in 1174, aged 56 (Ibn Khallikan, iii. 338).—W.

[2] Abû el-Hârith Shîrkûh el-Melek el-Mansûr Asad ed-Dîn was uncle of Salâh ed-Dîn. He was sent to Egypt by Nûr ed-Dîn in 1163-1164, and returned to Damascus in 1164 after defeating Darghâm, and restoring Shâwer to the vizierate. In 1167 he again went to Egypt, and fought the celebrated battle of *el-Bâbein.* He entered Egypt for the third time in 1168, and, when Shâwer was killed, became vizier to the Khalif, el-'Âdid. He died at Cairo in 1169, and was succeeded by Salâh ed-Dîn, who had accompanied him in all his expeditions (Ibn Khallikan, i. 626).—W.

[3] *Misr*, or *Masr*, as it is usually pronounced, is used both of old Cairo and of Egypt generally. *Misr el-Mahrûsah* probably refers to Cairo.

resources of the country. This took place in the year 558 (A.D. 1163). Asad ed-Dîn at once commenced preparations for the campaign, and when he set out for Egypt, took his nephew (Salâh ed-Dîn) with him. The latter went against his inclination, but his uncle required him to command the army and assist him with advice. They arrived at Misr, with Shâwer, on the second day of the month Jomada II. (May 8) of the above year. Their arrival caused a great sensation, and struck terror into the inhabitants. Shâwer, supported (by Asad ed-Dîn), triumphed over his rival, and was re-established in office. (Asad ed-Dîn) enforced the acceptance of a treaty on his own terms, and, having re-established (Shâwer's) authority, and collected exact information as to the condition and resources of the country, set out on his return (to Syria). The hope of making himself master of Egypt had taken root in his heart, for he saw that it was a land wanting in men (worthy of the name), and that the direction of public affairs was left to chance and imbecile management. He commenced his march to Syria on the 7th of Zu el-Hijja of the above year (November 6, 1164). He had come to no decision, and settled no question without first consulting Salâh ed-Dîn, so much did he think of the felicity and good fortune that seemed to follow him, and so highly did he esteem his nephew's good judgment and the success that attended all his undertakings. On his return to Syria, he gave himself up to making his plans and meditating on the means he might employ to justify his visiting Egypt again. His thoughts were entirely occupied with this project, and until the year 562 (A.D. 1166) he continued to discuss it, and to lay the ground-work of his plans, with (his sovereign) el-Melek el-'Âdel Nûr ed-Dîn ibn Zenghi.

CHAPTER II.

SECOND EXPEDITION INTO EGYPT, CALLED THE EVENT OF EL-BÂBEIN.[1]

ASAD ED-DÎN used very often to speak publicly about his plans with regard to Egypt. Shâwer heard of them, and, fearing lest the country should fall into the hands of the Turks,[2] and knowing full well that Asad ed-Din would most certainly invade the land and take possession of it, he wrote to the Franks and made an agreement with them. By this treaty they undertook to enter Egypt,

[1] In January, 1167, Nûr ed-Dîn sent Asad ed-Dîn Shîrkûh a second time to Egypt, with orders to take possession of the country. Shâwer, the vizier of the Khalif, hearing of Nûr ed-Din's preparations, concluded a treaty with Amalric (Amaury), King of Jerusalem, under which the Franks were to assist the Khalif with an army. Shîrkûh marched by the *Wâdi el-Ghazâl*, and, whilst crossing the desert, was caught in a violent storm. He lost many men, and, after abandoning baggage and provisions, his army arrived in a crippled state before *Atfih*, on the right bank of the Nile above Cairo. The Franks, whose policy it was to lengthen the war, remained near Cairo, and gave Shîrkûh's men time to recruit. At last they attacked Shîrkûh, and forced his entrenchments, but did not follow up their victory. Shîrkûh commenced his retreat to Syria, but, suddenly retracing his steps, fell upon the combined force of Franks and Egyptians whilst it was encamped at *el-Bâbein*, near *Tûra*, about six miles south of Cairo. He gained a complete victory—often referred to afterwards as the 'day,' or 'event,' of el-Bâbein—and all Egypt fell into his hands. He afterwards evacuated the country in consequence of a treaty with the Franks ; but in the following year (1168) he returned and permanently occupied Egypt.

The omission of any mention of the battle in this chapter is remarkable. Possibly the author was unwilling to enlarge upon a victory in which his hero only played a subordinate part.—W.

[2] Nûr ed-Dîn's father, Imâd ed-Dîn Zenghi was one of the most eminent emirs under the Seljûk Turks ; and Nûr ed-Dîn was regarded as a Turk by the Arabs in Egypt.—W.

4

which was placed in their hands without reserve, and
to give every assistance to the vizier, who would thus be
enabled to crush his enemies, and relieve himself of all
apprehension. Asad ed-Dîn and Nûr ed-Dîn became very
anxious when they heard this news, for they were afraid
that if the infidels once occupied Misr, they would take
possession of the whole country. Asad ed-Dîn began his
preparations for a campaign ; Nûr ed-Dîn furnished him
with troops, and constrained Salâh ed-Dîn, against his wish,
to accompany his uncle. They commenced their march
on the 12th of the month Rabi'a I., in the year 562
(January 6, A.D. 1167), and entered Egyptian territory
at the very same time as the Franks. Shâwer and all the
Egyptians with him joined the Franks to give battle to
Asad ed-Dîn. Many skirmishes and battles took place
between the two armies ; then the Franks and Asad ed-
Dîn both left Egypt. What decided the Franks to leave
was the news that Nûr ed-Dîn had invaded their territory
at the head of his forces, and taken El-Muneitera.[1] Fearing
for their possessions (in Syria), they left Egypt. Asad ed-
Dîn made up his mind to return on account of the smallness of his army compared with the combined forces of the
Franks and Egyptians, and on account of the fatigues they
had undergone, and the dangers they had encountered.
He did not retire until he had treated with the Franks for
the evacuation of the country. It was towards the end of
the (Moslem) year that he started for Syria. His ardent
desire to make himself master of Egypt was now
strengthened by the fear that the Franks would occupy
that country. He knew that they had informed themselves, as he had done, of the condition of Egypt, and were
as conversant as he was with all that related to it. He
waited, therefore, in Syria, full of unrest, his mind torn by

---

[1] *el-Muneitera*, 'the little watch-tower.' See p. 51, n. 2.

ambition, confident that Fate was leading him towards something (the possession of Egypt) which was reserved for another.[1]

CHAPTER III.

ASAD ED-DÎN'S THIRD EXPEDITION INTO EGYPT, AND CONQUEST OF THAT COUNTRY.

IN the month of Rejeb (April-May, A.D. 1167), after Asad ed-Dîn had departed (for Egypt), Nûr ed-Dîn took the castle of el-Muneitera, and demolished the fortress of Akâf in the Berrîya.[2] In the month of Ramadân (June-July), he met his brother Kotb ed-Dîn[3] (Prince of Mosul), and Zein ed-Dîn[4] (Prince of Arbela) at Hamah,[5] with a view of invading the enemy's territory. Having penetrated into the regions occupied by the Franks, they

[1] In 1167 King Amaury of Jerusalem was allied with the Fatimite Khalif of Egypt; but, after his marriage with Maria, grand-niece of Manuel Comnenos, he agreed with the Greek Emperor to attempt the conquest of Egypt. The Knights Hospitallers assisted, but the Templars refused to break the treaty with Egypt. Bilbeis was taken, November 3, 1167, but King Amaury retreated on hearing that Nûr ed-Dîn had again sent Shîrkûh to Egypt with a large force.

[2] The *Berrîya*, 'outer land,' or 'desert,' was a term applied to the region between Damascus and Emesa. *el-Muneitera* near Tripoli, according to Yâkût, was a fortress in Syria. *Akâf* is not known.

[3] Kotb ed-Dîn Maudûd, el-'Âraj, 'the lame,' son of Zenghi, succeeded his brother, Seif ed-Dîn Ghâzi, as Lord of Mosul in 1149, and died in 1170. He is noted as having imprisoned his vizier, the celebrated Jemâl ed-Dîn (Ibn Khallikan, iii. 458).—W.

[4] Zein ed-Dîn 'Ali Kuchuk was a Turkoman who had gained possession of Arbela (now *Erbîl*, about 52 miles from Mosul on the road to Baghdad) and other towns in that part of the country. He retained Arbela; and gave the other towns he had taken to the sons of Kotb ed-Dîn, the Lord of Mosul. Zein ed-Dîn was remarkable for his great strength and courage (Ibn Khallikan, ii. 535).—W.

[5] *Hamah*, the ancient *Hamath*, in the Orontes valley.

4—2

demolished the castle of Hûnîn,[1] in the month of Shawâl
(July-August) of the same year. In the month of Zu
el-'Kada (August-September), Asad ed-Dîn returned from
Egypt. The cause of this (the third expedition into Egypt)
was the action of the Franks, whom may God confound!
They assembled their footmen and horsemen, and marched
on Egypt, thus breaking all the promises they had made
to the Egyptians and Asad ed-Dîn when they agreed to
the treaty of peace; and this they did in the hope of
obtaining possession of Egypt. On receiving this news,
Nûr ed-Dîn and Asad ed-Dîn felt that they could no
longer remain inactive, and they began to organize a fresh
expedition to that country. Nûr ed-Dîn contributed his
share in money and men, but he did not take part in it
personally, being afraid that the Franks would invade his
own dominions, and also because he had just received from
Mosul news of a most important event—the death of Zein
ed-Dîn 'Ali,[2] the son of Bektikîn, who had died in the
month of Zu el-Hijja, in the year 563 (September-October,
A.D. 1168). This chief had granted to the Atabeg Kotb
ed-Dîn[3] all the strongholds he possessed, with the exception of Arbela,[4] a city which the Atabeg Zenghi had
bestowed upon him. Therefore, Nûr ed-Dîn turned his
ambition in this direction, and allowed the army to depart
(for Egypt). Asad ed-Dîn, for his part, contributed to the
strength of the army by his own presence, by supplies of
money, and by taking with him his brothers, the people of
his household, and the men whom he kept as retainers.

---

[1] *Hûnîn*, in Upper Galilee, 9 miles S.W. of Bânîas.

[2] See p. 51.

[3] Kotb ed-Dîn (see p. 51) was *Atabeg* or 'guardian' to a son of one
of the Seljûk Sultans.

[4] Arbela (*Erbil*) gave its name to the battle in which Darius was
defeated by Alexander. It is now a Turkish military post, and an
important road-centre.—W.

The Sultan (Saláh ed-Dîn) said to me one day: 'Of all men, I was the one who least wished to accompany the expedition, and it was not of my own accord that I went with my uncle.' Such is the meaning of the words of the Most High : ' *Peradventure that ye hate a thing while it is good for you* ' (Kurân ii. 213). When Shâwer learnt that the Franks were marching upon Egypt with the purpose (we have set forth), he sent to ask Asad ed-Dîn for immediate assistance. Asad ed-Dîn set out in all haste, and arrived at Misr in the course of the month of Rabi'a I., 564 (December, 1168—January, 1169). In the month of Moharrem (October) of this year, Nûr ed-Dîn obtained possession of the fortress of J'aber[1] from Ibn Mâlek, whom he had taken prisoner, in exchange for Serûj,[2] the Bâb Biza'a,[3] and El-Melûha. In the same month died Yarûk, a chief whose name is preserved in that of the village of el-Yarûkiya.[4] When the Franks learnt that Asad ed-Dîn had come into Egypt, they made a treaty with the government of that country, turned back, and were obliged to desist. Asad ed-Din remained there, and was visited frequently by Shâwer. This minister had promised to indemnify him for the expenses of the expedition, but he

---

[1] *Kaleh J'aber*, or *Dusar* (ancient Dausaria), on the left bank of the Euphrates, N. of *Rakka*, and about 1 mile from the river. It was taken by the Seljûk Sultan Melik Shah. Zenghi, the founder of the Zenghid Dynasty of Mosul, was murdered by his eunuchs whilst besieging it.—W.

[2] *Serûj*, the Serug of Gen. xi. 20, lies between Harrân and the Euphrates.

[3] *Bab*, or *Bap*, is about 20 miles from Aleppo, on the road to Membij. In a mosque on the hill above it are shown the tombs of *Nebi Haskil* (Ezekiel) and *'Akil*, a brother of the Khalif 'Ali. *Biza'a* is about a mile further on, and is apparently on an ancient site.—W.

[4] *El-Yarûkiya* was a large quarter lying outside Aleppo, in which Yârûk, one of the Turkoman Emirs of Nûr ed-Dîn, built a palace and lived.

gave him nothing. Then the claws of the *Lion of the Faith* (Asad ed-Dîn) fastened themselves upon Egypt. He knew that if the Franks found a favourable opportunity, they would take possession of the country; he felt that constant expeditions to drive them out would be unwise; he saw clearly that Shâwer was playing, now with him, now with the Franks; and he was convinced that, so long as the vizier remained, he would be unable to possess himself of Egypt. He therefore resolved to have him arrested on one of his visits. For all except Asad ed-Dîn used to visit Shâwer, and do him homage, but Shâwer himself paid visits to Asad ed-Dîn. On these occasions he used to come on horseback, with drums, trumpets, and banners, according to the custom of the viziers of that country, but none of the officers dared lay a hand upon him. It was Salâh ed-Dîn himself who arrested him, and in this wise : Shâwer had set out to visit them, and (Salâh ed-Dîn), having mounted his horse, went to meet him. He then rode by his side, and as they were going along, he seized him by the collar, and commanded his men to fall upon the vizier's retinue, who took to flight, and were stripped and plundered by the soldiers. Shâwer was led a prisoner to a tent set apart. Very soon the Egyptians sent a eunuch of the palace, bearing a written message, in which they demanded the head of the prisoner. Shâwer was beheaded, and his head sent to them. The Egyptians then sent a vizier's robe to Asad ed-Dîn, who put it upon him, and betook himself to the citadel, where he was accepted, and established as vizier. In this the Egyptians were acting in accordance with their custom of bestowing the vizier-ship on the man who conquered his adversary. Asad ed-Dîn's nomination took place on the seventeenth of the month Rabi'a II., 564 (January 18, A.D. 1169). From that time Asad ed-Dîn exercised supreme authority, and entrusted the general management of affairs to Salâh ed-Dîn, on account of his great abilities, and the wide knowledge, good judgment, and administrative talents he displayed.

CHAPTER IV.

DEATH OF ASAD ED-DÎN. THE CHIEF AUTHORITY DE-VOLVES UPON THE SULTAN (SALÂH ED-DÎN).

ASAD ED-DÎN was a very hearty eater, and was so fond of rich dishes that he frequently suffered from surfeit and indigestion. He used to recover, after suffering great pain ; but, when he was attacked by severe illness, it induced inflammation of the throat, of which he died. This took place on the 22nd of Jomada II. in the above year (March 23, A.D. 1169). After his death Salâh ed-Dîn was invested with supreme authority. The Sultan soon had the satis-faction of seeing his government respected, and order established on all sides. He spent money lavishly, won all hearts, and brought everyone into obedience to his rule. In recognition of the blessings which God had vouchsafed to him, he gave up wine and the pleasures of the world, and devoted himself to serious business and to work. He never abandoned the course he then adopted ; he showed an industry which increased day by day until God sum-moned him to appear before His mercy. I have heard him say, ' When God allowed me to obtain possession of Egypt with so little trouble, I understood that He purposed to grant me the conquest of the *Sâhel*,[1] for He Himself

---

[1] Under the word *Sâhel*, ' plain,' the author refers to those countries on the Syrian coast which were then occupied by the Franks. Arab historians often employ the word as a name for Palestine and Phœnicia. Henceforth this word is rendered *coast*.

implanted the thought in my mind.' Therefore, directly his authority was firmly established, he began to send expeditions into the territories of the Franks, in the district round el-Kerak and esh-Shôbek.[1] The clouds of his munificence and liberality poured down their waters so copiously that there has never been recorded in history munificence such as he displayed when he was a vizier, responsible to the Egyptian government. He took great pains to establish the true faith (*sunna*) more firmly (in Egypt),[2] by aid of the '*ulema*, jurists, dervishes, and fakirs. People came to visit him from every side, and flocked to his court from all parts. He never disappointed the hopes of a visitor, nor allowed him to depart with empty hands.

As soon as Nûr ed-Dîn heard that Salâh ed-Dîn was established as Sultan, he took away the city of Emesa[3] from the officers whom Asad ed-Dîn had left in charge. This occurred in the month of Rejeb, in the year 564 (April, A.D. 1169).

CHAPTER V.

THE EXPEDITION OF THE FRANKS AGAINST DAMIETTA, WHICH MAY GOD PRESERVE!

WHEN the Franks heard what had happened to the true believers and to their own armies, and saw the

---

[1] *Kerak*, on the precipice E. of the Dead Sea, was a strong castle built by King Fulk about 1140. *Shôbek*, N. of Petra, called Montreal by Franks, was built in 1116 by Baldwin I.

[2] Salâh ed-Dîn was a Sunnî Moslem of the Shaf'ai sect. The Fatimite Khalifs of Egypt were Shi'ah Moslems not recognising the Khalif of Baghdad.

[3] *Emesa*, now *Homs*, on the right of the Orontes, between B'albek and Hamath in Syria.

Sultan (Saláh ed-Dîn) establishing his authority in Egypt upon a firm basis, they were convinced that he would obtain possession of their dominions, would lay waste their dwelling-places, and wipe away all traces of their rule. Therefore they joined themselves with the Greeks, intending to invade the land of Egypt, and gain possession of it. They determined to commence by an attack upon Damietta, as the master of that place would command both land and sea ; and, if they could occupy it, the city would serve as a depôt and place of retreat. They brought with them mangonels, movable towers, arbalists, besieging engines,[1] and other machines.[2] The Franks in Syria, when they heard this news, took heart of grace, and surprised the Moslems in the fortress of 'Akkàr,[3] which they succeeded in taking, and made the governor prisoner. This man was one of Nûr ed-Dîn's memlûks; his name was Khotlokh, the standard-bearer. This took place in the month of Rabî'a II. of the same year (January, 1169). In the month of Rejeb (April) occurred the death of el-'Imâdi, an old follower of Nûr ed-Dîn and his grand chamberlain. He was then 'lord of B'albek and of Tadmor (Palmyra).

---

[1] For mangonels see p. 31. The movable towers, or 'belfreys,' were brought in pieces, which were framed together. They were then pushed across the ditch of the fortress, which was filled up with hurdles and fascines to facilitate their passage. The towers protected the 'besieging engines' with which the walls were battered, and the mining operations. The besieged made every effort to burn or overthrow them. The arbalists (Fr. *arbalèt*, Lat. *arcus balistarius*), or cross-bows, are supposed to have been introduced into France by the first Crusaders, and into the English army by Richard I. They killed point-blank at 40-60 yards, and with elevation at 120-160 yards.—W.

[2] Manuel Comnenos sent 150 galleys to aid King Amaury at Damietta. The town was not taken, and a treaty with Saláh ed-Dîn was signed in December, 1170.

[3] *'Akkâr*, on the Lebanon, N.E. of Tripoli.

When Nûr ed-Dîn learnt that the Franks had taken the field and sat down before the walls of Damietta, he resolved to distract their attention; therefore in the month of Sh'abân of this year (565, April-May, A.D. 1170), he blockaded the fortress of el-Kerak; then, hearing that the Franks of the coast were marching upon him, he raised the siege and advanced to meet them; but they did not give him time to come up. After this he received news of the death of Mejed ed-Dîn Ibn ed-Daya,[1] at Aleppo, in the month of Ramadân 565 (May-June, A.D. 1170). The event touched him nearly, for this officer was the chief of his rulers. Therefore he set out to return to Syria. On arriving at 'Ashtera,[2] he learnt that on the 12th of Shawâl this year a great earthquake had taken place at Aleppo and destroyed a great part of the country. He then set out for Aleppo, and heard that his brother Koṭb ed-Dîn[3] had just died at Mosul. This event occurred on the 22nd of Zu el-Hijja of the above year (6 September, A.D. 1170). He received these tidings at Tell-Bâsher,[4] and the same night he started for Mosul.

Sultan Salâh ed-Dîn, understanding that the enemy meant to attack Damietta with all the forces at their command, threw into that city footmen and horsemen of well-known courage, provisions for the garrison, engines of war and arms, and, indeed, everything that might enable it to hold out. He promised the troops whom he stationed

---

[1] He was Governor of Aleppo, and one of the ed-Daya family from India.

[2] *'Ashtera* is the present *Tell 'Ashterah* (Ashtaroth Carnaim) in Bashan, on the road from Kerak to Damascus. See p. 109.

[3] Kotb ed-Dîn Maudûd, son of Zenghi. See p. 51.

[4] *Tell Bâsher*, about two days' journey N. of Aleppo, is now *Salasi Kaleh*, a large mound with ruins near the village of *Tulbashar*. It is the *Turbessel* of the Crusaders, and the place to which Jocelyn II. removed when Zenghi took Edessa in 1144.—W.

there to bring them reinforcements and appliances of war, and to repulse the enemy if they took up a position threatening the city. The number of his gifts and presents (on this occasion) was immense, but he was at that time a vizier exercising absolute authority, whose commands were implicitly obeyed. The Franks, having encamped against Damietta at the date we have given above, made a vigorous assault on that place, but whilst engaged with the garrison on one side, they had to sustain the onslaught of the cavalry which the Sultan hurled against them on the other. God gave the victory to the Moslems through the instrumentality of the Sultan, and in consequence of his well-chosen measures for the reïnforcement of the garrison. The Franks, seeing the failure of their plans and the triumph of the true faith over the unbelievers, thought it prudent to withdraw from danger and save themselves alive ; so they departed, disappointed in their expectations and full of regret for having incurred so much useless expense. Our people set fire to their mangonels, plundered all their warlike stores, and inflicted great loss of men upon them. Thanks to the goodness of God and to His assistance, the city was saved, the sword of their violence was shattered, and the Sultan's authority was firmly reestablished.

CHAPTER VI.

RELATES HOW HE MET HIS FATHER.

HE then went to meet his father, that his happiness might be complete in the pleasure of seeing him, and wishing in this to imitate his namesake, the prophet Joseph. It was in the course of the month of Jomada II., in the year 565 (February-March, A.D. 1170), that his father, Nejm ed-Dîn Ayûb,[1] came to join him. Urged by the respect he had always felt for his father, he offered to yield up to him all the power he had acquired ; but Ayûb replied : ' My dear son, remember that God would not have chosen thee to occupy this position had He not judged thee capable of filling it. When good fortune is sent us, we must not alter its destination.' Then the Sultan bestowed upon him the management of all the treasure of the realm. Salâh ed-Dîn continued to exercise absolute authority as vizier until the death of el-'Âdid Abu Muhammad 'Abd-Allah,[2] the last of the Egyptian khalifs.

In the month of Moharrem 566 (September-October, A.D., 1170) Nûr ed-Dîn took the city of Er-Rakka,[3] and afterwards, towards the end of the same month, he captured Nisibin.[4] He took Sinjâr[5] in the month of Rabî'a II.

---

[1] Abû esh-Shukr Ayûb el-Melek el-Afdal Nejm ed-Dîn was the son of Shâdi, the Governor of *Tekrît*, on the Tigris. He succeeded his father as governor, but afterwards took service with Zenghi, Lord of Mosul, who made him Governor of *B'albck*, where he founded a convent of Sûfîs. He was next Governor of Damascus for Nûr ed-Dîn, and defended it against the Franks in 1148. He finally died at Cairo from a fall from his horse (1173).—W.

[2] Shortly before the death of el-'Âdid, who was Fatimite (Shî'ite) Khalif from 1160 to 1171, Nûr ed-Dîn, who was a Sunni Moslem, and attached to the interests of the 'Abbassides, instructed Salâh ed-Dîn to restore the name of the 'Abbasside Khalif, el-Mostadi, in the Friday sermon (*khotba*), and depose the Shî'ite Khalif.—W.

[3] *Rakka.* on the left bank of the Euphrates, at the junction of the *Belik* with that river, is about eleven hours below *Meskinch*, the head of steam navigation. Rakka is on the site of *Nicephorium*, and nearly opposite to it, on the right bank, was Thapsacus. Here Cyrus forded the Euphrates, and Alexander crossed the river in pursuit of Darius.—W.

[4] *Nisibin*, ancient *Nisibis*, is near the point where the Jaghjagha Su (*Mygdonius*) leaves the mountains. It was a famous town and fortress, and was at one period (B.C. 149—A.D. 14), the residence of the Armenian kings. Trajan derived his title ' Parthicus ' from its capture.—W.

[5] *Sinjar (Singara)* on the *Nahr Thathar*, which rises in Jebel Sinjar, is on the road from *Deir* to Mosul, and about 63 miles west

(December, 1170; January, 1171), and then marched towards Mosul, with no hostile intention, however. Having crossed the river (the Tigris) with his troops at the ford of Beled, he encamped upon the Tell facing Mosul, which is called the Castle[1] (El-Hisn). Then he sent a message to his nephew, Seif ed-Dîn Ghâzi,[2] prince of that city, informing him of his friendly intentions. He concluded a treaty of peace with him, and on the 13th of the month of Jomada I. (January 22, A.D. 1171), made his entry into Mosul, confirmed his nephew in the government of that city, and gave him his daughter in marriage. To his other nephew, 'Imâd ed-Dîn,[3] he gave the city of Sinjâr. Then, leaving Mosul, he set out on his return to Syria, and entered Aleppo in the month of Sh'abân (April-May) of the same year.

CHAPTER VII.

DEATH OF EL-'ÂDID.

EL-'ÂDID died on Monday, the 10th of Moharrem, 567 (September 13, A.D. 1171). A short time before his death, Salâh ed-Din, whose authority was by this time firmly established, had ordered the *khotba* to be read in the name

---

of the latter place. It was a strong border fortress of the Romans, and beneath its walls was fought a memorable battle between Constantius and Sapor. It was stormed by the Persians during the reign of Julian. —W.

[1] The mound of *Kuyunjik* (*Nineveh*).

[2] Seif ed-Dîn Ghâzi succeeded his father, Kotb ed-Dîn, as Lord of Mosul in 1170. He submitted to his uncle, Nûr ed-Dîn, and was confirmed in his government. He took the side of his cousin, es-Sâleh, Lord of Aleppo, and was defeated by Salâh ed-Dîn. He died in 1180 (Ibn Khallikan).—W.

[3] See pp. 28, 71.

of the Abbaside Khalif, el-Mostadi,[1] and nothing occurred to disturb the order that prevailed throughout the country. All the treasures of money in the palace he expended and disposed of as presents. On each occasion, when God opened unto him the treasure-house of any prince, he gave the contents up as spoil, keeping nothing for himself.

He then commenced preparations for an expedition into the enemy's territory, organizing it with the greatest forethought. Nûr ed-Dîn, for his part, had resolved to make war (on the Franks), and had invited his nephew, the Prince of Mosul, to give him his support. This prince arrived with his army, and served under his uncle. The expedition terminated in the capture of 'Arka,[2] which took place in Moharrem, 567 (September-October, A.D. 1171).

CHAPTER VIII.

FIRST EXPEDITION UNDERTAKEN BY THE SULTAN OUT OF EGYPT.

FOR a long while he had devoted all his strength to the promotion of justice, and to the scattering of benefits and boons upon the nation. In the year 568 (A.D. 1172-1173),

---

[1] El-Mostadi was Khalif from 1170 to 1180. The *Khotba* (*Khutba*) is the sermon delivered on Fridays at the time of mid-day prayer. It must be in Arabic, and must include prayers for Muhammad, the Companions, the reigning Khalif, and the Sovereign. Hence the mention of a man's name in the *khotba* is a sign of his assumption of sovereignty.—W.

[2] *'Arka* was about 12 miles north of Tripoli, and some 6 miles from the coast. It commanded the great coast-road, which ran between it and the sea, and the road up the valley of the Eleutherus to Emesa (*Homs*). The site, on a rocky hill, still bears the name 'Arka. Its capture secured to the Moslems access to the coast, and facilitated operations against the Christians.—W.

he marched at the head of his army upon el-Kerak and esh-Shôbek, having made up his mind to begin with those places, because they were nearest to Egypt, and lay on the road to that country. They thus prevented travellers from resorting thither. No caravan could pass through that district unless the Sultan marched out and escorted it in person. His object, therefore, was to make the road freer and more easy, to put the two countries[1] into communication, so that travellers might come and go without hindrance. He set out to lay siege to these places in the year 568, and engaged in many skirmishes with the Franks. He returned to Egypt without having gained any advantage in this expedition. Nevertheless, a recompense for undertaking it remained to him in God's hands. Nûr ed-Dîn took Mar'ash[2] in the month of Zu el-K'ada of this year (June-July, A.D. 1173), and overthrew Behnesâ[3] the month following.

CHAPTER IX.

DEATH OF NEJM ED-DÎN (AYÛB), THE SULTAN'S FATHER.

ON his return from this expedition, before he reached Misr, the Sultan received news that his father, Nejm ed-Dîn, was no more. He was sorely grieved not to have been with him in his last moments. Nejm ed-Dîn died

---

[1] Syria and Egypt.

[2] *Mar'ash*, near the foot of the Taurus, N. of Aleppo. It was a place of great importance during the border warfare between the Arabs and the Byzantines.

[3] *Behnesâ*, or *Behesnâ* (*Besne*), is about two days' journey N.E. of *'Aintâb*, on the road from *Mar'ash* to *Sumeisât*, on the Euphrates. The castle was regarded as impregnable until taken by Timûr in 1400.—W.

from a fall from his horse ; he was very fond of galloping at full speed, and playing *dira'a.*[1] At such a rate did he go that those who saw him used to say : ' That man is sure to die from a fall from his horse.' He died at Misr in the year 568 (A.D. 1172-1173).

In the year 569 (A.D. 1173-1174) the Sultan saw the strength of his army, and the great number as well as the courage of his brethren. He also heard that a certain man named 'Abd en-Nebi Ibn Mehdi had made himself master of Yemen and of the strongholds of that country, and that he had the *khotba*[2] preached in his own name, declaring that his empire would stretch over all the earth, and that he was destined to obtain supreme power. The Sultan was counselled to send his eldest brother, Shems ed-Daula el-Melek el-Mu'azzem Tûrân Shah,[3] against this man, a noble and lofty-minded prince, greatly distinguished by the fine qualities of his disposition. I have heard the Sultan praise his brother's noble disposition and fine qualities, ' in which he excels me,' he used to say. Tûrân Shah set out for Yemen in the month of Rejeb, 569 (February, A.D. 1174), and it was at his hands that God granted us the conquest of that country. He killed the heretic (*Khâreji*) who had established himself there, made himself master of the greater part of the country, and bestowed gifts and presents upon a great number of people.

---

[1] *Dira'a* is a second name for *Jerîd.* The word means the cubit, fore-arm, and among some tribes the fore part of a spear between the point and the fist holding it.—W.

[2] See p. 62.

[3] Tûrân Shah, who was at one time Governor of Damascus, made an expedition against Nubia in 1172-1173. He died at Alexandria in 1180.—W.

CHAPTER X.

DEATH OF NÛR ED-DÎN MAHMÛD, SON OF ZENGHI— MAY THE MERCY OF GOD BE UPON HIM!

LIKE Asad ed-Dîn, Nûr ed-Dîn[1] died of an affection of the throat which his physicians were unable to cure. His death took place on Wednesday, the 11th of Shawâl, 569 (May 15, A.D. 1174), in the castle of Damascus. He was succeeded by his son, el-Melek es-Sâleh Ism'aîl.[2] Salâh ed-Din gave me the following account : 'We had received information that Nûr ed-Din had declared his intention of coming to attack us in Egypt, and some of our council were of opinion that we ought to throw off the mask, declare ourselves in revolt, and openly break with him. They said : "We will take the field against his army in battle array, and will drive him back from hence, if what we hear he is planning ever comes to pass." I was the only one who opposed this idea, saying: "We must not even think of such things." The discussion continued among us until we received tidings of his death.'

CHAPTER XI.

TREACHERY OF EL-KENZ[3] AT ASWÂN IN THE YEAR 570 (A.D. 1174-1175).

THIS El-Kenz had been a general in the service of the Egyptian Government. He managed to escape, and estab-

---

[1] See p. 47.

[2] El-Melek es-Sâleh 'Imâd ed-Dîn Ism'aîl was only eleven years old when he succeeded his father. He died at Aleppo in 1181 when not quite nineteen, nominating his cousin, 'Izz ed-Dîn, son of Kotb ed-Dîn, as his successor.—W.

[3] According to some readings, *el-Kend.*

5

lished himself at Aswân,[1] where he set to work to organize a conspiracy. He gathered together the negroes, and made them believe that he was going to make himself master of the country and reinstate the Egyptian Government. These people were possessed by the spirit of faction which characterizes all Egyptians, and which reduces acts such as this man contemplated to the merest trifles in their eyes. When he had assembled together a great number of people and a host of negroes, he marched towards Kûs[2] and the dependent districts round it. The Sultan, informed of his movements, sent against the insurgents a strong, well-armed force, selected from men who, having tasted the sweetness of Egypt, were afraid it might be taken from them. At their head he placed his brother, el-Melek el-'Âdel Seif ed-Din, who marched out to meet the enemy, defeated them in a pitched battle, and killed a great number. Thus the evil was rooted out and the revolt extinguished. This took place on the 7th of the month Safer, in the year 570 (September 7, A.D. 1174). By this means the foundations of the Sultan's authority were greatly strengthened and renewed—may God be praised !

CHAPTER XII.

THE FRANKS ATTACK THE DEFENCES OF ALEXANDRIA— MAY GOD PROTECT IT !

THE Franks, hearing of the revolution in Egypt and of the change of government that had taken place, conceived the

---

[1] *Assuân* at the foot of the first cataract of the Nile.

[2] *Kûs*, or *Kos*, is on the right bank of the Nile, a little above Koptos, a town which it supplanted as the emporium of the Arabian trade. Kos itself afterwards gave place to *Kench*, as Myos-Hormos and Philoteras-portus, on the Red Sea, gave place to *Kosseir.*—W.

hope of conquering the country, and despatched a fully-equipped army by sea. Their fleet was composed of galleys (*shâni*), of transports (*tarîda*), of great ships (*botsa*[1]), and other vessels, to the number of six hundred. On the 7th of the month Safer, of this year (September 7, 1174), they took up their position before this frontier city. The Sultan sent a body of troops to relieve the place, and was so active in his opposition that the enemy, paralysed by the terror which God had placed in their hearts, were unable to resist him ; they departed with disappointed hopes, and having wasted all the money they had expended. They had closely besieged the city, and assaulted it with all their forces for three days, but God protected it. When they perceived that the Sultan was marching against them, they hastily abandoned their mangonels and other engines ; then the people of the city lost no time in sallying out to take possession of these machines, and set them on fire. This was a momentous event, and one of the greatest mercies ever granted (by God) to the Moslems.

CHAPTER XIII.

THE SULTAN GOES INTO SYRIA AND TAKES POSSESSION OF DAMASCUS.

AT his death Nûr ed-Dîn left a son, el-Melek es-Sâleh Ism'aîl, who at this time was at Damascus. The castle of Aleppo was occupied by Shems ed-Dîn 'Ali Ibn ed-Daya

---

[1] The word *botsa*, in the plural *botes*, is used by some Arab historians to denote a ship of great size. El-Makrîzi mentions a *botsa* which held 1,500 men. Quatremère shows the meaning of this word, and of the words *tarîda* and *shâni* very clearly in his extract from el-Makrîzi's ' Solûk,' published under the title of ' Histoire des Sultans Mamlouks.'

and by Shadhbakht[1] 'Ali (Ibn ed-Daya), who fòr his part
was laying ambitious plans.   El-Melek es-Sâleh, having
left Damascus, set out for Aleppo, and arrived outside that
city on the 2nd of Moharrem (August 3, A.D. 1174).   He
was accompanied by Sâbek ed-Dîn.[2]   Bedr ed-Dîn sallied
out from the town to receive him and arrested Sâbek ed-
Dîn.[3]   Having effected an entrance into the citadel, el-
Melek es-Sâleh arrested Shems ed-Dîn (Ibn ed-Daya), and
Hasan, his brother, and committed them all three to
prison.   On this same day, Ibn el-Khashâb Abu el-Fadl
lost his life in a tumult that took place in the city of
Aleppo.   It is said that he was killed the day before the
arrest of the two sons of ed-Daya, for it was they who
committed this murder.

The Sultan, having assured himself of the truth of the
report of Nûr ed-Dîn's death, and knowing that the
son of that prince was a young man unequal to the

---

[1] When Nûr ed-Dîn died, the emirs at Damascus appointed Gumishtikîn S'ad ed-Dîn, Emir of Mosul, the guardian of his young son, es-
Sâleh, and sent him and the prince to Aleppo. That town was then
torn by factions, part of the people being Fatimite (*Shî'ite*) and part
Abbaside (*Sunni*). Shems ed-Dîn, who had been one of Nûr ed-
Dîn's principal emirs, was governor, but his authority was confined
to the citadel, where he lived with his brother, Jemâl ed-Dîn Shadhbakht. The city was held by another brother, Bedr ed-Dîn Ibn ed-
Daya. The emirs were jealous of each other, and continually plotting
to get the sole government of the city, and to become guardian of the
young prince. In one of the tumults, Abû el-Fadl Ibn el-Khashâb,
who was Kadi and head of the Shi'ite party, was killed. When
Gumishtikîn arrived with es-Sâleh, he imprisoned the brothers ed-
Daya, and restored order. The ed-Dayas were natives of India, and
freed men of Nûr ed-Dîn ('Zobda el-Haleb,' a history of Aleppo, by
Kemâl ed-Dîn).—W.

[2] This is a mistake. The author should have written *S'ad ed-Dîn*,
the title given to Emir Gumishtikîn.

[3] This is another mistake. Emir Bedr ed-Dîn sallied out from the
town to meet S'ad ed-Dîn, and was arrested by him (Kemâl ed-Dîn's
'Zobda').

cares and responsibilities of sovereignty, and to the task of driving the enemies of God from the land, made preparations for an expedition to Syria, the root (or base) of all the lands of Islâm. He set out with a strong body of troops, after leaving a sufficient force in Egypt to protect that country, maintain order, and uphold the authority of the government, and he was accompanied by many of his kinsmen and retainers. As he had sent letters to the emirs and people of Syria, the supporters of el-Melek es-Sâleh were divided and had no settled plans. Each man distrusted his neighbour, and some were arrested by their colleagues. This inspired great terror among the others, and estranged the hearts of his people from the young prince. The state of affairs forced Shems ed-Din Ibn el-Mokaddem[1] to write to the Sultan, who hastened his march, with a view of demanding that el-Melek es-Sâleh should be given up to him. He would then take upon himself the education of that prince, the administration of government, and the re-establishment of order. There was no resistance on his arrival at Damascus, and the city was delivered up to him on Tuesday, the 30th of the month Rabi'a II., in the year 570 (November 27, A.D. 1174). He also obtained possession of the castle. The first house he entered was that which had belonged to his father. The people of the city assembled to see him and to receive him with expressions of joy. He distributed large sums of money that day, and showed the people of Damascus that he was as pleased to see them as they were to have him in their city. He then took up his quarters in the

---

[1] Shems ed-Dîn Ibn el-Mokaddem, who had been appointed guardian of es-Sâleh, became alarmed at the ambitious schemes of Gumishtikin at Aleppo, and sided with Salâh ed-Dîn, to whom he surrendered Damascus. He was killed at Mount 'Arâfât in a scuffle that arose out of a dispute about precedence with the chief of the pilgrim caravan from Irak.—W.

castle and thus established his authority in the city. He
set out shortly afterwards for Aleppo. On reaching
Emesa, he took up a position against that city, and
captured it in the month Jomada I. (December), in the
year 570. Without pausing to besiege the castle of that
place he pushed on, and on Friday, the 30th of the same
month, halted for the first time at Aleppo.

CHAPTER XIV.

SEIF ED-DÎN SENDS HIS BROTHER 'IZZ ED-DÎN[1] TO OPPOSE THE SULTAN.

SEIF ED-DÎN, Prince of Mosul, learning what had taken
place, saw that a man had appeared who was to be feared,
and was mighty and full of mastery. Fearing that, if the
Sultan met with no opposition, he would over-run the
country, establish his authority over it, and obtain supreme
power, he equipped a great number of men, and entrusted the
command of this powerful army to his brother, 'Izz ed-Dîn
Mas'ûd. The troops set out to oppose the Sultan with a
view of giving him battle, and driving him out of the land.
Salâh ed-Dîn, informed of their plans, left Aleppo on the
1st of Rejeb of this year (January 26, A.D. 1175), and
retreated in the direction of Hamah. On reaching Emesa,
he laid siege to the castle, and captured it. 'Izz ed-Dîn
came to Aleppo, and, after joining the garrison of that
city to his own army, renewed his march at the head of

---

[1] Abû el-Fath Abû el-Muzaffer 'Izz ed-Dîn, in the lifetime of his
brother, commanded the troops, and was defeated by Salâh ed-Dîn
in 1175. His cousin, es-Sâleh, made him his heir, and he reached
Aleppo in December, 1181. A few months later he exchanged Aleppo
with his brother, 'Imâd ed-Dîn, for *Sinjar*, etc. He succeeded Seif
ed-Dîn as Lord of Mosul in 1180, and died in 1193.—W.

an immense multitude. The Sultan, knowing that these troops were on the march, set out to meet them, and fell in with them at the *Horns of Hamah*.[1] He wished, if possible, to persuade their leaders to make peace, and entered into correspondence with them ; but in this he was unsuccessful. They preferred to risk a battle in the hope of attaining their chief object, and the fulfilment of their wishes. But the decision (of God) is other than the will (of man) ; the battle took place, and God granted that the troops (of Mosul) were utterly routed. Many of them were taken prisoners, but the Sultan afterwards gave them their liberty. This took place on the 19th of Ramaḍân, 570 (April 13, A.D. 1175). After this victory, the Sultan encamped before Aleppo for the second time, and its inhabitants were obliged to cede him el-M'aarra[2] and Kefr Tâb[3] as the price of peace. He also took (the fortress of) Bârîn[4] towards the end of the year.

CHAPTER XV.

SEIF ED-DÎN HIMSELF SETS OUT AGAINST THE SULTAN.

THE day on which this battle was fought, Seif ed-Dîn was besieging his brother, 'Imâd ed-Dîn,[5] in Sinjâr. He was

---

[1] Heights near the gorge of the Orontes at Hamath in N. Syria.

[2] *El-M'aarra en-Nu'mân*, so called from one of the companions of the Prophet who died there, is about eight hours from *Hamah* on the road from that place to Aleppo. It was first taken by the Crusaders in November, 1098, and plundered and destroyed by Bohemund in 1099. The village is still noted for its pistachios, olives, etc.—W.

[3] *Kefr Tâb* was a small town between M'aarra and Aleppo.

[4] *Bârîn* was a small town about one day's march S. of *Hamah*, and near *er-Rafaniya (Raphanea)*. It had a castle, built by the Crusaders about 1090.—W.

[5] See pp. 28, 81.

determined to wrest the city from him, and oblige him to
renew his allegiance ; for this prince maintained friendly
relations with the Sultan, and thought that would suffice
to protect him. Seif ed-Dîn beset the place very closely,
brought mangonels to play upon it, and made a great
breach in the walls. He was on the point of taking it,
when he heard the result of the battle. Fearing that his
brother would hear of this event, and be encouraged to
continue his resistance, he made proposals for peace, which
were accepted. Immediately after this, he set out for
Nisiba, where he exerted himself to assemble his troops,
and pay them. He then marched towards the Euphrates,
which he crossed near el-Bîra.[1] Having encamped on the
Syrian bank, he sent messengers to Gumishtikîn and el-
Melek es-Sâleh, proposing the terms of a treaty on which
he could join them. Gumishtikîn came to his camp, and
entered into negotiations which were interrupted and
renewed so many times that Seif ed-Dîn was often on the
point of returning home. At last it was agreed that he
should have an interview with el-Melek es-Sâleh, and he
set out for Aleppo. When he approached the city, the
young prince went out in person to welcome him, and the
meeting took place near the fortress. Seif ed-Dîn embraced
him, took him in his arms, and wept. Then he sent him
back to the fortress, and encamped close to the spring
called el-Mobâraka ('blessed'), where he remained for
some time, and where the Aleppo garrison came every day
to pay him respect. He visited the fortress, attended by
a company of his horsemen, and took a meal there (*lit.*,
eat bread there). After this he struck his camp, and

---

[1] *El-Bîra*, in modern Arabic, *Bir ;* in Turkish, *Birejik* (*Apamea
zeugma*), at one of the most important crossings of the Euphrates
N.E. of Aleppo.

repaired to Tell es-Sulṭân,[1] accompanied by the troops from Diarbekr, and a great number of people.

Whilst the Sultan was awaiting the arrival of the troops he had summoned from Egypt, the others (the supporters of el-Melek es-Ṣâleh) made no good use of their time either in action or in making arrangements, little suspecting that their negligence would be fatal. The army having arrived from Egypt, the Sultan resumed his march, and reached the Horns of Hamah. The others, when they heard that the troops had come, sent out their spies and secret emissaries, through whom they learnt that the Sultan had pushed forward with a small escort to the Turkoman's Well, and that the rest of the army was dispersed in different directions to water the horses. Had it been God's will to give them the victory, they would have marched upon the Sultan that very moment; '*but if God decrees, it was to be*' (Kurân viii. 43). Therefore they gave the Sultan and his troops time to water their horses, to concentrate, and prepare for battle, and on the following morning they took up their position to fight. It was on the morning of Thursday, the 10th of Shawâl, 571 (April 22, A.D. 1176), that the two armies encountered one another. Then followed a fierce conflict, in which the right wing of Seif ed-Dîn's army, commanded by Muzaffer ed-Dîn[2] (Kukbûri),

---

[1] About a day's march from Aleppo, on the road to Hamah.

[2] Abû Saîd Kukbûri el-Melek el-Mu'azzam Mozaffer ed-Dîn succeeded his father as Lord of Arbela in 1168. He was then only fourteen, and was imprisoned by his Atabeg, Mujâhid ed-Dîn Kâimaz, who placed his younger brother, Zein ed-Dîn, on the throne. Kukbûri, after visiting Baghdad, entered the service of Seif ed-Dîn, who gave him Harrân as a fief. He afterwards took service with Salâh ed-Dîn, who gave him Edessa and Sumeisât, and whose sister he married. He fought in most of Salâh ed-Dîn's battles, and displayed great bravery, especially at Hattîn. On the death of his brother, 1190, he succeeded him at Arbela, and was noted for his charitable works.

son of Zein ed-Dîn, overthrew the Sultan's left flank.
Salâh ed-Dîn then charged in person, put the enemy to
flight, and made prisoners a great number of their chief
officers, and Fakhr ed-Dîn 'Abd el-Mesîh (the vizier). He
restored the important persons to liberty. Seif ed-Dîn
returned to Aleppo, took the money which he had left
there, and crossed the Euphrates on his return to his
own country. The Sultan refrained from pursuing those
who had escaped. He spent the rest of the day in the
enemy's camp, where he found all their baggage just as
they had left it; their cooking utensils, their provisions,
their stables full of horses—all had been left. He distributed the horses and provisions amongst his officers and
men, and gave Seif ed-Dîn's tent to 'Izz ed-Dîn Ferrûkh-
Shah, nephew of that prince. Then, having sat down
before Membej,[1] he received the capitulation of that place
towards the end of the same month; after that he marched
upon the Castle of 'Âzâz,[2] and laid siege to it on the 4th
of the month of Zu el-K'ada, 571 (May 15, A.D. 1176).
It was here that the Ism'ailîya[3] tried to assassinate him;
but God preserved him from their treachery, and gave the
assassins into his power. This occurrence did not daunt
his determination; he remained before the place until he
took it on the 14th of Zu el-Hijja (June 24). He arrived

He brought water by an aqueduct to Jebel 'Arâfât, and built fountains
there for the Mecca pilgrims (Ibn Khallikan, ii. 535).—W.

[1] *Membej* (Bambyce), between Aleppo and Bîr.

[2] *'Âzâz* is to the N.W. of Aleppo, near the road to Killis, in a
fertile district.

[3] The Ism'ailîya or Assassins (*Hashshâshîn*, 'hemp-smokers'),
organized by Hasan el-Homeiri in 1090 at Alamût in Irak, had
established themselves in the N. Lebanon by the middle of the twelfth
century. The lower initiates were bound to carry out the Sheikh's
orders against Moslem or Christian alike. The mystical teaching of
the sect, tracing back to Ism'ail, the sixth Imâm, had reached Syria as
early as the ninth century.

before Aleppo on the 16th of the same month, and, having encamped there for some time, took his final departure. One of the daughters of Nûr ed-Din, quite a young girl, was sent to him by the Government of Aleppo to ask for the Castle of 'Âzâz as a gift at his hands ; this request he granted. Towards the close of the same month, his brother, Shems ed-Daula[1] (Tûrân Shah), arrived at Damascus on his return from Yemen. He remained there some time, and then returned to Egypt. He died at Alexandria on the 1st of Safer, 576 (June 27, 1180 A.D.). The Sultan also returned to Egypt to ascertain the condition of the country, and support those whom he had left in authority. It was in the month of Rabi'a I., 572 (September to October, A.D. 1176), that he set out for Egypt, leaving his brother, Shems ed-Daula, as his lieutenant in Damascus. Having spent some time in Egypt, restoring order in the administration of affairs, remedying defects in the government, and recruiting his army, he began his preparations for an invasion of the territories of the Franks, determined to penetrate to the sea-coast. He came into collision with the Franks at Ramla, whither they had advanced to meet him, early in the month of Jomada I., 573 (the end of October, A.D. 1177).

CHAPTER XVI.

DEFEAT SUSTAINED AT RAMLA.

PRINCE ARNÂT (Renaud de Chatillon), the leader of the Franks, had been ransomed at Aleppo, where he had been detained a prisoner since the time of Nûr ed-Dîn. This day (*i.e.*, that of Ramla) the Moslems sustained a severe defeat. This is the explanation the Sultan gave of the

[1] See p. 64.

cause of the disaster. Our troops had been drawn up in
order of battle, and the enemy was advancing, when some of
our people thought we ought to change the position of our
flanks,[1] so as to gain the protection of a well-known Tell in
the country of Ramla,[2] in our rear. Whilst our men were
executing this movement, the Franks charged, and, by
God's permission, put them to rout. As there was no
stronghold at hand to which they could retreat, the
Moslems fled in the direction of Egypt, and, losing their
way, were scattered far and wide. The enemy took a
great number of prisoners, amongst whom was 'Aisa,[3] the
jurist. This was a great reverse, but God repaired our
loss by the advantage we gained in the famous battle of
Hattîn.

Let us turn to el-Melek es-Sâleh. This prince's affairs
having fallen into disorder, he had Gumishtikîn, who
was really governor of the whole country, arrested, and
commanded him to give up the castle of Hârim.[4] On his
refusal to do so, he put him to death. The Franks, hearing that the minister was dead, laid siege to Hârim, in the
hope of taking it. This took place in the month of
Jomada II., in the year 573 (November - December,
1177 A.D.). The garrison, attacked on one hand by the
Franks, and threatened on the other by el-Melek es-Sâleh's

---

[1] The original is not clear. According to one translation, it means
that the right and left wings should interchange their positions.—W.

[2] This defeat of Salâh ed-Dîn occurred at Gezer (*Tell Jezer*), 5 miles
S.E. of Ramleh, on November 25, 1177. See Röhricht's ' Regesta Regni
Hierosolymitani,' No. 264.

[3] It was through the exertions of this man, who was both lawyer
and warrior, that Salâh ed-Dîn was able to rally round him the emirs
of Nûr ed-Dîn's army, when the Fatimite Khalif appointed him his
first minister, and honoured him with the title of *Sultan.*

[4] *Hârim* was an important border castle (called Harenc by the
Franks) E. of the Orontes, and E. of Antioch. Near it Nûr ed-Dîn
defeated the Franks in 1163.

army, surrendered the place to es-Sâleh during the last ten days of the month of Ramadân (the middle of March, 1178 A.D.). Upon this the Franks withdrew into their own territories, and es-Sâleh returned to Aleppo. Dissension still reigned all round him, for several of his nobles had shown a leaning towards the Sultan. On the 10th of Moharrem, 576 (June 6, A.D. 1180), he sent a body of troops against 'Izz ed-Dîn Kilîj,[1] who had revolted at Tell-Khâlid.[2] After this he received tidings of the death of his cousin, Seif ed-Dîn Ghâzi, Prince of Mosul, who died on the 3rd of Safer (June 29) this year. On the 5th of the same month 'Izz ed-Dîn Mas'ûd succeeded his brother Seif ed-Dîn upon the throne. Shems ed-Daula (Tûrán Shah, brother of Salâh ed-Din) died the same year at Alexandria.

CHAPTER XVII.

THE SULTAN RETURNS INTO SYRIA.

ON his return to Egypt after his defeat, Salâh ed-Din remained there whilst he remodelled his army; then, hearing of the grievous condition of Syria, he made up his mind to return thither to give battle to the infidels. At this time an ambassador came from Kilîj Arslân[3] (Prince of Iconium) to negotiate a treaty of peace and alliance with him, and to complain of the Armenians. He at once determined

---

[1] 'Izz ed-Dîn Kilîj had been one of Nûr ed-Dîn's emirs. He held in fee the fortress and lands of *Tell Khâlid*, in the province of Aleppo.

[2] *Tell Khâlid* was a castle about twelve miles N.W. of *Membej*.

[3] Izz ed-Dîn Kilîj Arslân II., the Seljûk Sultan of Rûm, whose capital was at Iconium (*Konia*). 'Izz ed-Dîn added largely to the Seljûk Empire of Rûm, but in 1188 divided it between his ten sons, and abdicated.—W.

to invade the country of Ibn Lâôn,[1] and support Kilîj Arslân. When he came to Kara-hissâr,[2] he encamped there and effected a junction with the troops from Aleppo, who had been sent to put themselves under his orders. Indeed, one of the conditions of the treaty of peace concluded with Aleppo was that he should be furnished with troops whenever he required them for any expedition. This contingent joined him on the banks of the Nahr el-Azrak[3] (the blue river), which flows between Behnesâ and Hisn Mansûr.[4] Having crossed this river, he advanced to Nahr el-Aswad[5] (the black river), which forms the boundary of the territories of Ibn Lâôn, where he captured the fortress[6] . . . from (the Armenians), and razed it to the ground. After this the enemy surrendered a number of prisoners to him as the price of peace, upon which the Sultan decided to withdraw. Kilîj Arslân pro-

---

[1] Ibn Lâôn was Rhupen II. (1174-1185), the grandson of Levon I. (Leo), the 'Thakavor' or Baron of Lesser Armenia. He waged war successfully against Byzantines, Seljûks, and Arabs, and largely extended the kingdom. He was treacherously captured by Bohemund, of Antioch, and abdicated in favour of his brother, Leo II., 'the great.'—W.

[2] *Kara-hissâr* is the name of a large meadow (*merj*) or plain to the N. of Aleppo.—W.

[3] The *Nahr el-Azrak* is the present *Geuk Su*, which falls into the Euphrates below *Sumeisât.*

[4] *Hisn Mansûr* is possibly the modern *Adiaman*, the chief town of the Hisn Mansûr Kaza.

[5] The Nahr el-Aswad is the *Kara Su*, which flows between the Giaour Dagh and the Kurt Dagh to the Lake of Antioch.

[6] The name of the fortress is omitted in the original, and the Arabic sentence is left incomplete. The course of this campaign cannot be clearly followed. It is difficult to understand why Salâh ed-Dîn should have passed Aleppo, and gone so far north as the Geuk Su before being joined by the Aleppo contingent. The fortress he took was apparently near the Kara Su, and perhaps near the Baghche Pass.—W.

posed that he should grant peace to all the Orientals.[1]
Salâh ed-Dîn consented to this, and on the 10th of the
month Jomada I., in the year 576 (October 2, A.D. 1180),
he swore to observe the terms of this treaty, in which
Kilîj Arslân was included, as well as the inhabitants of
Mosul and Diarbekr. This compact was signed on the
banks of the Senja,[2] a tributary of the Euphrates. The
Sultan then returned to Damascus, and thence into Egypt.

CHAPTER XVIII.

DEATH OF EL-MELEK ES-SÂLEH. 'IZZ ED-DÎN ENTERS ALEPPO.

IN the year 577 (1181-1182 A.D.) el-Melek es-Sâleh suffered
from a sharp attack of colic. He fell ill on the 9th of
Rejeb (November 18, A.D. 1181), and on the 13th of the
same month his condition became so serious that the gates
of the fortress were closed. He then summoned his chief
emirs, one by one, and made them swear to receive 'Izz
ed-Dîn, Prince of Mosul, as their lord. On the 25th of the
same month (December) he breathed his last. His death
created a profound impression on the minds of his subjects. Directly he was dead a messenger was despatched
post-haste to carry the tidings to 'Izz ed-Dîn Mas'ûd, son
of Kotb ed-Dîn,[3] and to inform him that the deceased
Prince had bequeathed the principality to him, making all

---

[1] Under the name *Orientals*, Kilîj Arslân included the Princes of
Mosul, of the Provinces of Mesopotamia, and of Diarbekr.

[2] It has been supposed that the *Senja* was the same as the *Nahr
el-Azrak* or *Geuk Su*, but it is probably the river *Sajur*, which falls
into the Euphrates below *Jerâblus.*—W.

[3] See p. 70.

the people swear to receive him as their lord. 'Izz
ed-Din set forth at once and rode in haste, fearing lest
the Sultan should occupy the city before him. The first of
his emirs to enter Aleppo were Mozaffer ed-Din, son of
Zein ed-Din,[1] and the Lord of Sarûj. With them came an
officer to administer the oath of allegiance to all the emirs
in the city. They arrived on the 3rd of Sh'abân (December 12, A.D. 1181). On the 10th of the same month 'Izz
ed-Din entered Aleppo, went up into the fortress, and took
possession of the treasures and stores which had been
lodged there. On the 5th of Shawâl (February 11,
A.D. 1181), of the same year, he married the mother of
el-Melek es-Sâleh.

CHAPTER XIX.

'IZZ ED-DÎN EXCHANGES [ALEPPO] FOR THE TERRITORY
OF HIS BROTHER, 'IMÂD ED-DÎN ZENGHI.

'IZZ ED-DÎN remained in the fortress of Aleppo until the
15th of Shawâl, but he recognised that it would be impossible for him to keep both Mosul and Syria. He was
afraid of the Sultan, and overwhelmed by the extravagant
demands of the emirs, who persisted in asking for increased allowances, which his limited means prevented
him from granting. Mojâhed ed-Din Kâimâz[2] also, his

[1] See p. 73.

[2] Abû Mansûr Kâimâz Mojâhed ed-Din was a eunuch, and en-
franchised slave of Zein ed-Din Ali, Lord of Arbela (p. 52). In 1164
he was entrusted with the management of affairs at Arbela. In 1175
he removed to Mosul, and became vizier to Seif ed-Din Ghazi, and
afterwards to his brother, 'Izz ed-Din. He was noted for the excel-
lence of his administration, and for his justice. He died in 1199 (Ibn
Khallikan, ii. 510).—W.

chief minister, was in a very uncomfortable position, for he was not accustomed to the unseemly ways of the Syrian emirs. Therefore 'Izz ed-Dîn left the castle of Aleppo, and repaired to er-Rakka, leaving his son and Mozaffer ed-Dîn (Kukbûri) behind. On his arrival at er-Rakka he met his brother 'Imâd ed-Dîn, as had been arranged. They determined upon exchanging Aleppo for Sinjâr, and 'Izz ed-Dîn ratified this arrangement with his oath. This came to pass upon the 13th of Shawâl (February 27, 1182). One agent was sent to Aleppo to take possession of the city on behalf of 'Imâd ed-Dîn, whilst another was despatched by 'Izz ed-Dîn to receive the city of Sinjâr. On the 13th of Moharrem, 578 (May 19, A.D. 1182), 'Imâd ed-Dîn made his entry into the fortress of Aleppo.

CHAPTER XX.

THE SULTAN RETURNS FROM EGYPT.

AFTER peace had been concluded, through the intervention of Kilîj-Arslân, the Sultan set out once more for Egypt, leaving his nephew 'Izz ed-Dîn Ferrûkh Shah as Governor of Damascus. It was in Egypt that he received news of the death of el-Melek es-Sâleh, and this decided him to return to Syria, to protect that country against the attempts of the Franks. Very shortly afterwards he was informed of the death of Ferrûkh Shah, which occurred in the month of Rejeb, 577 (November-December, 1181). This event confirmed him in his resolution to pass over into Syria. Having set out from Misr, he arrived at Damascus on the 17th of Safer (June 22, 1182), and at once commenced preparations for an expedition against the Franks. On his march from Egypt this time he had crossed through their territories, boldly and not peacefully.

6

He marched at once upon Beirût and laid siege to that place, but without success, for the Franks collected their troops and forced him to retire. On his return to Damascus he learnt that an embassy from Mosul had reached the Franks, and was stirring them up to make war upon him. He concluded from this that the people of Mosul had broken their oaths, and he determined to visit that country, so as to unite all the forces of Islâm in a common feeling of hostility against the enemies of God. He had commenced his preparations when 'Imâd ed-Dîn heard of them, and sent to Mosul to warn the government, and to beg them to send troops as quickly as possible. The Sultan set out on his march, and appeared before Aleppo on the 18th of the month Jomada I., where he remained for three days. On the 21st of the same month he resumed his march in the direction of the Euphrates. He had already made terms with Mozaffer ed-Dîn, who was at this time holding the city of Harrân,[1] and who was in fear of an attack from the government of Mosul. He was still more afraid of the designs of Mojâhed ed-Dîn (Kâimâz), and he joined the Sultan, as a means of protection. He crossed the Euphrates, and urged the Sultan to invade the country (Upper Mesopotamia), representing that the conquest of that district would be an easy matter. Salâh ed-Dîn crossed the Euphrates and took the cities of er-Roha[2] (Edessa), er-Rakka, Nisiba, and Sarûj.

[1] *Harrân*, 'the city of Nahor,' is about 24 miles S.S.E. of Edessa, on the *Belik*, a tributary of the Euphrates, and in the N. of Mesopotamia.

[2] *Er-Roha*, the Armenian name of Edessa, comes from *Callirhoë*, one of the classical names of the town. It was further corrupted by the Turks to *Urfa* or *Orfa*. Edessa is built on two hills, between which flows a small stream, and there are still many remains of the old wall and castle. During the first Crusade the town was taken by Baldwin (1097), who called himself Count of Edessa. In 1144 it was captured from Jocelyn II. by the Atabeg Zenghi, Lord of Mosul. It was in the hands of his grandson, 'Izz ed-Dîn, when taken by Salâh ed-Dîn.—W.

He placed a commission (*Shihna*) over the province of Khabûr,[1] and divided it into military fiefs.

CHAPTER XXI.

THE SULTAN APPEARS (ONCE MORE) BEFORE MOSUL.

THIS time he arrived before Mosul on Thursday, the 11th of Rejeb, 578 (November 10, 1182 A.D.). As I was then in this city, I had been sent a few days before to Baghdad to solicit the assistance of the Khalif. I went down the Tigris so quickly that I reached Baghdad in the space of two days and two hours. All I could obtain from the government of Baghdad was that they would send a despatch to the Sheikh of Sheikhs (chief of the 'Ulema), who was then with the Sultan as an accredited ambassador from the Khalif. In this letter he was commanded to have an interview with the Sultan, and to endeavour to bring about an arrangement between him and the people of Mosul. The latter had already sent an ambassador to ask help from Pehlevân (Prince of Azerbijân).[2] The answer they

---

[1] The province of *Khabûr* included the district lying between the Euphrates and the river Khabûr, the Biblical *Aram Naharaim*, and the classical *Osrhoëne*. It is a very fertile district, and supported many important towns, but is now abandoned to nomads. In the time of Salâh ed-Din it still retained much of its ancient fertility.—W.

[2] Shems ed-Dîn Pehlevân, Lord of Azerbijân, Arran, and Persian Irak, was the son of Shems ed-Din Ildukuz, the Atabeg to the Seljûk Sultan, Arslan Shah, who died in 1174. Pehlevân died in 1186. *Azerbijân* is a province in N.W. Persia, which corresponds to the ancient *Atropatene*. It is separated from Russia by the Araxes, and its principal towns are Tabriz, Urmia, Khoi, Dilman, etc. It is one of the most fertile provinces of Persia, and is noted for its excellent fruit.—W.

received from him contained conditions which would have been more oppressive than war with the Sultan. Salâh ed-Dîn remained at Mosul for several days ; then he saw that no advantage could be gained by besieging so great a city in this manner, and that if he would take it, he must get possession of the castle and country around, and that he would be weakened by the long delay. He therefore struck his camp, and, on the 16th of Sh'abân (December 15, 1182), took up his position against Sinjâr, which was occupied by Sheref ed-Dîn, son of Kotb ed-Dîn, with a certain number of men. He pressed this city so closely that, on the 2nd of the month Ramadân, he carried it by assault. Sheref ed-Dîn evacuated it unarmed, and he and his men were furnished with an escort to conduct them to Mosul. The Sultan gave Sinjâr to his nephew, Taki ed-Dîn, and departed for Nisiba.

CHAPTER XXII.

THE ACTION TAKEN BY SHAH-ARMEN, PRINCE OF KHELÂT.

THE government of Mosul had summoned Shah Armen[1] to their assistance, and thrown themselves into the arms of that prince; he therefore resolved to set out from Khelât,[2]

---

[1] Shah Armen Nâsr ed-Dîn Muhammad, who reigned fifty-seven years at Khelât (1128 - 1185), was grandson of Sokmân el - Kutbi. Sokmân, who was an old slave of the Seljûk prince of Azerbijân, seized Khelât, Manazgerd, Arjish, and the districts round them, and proclaimed himself king, with the Persian title, *Shah Armen,* ' King of the Armenians.' This title was borne by his successors.—W.

[2] *Khelât,* now *Akhlât,* is near the north-west corner of Lake Van. There are several old mosques and richly-ornamented octagonal tombs, dating from the Seljûk period. It was at one time besieged by a

to bring them relief. He pitched his camp at Harzem,[1] and dispatched a messenger to 'Izz ed-Dîn, Prince of Mosul, to inform him of his arrival. The latter left the city on the 25th of Shawâl, and set out to meet him. On his arrival he found the Lord of Mardîn[2] was with Shah-Armen. A body of troops belonging to the army quartered in Aleppo also came to join them. Their object in meeting was to march against the Sultan's forces. Shah-Armen sent Bektimor[3] to Salâh ed-Dîn to negotiate a treaty of peace, through the intervention of the Sheikh of Sheikhs, but this step was unproductive of any result. Then, when he heard the Sultan was advancing upon them, he retreated into his own country. 'Izz ed-Dîn set out to return to his own dominions, and the coalition was dissolved. Salâh ed-Dîn then marched against Amid,[4] and captured that city after a siege of eight days. This took place during the first ten days of Moharrem, 579 (April-May, A.D. 1183). He gave Amid to Nûr ed-Dîn, son of Kara-Arslân, and to Ibn Nikân[5] he granted all the money

Byzantine force commanded by an adventurer, bearing the name of Russel Baliol.—W.

[1] Ibn el-Athîr mentions *Harzem* several times in his ' Kamel' as a place in the neighbourhood of *Mardîn.*

[2] *Mardîn* has always played an important part in the history of the district. It is built on the side of a conical hill, the houses rising tier above tier, and is extremely picturesque. The town lies on the direct road from Orfa to Mosul. The Lord of Mardîn referred to was Kotb ed-Dîn el-Ghâzi, one of the Ortokid dynasty, who died in 1184.—W.

[3] Bektimor, who was a slave of the father of Sokmân Shah-Armen, seized the throne on Sokmân's death in 1185.—W.

[4] Amid (*Amida*) is the modern *Diarbekr*, situated on the right bank of the Tigris. It is still an important town, and the capital of a vilâyet. The town is surrounded by walls of basalt, and it has several old mosques and churches.—W.

[5] Ibn Nikân was chief minister of Nûr ed-Dîn Mahmûd, son of Kara Arslan, Lord of Amid, and exercised absolute authority in the city. Salâh ed-Dîn restored the city to the Ortokid prince.

and portable property in the city. He then returned to
Syria, directing his march on Aleppo. In the interval
'Imâd ed-Dîn had sallied out, and dismantled the fortresses
of 'Azâz and Kefr Lâtha ;[1] this last he had taken from the
emir Bekmish, on the 22nd of the month Jomada I., when
he had gone over to the Sultan. He also laid unsuccessful
siege to the fortress of Tell Bâsher, which belonged to
Dolderim el-Yarûki, who had ranged himself on the side
of Salâh ed-Dîn. Meanwhile, the Franks took advantage
of the conflicts which had taken place between the (Moslem)
troops to make inroads into the country, but God drove
them out. 'Imâd ed-Dîn, having repaired the fortress of
el-Kerzein,[2] returned to Aleppo.

CHAPTER XXIII.

THE SULTAN RETURNS TO SYRIA.

THE Sultan returned to Syria and commenced operations
by an attack on Tell Khâled, which he took by storm. This
took place on the 22nd of Moharrem, 579 (May 17, A.D.
1183). He then marched upon Aleppo, and took up a
position against it on the 26th of the same month. He
first encamped on the Meidân el-Akhdar ('green plain '),
and called in a number of troops from all parts, after which
he employed all his forces in storming the city. 'Imâd
ed-Dîn, wearied beyond endurance by the insolent demands
of his emirs, felt that he could not make a satisfactory

---

[1] *Kefr Lâtha* was about a day's journey from Aleppo, in the district
of Azaz.

[2] *Kerzein* lies near Rakka, about eight miles to the south of el-Bira
(Birejik).

resistance ; he therefore requested Hossâm ed-Din[1] to approach the Sultan in his behalf, and persuade Salâh ed-Dîn to grant him the territory he had formerly held in exchange for the government of Aleppo. This arrangement was concluded quite unknown to the people or the garrison of the city. When matters had been settled in this wise, and the news was made public, the soldiers demanded an explanation of 'Imâd ed-Din. He replied that it was true, and recommended them to make terms for themselves. They deputed 'Izz ed-Dîn Jurdîk en-Nûri (one of Nûr ed-Dîn's memlûks) and Zein ed-Dîn[2] to negotiate a treaty with the Sultan for themselves and the people of Aleppo. These ambassadors had an interview with the Sultan, which lasted until nightfall, and obtained terms for the garrison and inhabitants which Salâh ed-Dîn swore to observe. This was on the 17th of Safer (June 11, A.D. 1183). The garrison then came forth from the city to place themselves at the disposal of the Sultan, who remained in his camp in the Meidân el-Akhdar ('green plain '), and with them came the chief men of the city. The Sultan clothed them with robes of honour, and set all minds at rest. 'Imâd ed-Din remained in the fortress to settle his affairs, and to pack up his treasure and other property. Meanwhile, the Sultan dwelt in his camp in the Meidân el-Akhdar ; and there, on the 23rd of Safer, his brother Tâj el-Molûk died from a wound he had received. The Sultan was sorely afflicted by this loss, and sat in his tent that day to receive the public condolences of his officers. 'Imâd ed-Dîn also came the same day, to participate in the Sultan's grief, and to wait on him. The Sultan settled various matters with him, lodged him in his own

---

[1] Hossâm ed-Din was governor of the fortress of Aleppo.

[2] In Kemâl ed-Dîn's ' Zobda ' this man is called Balek. Zein ed-Din was his Arabic name.

.

tent, and gave him (splendid) gifts and several fine horses ; he also clothed with robes of honour a great number of chiefs who came in the suite of his guest. 'Imad ed-Dîn set out the same day for Kara-hissâr[1] on his way to Sinjâr. The Sultan was filled with joy at the success of his plans, and he went up to the castle, where Hossâm ed-Dîn Domân set a magnificent banquet before him. This officer had remained to collect the various things which 'Imâd ed-Dîn had left behind. Soldiers were sent by the Sultan to take possession of Hârim, and as the governor of that place made difficulties in order to create delay, the garrison sent to the Sultan and obtained a treaty ratified by his oath. Salâh ed-Dîn then set out for Hârim, and arrived there on the 29th of Safer. Having taken possession of the city, he remained there for two days to reorganize the government ; he appointed Ibrahîm Ibn Sherwa governor, and then returned to Aleppo, arriving there on the 3rd of the month Rabî'a I. His troops were granted leave to return to their homes, whilst he remained at Aleppo to reorganize the government, and preside over the affairs of the city.

CHAPTER XXIV.

EXPEDITION TO 'AIN JÂLÛT.

THE Sultan did not stay long in Aleppo. On the 22nd of the month Rabî'a II., in the year 579 (August 14, A.D. 1183), he set out for Damascus, preparatory to making an expedition into the infidel's territories. He called his troops together, proceeding on his march whilst they followed

[1] See p. 78.

him. He did not halt at Hamah, but advanced by forced marches, taking no provisions with him, until the 3rd of the month Jomada I. (August 24), when he reached Damascus. Here he passed some days making preparations, and on the 27th of the same month he pitched his camp by the Wooden Bridge, where he had ordered his troops to meet him. He halted here nine days, and then, on the 8th of Jomada II. (September 28), marched to el-Fawâr,[1] where he made his final arrangements before entering the enemy's country. From this place he pushed on to el-Kuseir,[2] where he spent the night. Quite early the next morning he reached the ford (over the Jordan), and, having crossed the river, marched as far as el-Beisân.[3] Its inhabitants had abandoned their dwellings, leaving behind all the property they could not easily carry, and the fruits of their harvest. The soldiers were allowed to pillage the place, and they burnt everything they could not take with them. The Sultan continued his march to el-Jâlût,[4] a prosperous village, near which there is a spring (*'ain*), and here he pitched his camp. He had sent forward a body of Nûri memlûks (who had formerly belonged to Nûr ed-Dîn), commanded by 'Izz ed-Dîn Jurdik and Jâweli, a memlûk (who had served) Asad ed-Din, to ascertain the whereabouts and movements of the Franks. These men fell in unexpectedly with contingents from el-Kerak and esh-Shôbek, on their way to reinforce the enemy. Our people attacked them, killed a great number,

---

[1] *El-Fawâr*, 'the bubbling spring.' Possibly the present village *Fu'ara*, 12 miles E. of Jordan, at the head of Wâdi Ekseir.

[2] *El-Kuseir*, 'the little fort.' The name survives in *Wâdy Ekseir* falling into the Jordan on the E., about 8 miles N. of Beisân.

[3] *Beisân* (Bethshean), 3 miles W. of the Jordan, near the mouth of the Valley of Jezreel.

[4] Now *'Ain Jâlûd*, 'Goliath's Spring,' in the Valley of Jezreel, a mile S.E. of Jezreel. It has a large pool of water.

and made more than a hundred prisoners; then they returned, without having lost a single Moslem, except a man named Behrâm esh-Shâwûsh. Towards the end of the day—the 10th of Jomada II. (September, 30, A.D. 1183)—the Sultan received news of the defeat of the Franks. His army showed their delight, and became firmly persuaded that they were destined to obtain victory and success. On Saturday, the 11th of the same month, the Sultan was informed that the Franks had quitted Seffûria, where they had mustered their forces, and were marching on el-Fûla,[1] a well-known village. As he meant to pit his forces against theirs in the field, he drew up his ranks in order of battle—right wing, left wing, and centre —and marched to meet them. The enemy advanced on the Moslems, and they came face to face (lit., eye to eye). The Sultan sent out the vanguard, composed of five hundred picked men, to attack them, and they made a great slaughter, and the enemy killed some. The Franks kept their ranks close, and their infantry protected their knights, and they neither charged nor stopped, but continued their march to the spring we mentioned above, and there camped. The Sultan halted opposite to them, and endeavoured to provoke them to quit their position and do battle by sending out skirmishing parties. Nevertheless, they remained where they were, seeing that the Moslems were in great force. As the Sultan could not draw them from their position, he resolved to retire, hoping that they would pursue him, and give him an opportunity of fighting a pitched battle. He therefore marched in the direction of et-Tôr (Mount Tabor) on the 17th of the same month,

---

[1] *El-Fûleh*, 'the bean,' called La Fève by the Franks, was a small fort 3½ miles N. of Jezreel. The outposts of the Franks were at Tubania ('*Ain Tubaûn*), a mile N.E. of 'Ain Jâlûd, and 5 miles S.E. of Fûleh.—'William of Tyre,' xxii. 27.

and took up a position at the foot of the mountain, watching for a favourable moment to attack them as soon as they began to move. The Franks started at dawn, and retreated. He pursued them, and tried in vain to provoke them to fight by a constant shower of arrows, and he continued to follow their march until they halted at el-Fûla, going back to their own country. The Moslems, seeing this, came to the Sultan, and advised him to retire, because their supplies were running very short. Besides, he had inflicted severe loss upon the enemy, both in killed and in the prisoners he had taken ; and had destroyed several of their villages, such as 'Aferbela, the stronghold of Beisân, and Zer'ain.[1] He therefore retired, victorious and triumphant, and halted at el-Fawâr, where he gave leave to such of his men as wished to return to their homes. He then marched back to Damascus, which he entered on Thursday, the 24th of the same month. The citizens testified the greatest delight at his return. What lofty ambition dwelt in his soul ! Even the capture and occupation of Aleppo did not deter him from undertaking another expedition ! His object in all his conquests was to enlarge his resources for carrying on the Holy War. May God grant him a splendid reward in the next life, even as, by His mercy, He allowed him to perform so many meritorious actions in this !

CHAPTER XXV.

HE UNDERTAKES AN EXPEDITION AGAINST EL-KERAK.

THE Sultan remained at Damascus until the 3rd of Rejeb, 579 (October 22, A D. 1183), and went out several

---

[1] *Zer'ain* is Jezreel. *'Aferbela* (Forbelet of the Franks) is unknown.

times towards el-Kerak. He had summoned his brother, el Melek el-'Âdel, who was at that time in Egypt, to join him at el-Kerak. As soon as he heard his brother had set out, he left (Damascus), and went to meet him, which he did quite close to el-Kerak. A great number of merchants and other people had travelled with el-'Âdel, who arrived on the 4th of Sh'abân (November 22, A.D. 1183). The Franks had received information that el-Melek el-'Âdel had taken the field, and they marched their men and knights towards el-Kerak to defend that place. When the Sultan heard that the army of the Franks was strong in number, he grew apprehensive of their marching in the direction of Egypt; and therefore he sent his nephew, el Melek el-Mozaffer Taki ed-Dîn, into that country. This occurred on the 15th of Sh'abân. On the 16th of the same month the Franks encamped at el-Kerak, and the Sultan, after vigorously assaulting the place, was obliged to retire. It was here that Sheref ed-Dîn Barghôsh (who had been one of Nûr ed-Dîn's memlûks) testified (to the faith) by death.

CHAPTER XXVI.

HE GIVES THE CITY OF ALEPPO TO HIS BROTHER, EL-MELEK EL-'ÂDEL.

AFTER the arrival of the Franks at el-Kerak, the Sultan abandoned the hope of taking that stronghold, and retired towards Damascus with his brother, el-Melek el-'Âdel. He arrived on the 24th of Sh'abân, and on the 2nd of Ramadân (December 19, 1183), he granted the Government of Aleppo to el-'Âdel, who had remained with him. At that time his son, el-Melek ez-Zâher, was in Aleppo, with Seif ed-Dîn Yazkûj, the regent, and Ibn el-'Amid.[1] El-Melek ez-Zâher was his favourite son, on account of the fine character with which God had endowed him. Exalted ambition, clear judgment, lofty intelligence, an upright spirit and a virtuous life—all the gifts which lead to pre-eminence were united in his person, and he showed his father untiring affection and obedience. Nevertheless, his father took the Government of Aleppo out of his hands, because he believed certain advantages would accrue from such a measure. The prince quitted Aleppo with Yazkûj as soon as el-Melek el-'Âdel arrived, and both went to attend the Sultan. On the 28th of Shawâl (February 13, 1184), they arrived at Damascus. Ez-Zâher remained with his father, and obeyed him and submitted unto him in all things. Nevertheless, he concealed in his heart a discontent that did not escape the Sultan's observation.

This same month I came to the Sultan as a member of a deputation sent by the Government of Mosul. We had previously applied to Khalif en-Nâsr ed-Dîn Illah, then at Baghdad, and had persuaded him to allow the Sheikh of Sheikhs, Bedr ed-Dîn, to accompany us, to act as ambassador and mediator. He was a most worthy man, highly respected not only at the Khalif's court, but throughout the country. The Sultan held this doctor in such esteem that during his stay at the court he went to visit him almost every day.

---

[1] Ibn el-'Amid (Naseh ed-Dîn ed-Dimashki) was head of the executive government, both civil and military (*divân*), at Aleppo.

CHAPTER XXVII.

OUR DEPUTATION ARRIVES AT THE SULTAN'S COURT.

THE Sheikh had visited Mosul on his way, and from thence had travelled with the Kâdi Mohi ed-Dîn, son of Kemâl ed-Dîn, who had been a friend from the days of his boyhood. I, too, was a member of the deputation. We continued our journey, and on our arrival at Damascus the Sultan came out to meet us, to welcome the Sheikh and the others of us who were of his company. After the interview, which took place some distance from Damascus, we made our entry into the city on Saturday, the 11th of Zu el-K'ada (February 25, 1184). The Sultan accorded us the most gracious and gratifying reception, and we spent several days in negotiations and attempts to make a final arrangement. But peace was not made on this occasion, and we departed to return to Mosul. The Sultan accompanied us as far as el-Kuseir,[1] where he bade the Sheikh farewell, and Bedr ed-Dîn that day made one last endeavour to effect a settlement. But his attempt failed in consequence of an objection raised by Mohi ed-Dîn. The Sultan stipulated that the Lord of Arbela and the Lord of el-Jezîra[2] should be free to choose his rule or that of Mosul, but the Kâdi declared they must sign the treaty (of peace). This condition put a stop to the negotiations, and we started on our journey on the 7th of Zu el-Hijja (March 22). During our visit the Sultan commissioned the Sheikh to offer me all the posts which Behâ ed-

---

[1] El-Kuseir, a ruined village with a tower, nine miles N.E. of Damascus.

[2] This is the city and principality of Jezîrat Ibn 'Omar.

Dimashki[1] had held in Misr. I refused his offer, fearing lest the ill-success of our negotiations should be attributed to me. From that time the Sultan had an opinion in his noble mind of myself of which I knew nothing until after I had entered his service. Saláh ed-Din remained at Damascus, and continued to receive the ambassadors who were sent to him from all parts. One came from Sinjâr Shah,[2] Lord of el-Jezîra, on whose behalf he swore faith with the Sultan. The plenipotentiary of the Lord of Arbela did the same, and took his departure with the other ambassadors. On the 4th of Zu el-Hijja (March 19), el-Melek el-'Âdel arrived from Aleppo to visit his brother the Sultan, and after being present at the Feast (of the Sacrifice),[3] on the 10th of Zu el-Hijja, he returned once more to Aleppo.

CHAPTER XXVIII.

THE SULTAN'S SECOND EXPEDITION AGAINST EL-KERAK.

THE Sultan had sent out messengers in all directions to collect troops. The first chief who came to join his standard was Nûr ed-Din, son of Kara Arslân, and Prince of Hisn Keifa. He arrived at Aleppo on the 18th of the month of Safer (May 31, 1184), and was received with the highest honours by el-Melek el-'Âdel. This prince took him into the fortress, where he entertained him most agree-

---

[1] El-Behá ed-Dimashki was principal professor in Menâzel el-'Izz College, in Old Cairo, and held the office of *Khatib*, or chief preacher, in the same city.

[2] This was the Atabeg prince, Mo'ezz ed-Din, son of Seif ed-Dîn Ghâzi, and Prince of Jezîrat Ibn 'Omar.

[3] *Zu el-Hijja* is the month of the *Háj*, and the sacrifice is one of the ceremonies at Mecca.

ably, and on the 26th of the same month set out with him for Damascus. The Sultan had been ill for several days, and God then restored him to health. As soon as he heard that the son of Kara Arslân was approaching, he hastened to meet him, for he was most generous in paying every honour to all men. They met in the Buk'aat 'Ain el-Jisr on the 9th of the month of Rabi'a I. (June 20, 1184). He then returned to Damascus, in advance of the son of Kara Arslân and of el-Melek el-'Âdel, and set about making preparations for another expedition. On the 15th of that same month he left Damascus and took up his position at the Wooden Bridge.[1] On the 24th el-'Âdel arrived at Damascus with the son of Kara Arslân, and after sojourning there some days, set out with him to join the Sultan. The latter had just left Râs el-Mâ[2] on his way towards el-Kerak, and halted for several days close to that stronghold to await the arrival of el-Melek el-Moz-affer[3] from Egypt. This prince joined the Sultan on the 19th of Rabi'a II. (July 30), and brought with him the household and treasures of el-Melek el-'Âdel, all of which the Sultan despatched to that prince, and commanded him and the other leaders to join him forthwith at el-Kerak. All the detachments arrived in close succession, so that by the 4th of Jomada I. (August 13) the fortress was completely invested. As soon as the contingents from Egypt, from Syria, and from el-Jezîra—the latter commanded by the son of Kara Arslân—had effected a junction, the mangonels were set up to batter the place. When the Franks received news of what had taken place, they set out with their

---

[1] Probably the bridge of el-Kesweh, nine or ten miles S.W. of Damascus.

[2] Râs el-Mâ lies between es-Sanemein and Shemeskîn, on the road from Damascus to Mecca. It is now called *Kefr el-Mâ*.

[3] This was the title of Taki ed-Dîn 'Omar, Salâh ed-Din's nephew.

knights and footmen to the relief of el-Kerak. This fortress was a source of great annoyance to the Moslems, for it so effectually commanded the road to Egypt that caravans could not travel without a strong military escort. The Sultan was resolved to put an end to this state of things and open the road to Egypt. When he heard that the Franks had come out, he prepared to meet them, ordering his men back to the heights of el-Kerak, and sending the baggage (away) into the country, that his troops should not be hampered in fighting. Then he marched against the enemy. As the Franks had halted at el-Wâleh,[1] he took up a position opposite to them, close to a village called Hesbân, but afterwards marched on to a place called M'äin ; the Franks remained in their position at el-Wâleh until the 26th of Jomada I. (September 4, 1184), when they moved their camp nearer to el-Kerak. A detachment of the Moslem army hung on their march, annoying their rear, till the end of that day. As soon as the Sultan saw that the Franks were bent on el-Kerak, he sent his army into the countries lying on the coast, which were left entirely unprotected in the absence of the troops. They carried Nâblus by storm, and pillaged the city, but did not succeed in taking the castle. Then they captured Jânin (Jenin), and returned to join the Sultan at Râs el-Mâ with the prisoners they had taken, pillaging, burning, and sacking the country that they had passed through.[2] Salâh ed-Din entered Damascus in triumph on Saturday, the 7th of Jomada II. (Septem-

---

[1] The Franks, sallying from Kerak, defended the pass of *Wadi Wâleh*, about 20 miles N. of the castle. Salâh ed-Din, at *Hesbân* (Heshbon), was about 15 miles to the N.E., and at *M'ain* (Beth Meon) about 10 miles N. of this position.

[2] Salâh ed-Dîn's army probably crossed the Jordan E. of *Nâblus* (Shechem), and marching N. by *Jenin* (*En Gannim*) would recross S. of the Sea of Galilee near *Beisân*.

ber 15), supported on either side by el-Melek el-'Âdel, and
by Nûr ed-Dîn, son of Kara Arslân. The latter he overwhelmed with honours and with tokens of his good-will
and esteem. This month an ambassador arrived from the
Khalif, bringing robes of honour for the Sultan, for his
brother (el-Melek el-'Âdel), and for the son of Asad ed-Dîn,[1]
and invested them therewith. On the 14th of the same
month the Sultan clad the son of Kara Arslân in the robe
he had received from the Khalif, and gave him leave to
depart ; he also dismissed the troops. About the same
time messengers came from Kukbûri, son of Zein ed-Dîn,
to ask the support of the Sultan. They brought news that
the Mosul army, assisted by the troops of Kizil (Prince
of Hamadân), under the command of Mojâhed ed-Din
Kâimâz, had threatened Arbela, and pillaged and burned
in all directions. Kukbûri had defeated them and put
them to flight.

CHAPTER XXIX.

THE SULTAN'S SECOND EXPEDITION AGAINST MOSUL.

ON receiving this news the Sultan set out from Damascus
for the country (of which Mosul is the capital), leaving
orders for the army to follow him. He reached Harrân,
after a meeting with Mozaffer ed-Dîn (Kukbûri) at el-
Bîra[2] on the 12th of Moharrem, 581 (April 15, A.D. 1185).
Seif ed-Dîn Ibn el-Meshtûb, by the Sultan's command, led
the vanguard of the army to Râs el-'Ain.[3] On the
22nd of Safer (May 25) the Sultan arrived at Harrân, and

---

[1] Prince Muhammad, son of Asad ed-Dîn Shîrkuh.
[2] See p. 72.
[3] *Râs el'Ain*, on the Khabûr river, S.E. of Harrân.

on the 26th he had Mozaffer ed-Dîn (Kukbûri), son of
Zein ed-Dîn, arrested for something he had done and for
certain words attributed to him by his ambassador, which
angered the Sultan, though, indeed, he had not thoroughly
investigated the matter.[1] The Sultan deprived him of the
governorship of the castles of Harrân and Edessa, and
kept him in prison to give him a lesson. Then, on the
first day of the month of Rabi'a I. he clad him with a robe
of honour, and received him once more into favour, restoring to him the castle of Harrân and the provinces he had
held, together with all the honours and dignities he had
formerly enjoyed. Everything was restored to him excepting the fortress of Edessa, and this place the Sultan
promised should be given back to him later on. On
the 2nd of the month Rabia' I. Salâh ed-Din came to Râs
el-'Aïn, where he received an ambassador from Kilij
Arslân, who brought tidings that the princes of the East
had sworn together to march against him, if he did not
withdraw from Mosul and Mardîn, and to do battle with
him should he persist in his designs. This information
determined the Sultan to march towards Doneiser.[2] On
the 8th of the month Rabi'a I. he was joined by 'Imâd
ed-Dîn, son of Kara Arslân, accompanied by the troops of
Nûr ed-Dîn, his brother, and the lord of Mardîn. The
Sultan went out to meet him and received him with great
honours. On the 11th of the same month he left Doneiser
on his way to Mosul, and encamped in a place called el-
Isma'îliyât, which was near enough to the city to enable

---

[1] According to Ibn el-Athîr, in his ' Kamel,' Kukbûri had offered
the Sultan the sum of fifty thousand dinars as an inducement to undertake another expedition against Mosul. He did not fulfil his promise,
and hence the Sultan's displeasure.

[2] *Doneiser*, according to the author of the ' Merased el-Ittilâ,' lies at
the foot of the hill upon which stands the city of Mardîn.

him to relieve the detachment engaged in the blockade on each succeeding day. 'Imâd ed-Dîn, son of Kara Arslân, received news at this time of the death of his brother, Nûr ed-Dîn, and obtained the Sultan's permission to depart, in the hope of securing the throne thus left vacant.

CHAPTER XXX.

DEATH OF SHAH-ARMEN, PRINCE OF KHELÂT.

SHAH-ARMEN, Prince of Khelât, died in the month of Rabi'a II., in the year 581 (July, A.D. 1185) and was succeeded by one of his memlûks, named Bektimor, the same who had come on an embassy to the Sultan at Sinjâr. His government was just, and conduced to the prosperity of the people of Khelât; he followed the Sûfi[1] path, therefore his subjects were submissive and devoted to him. The death of Shah-Armen and succession of Bektimor roused the ambition of the neighbouring kings, and induced Pehlevân Ibn Yeldokûz to march on Khelât. When Bektimor received news of his approach, he sent an ambassador to the Sultan, saying that he wished to surrender Khelât to Salâh ed-Dîn, and to be received amongst the number of his servants, and that he would give his Majesty all he should ask. The Sultan thereupon felt so strong a wish to possess himself of Khelât that he raised the blockade of Mosul, and marched in the direction of that city. At the same time he despatched two envoys to Bektimor, viz., 'Aisa, the jurist, and Ghars ed-Dîn Kilîj,

---

[1] The 'path' is a Sûfi term for the course of religious training leading to renunciation of all worldly desires and to union with God. The Sûfi 'path' seems to have been borrowed from the teaching of Buddhism.

to negotiate a treaty with him, the terms of which were to be committed to writing. These ambassadors fell in with Pehlevân a short distance from the city. Bektimor had frightened this prince by informing him that he thought of surrendering his territory to the Sultan, and Pehlevân had made terms with him, giving him one of his daughters in marriage, confirming him in his dominions, and restoring his country to him. Bektimor therefore made excuses to the Sultan's ambassadors, and they had to depart without effecting anything. The Sultan had already sat down before Miâfârekîn, besieging it, and fighting a great fight, and setting up his mangonels against it. There was a man in Miâfârekîn named Asad, who left nothing undone for the defence of the city ; but his endeavours could not overcome destiny. The place surrendered to the Sultan on the 29th of Jomâda I. Having now lost all hope of getting possession of Khelât, Salâh ed-Dîn retired and took up a position before Mosul for the third time, encamping at Kefr Zemmâr, not far from the city. The heat at that time was excessive. He occupied this camp for some time, and it was here that he received a visit from Sinjâr Shah,[1] from el-Jezira. He had an interview with this prince, and then sent him back to his own city. At Kefr Zemmâr he was attacked by so serious an illness that it caused him great anxiety, and he set out for Harrân. Although his condition was so serious, he would not allow himself to give way and travel in a litter. He reached Harrân very sick, and so exhausted that his life was despaired of, and a report of his death was circulated abroad. At this juncture his brother arrived from Aleppo, bringing his own physicians with him.

[1] See above, p. 95.

CHAPTER XXXI.

THE PEOPLE OF MOSUL MAKE PEACE WITH THE SULTAN.

'IZZ ED-DIN, the Atâbeg Prince of Mosul, had sent me to the Khalif to entreat his assistance, but the mission was unsuccessful. He then applied to the Persians, but was unsuccessful in that quarter also. On my return from Baghdad, I informed him of the answer I had received, and he then abandoned all hope of obtaining help and assistance. When the news of the Sultan's illness was received in Mosul, we saw that it was an opportunity that ought not to be neglected, for we knew how readily that prince lent his ear to an appeal, and how tender-hearted he was; so I was commanded to go to him, accompanied by Behâ ed-Din er-Rebîb. To me was entrusted the drawing-up of the oath to be sworn. 'Make every endeavour,' my instructions ran, 'to obtain favourable conditions quickly.' It was during the first ten days of the month of Zu el-Hijja (the end of February, 1186), that we arrived in the Sultan's camp, and there we found that his life had been despaired of by all. We were welcomed with all honour, and the Sultan, for the first time since his convalescence, held a reception at which we were presented. On the day of 'Arafa (9th of Zu el-Hijja)[1] we obtained for the government of Mosul all the district that lies between the two rivers, which he had taken from Sinjâr Shah. He and his brother el-Melek el-'Âdel swore the oath that I administered to them, which was couched in strong terms. The Sultan observed the condi-

---

[1] The day of *'Arafa* is that when the Mecca pilgrims visit Mount Arafat.

tions of this peace till the hour of his death—may God hallow his soul!—and he never once broke them. When we came to him at Ḥarrân, he had already begun to grow stronger. At this place he received tidings of the death of (his cousin) son of Asad ed-Dîn (that is to say, of Muhammad, son of Asad ed-Dîn Shîrkuh), prince of Emesa. He breathed his last on the day of 'Arafa (9th of Zu el-Hijja, March 3, A.D. 1186). El-Melek el-'Âdel held a reception on this occasion to receive expressions of public condolence. At this period a conflict was being waged between the Turkomans and the Kurds, which resulted in great loss of life.[1] During this month, also, we heard of the death of Pehlevân, son of Yeldokûz, who passed away on the last day of the month of Zu el-Hijja (February 23, 1186).

CHAPTER XXXII.

THE SULTAN RETURNS TO SYRIA.

WHEN the Sultan found that his recovery was assured, he set out for Aleppo, which he reached on the 14th of Moharrem, 582 (April 6, 1186). The delight of the people at seeing him again in their midst, and in good health, made it a memorable day. He remained there for four days, and then started for Damascus. At Tell es-Sulṭân[2] he met Asad ed-Din Shîrkuh, who had come out to meet him with his sister, and a numerous following. He

---

[1] This struggle was prolonged through several years, and Upper Mesopotamia, Diarbekr, Khelât, Syra, Azerbijân, and other countries, were deluged with blood. Mojâhed ed-Din Kâimâz at last succeeded in bringing about a reconciliation between the two nations (Ibn el-Athîr's ' Kamel,' under the year A.H. 581).

[2] Tell es-Sulṭân is about half-way between Aleppo and Hamah.

brought with him a great number of presents (for the Sultan). That prince granted him the government of Emesa,[1] and spent several days in that city to transfer the paternal heritage ; then he marched to Damascus, which he entered on the 2nd of Rabi'a I. (May 23). Never were such rejoicings seen as on that day. During this month numerous encounters took place between the Turkomans and the Kurds, in the district of Nisiba and elsewhere. A great number were killed on both sides. The Sultan, hearing that M'oîn ed-Dîn had revolted at er-Rawendân,[2] sent a written order to the army at Aleppo to besiege that place. On the 2nd of Jomada I. (July 21, 1186), M'oîn ed-Dîn came from er-Rawendân to join the Sultan's train, after surrendering that place to 'Alem ed-Dîn Suleimân. On the 17th of the same month el-Melek el-Afḍal arrived at Damascus. He had never visited Syria until that time.

CHAPTER XXXIII.

EL-MELEK EL-'ÂDEL GOES INTO EGYPT, AND EL-MELEK EZ-ZÂHER RETURNS TO ALEPPO.

THE Sultan deemed it necessary to send el-Melek el-'Âdel into Egypt, because that prince was more familiar with the condition and circumstances of that country than was el-Melek el-Mozaffer (Taki ed-Dîn). He used to hold long conversations with him on this subject during his illness at Ḥarrân, which was a great pleasure to el-'Âdel,

---

[1] The government of Emesa was entrusted to Muhammad, son of Shîrkuh, and might naturally descend to Muhammad's son.

[2] *Er-Rawendân* (Ravendal of the Franks) was a fortress on the *Nahr 'Afrîn*, about two days' journey N.W. of Aleppo.

who was deeply attached to Egypt. When the Sultan's
health was re-established, and after his return to Damascus, he despatched a courier to el-'Âdel to summon him
to that city. On the 24th of Rabi'a I. (June 14, 1186),
el-'Âdel set out from Aleppo with a small escort, and proceeded by rapid marches to Damascus. There he remained
in attendance upon the Sultan, and was admitted to several
conferences and interviews with him. By the beginning of
Jomada I. the main parts of the business were settled, and
it was decided that el-'Âdel should return to Egypt and
surrender Aleppo to the Sultan. El-'Âdel sent certain
of his friends to Aleppo to fetch his family. El-Melek
ez-Zâher—may God protect him![1]—was at this time with
his father the Sultan, together with his brother el-Melek
el-'Azîz. The Sultan had made it a condition of el-Melek
el-'Âdel's return to Egypt, that that prince should act as
atâbeg[2] (or guardian) to el-Melek el-'Azîz. He entrusted
the young prince to el-'Âdel, who was to undertake his
education. The government of Aleppo was given to el-
Melek ez-Zâher.

El-'Âdel himself told me : ' When this arrangement had
been concluded, I went to pay my respects to el-Melek
el-'Azîz and el-Melek ez-Zâher. I found them together,
and sat down between them, saying to el-Melek el-'Aziz :
" My lord, the Sultan has commanded me to enter your
service, and to set out with you for Egypt. I know that
there are a great number of wicked people, some of whom
will come to you, and will abuse me, and counsel you not
to trust me. If you intend to listen to them, tell me now,
so that I may not go with you (into Egypt)." He replied :

---

[1] This phrase in Arabic is never used except in speaking of a
reigning prince, and at the time when our author was writing el-Melek
ez-Zâher was Lord of Aleppo, and of the northern parts of Syria.

[2] *Atabeg*, Turkish from *Ata*, 'father,' and *beg* 'lord'—a guardian.

" I shall not listen to them ; how could I do so ?" I then
turned to el-Melek ez-Zâher, and said : " I know quite well
that your brother might listen to men who devise mischief,
and that, if he did cause me that grief, I could not rely
upon anyone but you." He answered : " Bless you ! all
will go well." ' A short time afterwards the Sultan sent
his son el-Melek ez-Zâher to Aleppo with the title of
Sultan, because he knew that this city was the basis (the
foundation) and the seat of his whole power. It was on
this account that he had made such great efforts to get
possession of it. Once he had established his supremacy
there, he relaxed his watch over the countries to the east-
ward (Upper Mesopotamia, Mosul, and Khelât), contenting
himself with their assurances of loyalty, and promises of
support in the Holy War. He entrusted this city to his
son, being confident in his tact, decision, and watchfulness,
and in the strength and nobility of his character. El-Melek
ez-Zâher set out for Aleppo, accompanied by Hossâm
ed-Dîn Bishâra, who was to act as *shihna* (governor of the
city), and 'Aisa Ibn Belashu as *vâli* (governor of the district).
At 'Ain el-Mobâreka (' Holy Spring '), he was received by
the inhabitants of Aleppo, who had come forth to welcome
him. This was at day-break, on the 9th of Jomada II.,
582 (August 27, 1186). Towards mid-day he went up to
the castle, whilst the city gave itself up to manifestations
of delight. He extended the wing of his justice over
them, and rained down his bounty upon them. We will
return to el-Melek el-'Azîz and el-Melek el-'Âdel. When
the Sultan had decided on the privileges and honours they
were respectively to enjoy, he wrote to el-Melek el-Mozâffer,
informing him that el-Melek el-'Azîz was setting out for
Egypt accompanied by his uncle, and commanding him to
return to Syria. This prince was so aggrieved by these
instructions that he could not conceal his dissatisfaction,

and he formed a plan of going over to the nomad Arabs of
Barka.[1] The chief officers of state reproved him loudly for
thinking of such a thing, and represented to him that such
a step would ruin him for ever with his uncle the Sultan,
'and God alone knows,' they said, 'what would be the
consequence.' He recognised the wisdom of this advice,
and sent an answer to the Sultan signifying his obedience.
When he had handed the province over to his successor,
he set out to present himself before the Sultan, who, on
his side, came as far as Merj es Soffer[2] to receive him.
Their meeting took place on the 23rd of Sh'abân that year
(November 8, 1186). The Sultan showed great satisfaction
at seeing him, and gave him the city of Hamah (as an
appanage). El-Mozaffer betook himself to that place. On
the 26th of the month of Ramadân (December 10), el-Melek
ez-Zâher married one of the daughters of el-Melek
el-'Âdel, to whom he had been betrothed. The marriage
of el-Melek el-Afdel with the daughter of Nâsr ed-Din
(Muhammad), son of Asad ed-Din (Shirkûh), took place in
the month of Shawâl (December to January, 1186-1187).

---

[1] He proposed to go and join Karakûsh, one of Salâh ed-Din's
generals, who had taken Barka in Cyrenaica, and, with the assistance
of the nomad Arabs of that country and Mauretania, was carrying on
a successful war of conquest in Tripolitania and Tunisia. Some slight
information about *Karakûsh* may be found in the second volume of
Baron de Slane's translation, entitled 'Histoire des Berbers.'

[2] Merj es-Soffer lay in the Haurân, about thirty-eight geographical
miles S.W. of Damascus.

CHAPTER XXXIV.

THE SULTAN MAKES PREPARATIONS FOR AN EXPEDITION AGAINST EL-KERAK.

AT the beginning of the month of Moḥarrem, 583 (March, A.D. 1187), the Sultan resolved to march against el-Kerak, and sent to Aleppo for the troops of that city. He left Damascus on the 15th of the same month, and encamped in the district of Ḳuneiṭera,[1] awaiting the arrival of the armies from Egypt and Syria. As each body of troops arrived, he ordered them to send out detachments into the countries on the coast to ravage and pillage wherever they went. This order was obeyed. He remained in the country round el-Kerak until the arrival of the caravan of Syrian pilgrims on their return from Mecca, whom his presence protected from the attacks of the enemy. Another caravan, coming from Egypt, brought all the people of el-Melek el-Mozaffer's household, and all the household-goods that he had left in that country. The army from Aleppo was delayed for some time, for they were watching the Franks in Armenia, the country of Ibn Laon. It happened that the king of the Franks had died, and bequeathed the chief power to his nephew.[2] El-Melek el-Mozaffer was at that time at Ḥamah. When the Sultan heard this news, he ordered the troops at Aleppo to invade the enemy's terri-

---

[1] *Kuneitera,* in the N. of the Haurân, between Damascus and Bâniâs.

[2] This is not quite exact. Baldwin IV. had died in 1185, and the child, Baldwin V., son of Sibyl, sister of Baldwin IV., died September, 1186. Salâh ed-Dîn took advantage of the dissensions between the party of Sibyl, who married Guy of Lusignan, and the party of Isabel, first married to the step-son of Renaud of Chatillon.

tory, so as to damp the zeal which animated the Franks. El-Mozaffer led the troops from Aleppo to Hârim, and there took up his quarters, to show the enemy that that part (of Syria) was not neglected. The Sultan (having left el-Kerak) returned to Syria, and on the 17th of Rabi'a I. (May 27, 1187) set up his camp at 'Ashtera.[1] Here he was joined by his son, el-Melek el-Afdel, and by Mozaffer ed-Dîn, son of Zein ed-Din, and the rest of the army. The Sultan had instructed el-Melek el-Mozaffer to conclude a treaty with the Franks, which should secure the neighbourhood of Aleppo from being disturbed. In this way he thought he should be free from any anxiety, and could give his whole attention to the enemy on the coast. El-Mozaffer made peace (with the people of Antioch) during the last ten days of Rabi'a I. (beginning of June), and then marched towards Hamah to join the Sultan, and take part in the projected expedition. He set out with all the troops from the East that he could collect—that is to say, with detachments from Mosul, under Mas'ùd Ibn ez-Z'aferâni, and from Mardin. The Sultan went out to meet them about the middle of Rabi'a II., and received them with great honours. He reviewed his troops shortly afterwards at Tell Tesîl,[2] preparatory to the expedition upon which they were starting, and ordered the leaders of the flanks and the centre to take up their positions.

[1] The water supply S. of *Tell 'Ashterah* is more abundant than elsewhere in the Haurân, and the position served as a base equally against Kerak or Galilee.

[2] *Tesîl*, about 5 miles S.W. of *Nâwa*, and N.W. of *Tell 'Ashterah*, in the Jaulàn, E. of the Sea of Galilee.

CHAPTER XXXV.

ACCOUNT OF THE BATTLE OF HATTÎN, AN AUSPICIOUS
DAY FOR THE FAITHFUL.

THE Sultan believed that it was his duty, above all things,
to devote his whole strength to fulfil the command we have
received to war against the infidels, in recognition of God's
mercy in establishing his dominion, in making him master
of so many lands, and granting him the obedience and
devotion of his people. Therefore he sent an order to
all his troops to join him at 'Ashtera. When he had
mustered and reviewed them, as we have narrated above,
he made his dispositions, and marched full speed upon the
enemy's territory—may God confound their hopes !—on the
17th of the month Rabi'a II. (June 26, 1187). He used
always to attack the enemy on a Friday, at the hour of
prayer, believing that the prayers that the preachers
were offering from their pulpits at that time would bring
him good luck, because their petitions that day were
generally granted. At this hour, then, he began his
march,[1] holding his army in readiness to fight. He heard
that the Franks, having received intelligence of his muster-
ing of troops, had assembled in the plain of Seffûria,[2]
in the territory of Acre, and meant to come out and meet

---

[1] Melek el-Afdal, advancing by the bridges S. of the Sea of Galilee,
towards Tabor and Nazareth, encountered the Templars and Hospitallers coming from Fûleh. In the ensuing fight the Grand Master of
the Hospital and the Marshal of the Temple were killed. A general
advance was then ordered by Salâh ed-Dîn. This happened near Kefr
Kenna on May 1. See 'Jacques de Vitry,' p. 100.

[2] *Seffûrieh* is 3½ miles N. of Nazareth. The springs where the
camp was fixed are 1 mile S. of the village. Hattîn was 10 miles to
the E.

him and give him battle. He therefore took up a position close to the Sea of Tiberias, hard by a village called es-Sennâbra.[1] He next encamped on the top of the hill that lies to the west of Tiberias. There he remained ready for battle, thinking that the Franks would advance and attack him as soon as they had ascertained his movements; but they did not stir from their position. It was on Wednesday, the 21st of this same month (June 30, 1187), that the Sultan pitched his camp there. Seeing that the enemy were not moving, he left his infantry drawn up opposite the enemy and went down to Tiberias with a troop of light cavalry. He attacked that city and carried it by assault within an hour, devoting it to slaughter, burning, and sacking. All that were left of the inhabitants were taken prisoner. The castle alone held out.[2] When the enemy heard the fate of Tiberias, they were forced to break through their policy of inaction, to satisfy this call upon their honour, and they set out for Tiberias forthwith to drive the invaders back. The pickets of the Moslem army discerned their movement, and sent an express to inform the Sultan. When he received this message he detached a sufficient force to blockade the castle, and then rejoined the army with his suite. The two armies met on the summit of the hill to the west of Tiberias. This was on the evening of Thursday, the 22nd of the same month. Darkness separated the combatants, who passed the night under arms in order of battle, until the following day, Friday, the 23rd (July 2, 1187). Then the warriors of

---

[1] Now *es-Sennâbra* (Sinnabris), a ruin W. of Jordan, at the S. end of the Sea of Galilee. Salâh ed-Dîn crossed by the *Jisr es-Sidd* bridge, called also *Jisr es-Sennâbra*. His march to Hattîn, on the plateau W. of Tiberias, was about 9 miles N.W. His base might have been threatened from Fûleh and Beisân. The advance from Seffûrieh to Hattîn was fatal, on account of want of water.

[2] The fortress was held by the wife of Raymond of Tripoli.

both armies mounted their steeds and charged their opponents; the soldiers in the vanguard discharged their arrows; and the infantry came into action and fought furiously. This took place in the territory belonging to a village called Lûbia.[1] The Franks saw they must bite the dust, and came on as though driven to certain death; before them lay disaster and ruin, and they were convinced that the next day would find them numbered amongst the dead.[2] The fight raged obstinately; every horseman hurled himself against his opponent until victory was secured, and destruction fell upon the infidels. Night with its blackness put an end to the battle. Terrible encounters took place that day; never in the history of the generations that have gone have such feats of arms been told. The night had been spent under arms, each side thinking every moment that they would be attacked. The Moslems, knowing that behind them lay the Jordan, and in front the territory of the enemy, felt that God alone was able to save them. God, having granted His aid to the Moslems, gave them success, and sent them victory according to His decree. Their infantry charged from all sides; the centre came on like one man, uttering a mighty cry; God filled the hearts of the infidels with terror (for He has said), ' *Due from Us it was to help the believers* ' (Kurân xxx. 46). The count (Raymond of Tripoli), the most intelligent man of that race ,and famous for his keenness of perception, seeing signs of the catastrophe impending over his brothers in religion, was not prevented by thoughts of honour from taking measures for his personal safety. He fled in the beginning of the action, before the fighting had become serious, and set out in the direction of Tyre. Several

---

[1] *Lûbia* was 9 miles E. of Seffûrieh, and 2 miles S.W. of Haṭṭin. The village is supplied only by rain-water cisterns.

[2] *Literally*, amongst those who visit the tombs.

BATTLEFIELD OF HATTIN.

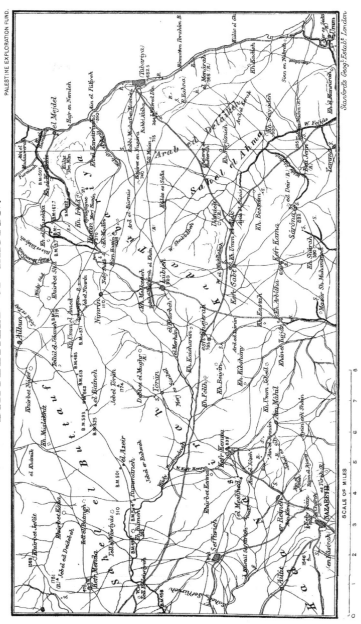

SCALE OF MILES

0   1   2   3   4   5   6   7   8

Moslems started in pursuit of him, but he succeeded in evading them ; true believers had nothing thereafter to fear from his cunning.[1] The upholders of Islâm surrounded the upholders of infidelity and impiety on every side, overwhelming them with arrows and harassing them with their swords. One body of the enemy took to flight, but they were pursued by the Moslem warriors, and not one of the fugitives escaped. Another band climbed Ḥaṭṭîn hill, so called from the name of a village, near which is the tomb of the holy patriarch Shu'aîb (Jethro).[2] The Moslems hemmed them in, and lighted fires all round them, so that, tortured by thirst and reduced to the last extremity, they gave themselves up to escape death. Their leaders were taken captive, and the rest were killed or made prisoners. Among the leaders who surrendered were King Geoffrey,[3] the King's brother,[4] Prince Arnâṭ (Renaud de Châtillon), Lord of el-Ḵerak, and of esh-Shôbek, the son of el-Honferi (Honfroi de Toron), the son of the Lord of Tiberias (Raymond of Tripoli), the chief of the Templars, the Lord of Jibeil,[5] and the chief of the Hospitallers. The others who

[1] He was killed soon after by the Assassins.

[2] The tomb of *Neby Shu'aîb* (Jethro) is still shown on the hill W. of the village of Haṭṭîn.

[3] Throughout his work our author makes the mistake of calling King Guy, *King Geoffrey.*

[4] Ibn el-Athîr also, in his ' Kamel,' says that the king's brother was amongst the prisoners. We read in 'Imâd ed-Dîn's ' Fatḥ el-Kossi ' : ' They brought before the Sultan King Guy, his brother Geoffrey, Hugh, Lord of Jibeil, Honfroi, Prince Arnaṭ, Lord of el-Kerak, etc.' According to the account of Raoul Coggeshale, who was present at the battle, the king's brother was amongst those taken prisoner, and from the continuator of William of Tyre we learn that Aimaury, the king's brother and constable of Jerusalem, was one of the prisoners made that day. He afterwards became King of Cyprus in succession to Guy. See ' Jacques de Vitry,' p. 107, where Geoffrey is noticed at the siege of Acre.

[5] His name was Hugh III. de l'Embriaco.

were missing had met their death ; and as to the common
people, some were killed and others taken captive. Of
their whole army none remained alive, except the prisoners.
More than one of their chief leaders accepted captivity to
save his life. A man, whom I believe to be reliable, told
me that he saw one soldier in the Haurân leading more
than thirty prisoners, tied together with a tent cord. He
had taken them all himself, so great had been the panic
caused by their defeat.

We will here narrate the fate of those leaders who
escaped with their lives. The count, who had fled,
reached Tripoli, and was there, by the grace of God,
carried off by pleurisy. The Hospitallers and Templars
the Sultan resolved to execute, and he spared not a single
one. Salâh ed-Dîn had sworn to put Prince Arnât to
death if he ever fell into his hands, and the reason he took
that oath is this : A caravan coming from Egypt, and
taking advantage of the truce, went quite close to esh-
Shôbek, where the prince then happened to be. Thinking
there was nothing to fear, they halted in the neighbourhood
of the place; but this man set upon them, in defiance of
his oath, and killed (a number) of them. The travellers in
vain besought him for mercy in the name of God, telling
him there was a treaty of peace between him and the
Moslems. He only answered by insulting the Holy Prophet.
When the Sultan heard what he had done, he was compelled by the Faith and by his determination to protect his
people to swear to take this man's life whenever he should
fall into his power. After God had granted him this
victory, he stayed at the entrance of his tent (for the tent
itself was not yet set up), and there he sat to receive
his soldiers, who came to win his approval of their
services, bringing the prisoners they had made and the
leaders they had found. As soon as the tent was pitched

the Sultan went to sit within, full of joy and gratitude for
the favour which God had just granted him. He then
commanded King Geoffrey, and his brother, and Prince
Arnât (Renaud) to be brought. He gave a bowl of sherbet
made with iced rose-water to the King, who was suffering
severely from thirst. Geoffrey drank part of it, and then
offered the bowl to Prince Arnât. The Sultan said to the
interpreter : ' Tell the King that it is he, and not I, who is
giving this man to drink.' He had adopted [the admirable
and generous custom of the Arabs, who grant life to the
captive who has eaten or drunk of their viands. He then
ordered his men to take them to a place prepared for their
reception, and, after they had eaten, he summoned them
again to his presence. He had only a few servants at that
time in his tent. He seated the King at the entrance, then
summoned the prince, and reminded him of what he had
said, adding : ' Behold, I will support Muhammad against
thee !'[1] He then called upon him to embrace Islâm, and,
on his refusal, drew his sabre and struck him a blow which
severed his arm from the shoulder. Those who were
present quickly despatched the prisoner, and God hurled
his soul into hell. The corpse was dragged out and thrown
down at the entrance of the tent. When the King saw the
way in which his fellow-captive had been treated, he
thought he was to be the second victim ; but the Sultan
had him brought into the tent and calmed his fears. ' It is
not the wont of kings,' said he, ' to kill kings; but that man
had transgressed all bounds, and therefore did I treat him
thus.' The conquerors spent that night in rejoicings ;
every voice chanted praise to God, and on all sides rose
cries of '*Allah Akbâr !*' ('God is most great !') and '*La
ilaha il' Allah !*' ('There is no other god but God !') till ·

---

[1] See p. 43.

dawn. On Sunday, the 25th of Rabi'a II. (July 4, 1187), the Sultan went down to Tiberias, and the fortress of that place was surrendered to him in the afternoon of the same day. He remained there until Tuesday, and then marched upon Acre. He arrived before that place on Wednesday, the last day of Rabi'a II. (July 8). On the following day, the first of Jomada I., he began the assault and took the city. He set free more than four thousand captives who had been detained there, and took possession of all the treasure, stores, and merchandise in the place, of which there were enormous quantities, for this city was a great centre of commerce. The troops were sent out in detachments to overrun the coast, taking the fortresses, castles, and strongholds. Nâblus fell into their hands, as well as Ḥaifa, Cæsarea, Ṣeffûria, and Nazareth, for all these places had been left defenceless by reason of the death or captivity of their protectors. The Sultan made arrangements for the government of Acre, and gave his soldiers a share of the booty and prisoners. He then marched in the direction of Tibnîn,[1] and sat down before that place on Sunday, the 12th of Jomada I. (July 20). As this was a very strong fortress, he set up his mangonels, and by frequent assaults reduced the place to the last extremity. The garrison was composed of men of tried valour and very zealous for their faith, therefore they held out with wonderful endurance; but God came to the Sultan's assistance, and he carried the place by storm on the 18th of the month, and led the survivors of the garrison into captivity. From this place he marched upon Sidon, which he captured on the day after his arrival. As soon as he had organized a regular government, he set out for Beirût, and took up a position to

---

[1] *Tibnîn* (Toron), in Upper Galilee, 17 miles S.W. of Bâniâs. The castle was built in 1107 by Hugh of St. Omer, Lord of Tiberias. See 'Jacques de Vitry,' p. 18.

attack that place on the 22nd of the same month. He set up his mangonels, storming the city several times, and maintaining the attack without any cessation until the 29th, when he succeeded in capturing it. Whilst he was occupied before Beirût, a detachment of his army had taken Jibeil.[1] Having completed the conquest of this district, he judged it expedient to march against Ascalon. He had made an attempt upon Tyre, but renounced it because his men were scattered through the districts on the coast, each soldier engaged in pillaging on his own account, and the army was growing weary of ceaseless fighting and continual war. Besides, all the Franks of the coast had collected in Tyre, therefore he thought it best to march against Ascalon, a city which he believed would be easy to take. On the 26th of Jomada II. (September 2) he encamped before the city, having taken on his march a number of places, such as er-Ramla, Yebna, and ed-Darûn.[2] He set up his mangonels against Ascalon, and, after a vigorous assault, succeeded in taking it on the last day of the same month. He remained encamped outside the city whilst detachments of his troops took Ghazza, Beit Jibrîn, and en-Natrûn,[3] which places surrendered without a blow. Thirty-five years had passed since the taking of Ascalon by the Franks; they had captured the city on the 27th of Jomada II., in the year 548 (September 19, A.D. 1153).[4]

---

[1] *Jibeil* (Gebal), N. of Beirût. This march cut the communication by land between Tyre and Tripoli.

[2] *Ed Darûn* is Darum now *Deir el-Belâh*, S. of Gaza, built about A.D. 1170.

[3] *Beit Jibrîn* (Gibelin), 18 miles E. of Ascalon, was fortified by King Fulk in 1134. For *Natrûn*, see p. 32.

[4] The final assault on the city appears to have been really on August 12, 1153.

CHAPTER XXXVI.

TAKING OF THE HOLY CITY (EL-KUDS ESH-SHERÎF).

HAVING taken Ascalon and the districts round Jerusalem (el Ḳuds), the Sultan devoted all his energies to preparations for an expedition against the city. He called together the various detachments of his army that were scattered through the coast-districts, and returned glutted with pillage and rapine ; and then marched upon Jerusalem, strong in the hope that God would uphold and direct him. He was anxious to make the most of his opportunities now that the door of success had been opened to him, following the advice of the Holy Prophet, who said : ' He to whom the door of success has been opened must take his opportunity and enter in, for he knows not when the door may be shut upon him.' It was on Sunday, the 15th of the month of Rejeb in the year 583 (September 20, 1187 A.D.), that he took up his position to the west of the city. The place was teeming with soldiers, both horse and foot, and their numbers, according to the best accounts, exceeded sixty thousand, without reckoning women and children. The Sultan shifted his position to the north of the city, thinking this would be best, and directed his mangonels against the walls.   Being very strong in bowmen, he pressed the place so closely by constant assaults and skirmishes that his miners were able to make a breach in one of the northern angles of the wall overlooking the Wâdi Jehennum.[1]   The enemies of God saw they were menaced by a disaster which they could not escape, and

---

[1] *Wâdi el-Jehennum* is the Moslem name for the Kidron Valley, E. of Jerusalem.

by divers signs it was revealed to them that the city would fall into the hands of the Moslems. Their hearts were filled with dread when they thought of their bravest warriors slain or taken captive, their strongholds destroyed or captured by the Moslems. Expecting to suffer the same fate as their brothers, and to die by the same sword that had cut them down, they adopted the only alternative, and asked for a treaty, that their lives might be spared. After messengers had several times passed backwards and forwards between the two parties, a treaty was concluded, and the Sultan was put in possession of Jerusalem on Friday, the 27th of Rejeb (October 2, 1187), on the anniversary of the night of the ascension (of the Holy Prophet into heaven), an event which is foreshadowed in the glorious Kurân (xvii. 1).[1] What a wonderful coincidence! God allowed the Moslems to take the city as a celebration of the anniversary of their Holy Prophet's midnight journey. Truly this is a sign that this deed was pleasing to Almighty God; and this mighty conquest was a testimony (for the Faith) to a multitude of people— learned men, dervishes, and fakirs—who were brought thither by the news of the Sultan's victories and successes in the lands on the coast, and by the report that he was going to undertake an expedition against Jerusalem. Therefore all men learned (in the law) came to join the Sultan, both from Egypt and from Syria; there was not a single well-known doctor but came to the camp. Every voice was raised in shouts, calling upon God, and proclaiming His unity and power. On the very day of the capitula-

---

[1] The Kurân says nothing of the legend of Muhammad's translation from Mecca to Jerusalem. The passage cited speaks of the prophet's going to the 'distant sanctuary' (*El-Haram el-Aksa*). The whole tradition of the night journey and ascent from the Sakhra to heaven is late, and Beha ed-Dîn therefore says only that it is 'foreshadowed' in the allusion cited.

tion Friday's prayer was solemnized in the city, and the khâṭib delivered the sermon.[1] The huge cross that rose from the dome of the Ṣakhra was thrown down. In this manner, by means of the Sultan, God accorded a magnificent triumph to Islâm. The chief condition stipulated by the treaty was that each man should pay ten Tyrian dinars as his ransom ; each woman five ; children, both boys and girls, were to pay only one dinar each. Every one who paid this ransom was to receive his freedom. God in His mercy delivered the Moslem prisoners who were in captivity in the city to the number of more than three thousand. The Sultan took possession of the whole of the booty, and distributed it amongst his emirs and soldiers. He also assigned a portion to the jurists, doctors of law, dervishes, and other people who had come to the camp. By his orders, all those who had paid their ransom were conducted to their place of refuge—that is to say, to the city of Tyre. I have been told that when the Sultan left Jerusalem he retained nothing whatever out of all these treasures, and yet they amounted to nearly two hundred and twenty thousand dinars. He left the city on Friday, the 25th of Sh'abán (October 30).

CHAPTER XXXVII.

HIS ATTEMPT ON TYRE.

THE Sultan, having established his supremacy upon a firm basis both in Jerusalem and on the coast, resolved to march against Tyre, for he knew that if he delayed in this undertaking, it would be very difficult to carry it to a

---

[1] Ibn Khallikân (ii. 634) has preserved this sermon for us.

successful issue. He repaired first to Acre, where he stopped to inspect the city, and then set out for Tyre on Friday, the 5th of Ramaḍân (November 8, 1187). When he came within sight of that city he pitched his camp, pending the arrival of his instruments of war. As soon as he had determined on undertaking this expedition, he had sent to his son el-Melek ez-Zâher, commanding him to join him. He had left that prince at Aleppo to protect that part of Syria whilst he himself was engaged in the conquest of the countries on the coast. Ez-Zâher reached the camp on the 18th of Ramaḍân, and his arrival gave his father the greatest satisfaction. As soon as the mangonels, moveable towers, mantelets, and other instruments of war had been brought in, the Sultan took up his position before the city on the 22nd of the month, and after completely surrounding it, began a brisk attack. The Egyptian fleet, which he had summoned to his assistance, blockaded the city by sea, whilst his army hemmed it in on the land side. His brother, el-Melek el-'Âdel, whom he had left behind in Jerusalem to settle affairs, received a command to join him, and reached the camp on the 5th of Shawâl (December 8). A body of troops, which the Sultan had detached to lay siege to Hûnîn, received the surrender of that place on the 23rd of the same month.

CHAPTER XXXVIII.

DESTRUCTION OF THE FLEET.

THE fleet was commanded by a certain man named el-Fâris Bedrân, a brave and clever sailor. 'Abd el-Mohsen, the High Admiral,[1] had instructed the ships to be watchful and

---

[1] *Râ-îs el-Baḥrein*, in Arabic, 'chief of the two seas'—that is to say, of the Mediterranean and the Red Sea.

vigilant, that the enemy might not find any opportunity of doing them harm ; but they neglected this advice, and omitted to keep a good watch during the night. Therefore the infidel fleet came out of. the harbour of Tyre, fell upon them unawares, took five of their ships with two captains, and killed a great number of Moslem sailors. This took place on the 27th of the month of Shawâl (December 30). The Sultan was much cast down by this occurrence, and as it was now the beginning of winter, and torrents of rain were falling, the troops were unable to fight any longer. He summoned his emirs to a council of war, and they advised him to strike camp, so as to give the soldiers a little rest, and to make preparations for renewing the siege later on.

He followed their advice and retired, dismounting his mangonels, and taking them with him. He ordered all that could not be transported to . be burnt. He took his departure on the 2nd of the month of Zu el-K'ada in the same year (January 3, 1188). He then dismissed the different bands that formed his army, and gave permission to the detachments to return to their respective homes. He himself with his own particular troops took up his quarters in Acre, and remained there until the year 584 (beginning of March, 1188 A.D.).

CHAPTER XXXIX.

HE LAYS SIEGE TO KAUKAB.

IN the beginning of that year he turned his attention to the fortresses which still remained in the hands of the Franks, and thought it would be best to get possession of these in order to discourage the garrison at Tyre. During the first ten days of the month of Moḥarrem (March 2-12) he encamped before Kaukab.[1] He began with this stronghold, because the troops he had stationed there, to prevent succours from being thrown in, had allowed themselves to be surprised by the Franks in a night attack. The Sultan set out from Acre with his own troops only, and sat down before the place; he had given leave to the rest of his army. His brother, el-'Âdel, had returned to Egypt, and his son, Ez-Zâher, to Aleppo. On the march they suffered severely from the cold and snow, but making it a point of honour to avenge his men, he encamped before the fortress, and kept up a smart attack for some time. It was at this place that I had the honour of being presented to him. In the year 583 I had performed the pilgrimage to Mecca, and was on the spot when Ibn el-Moḳaddem was mortally wounded at 'Arâfât, the very day that the pilgrims visit that hill. It occurred in consequence of a difference that arose between him and Tastikîn, the leader of the pilgrimage, on the subject of his right to beat cymbals and drums, which Tastikîn would not allow him to do. Ibn el-Moḳaddem was one of the chief emirs of Syria, and had distinguished himself by his honourable deeds, and the number of his campaigns; therefore God had decreed that he should be wounded at 'Arafa on the day of 'Arafa; that he should be carried, wounded as he was, to Mena; that he should die in that place on Thursday, the day of the great feast; that his funeral oration should be pronounced that same evening in the mosque of el-Khaif, and that he should be buried in el-M'ala.[2] He could have had no happier fate. This

---

[1] *Kaukab* (Belvoir), see p. 25.

[2] The allusions are to the rites of the Hâj, including the visit of pilgrims to Mount 'Arâfât, the Valley of Mena, etc., close to Mecca.

occurrence touched the Sultan deeply. On my return from the pilgrimage I took the road to Syria, intending to go to Jerusalem, and visit both (the shrine of) the Holy Prophet (the Sakhra), and (that of) the patriarch Abraham—peace be upon him!—(at Hebron). I left Damascus, and set out for Jerusalem. When the Sultan heard of my arrival, he thought I had come on an embassy from the government of Mosul. He summoned me to his presence, and received me with every mark of consideration. After I had taken leave of him, and was about to proceed to Jerusalem, I received a command through one of his officers to wait upon him again on my return from that city. I thought he wished to give me some important message for the Mosul government, and I arrived, on my return from Jerusalem, on the very day that he raised the siege of Kaukab. He saw that it would be necessary to employ a great number of troops to reduce this place, for it was very strong, most amply provisioned, and garrisoned by determined men whom, so far, the war had spared. He entered Damascus on the 6th of Rabi'a I. (May 5, 1188), the very day that I arrived there on my return from Jerusalem. He had been absent sixteen months from Damascus. On the fifth day after his arrival, he heard that the Franks had marched upon Jibeil with a view of surprising that place. As soon as he received this news, he lost not a moment, but left the city forthwith, and marched towards Jibeil, sending out in all directions to summon his troops. When the Franks heard he had taken the field, they gave up their attempt. At this time the Sultan received a message, saying that 'Imâd ed-Dîn (Zenghi, son of Maudûd, Prince of Mosul), and Mozaffer ed-Dîn (Kukbûri) had just arrived at Aleppo with troops from Mosul, to place themselves under his orders, and take part in the Holy War. He then marched towards the fortress of the Kurds,[1] on his way to the upper sea-coast (the maritime districts of Upper Syria).

CHAPTER XL.

HE ENTERS THE LANDS OF THE UPPER SEA-COAST, AND TAKES LAODICEA,[2] JEBELA, AND OTHER CITIES.

ON the first day of the month Rabi'a II. (May 30, 1188), he took up his position on a hill facing the fortress of the Kurds, and dispatched couriers to el-Melek ez-Zâher, and el-Melek el-Mozaffer, commanding them to join their forces, and take up a position at Tîzîn,[3] to cover the districts round Antioch. The troops from the eastern provinces mustered in the place where the Sultan was encamped, and put themselves under his command. It was here that I came upon him, just as I was setting out on my journey to Mosul. When I presented myself before him, he seemed very glad to see me again, and gave me the most gracious reception. During my stay in Damascus I had compiled a treatise on the Holy War, in which I had inserted all the laws and customs in any way connected with it. I presented this book to him, and he accepted it with pleasure, and made it a frequent study. I kept asking for permission to depart, but he always put me off, and meanwhile summoned me constantly to his presence. He even commended me in public, and spoke very favourably of me, as I have been told by people

---

[1] *Hosn el-Akrâd*, 'castle of the Kurds' (called by the Franks Crac), on the slope of Lebanon, half-way from Emesa to Tripoli, a castle of the Knights Hospitallers.

[2] Read : And takes Antartus.

[3] Tîzîn lies about 30 geographical miles N.E. of Antioch.

who were present. He remained encamped on the same
spot during the whole of the month Rabi'a II. (June),
and during the course of that month marched to the
fortress of the Kurds, and blockaded it for a day to
reconnoitre the ground. He thought he had not time
to besiege the place, and as the troops he had called out
had now mustered round his standard, he sent two expeditions into the districts round Tripoli. They were
ordered to pillage, and to ascertain the military strength
of the country, and he proposed to apply the spoils to
the maintenance of his army. Towards the close of this
same month he issued the following order : 'We are going
to enter the districts on the coast ; provisions are scarce
there, and as the enemy will meet us on their own ground,
they will surround us on every side. Therefore you will
have to provide yourselves with sufficient- food for one
month.' He then instructed 'Aisa the jurist to inform
me that he did not intend to allow me to return to Mosul.
Since God had filled my heart with a great affection for
the prince from the moment I first saw him, and because
I had observed his devotion to the Holy War, I consented
to remain. It was on the first day of the month Jomada I.,
in the year 584 (June 28, 1188 A.D.), that I entered his
service, and on the same day he marched into the coast-
lands.

All that I have narrated thus far is founded on what I
have been told by trustworthy persons, who were present
at the occurrences they described. Henceforth I shall write
nothing but what I myself have witnessed, or have gleaned
from people worthy of credit, whose words seemed to me
as deserving of belief as the testimony of my own eyes.
May God in His mercy assist us !

On Friday, the 4th of Jomada I., the Sultan drew up
his troops in order of battle, and marched against the

enemy. Each part of the army had a special position assigned to it : the right wing, under 'Imâd ed-Din Zenghi, led the van ; the centre followed ; then came the left wing, under Mozaffer ed-Din, son of Zein ed-Din. The baggage was placed in the centre, and advanced with the army. When we reached the appointed place, we halted, and passed the night in the enemy's country. On resuming his march, the Sultan next halted at El-'Orima ('the little sand-dune'), but made no hostile demonstration ; and on the 6th of the same month (July 3), he arrived before Antarsûs (Tortosa). He had not intended to stop here, Jebela[1] being the object of his march ; but as Antarsus appeared to be easy of capture, he resolved to attack it. He recalled the right wing, and ordered it to take up a position on the shore (on one side of the city), and the left wing he stationed on the shore on the other side. He himself took up a position between the two, so that the army completely surrounded the place by land, both flanks resting on the sea. The city of Antarsus was built close to the sea, and was protected by two strong towers almost like castles. The Sultan rode up close to the city and gave the order to begin the assault. The troops ran to arms (*literally*, donned the breastplate of war), and stormed the place so vigorously that the garrison were soon at their last gasp. Before they had finished pitching the tents the Moslems had scaled the walls and carried the place by storm. The conquerors seized everything in the city, both men and goods, and evacuated it, carrying off many captives and great riches. The servants, whose duty it was to pitch the tents, left their work and joined in the pillage. The Sultan had said : ' To-night, please God, we will sup in Antarsus ;' and his words came to pass. He returned

---

[1] *Jebela*, or Jebâl, N. of Tortosa.

to his tent rejoicing, and we presented ourselves before
him to congratulate him on his success. Then, according
to his custom, he crdered a meal to be served, of which
everyone partook; afterwards he laid siege to the two
towers. Mozaffer ed-Din, to whom he committed the
reduction of one of the forts, attacked it without ceasing
until he had laid it in ruins, and taken the garrison captive.
The Sultan ordered the walls to be razed, and assigned to
each of his emirs the task of throwing down a certain
portion of the earthworks. Whilst they were thus occupied,
the troops began to besiege the other tower, which was
very strong, as it was built in an inaccessible place, and its
walls were constructed of solid masonry ; it was garrisoned
by all the knights and footmen belonging to the city ; round
it ran a ditch full of water, and it was furnished with huge
arbalists[1] that wounded people at a great distance, whilst
the Moslems had no means of injuring (their opponents).
Therefore the Sultan saw that he would have to postpone
the attack, and turn his attention to more important
matters. He occupied himself with the destruction of the
city until it was utterly demolished. The church, held in
such great reverence by the Christians, and visited by
pilgrims even from distant lands, was razed to the ground.
The Sultan ordered the rest of the city to be set on fire,
and all its buildings were devoured by the flames. Whilst
they were engaged in this work, the conquerors shouted
strenuously, glorifying the one and only God. The Sultan
remained here to complete the destruction of the city until
the 14th day of the month, and then marched upon Jebela.
On the road he met his son el-Melek ez-Zâher, whom he
had summoned from Tîzîn, and who brought with him all
the troops that had been stationed in that district.

[1] See p. 57.

CHAPTER XLI.

CAPTURE OF JEBELA AND LAODICEA.

THE Sultan arrived before Jebela on the 18th of the month Jomada I., and he had scarcely drawn up his army before he obtained possession of the town. There happened to be Moslem residents there with a kâḍi to settle their disputes, and to him the government of the city had been entrusted. This official offered no resistance to the Sultan, but the castle held out. The Sultan made one onset against the place in order to furnish the garrison with a pretext for surrendering, and on the 19th of the month (July 16, 1188) the castle capitulated. He remained at Jebela until the 23rd, when he set out for Laodicea, and took up a position before that place on the following day. This is a beautiful city, very pleasing to the eye, as is well known ; it possesses a celebrated harbour, and two castles, lying side by side, on a hill overlooking the town. The Sultan at once invested both the city and the castles, but did not place his troops between the hill and the city. Then followed a sharp attack, our men assaulting the city furiously, whilst cries and shouts filled the air on every side. This continued until the end of the day, which was the 24th of the month, and the city was taken, though the castles still held out. The booty was enormous, for it was a commercial city, and full of treasure and merchandise. The fall of night parted the combatants. On Friday morning the attack on the castles was resumed, and a breach made on the north. They made this breach sixty cubits deep and four wide, as I have been told. Then they climbed the hill, and, getting close to the wall, began a brisk assault. The struggle

9

raged continuously, and either side threw stones at their opponents with their hands. When the garrisons saw the ferocity with which our men were attacking them, and how close they had approached, they offered to surrender. This was on Friday, the 25th of the month. The Sultan granted the request of the besieged, and allowed the kâdi of Jebela to go to them and draw up the treaty. He never refused to grant terms when an enemy wished to surrender. The besiegers then returned to their tents, worn out with fatigue. Very early the following day, Saturday, the kâdi was sent to the besieged, and helped them to arrange the conditions of their treaty. It provided that they should be permitted to go free with their families and their belongings, but they were to leave to the victors all their stores of corn, their military treasure, arms, horses, and instruments of war. Still they were allowed a sufficient number of beasts to carry them to a place of safety. As day drew to a close, the victorious banner of Islâm floated over the wall of the stronghold. We remained there until the 27th of the month.

CHAPTER XLII.

CAPTURE OF SAHYÛN.

WHEN the Sultan departed from Loadicea, he marched upon Ṣahyûn, on the 29th of Jomada I. surrounded the place with his army and set up six mangonels to play on the walls. Sahyûn[1] is a very inaccessible fortress, built on the steep slope of a mountain. It is protected by wide ravines of fearful depth ; but on one side its only defence

---

[1] *Sahyûn*, called Saone by the Franks, a strong castle on a hill S.E. of and in sight of Latakîa, a fortress of the Knights Hospitallers.

is an artificial trench about sixty cubits deep cut out of the rock. This fortress has three lines of ramparts, one round the precincts, another protecting the castle itself, and a third round the keep. On the summit of the keep rose a lofty turret, which I noticed had fallen to the ground when the Moslems drew near. Our soldiers hailed this as a good omen and felt certain of victory. The fortress was attacked very smartly from all sides at once, and el-Melek ez-Zâher, Lord of Aleppo, brought his mangonel into play. He had set it up opposite the stronghold, quite close to the wall, but on the other side of the ravine (*Wadi*). The stones hurled from this engine always reached their mark. The prince continued to play upon the place till he had made a breach in the wall large enough to enable the soldiers to climb the rampart. On Friday morning, the second day of the month Jomada II., the Sultan gave the command to assault, charging the men who had the management of the mangonels to shoot without ceasing. Then there arose mighty cries and a terrible noise, whilst our men shouted the tahlîl and the takbîr.[1] An hour afterwards the Moslems had scaled the wall and burst into the courtyard. I saw our men seize the pots and eat the food that had just been cooked, without leaving off fighting. The people in the courtyard fled into the keep, leaving everything behind them, and all they abandoned was promptly given up to pillage. The besiegers surrounded the walls of the keep, and the garrison, thinking they would be annihilated, asked for quarter. As soon as this was reported to the Sultan, he granted their prayer and allowed them to depart with their household goods, but demanded a ransom of ten pieces of gold from each man, and five pieces from each woman ; the

---

[1] The *tahlîl* is the expression *Lâ ilâha'il 'Allah âh*, 'there is no deity but God'; the *takbîr* the expression *Allâhu akbâr*, 'God is most great.'—W.

children were to pay two. Then he took possession of the fortress, and remained there whilst his troops took several others, such as El-'Aîd, Fîha, Blâtanîs[1] (Platanus), etc. These castles and little forts were surrendered to (the Sultan's) deputies.

CHAPTER XLIII.

CAPTURE OF BEKÂS.

HE then set forth upon his march, and on the 6th of Jomada II. we arrived at Bekâs, a strong fortress built on one bank of the Orontes, from the foot of which springs a little brook. The army encamped close to the river, and the Sultan with a small body of men went up nearer to the stronghold. It lies on a lofty hill commanding the Orontes. His army invested it on all sides, battering it with their mangonels ; and they pressed it so close, that on the 9th of the month, by the grace of God, they carried it by storm. All those of the garrison who had not been killed in the assault were led into captivity, and the contents of the place given up to pillage. Close to Bekâs there was a smaller subordinate fort, which was reached by means of a bridge. It is called Esh Shoghr.[2] It was very difficult of access, for there was no road up to it. The Sultan ordered

---

[1] The castle of *Blâtanîs*, or *Balâtunus* (*Mansio Platanus*), was close to the coast, near *Jebel el-Akra* (Mons Casius), and was regarded as impregnable. It was said to be connected with a small port by a tunnel, through which a man could ride. Platanus was 40 M.P. from Laodicea on the road to Daphne (*Beit el-Mâ*), near Antioch.—W.

[2] *Esh-Shoghr* and *Bekâs* were two castles on heights about a bow-shot apart, and separated by a fosse-like ravine. They were on the direct road from Latakîa to Aleppo, and not far from the bridge of Kashfahân across the Orontes. The ruins of the two castles, now called *K. el-Harûn* and *K. es-Sultân*, may still be seen at *Esh-Shughr*, a considerable Moslem village on the Orontes.—W.

his mangonels to play upon it from all sides, and as the garrison had no hope of succour they asked for terms. This was on the 13th of the same month. They obtained a respite of three days in order that they might obtain permission to surrender from the government of Antioch, and then they delivered the castle to the Sultan. His banner was unfurled on the keep on Friday, the 16th of the month. Ṣalâḥ-ed-Dîn then rejoined the baggage-train and despatched his son, el-Melek ez-Zâher, against the fortress of Sermâniya.[1] Ez-Zâher attacked the place very smartly and reduced it to such extremities that he succeeded in taking it on Friday, the 23rd of the same month. Since the capture of Jebela, of Sermâniya, and of other places in the coast lands took place, in each instance on a Friday, it was evident that God had heard the prayers of the Moslem preachers and looked with favour upon the Sultan's undertakings, because a good deed accomplished on that day received a double reward. This series of conquests, each effected on the Friday of successive weeks, is a thing so extraordinary that its parallel has never been recorded in history.

CHAPTER XLIV.

CAPTURE OF BURZIA.

THE Sultan, attended by an escort of light cavalry, then marched to Burzia,[2] a very strong and almost inaccessible

---

[1] *Sermâniya*, or *Sermîn*, is about a day's journey S. of Aleppo on the road to *Hama*. It was noted for its perfumed soap and cotton stuffs. The water supply is from rain collected in cisterns, many of which are very ancient.—W.

[2] *Burzia*, or *Burzûya*, lay to the N.W. of *Afâmia* (Apamea, now *Ḳal'at el-Mudîk*) and on the opposite side of the marshy valley of the Orontes. It was about a day's march S. of *esh-Shughr*, and was so strong that its impregnability passed into a proverb.—W.

fortress. It was built on the crags of a high mountain,
and was proverbial in all Frank and Moslem lands. Valleys
surrounded it on all sides, and their depth was more than
five hundred and seventy cubits. The Sultan's intention
to besiege this place was strengthened after he had seen
it; he ordered the baggage-train forward, and posted it,
with the rest of the army, at the foot of the mountain
on which the stronghold was built. This was on the
24th of the month. On the 25th, very early, he ascended
the mountain at a great pace, followed by his soldiers,
his mangonels, and instruments of war. Having surrounded
the castle, he attacked it from all sides, and played upon
the walls with the mangonels, both night and day, without ceasing. On the 27th of the month he divided his
troops into three sections, each of which was to fight in
turn for a certain time every day and then rest. In this
way he contrived that there should be no interruption
whatever in the attack. 'Imâd ed-Dîn, Prince of Sinjâr,
led the division first on duty; they fought with all their
strength until the time came for their relief, and the
people returned and whetted their teeth for battle. The
Sultan took command of the second division himself, and
riding out several paces called upon his men. They
rushed forward like one man with great shouts, and ran
up to the wall from all sides. In less than an hour they
had scaled it, and burst into the castle, which they carried
by storm. The garrison asked permission to surrender,
but they had already fallen into the hands of the victors.
*Their faith was of no avail to them when they saw our
violence* (Kurân xl. 85). All that the place contained
was given up to pillage, and the men who were taken
were led into captivity. A great number of people had
taken refuge there. Burzia was one of their most celebrated
fortresses. Our troops returned to their tents laden with

booty, and the Sultan rejoined the baggage-train, overcome with joy and delight.   The governor of the fortress,
a person of importance amongst the Franks, and seventeen
members of his family, were brought before the Sultan.
The Sultan took compassion upon them, and, having
granted them their freedom, sent them away to the Lord
of Antioch, to whom they were related.   He endeavoured
by this means to conciliate that prince.

CHAPTER XLV.

CAPTURE OF DERBESÁK.

SALÂH ED-DÎN next marched to the Iron Bridge,[1] where
he remained several days, and then set out for Derbesâk.[2]
It was on Friday, the 18th of the month of Rejeb (September 12, 1188), that he arrived before that fortress,
which lies close to Antioch.   He attacked it stoutly with
his mangonels, keeping up a very strict blockade.   He
undermined one of the towers with such success that it
gave way.   The besieged stationed men at the breach
to prevent an entrance, and their warriors stood in the
gap itself to hinder our men from gaining that position.
I saw them myself, and noticed that every time one of
them was killed another stepped forward and took his place.
They stood as motionless as the wall itself, with absolutely
no protection.   Seeing full well the extremity to which
they were reduced, they asked permission to capitulate,

---

[1] *Jisr el-Hadîd*, 'the iron bridge' over the Orontes E. of Antioch.

[2] *Derbesâk* was a village with springs and gardens and a lofty castle.
It lay on the W. side of the Valley of the *Kara Su* or *Nahr el-Aswad*,
and a little to the N. of the eastern entrance to the Beilân Pass over
the *Giaour Dâgh*.—W.

and obtained leave to retire to Antioch. One of the conditions of the treaty was that they should carry nothing with them when they left the fortress, excepting the clothes they wore. The Moslem standard was set up on the castle on the 22nd of Rejeb. On the following day the Sultan departed, having given the place (as a fief) to Suleimân Ibn Jender.

CHAPTER XLVI.

CAPTURE OF BAGHRÂS.

BAGHRÂS,[1] a strong castle lying nearer to Antioch than Derbesâk, was well provisioned and garrisoned by a large force. The army encamped in the neighbouring plain, and several detachments of light-armed soldiers were sent forward to invest the place. We were at the same time obliged to detach an advanced guard in the direction of Antioch to protect us against an attack, lest the people of that city should fall upon us unawares. This detachment was pushed so close to the gates of Antioch that nothing could leave the city without its knowledge. I had gone with them, and remained several days to see the city and visit the tomb of Habîb en Nejjâr, a holy man who lies buried there. Baghrâs was subjected to such a smart attack that the garrison surrendered, with the permission of the government of Antioch, and on the 2nd of Sh'abân (September 26) the Moslem banner floated from the turrets. The evening of the same day

---

[1] *Baghrâs* (ancient *Pagrae*) was a fortress of great importance, as it lay about half-way between Antioch and Alexandretta (*Skanderûn*), and commanded the entrance to the Beilân Pass. The ruins of the castle are still called *Kal'at Baghrâs.*—W.

the Sultan returned to camp, and there he received a message from the people of Antioch asking for peace. The Sultan, taking into consideration the fatigues and hardships that the army had undergone, and being worried by the reiterated demands of 'Imâd ed-Dîn, Lord of Sinjâr, who persisted in his desire to return home, concluded a treaty of peace with Antioch—in which the other cities occupied by the Franks were not included—on condition that the Moslems kept prisoner in that city were set at liberty. This peace was to last seven months, and at the end of that time the city was to be delivered into the Sultan's hands unless it had in the meantime received assistance from outside. The Sultan then departed for Damascus, and at the request of his son, el-Melek ez-Zâher, took Aleppo on his way, arriving there on the 11th of Sh'abân. He lodged in the castle for three days, and his son entertained him with the greatest magnificence. Every soldier received some present at the hands of the young prince, who was so liberal, that to spare his revenues the Sultan left for Damascus. His nephew, el-Melek el-Mozaffer Taki ed-Dîn, came out to meet him, and conducted him to the castle of Hamah, where a magnificent repast was set before him, and he listened to the Ṣûfis who were presented to him. The Sultan remained one night there, and gave the cities of Jebela and Laodicea to his host. Then he resumed his journey, taking the road that runs through B'albek, and halting for a day in the plain near that city. There he took a bath, after which he departed for Damascus, and reached that city a few days before the beginning of the month of Ramaḍân. He did not think it right (in this month set apart for fasting) to neglect the duty of fighting the infidels; he considered he was bound to do this whenever he could, and, above all, since there still remained several fortresses untaken near the Haurân, which threatened that district. Among these were Sâfed and Kaukab. Therefore, although he was observing the fast, he thought it necessary to turn his attention to those two places, and to get possession of them.

CHAPTER XLVII.

CAPTURE OF SÂFED.

ON one of the early days of the month of Ramadân (end of October), the Sultan set out from Damascus on his way to Sâfed.[1] He was not deterred by the thought that he was leaving his family, his children, and his home during a month when everyone, no matter where he may be, is anxious to return to the bosom of his family, and for that purpose will even undertake a long journey. It is true that the Sultan submitted to this privation in order to obtain a glorious reward,—Thy favour (oh, God !). Sâfed is a very inaccessible fortress, the ground all round being broken up by (deep) ravines. The army invested the place, and placed its mangonels in position. This was in the month of Ramadân ; rain was falling in torrents, and the ground became a swamp ; but this did not affect the Sultan's determination. As I was then on duty, I spent a night in his tent. He had just been marking out the positions on which five mangonels were to be erected, and he said : ' I shall not go to sleep until all have been set up.' He had allotted a certain number of workmen to each mangonel, and his messengers went backwards and forwards continuously to see what they were doing, and report their

[1] See p. 31.

progress to the Sultan. This went on until daybreak. By
that time the work was finished, and nothing remained
but to fix the khanzîrs[1] to the mangonels. I took this
opportunity of quoting to him the well-known tradition
recorded in genuine collections, saying that the promise of
this tradition would be fulfilled in his case. The text
runs: *The Holy Prophet said: There are two eyes that the
fire of hell will never touch: the eye that has kept watch in
the service of God, and the eye that has wept in fear of Him.*
The attack on Ṣâfed was maintained without interruption
until the place surrendered. The capitulation took place
on the 14th of Shawâl (December 6, 1188). During the
course of the month of Ramaḍân the Sultan obtained
possession of el-Kerak, the officers in command surrendering the fortress in order that their lord[2] might be set at
liberty. He had been taken captive at Haṭṭin.

CHAPTER XLVIII.

CAPTURE OF KAUKAB.

THE Sultan then marched towards Kaukab, encamped on
the mountain plateau, and surrounded the fortress with
light-armed troops. He pressed so close to the place that
the arrows and bolts of the besieged passed over the
spot he occupied. The wall built of stones and clay
afforded perfect protection to those behind it ; so that no
one could appear at the entrance of his tent without putting
on his armour. Rain fell without ceasing, and the mud
was so thick that it was almost impossible to get about
either on foot or on horseback. We suffered terribly from

---

[1] See note, p. 31.   [2] Humphrey IV. of Toron.

the violence of the wind and the ·heaviness of the rain, as
well as from the proximity of the enemy, who from their
position necessarily commanded our camp, killing and
wounding a great number of our men. The Sultan being
determined to accomplish the taking of the castle, so conducted his operations as to enable the miners to effect
a breach in the wall. The enemy—may their hopes be
ever confounded!—saw that they would be taken, and
asked for terms. The Sultan granted them the favour they
begged, and took possession of the place on the 15th of
Zu el-Ḳ'ada (January 5, 1189). The baggage, which had
been on the plateau, was transported, on account of the
mud and the wind, into the Ghôr.[1] During the remainder
of this month his brother, el-Melek el-'Âdel, had several
interviews with him on private matters. At the beginning
of the month of Zu el-Hijja (January 21, 1189) he dismissed the troops he had called together, and set out for
Jerusalem with his brother that he might bid el-Melek
farewell, and visit the Holy Places in that city. His
brother was to start from that place on his return to
Egypt. They arrived at Jerusalem on Friday, the 8th of
Zu el-Hijja, and were present at public prayer in the Dome
of the glorious Rock (Ḳubbet es Ṣakhrat esh Sherîfa). On
the day of the great feast,[2] which was a Sunday, they
worshipped there again. On the 11th of this month the
Sultan left for Ascalon, to look into the condition of that
city, and he spent several days there re-establishing
order in every department, and arranging everything on
a satisfactory basis. He then set out for Acre, taking
the road through the coast lands, with the view of
inspecting the cities he should pass through, and rein-
forcing them with men and supplies. He arrived at Acre,

---

[1] The Valley of the Jordan.

[2] The 'Îdu el-Azha, 'the Feast of Sacrifice,' is celebrated on the
tenth day of Zu el-Hijja.

and spent the greater part of the month of Moharrem of the year 585 (February-March, 1189) in that city. He left Behâ ed-Dîn Karakûsh[1] as governor there, charging him to repair the fortifications, and to give unremitting attention to that business. He left Hossâm ed-Dîn Bishâra with him. Then, having set out for Damascus, he entered that city on the 1st of Safer in the year 585 (March 21, 1189).

CHAPTER XLIX.

THE SULTAN MARCHES AGAINST SHAKÎF ARNÛN. THIS EXPEDITION IMMEDIATELY PRECEDED THE EVENTS AT ACRE.

THE Sultan remained in Damascus till the month Rabi'a I. (April 19, 1189), when he received a message from Khalif en-Nâsr li-Dîn Illah, who had appointed his son to succeed him, and therefore sent an injunction, commanding that his name should be inserted in the khotba. The Sultan carried out this order, and then determined to march against Shakîf Arnûn, a very strong fortress in the neighbourhood of Bâniâs. He left Damascus on the 3rd of the aforesaid month, and came to a halt in the meadow (merj) of Felûs (*or* Kalûs). On Saturday morning he set out from thence and marched to the meadow of Berghûth,[2] where he remained until the 11th of the month to await his troops. Detachments arrived one after another. He

---

[1] Behâ ed-Dîn Karakûsh, a eunuch, was a freedman of Shirkûh, on whose death he assisted 'Aisa (p. 173) to make Salâh ed-Dîn vizir. Salâh ed-Dîn made him his lieutenant in Egypt, and he built the citadel, and the walls enclosing old and new Cairo (Ibn Khallikan, ii. 520).—W.

[2] *Merj el-Felûs,* 'meadow of coin'; *Merj el-Berghûth,* 'meadow of the flea,' places on the S. of Mount Hermon.

then set out for Bâniâs, from which place he marched to
the Merj 'Ayûn; he arrived and pitched his camp there on
the 17th. This plain lies so close to Shakîf-Arnûn[1] that
the Sultan used to ride out with us every day to inspect it.
Meanwhile reinforcements and supplies arrived in the camp
from all sides. The Lord of Shakîf,[2] knowing that these
preparations certainly betokened his ruin, decided to come
to an arrangement with the Sultan which would relieve him
from danger. He came down from his fortress and presented himself at the entrance to the Sultan's tent before
we had heard of his arrival. The Sultan had him admitted
and received him with great respect and with every mark
of honour. This man held high rank amongst the Franks,
and was distinguished for his keen intellect. He knew
Arabic, and was able to speak it; he also possessed some
knowledge of history. I had heard that he had a Moslem
in his suite, whose duty it was to read to him and expound.
His manners were truly charming. He presented himself
before the Sultan, ate with him, and then, in a private
interview, declared that he was his servant (memlûk), and
that he would surrender the place to him without giving
him the trouble to fight. As a condition, he stipulated
that an asylum should be provided for him at Damascus,
for he could no longer dwell amongst the Franks, and that
a certain income should be granted him in the same city
as a provision for himself and his family. He added that
he would wish to be permitted to remain where he was,
and that in the course of three months, beginning from the
day on which he was speaking, he would present himself
in due course and wait upon the Sultan; he needed this

---

[1] *Shakîf Arnûn*, a strong Templar fortress built before 1179 (Belfort; see Burchard, p. 13) on the N. bank of the Leontes, 10½ miles
N.W. of Bâniâs. *Merj 'Ayûn* is the open valley to its E.
[2] Renaud of Sidon.

time to remove his family and dependents from Tyre. The Sultan consented to all his proposals, and from that time received frequent visits from him. He argued with us on the subject of our religion, and we reasoned with him in order to show him the vanity of his beliefs. He talked very well, and expressed himself with great moderation and courtesy.

In the month Rabi'a I. (April - May) we received tidings of the capture of esh - Shôbek. This place had been blockaded for a whole year by a strong body of troops sent thither by the Sultan, and the garrison capitulated when all their provisions were expended.

CHAPTER L.

THE FRANKS COLLECT THEIR TROOPS TO MARCH UPON ACRE.

THE Sultan had promised to set the king (of Jerusalem) at liberty on his ceding Ascalon to him, and as the king had caused his officers to surrender this place and demanded to be released, the Sultan suffered him to depart from Anṭarsûs,[1] where he had been kept prisoner. At that time we were encamped near the castle of the Kurds. Amongst the conditions he imposed upon the king, was that he should never again draw sword against him, and should always consider himself the servant (memlûk) and bondsman of his liberator. The king— God curse him!—broke his word, and collected a body of troops, with which he marched to Tyre. As he was unable to gain admittance into this city, he encamped

[1] Antaradus, Tortosa, the modern *Tartûs.*

outside the walls, and entered into negotiations with the marquis (of Montferrat),[1] who happened to be there at the time. The marquis—a man accurst of God—was an important personage, distinguished by his good judgment, the energy and decision of his character and his religious zeal. He replied to the king: 'I am only the lieutenant of the kings beyond the seas, and they have not authorized me to give the city up to you.' After prolonged negotiations an arrangement was made to form an alliance against the Moslems, and with the object of uniting the troops of Tyre with those of the other cities occupied by the Franks. The king's army was to remain outside the gate of Tyre.

CHAPTER LI.

THE SKIRMISH IN WHICH AIBEK EL-AKHRESH TESTIFIED (FOR THE FAITH).

ON Monday, the 17th of Jomada I. in the aforesaid year (July 3, 1189), the Sultan received news from the advanced guard that the Franks had just crossed the bridge which lies on the boundary between the territories of Tyre and Sidon.[2] It was in the territory of this latter place that we found them. The Sultan mounted his steed, and the jâwûsh[3] called (to arms). The cavalry mounted so as

---

[1] Conrad, of Montferrat, married Isabel, half-sister of Sibyl, wife of King Guy, who became heiress, in 1189, of the kingdom of Jerusalem, and Conrad was declared king in 1192, but assassinated at Tyre on April 28 of that year. The English chroniclers speak badly of him, as he opposed the policy of King Richard I. See pp. 303, 317.

[2] The bridge over the *Kasimiyeh* or Leontes river between Tyre and Sidon.

[3] This seems to be the Turkish *Chaúsh*, a term now used for a sergeant or non-commissioned officer.

SYRIA
IN THE MIDDLE AGES
after the
ARAB GEOGRAPHERS

.

to join the advanced guard, but when they got up, the affair was at an end. This is what had taken place. When a numerous body of the Franks had crossed the bridge, the Moslem advanced guard rushed upon them and assailed them vigorously, killing a great number, wounding twice as many, and driving others into the stream, where they were drowned. Thus did God come to the assistance of Islâm and the Moslems. None of the latter were killed, excepting one of the Sultan's memlûks called Aibek el-Akhresh, who had the good fortune to receive a martyr's death. He was very brave and daring, and an experienced soldier. His horse was killed under him, and he then set his back against a rock, and fought until his quiver was empty ; then he defended himself with his sword, and killed several of the enemy ; but he succumbed at last, overwhelmed by numbers. The Sultan was much grieved by the loss of so brave a servant. After this he set out once more with an escort of light cavalry, and repaired to the camp which had been pitched by his orders close to this place.

CHAPTER LII.

A SECOND SKIRMISH, IN WHICH A NUMBER OF MOSLEM FOOT SOLDIERS EARN MARTYRDOM.

THE Sultan remained in this camp, and on the 19th (of Jomada I.) he rode out to inspect the enemy's position according to his custom. A number of footmen, volunteers, and servants followed his escort, and, in spite of his express orders and the blows he commanded to be given them, they refused to return. He feared lest something should happen to them, because the place for which they were

making was very difficult to cross, and afforded no protection whatever for men on foot. These men rushed
towards the bridge and discharged arrows at the enemy,
whilst a number of them crossed over it. Then followed a
furious struggle, for a company of the Franks had surrounded
them before they perceived their position. The enemy,
feeling sure there was no ambuscade to be feared behind
this venturesome body, charged them like one man, without
the Sultan's knowledge. He was far from the scene of the
combat, and had no army with him, for he had not gone
out that day with troops in battle array; he had only
ridden forth to reconnoitre, as was his daily custom.
Seeing by a cloud of dust that a fight was going forward,
he sent the troops he had with him to bring back those
rash men. This detachment saw that the action had
become very serious, and that, as the Franks were now
superior in numbers, they had everything to apprehend.
The enemy gained a complete victory over these footmen,
and a fierce combat then took place between them and the
detachment. A number of foot soldiers were killed, and
others taken prisoner. The number of those who found
martyrdom on the field of battle was altogether one hundred
and eighty. The Franks on their side had many killed and
drowned. Amongst their dead was the leader of the
Germans, an important personage with them. In the
number of the Moslem martyrs, whose names could be
ascertained, was Ibn el-Bessâru, a fine young fellow of
great courage. His father, reckoning him for God's cause,
shed not a single tear. So I have been told by several
who were there. Of all the battles at which I was present, there was none in which the Franks obtained more
advantage. Never had they killed so many Moslems, nor
in so short a time.

CHAPTER LIII.

THE SULTAN MAKES ALL SPEED TO REACH ACRE. HIS MOTIVE.

THE Sultan, after this extraordinary blow had fallen upon the Moslems, called his emirs together, and consulted them on the subject. It was decided that they should cross the bridge and throw themselves upon the Franks, and should not cease the slaughter until they were all exterminated. The enemy had just left Tyre and taken up their position close to the bridge, which lies a little more than a parasang (to the north) of that city. The Sultan, having determined to attack them, mounted his horse on the morning of Thursday, the 17th of Jomada I.,[1] and set forth, followed by his troops, and also by volunteers, and all the camp followers. When the force in rear came up, it met the advanced guard in front returning with their tents. When these men were questioned as to why they had left their position, they replied that the Franks had withdrawn to Tyre, either to seek protection within the walls of that city, or to intrench themselves in the neighbouring plain. ' When we heard this,' said they, ' we turned back, for we knew that an advanced guard was no longer necessary there.' When the Sultan received this news, he determined to go to Acre to inspect those portions of the fortifications which he had ordered to be rebuilt, and to hasten the completion of that undertaking. On his arrival at Acre he re-established order, and commanded that the ramparts should be repaired in the most solid fashion. Then, having

---

[1] This date does not agree with the one last given. Our author probably intended to write the 27th.

10—2

charged the garrison to use the utmost vigilance, and keep
the strictest watch, he returned to the army, which had meanwhile remained encamped in the Merj 'Ayûn, and there he
awaited the expiration of the time he had granted to the
Lord of esh-Shakîf—that man accurst of God.

CHAPTER LIV.

ANOTHER SKIRMISH.

ON Saturday, the 6th of Jomada II. (July 22, 1189), the
Sultan received information that a detachment of foot-
soldiers from the enemy's army had become bolder, and
was going to the hill of Tibnîn to cut firewood. As the
disaster which the Moslem infantry had lately sustained
was still on his mind, he determined to lay an ambush into
which he hoped these Franks would fall. He knew that a
body of knights was coming out behind this detachment
to protect them, and he laid a snare to catch them both.
He commanded the garrison at Tibnîn to send out a
small body of troops to attack the footmen, and retire
to a place he pointed out as soon as they saw the
enemy's cavalry coming down upon them. This was
to take place on the morning of Monday, the 8th of
Jomada II. He also commanded the garrison at Acre
to pursue the enemy, and raid their camp, if they should
turn out to succour their comrades. Very early on Monday he rode out with his bodyguard, all lightly armed,
without either baggage or tents, and repaired to the spot
he had pointed out to the people of Tibnîn as that to
which they were to direct their flight. He continued his
march until he had passed Tibnîn, and then divided his

troops into eight sections, taking from each of these sections about twenty horsemen well mounted and of tried valour. He ordered this picked body to show themselves to the enemy so as to attract their attention, then to discharge a few arrows among them, and to flee precipitately towards his place of ambush. They did so, and they saw before them almost all the forces of the Franks. For they had received information of what was going forward, and had marched out, and were advancing in order of battle under their king. A terrible fight ensued between this army and the Moslem detachment, which, too proud to retreat before the Franks, was urged by a feeling of honour to disobey the Sultan's commands, and to close with the body of the enemy, in spite of their own small numbers. The fight raged till the close of the day ; it was Monday, and not one of the Moslems returned to the camp with tidings of what had occurred. The Sultan did not hear of the encounter until it was almost ended, and, as night was at hand, he sent out a few detachments, knowing that it was too late for a pitched battle, and that the opportunity for surprising the enemy had gone by. The Franks, when they saw the first reinforcements appear, were seized with terror, and retreated. Both sides had fought furiously. I learnt from one of those who was present (for I myself was not there) that the Franks had more than ten men killed, and the Moslems six, two of whom belonged to the advanced guard, and four to the Arab auxiliaries. One of the latter was the emir Zâmel, a fine young fellow of good character, and chief of his tribe. His horse being killed under him, his cousin gave him his, and this likewise was killed. He was made prisoner, with three of his kinsmen. When the Franks saw the Moslem reinforcements arrive, they killed their prisoners, lest they should be carried off. There were a great number of wounded on both sides, both men and horses. A very singular thing happened in this encounter: one of the Sultan's memlûks was riddled with wounds, and fell amongst the dead, where he remained all night, drenched in his own blood. On Tuesday morning his comrades noticed that he was missing, and, as they could not find him, they informed the Sultan. He gave orders for a fresh search to be made, and he was found lying among the heap of the slain in the state we have described. He was carried into the camp, and so well nursed that God restored him to health. On Wednesday, the 4th of the month, the Sultan returned to camp.

CHAPTER LV.

THE LORD OF SHAKÎF IS MADE PRISONER. CAUSE OF HIS ARREST.

AFTER this a report spread through the army that the Lord of esh-Shakîf had asked for a delay only to deceive us, and was not acting uprightly. Several things showed that he was only seeking to gain time, such was his eagerness to procure supplies for his castle and to strengthen the gates. The Sultan thought it necessary to take up a position on the mountain plateau that he might observe the place more closely, and prevent the introduction of any succours or provisions. He gave out as a pretext that he was anxious to escape the great heat which then prevailed, and the unhealthy air of the Merj. It was the 12th of that month, and at the beginning of the second quarter of the (preceding) night, he went up to the mountain, and scarcely had day dawned when the Lord of esh-Shakîf perceived the Moslem camp pitched quite close at hand.

A portion of the army remained in the Merj as before.
Seeing the troops so near him, and knowing that the
respite which had been granted him would expire towards
the end of Jomada II.—that is to say, within a few days—
he flattered himself that if he visited the Sultan he could
cajole him into allowing a prolongation of the time. He
imagined, from what he had seen of the Sultan's character
and of his courtesy, that this favour would be granted
him. He therefore went to pay his respects, and offered
to give up the place, adding that the fatal day would soon
arrive, and that it was a matter of indifference to him
whether the Sultan should be put in possession to-day or
to-morrow. He also pretended that several of the members of his family had not yet left Tyre, and that they
would do so in a few days. He spent the day in the
Sultan's presence and returned to the castle towards night-
fall. The Sultan did not let him see what he felt, but
received him just as before, for he was anxious to fulfil the
obligation which the respite imposed upon him. A few
days afterwards, when the term was just at an end, the
Christian came down once more from his castle, and, having
been granted a private interview with the Sultan, asked
him to prolong the respite for a further period of nine
months, in order to make it a complete year. The Sultan
knew by this that the man meant to deceive him, but,
fearing to provoke him by a refusal, he postponed giving
an answer until another day. 'We will reflect on the
matter,' he said ; 'we will take the advice of our council,
and let you know our decision.' He then ordered a tent to
be pitched for him by the side of his own, and, whilst he
continued to treat him with the greatest honour, he had this
tent watched quite unknown to its occupant. Discussions
on this subject and messages between the parties occupied
all the time until the expiration of the respite. The Sultan

then demanded the surrender of the place, saying to him openly : 'You always meant to deceive us ; you have repaired your fortress and introduced fresh supplies.' The other denied the fact, and then arranged with the Sultan that each of them should appoint a trustworthy person, and that the two agents should repair to the castle to receive its surrender and ascertain on the spot whether it had lately been repaired or not. When they presented themselves before the fortress, the garrison refused to comply with their demand, and the envoys remarked that the gate in the walls had lately been repaired. Orders were forthwith issued for a strict guard to be kept over the (chief deceiver), and he was now openly watched, and forbidden to enter the Sultan's presence. He was informed : 'The term of the respite is at an end ; you must absolutely deliver up the place.' Once more he tried to play upon their credulity, and could not be made to give a definite answer ; then he sent his confidential servant with a message to the people in the castle, charging them to surrender the place. But they declared most resolutely that they would not obey. ' We are the Master's servants,' they said, ' and not yours.'[1] A guard was then placed upon the castle to prevent anyone going in or coming forth. On the 18th of Jomada II. the Christian acknowledged that the respite had expired, and said that he would go himself to the castle and see that it was delivered up. He mounted his mule and set out with several of our officers. On his arrival at esh-Shaḳîf he commanded his people to surrender the place, but they refused to do so. A priest then came out and conversed with him in their language, after which he returned into the castle, and from that moment those who were within maintained a still stouter resistance. It was

---

[1] The defenders meant the Master of the Templars. The Knights were forbidden ever to retreat without superior orders.

thought that the chief had charged the priest to encourage them in their refusal. He spent the remainder of the day in sending messages to the people in the castle, and, as they paid no manner of heed, he was brought back to the camp. That same night he was sent to the castle of Bâniâs,[1] there to be kept a prisoner. The army surrounded esh-Shakîf, and effectually blockaded it. The lord of the castle remained at Bâniâs until the 6th of Rejeb. The Sultan was very wroth with this man, who had caused him and his whole army to waste three months, during which time they had done nothing at all. The prisoner was brought back to the camp, and on the night of his return terrible threats were used to make him yield, but without effect. On the following day, the 8th of Rejeb, the Sultan had his tents carried up to the plateau, and ordered them to be pitched on a spot from which he could command the castle better than from the position he had just left, and which was also still further raised above the exhalations of the plain, that were already beginning to affect his health. After these things had taken place, we were informed that the Franks of Tyre, together with those in the army of the king, were marching towards en-Newâkîr on their way to Acre. We also heard that a body of Franks had disembarked at Iskanderûna,[2] and established themselves there, after losing a few men in a skirmish with the Moslem infantry.

---

[1] The castle (*Kal'at es-Subeibeh*) on the hill E. of Bâniâs, taken by Nûr ed-Dîn from the Franks in 1164.

[2] *Iskanderûna* is 8 miles S. of Tyre, the older Alexandroschene, and Scandalion of the Franks. *En-Nawâkîr* (plural of *en-Nakûrah*, 'the cutting') is the Ladder of Tyre, 6 miles S. of the preceding, and 12 miles N. of Acre.

CHAPTER LVI.

THE WAR AT ACRE.

WHEN the Sultan heard that the Franks were marching upon Acre,[1] he felt the greatest anxiety; but he did not think it expedient to hasten his departure, for this manœuvre was in all probability only a feint to induce him to remove from esh-Shakîf. He therefore remained where he was, awaiting the course of events. On the evening of the 12th of Rejeb (August 26, 1189), a courier came in with the tidings that the Franks were on the march, and had just halted at 'Ain Bassa, whilst they had thrown their advanced guard forward as far as ez-Zîb.[2] This news appeared to him so serious that he wrote to all the neighbouring governors, commanding them to come with their troops to the place where his army was encamped. And he despatched other letters to them almost immediately, even more urgent than the first, and ordered that the baggage should start that very night. By the morning of the next day, the 13th of Rejeb, he was on his way to Acre, taking the road through Tiberias,[3] because there was no other in that district practicable for an army. He ordered a small detachment, however, to take the Tibnîn road, that they might watch the enemy's movements more closely, and send him information at regular

---

[1] This force was the army of King Guy, aided by the ships sent by King William of Sicily, the former marching from Tyre, the latter landing at Scandalion.

[2] *'Ain Bassa*, the spring S. of el-Bassah (Basse Poulaine of the Franks), 12 miles N. of Acre, 2 miles from the sea. *Ez-Zîb* (Achzib, or Ecdippa), 10 miles N. of Acre on the shore.

[3] Salâh ed-Dîn marched down the Jordan Valley from Belfort.

intervals. We marched as far as el-Ḥûla,[1] where we arrived at mid-day ; there we halted an hour, and set out again, marching all through the night. On the following morning, the 14th of the month, we reached a place called Minya.[2] There we heard that the Franks had taken up their position before Acre on Monday, the 13th (August 27). The Sultan sent the Lord of esh-Shaḳîf to Damascus, after upbraiding him most bitterly for his perfidy. He then set out for the plain of Ṣeffûria, attended by a small escort, to meet the detachment that had been sent round by way of Tibnîn with orders to await him there.[3] He had given instructions that the baggage also was to meet him at that place. He continued to push forward until, at el-Kharrûba,[4] he could overlook the enemy. He then sent a detachment forward to Acre, which succeeded in getting into the city without the knowledge of the enemy. He kept on sending detachments, one after another, until the city was filled with men and provisions of all kinds. Then he drew up his army in order of battle, by right wing, left wing, and centre, and set out for el-Kharrûba, which he reached on the 15th. He proceeded thence to Tell Kîsân,[5] which lies at the entrance to the plain of Acre, and here his troops encamped in their appointed order. The extreme left of the left flank rested on the bank of the Nahr el-Halu,[6] whilst the extreme right of the right flank was encamped close to the hill (*tell*) of el-'Aiâdîya.[7] The

---

[1] The *Hûleh* lake, or Waters of Merom.

[2] *Khân Minyeh,* on the N.W. shore of the Sea of Galilee, on the road to Tiberias.

[3] The road from *Tibnîn* (Toron) over the mountains to Seffûrieh led probably along the watershed to Sâfed, and thence S.W.

[4] *El-Kharrûba,* see p. 28.

[5] *Tell Kîsân* lies 5½ miles S.E. of Acre.

[6] *Nahr el-Halu,* 'sweet river,' is the Belus flowing to the sea S. of Acre.

[7] *El-'Aiyadîyeh* is 5 miles E. of Acre, N. of the Belus.

Moslem army surrounded the enemy, and occupied all the
roads that led to their camp.   Their numbers were increased by the continual arrival of fresh reinforcements.
An advanced guard was always stationed close up to the
enemy, and the marksmen harassed them by maintaining
a constant discharge.   The Franks were blockaded in the
camp on every side, so that no one could come forth without being killed or wounded.   They were encamped on
one side of Acre, and the king's tent was pitched on Tell
el-Mosallîyîn[1] ('the hill of those who pray '), a hill which
rises close to the gate of the city.   They had two thousand
horsemen, and thirty thousand footmen.[2]   I have never
met anyone who estimated their numbers at less than this,
whilst many, on the other hand, held they were still
stronger, and they constantly received reinforcements by
sea.   Skirmishes occurred very frequently between their
army and our advanced guard, and were obstinately dis-
puted.   The Moslems were most anxious to push on and
attack the enemy, but the Sultan kept them in hand.
Contingents from the different Moslem provinces kept on
arriving, as well as princes and emirs from the different
districts.   The first to appear was Mozaffer ed-Dîn, the
great emir, son of Zein ed-Dîn, and after him came el-
Melek el-Mozaffer, Lord of Hamah.   This was the position
of affairs when Hossâm ed-Dîn Sonkor el-Akhlâti died of
a flux.   His loss was a source of great grief to the Moslems,
for he was distinguished both for his bravery and his piety.
The numbers of the Franks kept on increasing, until at

[1] *Tell el-Mosalliyîn*, now called *Tell el-Fokhkhâr*, a large sandy
hillock a mile E. of Acre.

[2] Jeoffrey de Vinsauf (l. xxv.) makes King Guy's army number
9,000 men, with 50 Pisan galleys.   The Danes and Frisons who joined
him numbered 12,000.   An English and Flemish fleet arriving in
October, 1190, increased this force before the arrival of the French
and English armies.

last they were sufficiently strong to blockade the city,
and prevent anyone from going in or coming out. The
investment of Acre was completed on Thursday, the last
day of the month of Rejeb. The Sultan recognised the
gravity of the situation, and grew anxious; he endeavoured
to devise a means of breaking a way through them, in
order to introduce supplies and reinforcements into the
besieged city. He summoned his emirs and councillors of
State to consider his plan, which was to close up round
the enemy and hem them in. It was resolved at the
council to attack the Franks with all our strength and to
overwhelm them, in order to effect a passage. On the
morning of Friday, the 1st of the month of Sh'abân, 585
(September 14, 1189), he began to move his army, which
marched in order of battle, by right wing, left wing, and
centre, and when they came to close quarters with the
enemy, they rushed on them furiously. The attack was
commenced after the hour of Friday's prayer, in order that
we might benefit by the supplications of the preachers
from their pulpits. Several terrible charges were made,
and the battle raged, with many vicissitudes of fortune,
until night closed in and separated the combatants. Both
sides spent the night under arms, as each army expected
to be attacked by the other.

CHAPTER LVII.

THE MOSLEMS BREAK THROUGH TO ACRE.

DURING the morning of Saturday the troops were held in
readiness to fight, and the Sultan sent a detachment of
picked men towards the shore on the north side of the
city. The enemy's camp did not extend as far as that,

but the unoccupied space was held by platoons of light cavalry. Our soldiers charged and routed them, and killed a great number. Those who escaped death fled to their camp, and the Moslems pursued them right up to the entrance. Thus a passage was opened to the city, and its walls were freed from the enemy from the tower gate called Ḳal'at el-Melek[1] as far as the gate rebuilt by Ḳara-kûsh, which bears his name. Now that the road was thrown open, provision merchants went in with their wares, and a single man or woman could pass in safety ; for the Moslem advanced guard was posted between the road and the enemy's camp, completely blockading the latter. This same day the Sultan went into Acre and walked on the wall, from whence he could see the enemy's camp pitched at the foot of the ramparts. The Moslems gave them-selves up to rejoicing, seeing that God had come to their aid. The garrison, led by the Sultan, made a sortie, and the Franks were thus surrounded by the Moslems on every side. This manœuvre was executed after the noon-day prayer. Then the Moslems ceased fighting, that they might water their horses and take a little rest ; permission to desist had been granted them on condition that they should return to the fight directly they had refreshed themselves a little. However, as there was but a short time before them, and they were worn out with fatigue, they did not return to their posts that day, and lay down thinking that on the morrow, Sunday, they would attack the enemy in such a way as would bring on a general action. The Franks, on their side, remained in the shelter

---

[1] *Ḳal'at el-Melek*, 'King's Castle.' On Marino Sanuto's map of Acre the 'King's New Tower' is immediately west of the 'Cursed Tower,' which was at the N.E. angle of the old walls. Mount Musard, the N. quarter of Acre in the thirteenth century, did not exist in Salâh ed-Dîn's time.

of their camp, and not a single man was to be seen. On Sunday morning, the 3rd of Sh'abân (September 16, 1189), the army prepared for the fight, and, surrounding the enemy, resolved to storm their camp. The emirs and the greater part of the men were ordered to dismount, so that they might fight the Franks at their very tents. All the arrangements had been made, when some of the emirs advised that the attack should be postponed until the morning of Monday, the 4th of Sh'abân, and that the foot soldiers should be thrown into Acre so as to make a sortie from the city with the garrison ; then they were to attack the enemy in the rear, whilst the Moslems outside were to mount and rush from all sides with one accord against the camp. The Sultan led the army in person, and took an active part in the battle ; wherever the fight was keenest he was to the fore. Indeed, his eagerness and anxiety throughout was like that of a mother robbed of her infant. I have been told by one of his body-physicians, that from the Friday to the Sunday he ate hardly anything, his mind was so preoccupied. The plan of attack was carried out, but the enemy maintained a stout resistance in their camp. The battle raged until Friday the 8th of Sh'abân ; it was a market in which everyone sold his life to gain a great profit (Paradise) ; it was a sky raining down a shower, every drop of which was the head of a chief or a leader.

CHAPTER LVIII.

THE ARMY WITHDRAWS TO TELL EL-'AIÂDÎYA.

On the 8th of Sh'abân (September 21, 1189) the enemy left their camp in a body—infantry and cavalry—formed in

line on the top of the hill, and began to march quite
quietly, and without the least hurry. They advanced
within the outer ring formed by their foot soldiers, which
surrounded them like a wall, and came on until they
reached the tents of our advanced guard. When the
Moslems perceived the enemy advancing upon them, their
warriors called out to one another, the heavy cavalry prepared to charge, and the Sultan cried to the Moslem
soldiers : *On for Islâm !* The horse soldiers sprang to their
saddles, the foot soldiers were as eager as the cavalry, the
young warrior as resolute as the veteran ; they hurled
themselves like one man on the enemy, and drove them
backwards. The infidels rallied, and a close sword fight
ensued ; those who escaped with their lives were wounded ;
those who were killed were left where they fell ; the
wounded stumbled over the dead, and each man
thought only for himself. Those of the enemy who
escaped from the massacre fled to their camp, and
would not fight for several days. Indeed, they sought
only to avoid death, and to keep themselves out of danger.
Now that the road to Acre was clear, the Moslems went
to and fro, and I also went into the city. I climbed to the
top of the wall, as everyone did, and from thence I hurled
at the enemy the object nearest to my hand. Fighting
was kept up night and day between the two sides until the
11th of Sh'abân (September 24). Then, with a view of
extending the circle in which the Franks were enclosed,
and thus enticing them out of their camp to a place where
they might all be massacred, the Sultan ordered the
baggage to be removed to Tell el-'Aiâdîya, a hill opposite
to Tell el-Moṣalliyîn, from which watch could be kept both
over Acre and over the enemy's camp. It was at el-'Aiâdîya
that Ḥossâm ed-Dîn, one of our chief warriors, died. He
was buried at the foot of the hill. I delivered the funeral

prayer over his body, together with several other doctors of law. This ceremony took place during the night preceding the 15th of Sh'abân.

CHAPTER LIX.

BATTLE BETWEEN THE ARABS AND THE ENEMY.

WE received information that a party had left the enemy's camp to forage on the banks of the river. The Sultan posted a detachment of Arabs in ambush to surprise them. He chose Arabs because they are so swift of movement on horseback, and because he trusted them. The detachment of Franks had left the camp, and were not expecting any attack, when the Arabs fell upon them, killing a great number and taking many prisoners. When the soldiers brought the heads to the Sultan, he gave them robes of honour and rewarded them liberally. This was on the 16th of the month. In the evening of the same day a furious fight took place between the enemy and the garrison, and a great number were killed on both sides. Hostilities were kept up for a long time, and not a day passed but some were killed, wounded and made captive. The soldiers of both sides grew so accustomed to meeting that sometimes a Moslem and a Frank would leave off fighting in order to have a conversation ; sometimes the two parties would mingle together, singing and dancing, so intimate had they become, and afterwards they would begin fighting again. One day, wearying of this constant warfare, the soldiers of both sides said to one another : ' How long are the men to fight without allowing the boys their share in the pleasure ? Let us arrange a fight between two parties of young fellows, the one from your side, the

other from ours.' Boys were fetched from the city to
contend with the Frankish youths. The two bands fought
furiously, and one of the young Moslems seized a young
infidel, raised him in the air, and threw him to the ground,
making him prisoner. A Frank ransomed the prisoner for
two gold pieces. 'He is your prisoner,' he said to the
victor; therefore he took the two gold pieces as his ransom.
This is a strange occurrence such as very seldom happens.
A ship arrived laden with horses for the Franks; one of
these animals leapt into the sea and swam to the harbour
of the city, despite their efforts to alter his direction, and
he fell into the hands of the Moslems.

CHAPTER LX.

THE GREAT BATTLE OF ACRE.

ON Wednesday, the 21st of the month (October 4, 1189),
an unusual degree of movement was observed to be taking
place in the Frank army; cavalry and infantry, veterans
and recruits, were drawn up in line outside the camp,
formed in a centre with right and left flanks. Their king
was in the centre, and in front of him were borne the
Gospels, protected under a canopy of satin, held up at the
four corners by four men. The right wing of the Franks
extended the whole length of the Moslem left; while their
left, in like manner, was drawn up exactly opposite our
right. They occupied the ridge of the hills, their right
resting on the river, their left on the sea. The Sultan
ordered his heralds to proclaim through the ranks of the
Moslems : ' *O Islâm and the army of the servants of the One
God !*' The soldiers sprang to their saddles, determined to
purchase paradise with their lives, and they remained

motionless in front of their tents. Their right wing stretched to the sea, and their left rested on the river, just as with the Frank army.[1] The Sultan had made his troops encamp in order of battle, the right wing, the left, and the centre drawn up separately, so that in case of an alarm no manœuvring would be necessary to form up in their appointed places. He himself took up his position in the centre ; his son, el-Melek el-Afdal, was in the right centre ; and next to him his son, el-Melek ez-Zâfer, brother of el-Afdal ; then came the Mosul troops under Zâher ed-Dîn Ibn el-Bolenkeri ; then the troops from Diarbekr, commanded by Kotb ed-Dîn, son of Nûr ed-Dîn and Lord of Hisn (Keifa) ; next came Hossâm ed-Dîn Ibn Lajîn, Lord of Nâblus ; then Kâimâz en-Nejmi, the Tawâshi (*eunuch*), who was stationed at the extreme end of the right flank with a great number of men. The other end of the right wing, which rested on the sea, included the army of el-Melek el-Mozaffer Taki ed-Dîn and his own personal troops. On the left wing, in the part nearest the centre, Seif ed-Dîn 'Ali el-Meshtûb came first, a great prince and chieftain of the Kurdish people ; then Emir Mojelli, with the Mehrân and Hekkar (Kurdish tribes) contingents ; next Mojâhed ed-Dîn Berenkash at the head of the troops from Sinjâr and a party of memlûks ; then Mozaffer ed-Dîn, son of Zein ed-Dîn, with his personal troops and the army under his command. On the extreme left of the left wing were the chief officers of Asad's body of memlûks (formed by Asad ed-Dîn Shîrkuh)—to wit, Seif ed-Dîn Yazkoj, Arslân Bogha, and many another of Asad's old warriors, whose bravery has passed into a proverb ; Doctor

---

[1] The Franks had built earthworks, cutting off Acre from the land side, but Salâh ed-Dîn's line of battle is remarkable. As at Hattîn, he again was almost facing his line of retreat to el-Kharrûba. The defeat of his left imperilled his right, thrown far W. to the N. of Acre.

'Aisa and his personal followers were in the centre, which
was under that chief's command. The Sultan went through
the ranks in person, spurring his men to the fight, encouraging them to go down to the field of battle, and urging
them to believe that the religion favoured by God would
gain the victory. The enemy continued to advance and
the Moslems kept moving to meet them until the fourth
hour after sunrise. Then the left wing of the Franks
rushed on against our right, and el-Melek el-Mozaffer sent
his vanguard to meet them. Thereupon followed a fight
with varying fortune, until el-Melek, who occupied the
extreme right of the right wing on the sea-shore, seeing
the great number of his opponents, made a backward
movement ; he hoped by this means to entice them far
enough from their main army to enable him to give them
a decisive defeat. The Sultan, seeing this movement,
thought the prince was unable to maintain his position,
and sent several battalions from the centre to his support.
The enemy's left wing then drew back and came to a stand
on the top of a hill overlooking the sea. When the enemy
perceived that those battalions had been withdrawn from
the centre, they took advantage of the consequent weakness of that part of our line and charged the right flank of
the centre, both infantry and cavalry rushing on together
like one man. I myself saw the infantry advancing, keeping
pace with the knights, who did not outstrip them, and for a
while were even left behind. The stress of this charge fell
on the Diarbekr troops, who were unprepared to withstand
an attack ; therefore they gave way before the enemy and
fled in confusion. The panic spread until the greater part
of the right wing retreated in disorder. The Franks
pursued the fugitives right up to el-'Aiâdîya,[1] and surrounded that hill, whilst one body of their soldiers climbed

---

[1] The Franks thus cut off Salâh ed-Dîn's right.

up to the Sultan's tent and killed one of his water-carriers there. During the day Ism'aîl el-Mokabbis, and Ibn Rewâha also, won a martyr's death. The left wing maintained its position, for the enemy's charge did not affect it. During all this time the Sultan was going from battalion to battalion encouraging the men, promising them magnificent rewards, and urging them to continue the fight for God. ' On !' he cried, ' for Islâm !' He had only five of his suite left, but he continued to go from battalion to battalion, from rank to rank ; then he withdrew to the foot of the hill on which his tents were pitched. The fugitives continued their flight as far as el-Fakhwâna,[1] crossing the bridge at Tiberias, and some of them went as far as Damascus. The enemy's cavalry pursued them as far as el-'Aiâḍiya ; then, seeing that they had reached the top of the hill, they left them there and returned to their army. On their way they fell in with a band of servants, mule-drivers, and grooms, who had taken to flight on the baggage-mules, and they killed several of these men ; when they reached the entrance to the market-place, they made a further slaughter, but suffered considerable loss themselves, for there were a great number of men there and all well armed. The Franks who had gone up to the Sultan's tents found absolutely nothing there, but they killed the three mentioned above. Then, seeing that the left wing of the Moslem army maintained its position, they saw we were not completely discomfited, and they came down from the hill to rejoin their main army. The Sultan remained at the foot of the hill, attended by only a few men, and tried to rally

---

[1] The bridge S. of the Sea of Galilee (*Jisr es Sidd*) is intended. *Fakhwâna* appears to be for *Kahwâna* (by the dots of the Arabic being too far apart over the first two letters), namely, the region immediately E. of the bridge. This agrees with the flight to *Fîk* (Aphek) on the E. side of the Sea of Galilee.

his soldiers and hurl them once more against the enemy. The men whom he had succeeded in collecting were eager to attack the Franks who were coming down from the hill; but the Sultan commanded them to remain where they were until the enemy had turned their backs upon them on their way to rejoin their main body. Then he shouted his war-cry, and his men rushed on the band, laying several of them low. The rest of the Moslem soldiers, seeing that these men would be an easy prey, rushed up in great numbers and pursued them until they had regained the main body. When the latter saw their fellow-soldiers in flight before a great force of Moslems, they imagined that the whole division which had charged had been cut to pieces, and that none but these fugitives had been able to escape. Thinking that they too would be destroyed, they fled on all sides, and our left wing pressed down on them; el-Melek el-Mozaffer came up at the same moment with the troops that had formed the right wing. Our men assumed the offensive once more, coming up from all sides and cheering one another on. God rebuked Satan, and caused the true faith to triumph. Our warriors did not cease killing and cutting down, striking and wounding until those fugitives who escaped had reached their main body. The Moslems attacked the camp, but were driven back by several battalions which had been stationed there for that purpose by the enemy, and who now came out to meet them. The soldiers were worn out with fatigue and bathed in sweat. The hour of the 'Asr prayer[1] had just sounded when our men drew off and returned to their tents, uttering shouts of joy as they marched over the plain, covered with dead and drenched with blood. The Sultan returned to

ı 1 See p. 21.

his tent and received his officers, who came to report the names of their missing comrades. One hundred and fifty unknown youths were stated to have fallen; among the well-known warriors who earned a martyr's death was Zâher ed-Dîn, brother of Doctor 'Aisa. I watched the doctor whilst he was receiving the condolences of his friends; he heard them with a smile, saying he did not need them. 'To-day,' said he, 'is a day of rejoicing and not of mourning.' Zâher ed-Dîn had fallen from his horse; those who were near him had placed him in his saddle again, and several of his relations lost their lives in defending him. Emir Mojelli also met his death that day. These were the Moslems who were killed; the confounded enemy's loss, on the other hand, was estimated at seven thousand men; but I saw them carrying the bodies down to throw them into the river, and I do not think the number could have been so great. At the time the Moslems were fleeing in confusion the servants, who had been left in the camp, seeing the tents were abandoned and that there was no one to hinder them, began to rifle and pillage. It was left, indeed, quite unprotected, one division of the army having fled, and the other being fully occupied in fighting. Therefore the servants, thinking the army had been utterly defeated and that the enemy would seize whatever was in the camp, laid hands on all they could find, and carried off great stores of money, clothes and arms. This was a much greater disaster than defeat. As soon as the Sultan returned to camp and saw the consequences of the panic and the pillage, he took prompt measures to remedy this misfortune. He first of all wrote letters and sent men out to bring back the fugitives and to pursue the deserters. These messengers overtook them at the ascent of Fîk[1] and stopped their flight by shouting, ' Back to the

---

[1] *Fîk* (Aphek), see note, p. 165.

charge! To the rescue of the Moslems!' and they succeeded by this means in bringing them back to the camp.
The Sultan ordered all that they had stolen to be taken
away from the camp-servants and deposited in front of
his tent; everything was placed there, even down to the
coverlets and saddle-bags. He then seated himself, whilst
we formed a circle round him, and invited those who
could recognise their property to swear to it, and to take
their goods away. All this while he displayed the greatest
resolution and good humour, with unruffled serenity and a
discrimination that was never at fault; his trust in God
never faltered, nor did he waver in his determination to
uphold God's religion. The enemy, for their part, returned
to camp, having lost their bravest men and leaving their
most valiant chiefs on the field. The Sultan sent a number
of carts from Acre to take up the bodies of the Franks
who had fallen, and cast them into the river. I have
been informed by one of the men who superintended this
operation that the number of dead belonging to the enemy's
left wing amounted to four thousand one hundred odd; but
he had been unable to reckon the number of dead on the
right wing and in the centre, because another man had
been entrusted with the task of carrying these bodies to
the river. The remnant of the enemy shut themselves up
in their camp and confined themselves to the defensive,
paying no heed to the Moslem troops. Numbers had
taken to flight in the panic; only those who were known
by name returned to the camp, because they dreaded
punishment; but the others fled straight on. I was
present when the Sultan had all that was stolen collected
and returned to the rightful owners; this was on Friday,
the 23rd of Sh'abân; the gathering was like a close-
thronged market, where justice was the only merchandize; never had so great a multitude been collected

together. When the tumult following on the battle had
subsided, the Sultan ordered the baggage-train back as far
as el-Kharrûba, fearing that the effluvia from the heaps of
dead might injure the health of the troops. This place lay
near to the field of battle, but further off than the ground
they had been occupying. The Sultan's tent was pitched
close to the baggage, and he commanded the advanced
guard to occupy the ground where the camp had stood
the day before. This was on the 29th of the month.
On the following day the Sultan summoned his emirs
and councillors, I being of the number; he commanded
their attention, and spoke as follows: ' In the name of
God! Praise be to God! May the blessing of God rest
upon His messenger! The enemies of God and of our
race invaded our land and trampled the soil of Islâm
under their feet; but already we see a foreshadowing of
the triumph with which we shall overcome them, if it be
God's will. There remain but a small number of our
enemies; now is the time to utterly exterminate them. I
take God to witness that that is now our duty. You know
that the only reinforcements we can expect are those that
el-Melek el-'Âdel is now bringing us. There is the enemy;
if we leave them in peace, and they remain there till the
sea is open for ships, they will receive large reinforcements.
The opinion I hold, and which seems to me decidedly the
best, is that we should attack them forthwith, but let each
of you say what he thinks.' This speech was delivered
on the 13th Teshrin of the solar year (October 13). The
council was divided in opinion, and an animated discussion
ensued; it was finally determined to withdraw the army as
far as el-Kharrûba. ' The troops will remain there,' they
said, ' for several days, to give the men time to recover,
for they are worn out by the weight of their arms. This
will enable them to recover their strength and to give their

horses rest. They have been fifty days under arms and in
the saddle; the horses, too, have had their share of fighting
and are tired out. After they have had a little rest their
spirits will revive; el-Melek en-Nâṣr will come to our help
both with advice and by action; we shall be able to fetch
back the deserters and collect the foot-soldiers again, to
lead against the enemy's infantry.' The Sultan at this
time was suffering from a serious indisposition, brought on
by the anxiety which oppressed him, and also by the weight
of his armour, which he had now worn for a long time;
therefore he was persuaded, in the end, to adopt this
counsel. On the 3rd of Ramaḍân the rest of the troops
joined the baggage. The Sultan followed them the same
night, and remained there, nursing himself and collecting
his troops, whilst he awaited the coming of his brother,
el-Melek el-'Âdel, who arrived on the 10th of the month.

CHAPTER LXI.

WE RECEIVE TIDINGS CONCERNING THE KING OF THE GERMANS.

AT the beginning of the month of Ramaḍân, 585 (October,
1189 A.D.), the Sultan received letters from Aleppo, from
his son el-Melek ez-Zâher—may God increase his glory!
In these he announced, as an unquestionable fact, that the
king of the Germans[1] was marching on Constantinople at
the head of an immense army, with a view of invading the
territories of the Moslems. This news made the Sultan
exceedingly anxious, and he thought it his duty to summon

[1] The Emperor Frederic Barbarossa had been drowned in June
1189, in the Geuk Su on his march to Seleucia from Laranda.

everyone to the Holy War, and to inform the Khalif of what was going forward. He entrusted this mission to me, and commanded me to repair to the Lords of Sinjâr, of Jezîrat Ibn 'Omar, of Mosul, and of Arbela, calling upon each of them to come in person at the head of his troops to give battle to the infidel. He also charged me to repair to Baghdad, and carry this news to the Khalif, in order to induce him to come to our assistance. The throne of the Khalifate was then occupied by en-Nâsr li-Din Illah Abu el-'Abbâs Ahmed, son of el-Mostadi bi-Amr Illah. I set out upon this embassy on the 11th of the month of Ramadân, and by God's grace was permitted to see them all, to deliver the message with which I had been entrusted, and to receive from their own lips their assurance of effectual help. The first to march was 'Imâd ed-Dîn Zenghi, Lord of Sinjâr, who started with his troops before the end of the year. His cousin Sinjâr Shah, Lord of Jezîrat Ibn 'Omar, marched in person at the head of his army. The Lord of Mosul sent his son, 'Âlà ed-Din Khorrem Shah, and the Lord of Arbela also set out on the march with his troops. On my arrival at Baghdad, I presented myself at the Khalif's divan, and informed him of the object of my visit, in accordance with my instructions, and he made me most liberal promises. On Thursday, the 5th of Rabi'a I., in the year 586 (April 12, 1190), I returned to the Sultan's service, arriving before any of the troops that were on the march, and informed him of the satisfactory replies that the princes had given, and of their preparations to join him. This news afforded him the greatest satisfaction.

CHAPTER LXII.

SKIRMISH ON THE SANDS BY THE RIVER-BANK AT ACRE.

In the month of Ṣafer (March—April) this year the Sultan left the camp on a hunting expedition, his mind being perfectly easy, for the troops were encamped at some distance from the enemy. He went further than he had intended in the eagerness of the chase, and the Franks, informed that the Moslems were not keeping a strict watch, thought that this would be a good opportunity to surprise them. They collected their forces, and came out; but el Melek el-'Âdel perceived their intention, and called to arms. Our men sprang into the saddle, and rushed on the enemy from all sides, engaging them in a hand-to-hand fight, so that many lives were lost. Some few also were wounded, but the Moslems lost no one of consequence except Arghish, one of the Sultan's memlûks. This officer, distinguished for his piety and valour, had the good fortune to earn a martyr's death. When the Sultan heard what was happening, he left the chase, and returned to his army; but he found that it was all finished, both sides having returned to their respective camps. The enemy withdrew, after an unsuccessful attempt, with considerable loss. Praise be to God! He is the author of all mercy. I was not present at this skirmish, being at that time on my travels. The battles I have previously described I saw as closely as a man of my profession could see them; with regard to the others, I have had them described to me in so much detail that it is as if I had witnessed their various developments. A curious thing happened in this last skirmish: a certain man named Ḳara Sonḳor, one of the Sultan's memlûks, and a brave soldier, had killed several of the enemy, and the comrades of the dead men set a snare for him. Some of them hid, whilst others went out and showed themselves. The memlûk rushed on in pursuit of them, but they threw themselves on him from all sides, and made him prisoner. One of these men seized him by the hair, and another prepared to cut off his head with his sabre. The blow struck the arm of the man who was holding the memlûk, and severed his hand from the wrist ; the captive escaped, and succeeded in rejoining his comrades in safety. The Franks ran after him, but could not overtake him. '*God drove back the misbelievers in their rage ; they gat no advantage*' (Kurân, xxxiii. 25).

CHAPTER LXIII.

DEATH OF DOCTOR 'AISA.[1]

I HEARD of this occurrence by public report, because I was not on the spot at the time. He used to suffer from periodic attacks of asthma, and then he was seized with a flux, which weakened him very much, and to which he finally succumbed. Throughout his illness he retained his power of will and intellect. He was a generous, brave man, and lived a virtuous life. His zeal for the Moslem cause was unflagging. He passed away on Tuesday, the 9th of Zu el-K'ada, 585 (December 20, 1189), just as day was dawning.

[1] Abû Muhammad 'Aisa el-Hakkâri, surnamed Diâ ed-Din, was a Kurd who had studied law at Aleppo. He was a lawyer (*fakih*), and was Imâm to Shîrkûh, with whom he went to Egypt. With the assistance of Beha ed-Dîn Karakûsh, he conducted the intrigue which raised Salâh ed-Dîn to the post of vizir on Shîrkûh's death. Salâh ed-Dîn was grateful, and placed implicit confidence in him as a counsellor (Ibn Khallikan, ii. 430).—W.

CHAPTER LXIV.

ON Sunday, the 15th of the month Rabi'a I. (April 22, 1196), the Franks, who composed the garrison of esh-Shakîf, saw that nothing could save them from the fate God had appointed, and that their heads would be cut off if the place were carried by storm. They therefore offered to capitulate. Several meetings took place to discuss the terms of the treaty ; but as they knew their lord was undergoing a very severe punishment, they consented to surrender the fortress on condition that he should be set at liberty, and that all those who were within should be allowed to go free. They were, nevertheless, obliged to leave behind all the treasures and supplies that had been accumulated in the castle. The Lord of Sidon[1] repaired to Tyre, accompanied by all the Franks who had been with him in esh-Shakîf. The Sultan saw how important a thing the possession (of Acre) was in the eyes of the Franks from all parts, and how their attention was always fixed on that city ; he therefore took advantage of the winter season, when ships cannot travel on the sea, to throw such quantities of provisions and stores, of engines of war, and of soldiers into the place as, under God, to ensure its perfect safety. He also sent to Egypt to command his lieutenants to equip a fleet sufficient to carry a great number of people. He then set out for Acre, and entered the city with great display, to the chagrin of the enemy. After this he dismissed his troops, that they might rest until the end of the winter and regain their strength, and he himself remained in the face of the enemy with a very small body of men. At

---

[1] Renaud of Sidon, Lord of esh-Shakîf.

this time the ground between the two armies was covered with mud so deep that they were unable to get at one another.

CHAPTER LXV.

AN ANECDOTE.

WHEN the Sultan received tidings that the Franks intended to march on Acre, he summoned his emirs and councillors together to consult them as to what course he should pursue. He was at this time in the Merj 'Ayûn. He was of opinion that it would be best to attack the enemy and prevent them from establishing themselves in front of the city, 'for,' said he, ' in that case, their infantry would protect them like a wall ; they would intrench themselves behind it so that we could not get at them, and then the city might be taken.' The council was not of his opinion. ' Let them take up their position,' they said, 'and collect their troops together ; we will cut them to pieces in one day.' Events proved that the Sultan was right. I heard his words myself, and was witness of what happened. This is what is meant by the word of the Holy Prophet : ' Among my people there are some who can decide and speak, and 'Omar is one of them.'

CHAPTER LXVI.

ARRIVAL OF THE KHALIF'S AMBASSADOR.

THE Sultan neglected no opportunity of introducing supplies and stores, arms and troops into Acre; then, when the fighting season recommenced with the close of winter,

which opened the sea once more to traffic, he sent into all
the neighbouring countries, commanding them to dispatch
their contingents forthwith. After receiving the first of
these reinforcements, the Moslem army marched nearer to
the enemy, and encamped on Tell Kîsân. This took place
on the 18th of Rabi'a I. in the year 586 (April 25, 1190).
He drew up his troops in a right wing, left wing and centre,
and stationed his son el-Melek el-Afdal in that part of
the right wing nearest the centre. The contingents and
auxiliaries kept on coming in, one after another. An
ambassador arrived from Baghdad on a mission from the
Khalif. He was a young man belonging to one of the
families descended from Muhammad. He brought with
him a body of experts, skilled in throwing naphtha, as well
as two loads of that inflammable substance. He also bore a
warrant from the Khalif, authorizing the Sultan to borrow
the sum of twenty thousand gold pieces from the merchants
as a contribution to the expenses of the Holy War, in
payment of which he was to draw bills on the August
Divan (the Court of Baghdad). The Sultan accepted all
that the ambassador brought with him, but refused to make
use of this warrant, lest it should oppress the provinces over
which he ruled. This same day he heard that the Franks
were on the point of attacking the city, and had invested
it closely; he therefore mounted his horse and marched
against them, to divert their attention from the city by an
attack on his part. The fight that ensued was stubbornly
maintained until night separated the combatants. Both
sides returned to their own camps. The Sultan, seeing
that, though the Moslem army was now in full force, his
camp was a long way from the enemy, felt that the city
might easily be taken by storm; he therefore removed the
army and all the baggage to Tell el-'Ajjûl.[1] This was

---

[1] *Tell el-'Ajjûl*, W. of el-'Aiyâdîya.

effected on the 25th of the same month. During the morning of that day a man swam out from the city bringing letters, which said ·that the enemy had filled up part of the moat, and seemed determined to storm the place. The Sultan thereupon sent further messages to the reinforcements that had not yet arrived, urging them to hurry forward ; then he drew up his troops in order of battle, and marched nearer to the enemy so as to withdraw their attention from the city by occupying them in another direction. At dawn on Friday, the 27th of the month Rabi'a I. in the year 586 (May 4, 1190), el-Melek ez-Zâher Ghîâth ed-Dîn Ghâzi, Lord of Aleppo, with only a small escort, came in in hot haste to see the Sultan, his father. He had left his troops encamped at some distance. The next day, when he had paid his respects to the Sultan and satisfied his longing to see him once more, he returned to his army and brought it in to the camp. These troops were so well equipped and armed that the sight of them filled the hearts of the Sultan's army with joy. They passed in review before the Sultan, who had ridden out to meet them on the plain. He forthwith led them quite close to the enemy, that the sight of such numbers of the soldiers of God, so well equipped, might inspire their hearts with terror, and fill them with apprehension. Towards the close of the same day Mozaffer ed-Dîn, son of Zein ed-Dîn, attended by only a few followers, paid a flying visit to the camp to pay his respects to the Sultan. He set out again at once to rejoin his troops, and led them into the camp on the following Sunday. The Sultan reviewed these troops, and halted with them in sight of the enemy, then he sent them to take up their appointed position. Each time reinforcements came in, he made a point of reviewing them, and marching them close to the enemy ; then he used to lead them back to the camp, and give them a meal, and, as all these soldiers were strangers to him, he would load them with presents in order to win their affection. After this, they would withdraw, over-whelmed with marks of his favour, and encamp in the place he allotted to them.

CHAPTER LXVII.

OF THE GOOD FORTUNE GRANTED TO EL-MELEK EZ-ZÂHER, THE SULTAN'S SON.

THE enemy had erected three towers, built of wood and iron, and had covered them with hides soaked in vinegar, to prevent their being set on fire by the combustibles hurled at them by the besieged. These towers were as huge as mountains; we could see them from the place where we were; they commanded the city walls. They were set on wheels, and could each, according to report, accommodate more than five hundred men ; their roofs were broad, and were constructed to carry one mangonel on each. The sight of these engines created a profound impression on the Moslems; they inspired them with a terror that defies description, and they gave up all hope of being able to save the city. All was ready, and the besiegers had only to wheel these towers close up to the walls, when the Sultan, who had been reflecting on the best means of setting them on fire, called together his throwers of naphtha, and promised them rewards in money and gifts if they could successfully accomplish this. They tried to do it, but in vain, in spite of all their skill. Amongst those who were looking on there was a certain young man, a native of Damascus, and a caldron-maker by profession. He said that he knew a way of setting the towers on fire,

and that if they would send him into the city and furnish
him with certain materials which he specified, he would
undertake to do it. He was given the materials he asked
for, and, thus equipped, went into the city. He then
boiled these substances in naphtha and placed them in
copper pots, each of which was thus full of fire. On the
very day that el-Melek ez-Zâher, Lord of Aleppo, the
Sultan's son, came into the camp, this man hurled one of
the pots of fire against one of the towers, and the erection
took fire immediately and became a mass of flames. The
Moslems raised great shouts in praise of the one true
God (the *tahlîl* and the *takbîr*), and almost lost their senses
in the exuberance of their joy. Whilst we were watching
and rejoicing at this first conflagration, the man threw a
second pot at another tower, and directly it was struck it
burst forth into flames like the first. Then a great tumult
arose in both armies, and their shouts mounted to the
skies. Barely an hour after this he struck the third tower
with another pot and set that also on fire. I cannot
describe the delight with which our whole army watched
its burning. The Sultan mounted his horse towards the
end of the day, and the troops did the same in the order in
which they were drawn up, by right wing, left wing, and
centre. They advanced close to the Franks, hoping to entice
them from their camp and engage them in battle; but they
would not stir from their tents, and night coming on prevented the two armies from joining in battle. Our people
attributed this (the destruction of the towers) to the arrival
of el-Melek ez-Zâher and to the good fortune granted
him; his father rejoiced to have a son so distinguished,
and firmly believed that what had happened was the result
of the good fortune that always smiles on a virtuous heart.
Every day the Sultan rode out in sight of the enemy, in
the hope of persuading them to come out and fight, but

they kept close in their camp. Meanwhile, reinforcements kept on arriving in the Moslem quarters.

CHAPTER LXVIII.

ARRIVAL OF 'IMÂD ED-DÎN ZENGHI, PRINCE OF SINJÂR, AND OF SEVERAL OTHER CHIEFTAINS.

ON the 23rd of the month Rabi'a II. (May 30, 1190) Prince 'Imâd ed-Dîn Zenghi, son of Maudûd and Lord of Sinjâr, came into the camp with great pomp and display, followed by an army splendidly equipped in every particular. The Sultan received him with every honour, and drew up his troops in line of battle so as to go out and meet him. The ḳâḍis and (government) secretaries were the first from our army to appear before the prince ; then came the Sultan's sons, and, finally, the Sultan himself, who at once led his guest to a spot in full view of the enemy, and, after halting there some time, brought him back to the camp and welcomed him to his own tent. He set a magnificent banquet before him, and presented him with a number of rare and curious things that surpass my powers of description. He had a cushion placed only for him by the side of his own, and a satin cloth laid on the ground of the tent for him to walk upon. Then he ordered a tent to be pitched for him on the extreme left of the left wing, close to the river. On the 7th of the following month, Sinjâr Shah, Lord of Jezîrat Ibn 'Omar, son of Seif ed-Dîn Ghâzi Ibn Maudûd Ibn Zenghi, came into the camp. He came at the head of a fine army, splendidly equipped. The Sultan received him with the greatest honour, welcomed him in his tent, and then had one pitched for him next to the quarters occupied by his uncle, 'Imâd ed-Dîn. On the 9th of the same month arrived 'Alâ ed-Dîn Khorrem Shah, son of Mas'ûd, Prince of Mosul; he represented his father, whose troops he brought to the Sultan. Salah ed-Dîn showed the greatest joy when he heard of his approach, and rode out a considerable distance to meet him. He made him dismount, and led him into his own tent, where he gave him a magnificent present; then he commanded a tent to be pitched for him between those occupied by his own sons, el-Melek el-Afdal and el-Melek ez-Zâher.

CHAPTER LXIX.

ARRIVAL OF THE MOSLEM FLEET AT ACRE.

THE same day (June 12), at noon, we sighted a great number of sail out at sea. The Sultan was expecting the arrival of the fleet from Egypt, for he had given orders that it should be equipped and sent to him. He therefore mounted, with such of his officers as were on duty, and drew up his troops in battle array with the view of attacking the enemy and preventing their operating against the fleet. The Franks, on their side, prepared to oppose it, and made their ships ready to send out against the Moslem fleet, which they saw approaching. They were determined to prevent its coming into the harbour. When their fleet had put out to sea, the Sultan attacked them on the land side, and our people marched down to the beach to encourage the Moslem fleet and succour the crews. The two squadrons met at sea, whilst the two armies were fighting on shore; the fire of war was kindled, its flames burst forth; a furious engagement took place between the two fleets, which ended in the defeat of the enemy. One of the enemy's galleys was captured, and its crew massacred, and we also took a ship that came from Constantinople. Our victorious fleet entered the harbour, bringing with it a number of coasting-boats laden with provisions and supplies of all kinds. The arrival of these was a great relief to the people in the city, and completely restored their confidence, for the close blockade which they had suffered had reduced them to the greatest extremity. Outside the city the battle between the two armies raged until nightfall, when either side returned to its own camp. The enemy suffered great loss in killed and wounded, for they had to fight in three several places. The people in the city had made a vigorous attack on them to prevent their opposing the Moslem fleet, the two fleets had engaged one another; and the Moslem army had fought them on the land side, and in each instance we had carried off the victory. After these events, during the last ten days of the month Jomada I., Zein ed-Dîn, Lord of Arbela, arrived in the camp with a large body of troops splendidly equipped. This chieftain's name was Yûsuf Ibn 'Ali Ibn Bektikîn. The Sultan received him with great honour, and entertained him in his tent with magnificent hospitality; then he had a tent erected for him close to that of Mozaffer ed-Dîn (so that the two brothers might be together).

CHAPTER LXX.

TIDINGS OF THE KING OF THE GERMANS.

AFTER this we received continual reports of the movements of the king of the Germans, who had just entered the dominions of Ḳilîj Arslân.[1] We heard that a great number of Turkomans had gone out to meet him, to prevent his crossing the river[2]; but that, having no leader to direct their operations, and seeing an immense army drawn up against them, they found it impossible to accomplish their purpose. Ḳilîj Arslân pretended to oppose the king, whilst, in reality, he was on good terms with him. Therefore, as soon as the king had entered his territory, he openly showed the sentiments he had previously cherished in secret, and became a partner in his plans, giving him hostages which the king was to keep until Ḳilîj Arslân's guides had conducted the German army into the dominions of Ïbn Laon.[3] The troops suffered greatly on the march; their provisions were exhausted, and they lost the chief part of their baggage animals. Therefore they were forced to abandon a great quantity of baggage, and a number of cuirasses, helmets, and arms, for want of transport. It is said that they burnt a great number of things of this kind, lest they should fall into the hands of the Moslems. They marched on in this sorry plight until they came to a city called Tarsus[4]; then they halted on

---

[1] This was 'Izz ed-Dîn, Ḳilîj Arslân II., who had just divided his empire between his ten sons. The actual ruler at *Konia* (Iconium) during the march of Barbarossa was Kotb ed-Dîn Melek Shah II.— W.

[2] Probably the Maeander is intended.

[3] See note, p. 78. Geoffrey de Vinsauf (i. 14-17) says that Ḳilîj Arslân was treacherous in his dealings and an enemy of the Christians.

[4] Tarsus was in the territory of the King of Armenia (Leo II.). There is a confusion here between the fever caught by Alexander when bathing in the Cydnus and the death by drowning of Barbarossa. The Emperor Frederic Barbarossa (here called king of the Germans) was drowned in the Calycadnus (*Geuk Su*) whilst on the march from Laranda (*Karaman*) to Seleucia (*Selefke*). (See Jacques de Vitry, p. 111, P.P.T. translation.)

the bank of a river, and made ready to cross. The king suddenly determined to swim across, and, although the water was very cold, he jumped in, worn out as he was by the fatigues and anxieties he had undergone. The consequence was an illness to which he finally succumbed. When he realized the gravity of his condition, he delegated his authority to the son who had accompanied him on the expedition. After his death his officers resolved to steep his body in vinegar, and carry his bones to Jerusalem in a casket, in order that they might receive burial in that city. His son was installed in his stead, in spite of some slight opposition, for most of his officers inclined towards the eldest son of the king, who succeeded his father in his dominions[1]; but the younger son, being on the spot, obtained command of the army. Knowing the reverses they had suffered, and the havoc that famine and death had made in their ranks since the king's death, Ibn Laon held back and did not join them[2]; in the first place he could not tell how things would turn out, and in the second they were Franks, whilst he was an Armenian. Therefore he shut himself up in one of his strongholds in order to get out of their way.

[1] Henry VI. succeeded as emperor. Frederic, duke of Suabia, was with his father in Cilicia.

[2] This is contrary to the Frank accounts, which represent Leo II. and the Armenians as receiving the army hospitably after Barbarossa's death. In 1198 Leo was crowned king at Tarsus by the archbishop of Mayence.—W.

CHAPTER LXXI.

CONTENTS OF A LETTER RECEIVED FROM THE ARMENIAN CATHOLICOS.

THE Sultan, meanwhile, had received a letter from the Catholicos,[1] that is to say, from the chief of the Armenians, who was Lord of Kal'at er-Rûm,[2] a stronghold on the banks of the Euphrates. The following is a translation of this dispatch : 'With most cordial good wishes, the Catholicos sends the following particulars for the information of our lord and master, the Sultan strong to help, who has reunited the faithful, who bears aloft the banner of justice and benevolence, who is the prosperity (*Salâh*) of the world and of the Faith (*ed-Dîn*), Sultan of Islâm and of the Moslems—may God prolong his prosperity, magnify his glory, preserve his life, confirm him for ever in good fortune, and lead him to the goal of all his desires ! I write concerning the king of the Germans and those things he has done since his appearance. When he left his own dominions he forced his way through the territory of the Hungarians, and obliged their king to acknowledge his supremacy. He carried off from him by force such money

---

[1] The word is written *Kâtoghikos;* from the Armenian *Gath'oughigos* (Greek Καθολιχός). The Catholicos was the head of the Armenian Church. In 1065 the Catholicos, in consequence of the state of Armenia, resided in Lesser Armenia ; and until 1441 the Catholicoi resided at, and exercised their jurisdiction from, several different towns in Cilicia and Northern Syria. Hrhomgla (*Kal'at er-Rûm*) was purchased by the Catholicos, Gregory III., from the son of Jocelyn, count of Edessa, in 1150, and it was the residence of the Catholicoi till 1298.—W.

[2] *Kal'at er-Rûm*, the Turkish Rûm Kaleh, N. of Bir, is built on a cliff at the junction of the *Merziman Chai* with the Euphrates.

and men as he thought fit ; then he entered the country of the chief of the Greeks, took and pillaged several of his cities, and established himself therein after driving the inhabitants out. He forced the king of the Greeks[1] to come and do him homage ; he took away the king's son and brother as hostages, as well as about forty of the prince's most confidential friends. He also exacted from him a contribution of fifty quintals of gold, and as many of silver, as well as silken stuffs to an immense amount. He seized all his ships to transport his army from that coast (that of the Hellespont), bringing the hostages with him and retaining them until he had entered Ķilîj Arslân's dominions. He continued his march, and for three days the Awaj Turkomans maintained a friendly intercourse with him, supplying him with sheep, calves, horses, and other necessaries. Then they saw their opportunity to attack him, and troops came up from all sides and joined their forces ; then they fell upon the king and hung upon his march for three and thirty days. When he neared Iconium, Ķoṭb ed-Dîn,[2] son of Ķilîj Arslân, collected his troops together and marched upon him. A great battle ensued in which the king took the prince prisoner, and completely routed the army of Iconium. Then he advanced until he came within sight of that city. The Moslems came out in great numbers to oppose him, but he repulsed them and forced his way into the city, where he massacred a great number of Moslems and Persians, remaining there for five days. Ķilîj Arslân sued for peace, which the king granted, and received from him twenty

---

[1] Isaac Angelos, who acceded as emperor of Byzantium after the revolution in 1185, was an enemy of the Latins, who were massacred in Constantinople in 1183.

[2] Melek Shah II. Ķoṭb ed-Dîn was the son to whom Ķilîj Arslân II. had given Konia. See p. 183.

hostages of the nobility of the land. When he set out once more on his march, he followed Ḳilîj Arslân's advice and took the road leading to Tarsûs and el-Miṣṣîṣa[1]; but before entering that country he sent a messenger forward with a letter, announcing who he was and what he purposed doing ; he also gave an account of what had happened on his way thither, declaring that he was determined to march through their land—if not as their friend, then as a foe.[2] This occasioned the sending of Ḥâtem,[3] the memlûk, with instructions to grant the passage the king had demanded. This officer was accompanied by several persons of high rank, and bore the answer to the (king's) letter. According to their instructions, they were to endeavour to persuade the king to return to Ḳilîj Arslân's dominions. When admitted into the great king's presence, they gave the answer into his hands, at the same time informing him that the chief object of their mission was to persuade him to depart. Then the king collected all his troops together, and took up his position on the bank of a river. After he had eaten and slept, he was seized with a desire to bathe in the cool water, which he accordingly did. But, by the ordinance of God, when he came out of the water, he was seized with serious illness, occasioned by the chill of his bath, and, after languishing several days, he

---

[1] *Missis*, the ancient *Mopsuestia*, stood on both banks of the *Jihûn* (ancient *Pyramus*), and occupied an important position on the great road from the Cilician to the Syrian Gates. It frequently changed hands during the wars between the Christians and Moslems.—W.

[2] Tne greater portion of Cilicia was at this period in the hands of Leo II., king of Lesser Armenia. The Sultans of Rûm did not then possess any place on the coast.—W.

[3] Possibly *Haithon*, a common Armenian name. Amongst those sent to meet and compliment the German emperor was S. Narses of Lampron.—W.

died.[1]   Ibn Laon was on his way to visit the king when
he met his own messengers, who directly after this occurrence (the king's death) had promptly left the (German)
camp.   When he learnt from them what had just taken
place, he threw himself into one of his strongholds and
kept close within its walls.   The king's son had been
named by his father to replace him, when he first set out
to invade these countries, and, in spite of certain difficulties
that were raised, he succeeded in establishing himself.
When he heard of the flight of Ibn Laon's ambassadors,
he sent after them and brought them back.   Then he addressed them as follows : " My father was an old man, and
nothing would have induced him to come to this country,
but the desire of performing the pilgrimage to Jerusalem.
I, who have suffered so much on this journey, am now
master.   Therefore, unless Ibn Laon obeys me, I shall invade
his dominions."   On this Ibn Laon saw that he would be
obliged to yield and visit the king in person, for he was
at the head of an immense army ; he had lately reviewed
them, and found that there were forty-two thousand horsemen, equipped with all sorts of arms, and an innumerable
company of foot-soldiers.   It was a multitude of men of
divers nations and strange to look upon ; they were strict
in the performance of their duty, and kept under the
severest discipline.   Anyone who disgraced himself was
slaughtered like a sheep.   One of their chiefs had ill-
treated a servant by beating him unmercifully, and a
meeting of priests was called to try him.   It was an offence
punished by death, and he was unanimously condemned
by his judges.   A great number of people interceded with

---

[1] According to S. Narses, the emperor was carried away by the
rapidity of the river *Selef* (Calycadnus) and drowned.   According to
some accounts, the accident occurred on the march from Laranda ;
according to others at *Selefke.*—W.

the king in his behalf, but the prince was inflexible, and
the chief paid the penalty of death. These people deny
themselves every enjoyment. If one of them indulges in
any pleasure, he is avoided by his fellows and reprimanded.
This is all in consequence of the grief they feel at the state
of the Holy City. I havé been credibly informed that for
a long while some of them vowed to wear no clothing at
all, and were clad in nothing but their mail ; this, however,
was forbidden by their leaders. The patience with which
they bear suffering, hardship, and fatigue is carried to a
marvellous length. Your humble servant (*literally* memlûk),
sends you this account of the state of affairs. When anything fresh occurs, God willing, he will send you intelligence thereof. This is the letter of the Catholicos.' This
word means *vicar*. The name of the writer of this letter
was Bar Kríkur Ben Bâsîl.[1]

CHAPTER LXXII.

THE TROOPS MARCH TOWARDS THE FRONTIER TO MEET THE KING OF THE GERMANS.

WHEN the Sultan knew for certain that the king of the
Germans had entered the territory of Ibn Laon, and that
he was advancing on the Moslem dominions, he called the
emirs and councillors of his Empire together, to hear their
opinion on the course that he should pursue. They all
agreed in advising that part of the army should be sent
into the districts bordering on the enemy's line of march,
whilst the Sultan should remain with the rest of his army

---

[1] *Parsegh*, or Basil, bishop of Ani, was the son of Gregory, who
was nephew of Basil I. He belonged to the Arsacid family, and was
Catholicos at *Rûm Kaleh* (1180-1193).—W.

to oppose the enemy encamped (at Acre). The first of the emirs to set forth was Nâṣr ed-Dîn, son of Taḳi ed-Dîn, and Lord of Manbej.[1] After him went 'Izz ed-Dîn Ibn el-Moḳaddem, Lord of Kefr Tâb, Barîn, and other places. Mejed ed-Dîn, Lord of B'albek, followed him, and then went Sâbek ed-Dîn, Lord of Sheizer.[2] The Yarûkidi Kurds belonging to the army from Aleppo went next, and afterwards the troops from Hamah. El-Melek el-Afdal, the Sultan's son, also set out, followed by Bedr ed-Dîn, Governor (shihna) of Damascus. After them went el-Melek ez-Zâher, the Sultan's son; he was sent to Aleppo to keep a watch on the enemy's march, to gather information, and to protect the districts all round. Next went el-Melek el-Mozaffer (Taḳi ed-Dîn, the Sultan's nephew ·and Lord of Hamah), charged to protect the districts round his city and to keep a watch on the Germans as they marched past that place. This prince was the last to depart; he set out on the night preceding Saturday, the 9th of Jomada I. 586 (June 14, 1190). The withdrawal of these troops very much weakened the right wing, which had furnished the greater part of them; the Sultan therefore commanded el-Melek el-'Âdel to transfer himself to the extreme right of the right flank, and occupy the position left vacant by Taḳi ed-Dîn. 'Imâd ed-Dîn was posted on the extreme left of the left wing. An epidemic broke out in the army about this time, and Mozaffer ed-Dîn, Lord of Harrân, sickened of it, but recovered; it was next the turn of el-Melek ez-Zâfer, but he also recovered. A great number of people, chiefs and others, were seized with it; but, thanks be to God, the

---

[1] *Membej.* See p. 74.

[2] *Sheizer* is Cæsarea, immediately S. of Apamea, on the Orontes, and otherwise called Larissa. See Jacques de Vitry, p. 24, P.P.T. translation.

illness took a very slight form. The same epidemic also
appeared among the enemy, but with them was both
more wide-spread and more severe, and occasioned great
mortality. The Sultan maintained his position and kept
watch over the enemy's movements.

CHAPTER LXXIII.

ACCOUNT OF THE KING OF THE GERMANS CONTINUED.

THE king's son had replaced his father, but he was seized
with a serious illness, which forced him to halt in the
country of Ibn Laon. He retained with him five-and-
twenty knights and forty Templars (*Dâwia*), sending the
rest of the army forward to occupy the road to Antioch.
As his forces were very numerous, he divided them into
three divisions. The first, under a count of high rank
among them, was marching close to the castle of Baghrâs,
when the garrison of that place, though numbering but a
few men, succeeded in carrying off two hundred of his
soldiers by force and strategy. They then sent word that
the enemy was much exhausted, that they were suffering
from sickness, that they had but few horses and beasts
of burden, and that their stores and supplies were almost
entirely expended. The lieutenants, posted by the Sultan
in the different cities of Syria, were informed of this state
of things, and dispatched troops to find out what the
enemy were doing. These men fell in with a large body
(of Germans), who had left their camp on a foraging
expedition ; they attacked them smartly, inflicting a loss
of upwards of five hundred men in killed and captives.
That, at any rate, was the report made by our correspon-

dents in their dispatches. A second messenger came from the Catholicos, and was received by the Sultan ; in this interview, at which I was present, he informed us that, though the Germans were very strong in numbers, they were in a very weak condition, for they had hardly any horses or supplies, and the chief part of their baggage was being carried by asses. ‘I took up my position,’ said he, ‘on a bridge they had to cross, to get a good view of them, and I saw a great number of men march past, almost all without cuirasses or lances. I asked them the reason of this, and they replied, “We have been spending several days in an unhealthy plain ; our provisions were exhausted as well as our wood, and we have been obliged to burn a great part of our stores. We have also suffered great losses by death. We have been obliged to kill and eat our horses, and burn our lances and stores for want of wood.” ’ The count who commanded their advanced guard died when they reached Antioch. We learnt that Ibn Laon, hearing of the exhausted condition of their army, was filled with the hope of gaining some advantage thereby, and, knowing that the king was ill, and had retained but very few men with him, he contemplated spoiling him of his treasures. The Prince of Antioch, too, we were told, hearing of this, went out to meet the king of the Germans and bring him into the city, with the view of appropriating these same treasures himself, if the king happened to die in the city. News kept coming in concerning the enemy, and we heard that the epidemic was rife among them, and weakening them more and more. After this el-Melek el-’Âdel fought a battle with the enemy on the sea-shore.

CHAPTER LXXIV.

THE BATTLE FOUGHT BY EL-'ÀDEL.

On Wednesday, the 20th of Jomada II. (July 25, 1190), the enemy heard that several bodies had been detached from our army, and that the right wing had been much weakened by the departure of the troops belonging to the various districts through which the enemy (the Germans) proposed to march. They (the Franks) therefore resolved to come out (from their entrenchments), and fall upon that wing whilst they were not expecting an attack. But they became the sport of the vain hopes they had entertained. The hour of noon had just passed when they issued forth, deploying by right wing, left wing and centre, and then rushing forward. As they were in strong force, they thought that the right wing, where el-Melek el-'Àdel was encamped, would be unable to withstand them. When our people saw them coming out in order of battle, they called to arms, and rushed out of their tents as a lion springs from his lair. The Sultan sprang to his horse, crying: 'On for Islâm!' Our horsemen leapt into their saddles, and the battalions formed without delay. The Sultan had just left his tent when I saw him; he had only a few officers with him. Some of the men had not yet mounted their horses when he came galloping up, as anxious as a mother who has lost her only son. He ordered his drum to be beaten, and his emirs replied by ordering theirs to be sounded from the different positions where they were posted. Everyone was now in the saddle; but by this time the Franks had hurled themselves on the right wing, and pushed on as far as el-Melek el-'Àdel's tent. They

13

seized everything that they found in the tents and market-
place, killing and pillaging right and left.   They reached
the store-tent, and carried off part of the liquors that were
kept there.   When el-Melek el-'Âdel was informed of what
was taking place, he came out of his tent and mounted
his horse, commanding those of the right wing who were
near him to do the same.   His order was obeyed by
Kâimâz en-Nejmi the eunuch (*tawâshi*), and by other
champions (lions) of Islâm as brave as himself.   He held
himself in readiness, watching for an opportunity of surprising the enemy, and he was not long in finding it.   The
Franks, carried away by their cupidity, were engaged in
pillaging the camp, and loading themselves with furniture,
fruit, and provisions.[1]   When he saw them thus fully
occupied, he commanded his men to charge, and he himself rushed forward, followed by all the soldiers of the right
wing who were on the spot.   The whole of the right wing
was already engaged, when the Mosul troops, who had
been summoned afterwards, hurled themselves on the
Franks like lions springing on their prey.   God delivered
the enemy into their hands.   They were completely routed,
and fled headlong back to their camp, whilst the sword
of God did execution upon them, separating their souls
from their bodies, and severing their heads from their
shoulders.   The Sultan seeing, by the dust of battle that
arose, what was going on in his brother's camp, his heart
burning with zeal and brotherly love, and alarmed at the peril
of his kindred, flew eagerly to help the cause of God's Faith.
And the criers cried to the people: "On for Islâm, ye
champions of the one God!   The enemy of God is given
into our hands.   He has dared in his greediness to enter
your camp."   His memlûks, his friends, and his special guard

---

[1] This agrees with De Vinsauf's account.   The Franks were suffering from starvation.

(*halka*) responded to his appeal ; the Mosul army, under
'Alâ ed-Dîn, son of 'Izz ed-Dîn, came up to join him, and
afterwards the Egyptian army, led by Sonḳor el-Ḥalebi.
Other bands came in one after another, each brave warrior
answering his comrades' call. The Sultan took up his
position in the centre, fearing lest it should occur to the
enemy to attack him there, as they knew that part of the
army had been weakened by the withdrawal of great numbers
of troops. As detachments kept coming up one after
another, the fight was maintained without interruption,
and scarcely an hour had passed before we saw our enemies
prostrate as though they were palm-trees thrown down
(Kurân lxix. 7). The whole ground between el-Melek
el-'Âdel's camp and that of the enemy, a distance of a
parasang, or perhaps a little more, was covered with bodies.
Very few of their people escaped. Mounted on my mule,
I passed through a sea of blood, and tried to count the
number of dead, but there were so many that I could
not reckon them.[1] I noticed the bodies of two women.
Someone told me that he had seen four women engaged
in the fight, two of whom were taken prisoners. The
number of men made captive that day was very incon-
siderable, for the Sultan had commanded his troops to
spare none who should fall into their hands. The alarm
did not reach the left wing until the battle was at an end,
so great a distance was there between their camp and the
scene of the fight. This battle took place between the
Zuhr and '*Asr* (between the mid-day and afternoon prayers).
So great was the defeat of the enemy, that some of the
Moslems who pursued them are said to have penetrated
right into their camp. The Sultan, seeing that fortune

---

[1] A letter by the chaplain of Baldwin, Archbishop of Canterbury,
reckons the Christian loss on July 25, 1190, at 4,000 men. See Archer's
' Crusade of Richard I.,' p. 18.

had favoured him, called his men back from the pursuit.
During this battle the Moslems lost only ten men, and
these were all people of no rank.   When the soldiers of
God, who were stationed in Acre, saw what had befallen
the enemy, they sallied out and attacked their camp.   A
desperate fight ensued, the Moslems carrying off the victory.
They burst into their camp, pillaged their tents, and
carried off several women, together with a quantity of
furniture, and even the pots in which they were then
cooking their food.   A letter from the city informed us
of this victory.   It was, indeed, a bitter day for the infidels.
Different authorities are not agreed as to the number of
their dead ; some say eight thousand, others seven.   I
myself saw five rows of bodies, beginning from el-'Âdel's
camp, and running right up to that of the enemy.   I met
an intelligent man, one of our soldiers, who was going up
and down the lines counting the dead, and I asked him
how many he had counted.   He replied : ' So far there
are four thousand and sixty odd '   He had counted two
lines, and was engaged on the third, but in those that
remained to be computed the dead lay still more thickly.
This Wednesday witnessed the most brilliant triumph that
Islâm could possibly obtain.   On the following day, the
21st (July 26), at the hour of the *'Asr* prayer, a courier
from Aleppo arrived on a dromedary, having accomplished
the journey in five days.   The despatch he brought informed us that a strong force of the enemy, being part of
those who had come from the north, had made an incursion into Moslem territory with a view of pillaging all
they might find, and that the troops in Aleppo had taken
the field and cut off their retreat, so that but very few
of these (freebooters) had effected their escape.   This news
arrived immediately after the battle (of Acre).   It was
announced to the sound of music, and to the great joy

of the Moslems, who were filled with delight at the thought
of one splendid victory after another. Towards the close
of the same day Kâimâz el-Harrâni came in from the outpost and informed us that the enemy, finding themselves
terribly exhausted, had expressed a wish that the Sultan
should send them a representative, empowered to confer
with them on the subject of a treaty of peace. From that
time the enemy of God remained with broken wings, until
there arrived a count called Count Heri.[1]

CHAPTER LXXV.

ARRIVAL OF COUNT HENRY.

THIS count was one of the greatest princes among the
Franks. He came by sea, with a number of ships laden
with money and supplies, victuals and arms, and great
numbers of men. His presence inspired the besiegers with
courage, gave new strength to their hearts, and they even
indulged the hope of surprising the Moslem army by a
night attack. They spoke so openly of this project, that
the strangers who were allowed to visit their camp got
wind of it, as well as the (Sultan's) spies. Therefore the
Sultan called his emirs and councillors together, and consulted them as to what should be done. After discussing
several plans, they finally decided to enlarge the circle and
to withdraw further from the city, with a view of enticing
the besiegers to come out of their camp, and then, when
they had got some distance from it, God would deliver them
into the hands of the Moslems. This decision pleased the
Sultan, for God had decreed that it should find favour in

---

[1] Henry of Troyes, count of Champagne.

his sight. He therefore set out for Mount Kharrûba
with all his army. This was on the 27th of Jomada II.
(August 1). In the position they had just quitted he left
only about one thousand horsemen as an advanced guard ;
these men kept watch each in his turn. We continually received letters from Acre, and sent answers
back to the city ; these were carried by pigeons, by men
swimming, or by lightly-built boats that put off at night
and entered the harbour unknown to the besiegers. We
received constant tidings also of the movements of the
enemy, who were advancing from the north ; they were in
great want of both horses and supplies, and were suffering
severely from mortality and sickness. The whole army
had succeeded in reaching Antioch, but had been unable
to provide themselves with horses. We also heard that our
fellow-soldiers in Aleppo were employed in seizing any of
the enemy's troops that came out for grass or wood, and
were carrying off every individual who even showed himself
outside the camp.

CHAPTER LXXVI.

A LETTER IS RECEIVED FROM CONSTANTINOPLE—MAY
GOD GRANT US THE CONQUEST OF THAT CITY !

THE Sultan kept up a correspondence with the king of
Constantinople, each prince sending letters and ambassadors to the other. In the month of Rejeb, 585 (August-
September, 1189), whilst the Sultan was encamped on the
plain of Merj 'Ayûn, a messenger arrived from the king
bringing a (favourable) answer to a request that he had
made through his ambassador. The Sultan was desirous of
obtaining permission to have the *khotba* said in due form in
the mosque at Constantinople, now that the preliminaries

(of a treaty with the king) had been arranged. He had therefore dispatched an ambassador to provide for the celebration of the *khotba* in that mosque, and this man had been most honourably received and cordially welcomed by the king. In the ship in which he had performed the journey he had taken a preacher with his pulpit, a band of muezzins (to call to prayer) and several readers (whose duty it was to chant the Kurân). The day they entered Constantinople was a great day among the days of Islâm; great numbers of merchants and travellers were present. The preacher ascended his pulpit, and, surrounded by all the Moslems and merchants who were staying in the city, he delivered the Moslem invocation (*khotba*) in the name of the Abasside khalif. Our ambassador then returned, accompanied by the (Greek) ambassador, who was sent to inform us that the matter had been arranged in accordance with the Sultan's wishes. The Greek stayed with us some time. I was present when he came before the Sultan, attended by an interpreter, to deliver the message with which he was charged. He was the finest of old men, and wore the dress peculiar to his rank. He brought a certificate (credentials), and a letter sealed with gold. He stayed with us for some time, and then died. When he received news of his death, the king of Constantinople dispatched another ambassador to conclude the mission. This envoy brought a letter about the matter under consideration. We will describe this document, and give a copy of the translation. It was written in wide lines, but narrower than in the writing of Baghdad. The translation on both back and front was in the second section[1]; between

---

[1] Documents are extant, emanating from the Byzantine Chancery, in which a Latin translation is appended underneath the Greek text. In the document described by Behâ ed-Dîn the text was accompanied by a translation into Arabic.

the two the seal had been affixed. This seal was of gold, and had been stamped with a portrait of the King just as wax is impressed with a seal ; it weighed fifteen dinars.[1] The two sections of the letter ran as follows : ' From Aîsâkiûs (*Isaac*) the King, servant of the Messiah, crowned by the grace of God, ever glorious and victorious *Afghakûs* (imperial), ruling in the name of God, the invincible conqueror, the autocrat of the Greeks, Angelos, to His Excellency the Sultan of Egypt, Ṣalâḥ ed-Dîn, sincere affection and friendship. The letter written by Your Excellency[2] to My Empire[3] has been safely received. We have perused it, and have been informed thereby of the death of our ambassador. This has occasioned us great grief, more especially because he died in a strange land, leaving unfinished the business with which My Empire had charged him, and on which he was to confer with Your Excellency. Your Excellency doubtless intends sending us an ambassador to inform our Empire of the decision that has been made relative to the business with the arrangement of which we charged our late ambassador. The property he has left, or which may be recovered after his death, must be sent to My Empire, that it may be given to his children and relatives. I cannot believe that Your Excellency will give ear to malicious reports of the march of the Germans through my dominions ; it is not surprising that my enemies should propagate lies to serve their own ends. If you wish to know the truth, I will tell you. They suffered themselves more hardship and fatigue than they inflicted

---

[1] This would make it worth about £6 10s.

[2] The Greek equivalent would be εξοχότης.

[3] In official documents issued from the Byzantine Chancery, the prince refers to himself under the phrases βασιλεία μου or τὸ ἡμέτερον χράτος, rendered in the Latin translations as *imperium meum* or *nostrum imperium* (Wescher).

on my peasant population. Their losses in money, horses and men were considerable ; they lost a great number of soldiers, and it was with great difficulty that they escaped my brave troops. They were so exhausted that they cannot reach your dominions ; and even if they should succeed in reaching them, they could be of no assistance to their fellows, nor could they inflict any injury on Your Excellency. Considering these things, I am much astonished that you have forgotten our former (good) relations, and that you have not communicated any of your plans and projects to My Empire. It seems to My Empire, that the only result of my friendship with you has been to draw down upon me the hatred of the Franks and of all their kind. Your Excellency must fulfil the intention, announced in your letter, of sending me an ambassador to inform me of the decision in the business upon which I have corresponded with you for a long time past. Let this be done as soon as possible. I pray that the coming of the Germans, of which you have heard so many reports, may not weigh heavily on your hearts ; the plans and purposes they entertain will work their own confusion. Written in the year 1501.'[1] When the Sultan heard the contents of this letter, he received the ambassador with every mark of honour, and assigned him a lodging suitable to his rank. He was an old man of noble carriage, and very accomplished, for he knew Arabic, Greek, and the Frankish (tongues).

Some time after this the Franks renewed the siege of Acre with fresh energy, and pressed the city very close. They had been reinforced by the arrival of Count Henry[2] with ten thousand warriors. Other reinforcements reached

---

[1] The year 1501 of the Alexandrian era corresponds with the year 585 of the Hejira (A.D. 1189).

[2] See pp. 35, 197.

them by sea, and revived their drooping courage; therefore,
they made a furious attack on the city.

CHAPTER LXXVII.

BURNING OF THE ENEMY'S MANGONELS.

THE enemy, feeling themselves strong—strong again on
account of the reinforcements that continued to come in,
set their hearts with renewed determination on winning the
city.   They brought up their mangonels and placed them
in position on all sides, playing on the walls both day and
night, for as soon as the men on duty were weary, fresh ones
were sent to relieve them : thus a constant shower of stones
was kept up without intermission.   This was in the month of
Rejeb (August, 1190).   The people in the city, being thus
hard pressed by the enemy, gave free rein to that pride of
religion which Islâm alone could have inspired.   Their
leaders at that time were, first, the governor specially
appointed for the defence of the city, and, secondly, the
commandant of the garrison.   The former of these officers
was the great emir Behâ ed-Dîn Karâkûsh, the latter the
great *isfahsalâr* (general in chief) and emir Hossâm ed-
Dîn Abu el-Heija.   Hossâm was distinguished both
for his munificence and valour ; he was of high rank
amongst his own people (the Kurds), and the plans he
formed bore witness to the stoutness of his heart.   These
leaders agreed on the advisability of a general sortie,
taking advantage of the enemy's carelessness to fall upon
them when least expected.   The gates of the city were
thrown open, and the besieged rushed out simultaneously
on every side, penetrating into the very midst of the enemy
before they were aware of their approach.   The Moslems

charged the infidels, who, seeing their camp invaded, did not think of guarding and protecting their mangonels, and the pyrotechnists were therefore enabled to use their implements with good effect. Before an hour had passed those engines had been set on fire and completely burnt to the ground. In this engagement seventy of the enemy's cavalry were killed, and a number of prisoners taken. One of their leaders happened to be among the latter ; the soldier who took him prisoner was not aware of his rank, and it was not until after the battle, when the]Franks inquired whether their countryman were alive or dead, that he knew he had captured one of their chief men. When he learned who his prisoner was, fearing lest he should be carried off by force, he lost no time in dispatching him. The Franks offered a large sum of money as the price of his body, and persisted in their demand with the greatest importunity until at last the body was thrown down to them (from the wall). When they saw him dead, they threw themselves on the ground and covered their heads with dust. This occurrence damped their ardour. They never let us know the name of the chief they had lost. From this time forth the Moslems lost all fear of the enemy and the Arabs got into the habit of going in and out of their camp to pilfer and steal, killing and taking prisoner those they met. The count had had a great mangonel built, on which he expended fifteen hundred gold pieces, according to information we received from the spies and people who were allowed to visit the enemy's camp. This engine, which was quite ready to be brought up to the walls, had escaped burning in the sortie, because it was at some distance from the city, beyond the furthest point our men touched. But, on the night preceding the 15th of Sh'abân (September 17) some pyrotechnists and soldiers sallied out of the city, and laid their plans so well

that they succeeded in getting up to the mangonel, and
setting it on fire. At sight of the conflagration a great
cry went up from both armies, and the enemy seemed
paralyzed by the disaster; as the fire broke out at a
distance from the city, they thought they were being
attacked from all sides. By this means God increased the
strength of the Moslems very notably. The flames from
the great mangonel caught another smaller one that was
standing close by, and destroyed it as well.

CHAPTER LXXVIII.

STRATAGEM, BY MEANS OF WHICH A LARGE SHIP FROM
BEIRÛT SUCCEEDED IN MAKING HER WAY INTO THE
HARBOUR.[1]

THE Franks—may God confound them!—had blockaded
the harbour of Acre to prevent Moslem ships from entering. A great famine therefore reigned in the city; so
some Moslems embarked in a large ship at Beirût, loading it with four hundred sacks of corn and a quantity of
cheeses, onions, sheep and other victuals. They dressed
themselves like Franks, and shaved off their beards that
they might look more like the enemy; they even put pigs
on the bridge of the ship, so that they could be plainly
seen, and set up crosses in conspicuous places. They then
made towards the city, as though they had come a long
voyage, and ran into the midst of the enemy's ships, when
several sloops and galleys came up alongside. The crews
of these boats said to them: 'You seem to be making for
the city,' for they took them for their fellow-countrymen.

---

[1] This chapter is wanting in the Oxford manuscript.

The others replied : ' Do you mean that you have not taken it ?' ' No,' they answered, 'not yet.' 'Very well,' said the disguised Moslems ; 'we will make for the army (of the Franks) ; but there is another ship close behind us, coming on with the same wind ; you must warn them not to enter the harbour.' There really was a Frank ship behind them, that was steering towards the enemy's camp. The people in the boats looked in the direction indicated, and, seeing a ship, they made towards her to warn her of the danger. The Moslem ship, being thus free to proceed, took advantage of a favourable breeze and entered the harbour in safety ; praise be to God therefore ! Its arrival caused the greatest rejoicing in the city, for the inhabitants were beginning to feel the approach of famine. This took place during the last ten days of the month of Rejeb (end of August and beginning of September).

CHAPTER LXXIX.

ACCOUNT OF 'AISA THE SWIMMER.

A VERY curious and noteworthy thing occurred during this siege ; a Moslem, named 'Aisa, used constantly to swim to the city, taking letters and money, which were tied round his loins. He used to go by night, taking advantage of the carelessness of the enemy, sometimes diving under their ships and coming up on the other side. On one particular night he had put on his girdle—which held three purses, containing a thousand pieces of gold and a packet of letters for the army—and started swimming for the city with his burden ; but he met with an accident, and lost his life. For some time we did not know what had happened to him, for the bird, which he used to let fly to tell us when he reached the city, did not arrive. By this we knew that the man must have perished. Some days afterwards some people who happened to be on the shore inside the city, found the body of a drowned man that had been cast up on the beach by the waves. They examined it, and found that it was 'Aisa, the swimmer. Tied round his loins they found the money and the letters, the latter having been enclosed in oiled silk. The gold had been sent to pay the troops. Never before have we heard of a dead man delivering a message entrusted to his care. This also took place during the last ten days of the month of Rejeb.

CHAPTER LXXX.

FIRING OF THE MANGONELS.

THE enemy had brought several large mangonels into play on the walls of the city, and the stones hurled by these engines were not without their effect on the ramparts. Fear was felt lest the wall should give way. They therefore took two large arrows, such as are shot from a great arbalist,[1] and making their heads red-hot, aimed them at one of the mangonels. They stuck in it and set it on fire. The enemy tried in vain to extinguish the flames, which were fanned by the violence of the wind. They caught the other mangonel, and it also was soon in a blaze. The heat was so intense that no one dared come near to stop the spreading of the flames. This was a great day for the Moslems; they gave themselves up to rejoicing, whilst the infidels were occupied in meditating on the ill-success of their efforts.

[1] Cross-bow. See p. 57.

CHAPTER LXXXI.

ACCOUNT OF THE MOVEMENTS OF THE KING OF THE GER-
MANS CONTINUED. STRATAGEM EMPLOYED BY THE
MARQUIS.

THE king of the Germans, having once set foot in Antioch,
seized that city out of the hands of its lord. He first began
to make his power felt by forcing that chief to execute his
commands ; then he took possession of the castle by
stratagem and treachery, and deposited his treasures there.
On the 25th of the month of Rejeb he set out for Acre, at
the head of his army and followers, and, passing through
Laodicea, came to Tripoli. The marquis, Lord of Tyre,
one of the wiliest and most influential of all the princes of
the Franks, left the place where they were encamped and
came to meet him. It was chiefly through the instrumentality of the marquis that foreign nations were stirred up to
come and fight us. He had had a great picture painted,
representing the city of Jerusalem ; you could see the
Komâma,[1] the goal of their pilgrimage, a building they
hold in the greatest reverence, for in it is the chapel of
the tomb in which they assert that the Messiah was laid
after His crucifixion. This tomb is the chief object of
their pilgrimages, and they believe that a light descends
upon it every year on the occasion of one of their feasts.
In this picture a Moslem horseman was represented as
trampling the tomb of the Messiah under his horse's hoofs,
whilst his beast was desecrating the monument with his
urine. The marquis had this picture carried beyond the
sea, and shown in all the market-places and wherever a

---

[1] The Church of the Resurrection is called in Arabic *el-Kiâma.*
The Moslems, to show their contempt, call it *el-Komâma*, 'dung.'

number of men met together.   Priests, clad in hair-cloth, with their heads uncovered, carried it with mourning and groans : and by the picture he wrought on their hearts, for this is the root of their religion ; and how many thereby became pilgrims God only knows.   Among the number was the king of the Germans and his army.   The marquis, as he had been the principal in exciting him to this war, went forth to meet him, to keep up his courage, and to help him on the way.   He took him by the coast-road, in order to avoid being attacked by the Moslems, who would have swarmed up in all directions had he tried to pass through the districts of Aleppo and Hamah ; in those parts the word of truth (the religious zeal of the Moslems) would have risen up against him on every side.   He would, moreover, have been in danger of being attacked by our leaders.   El-Melek el-Mozaffer, Lord of Hamah, marched against him at the head of a large body of troops that he had collected.   He came up with the Germans, and his vanguard attacked them on both flanks.   Had el-Melek ez-Zâher, Prince of Aleppo, come up in time with his army, the fate of the Germans would have been sealed : but *for every period there is a book* (Kurân xiii. 38).   Accounts do not agree as to the number of men in the German army, but I learned from the letters of one of our military correspondents that he computed them at five thousand, horse and foot together ; and according to all reports this army was two hundred thousand strong when it first took the field.   When the Germans set out from Laodicea on their march to Jebela, they left about sixty horses behind, so broken down by fatigue and want of food that they were nothing but skin and bones.   They continued their march, closely followed up by the Moslems, who harassed them by pilfering their goods, and killing and carrying off their men.   This state of things continued until they reached Tripoli. The Sultan received tidings of their approach on Tuesday, the 8th of Sh'abân, 586 (September 10, 1190), quite early in the morning. He heard the news with great calmness, and did not stir from the position he had taken up, refusing to divert his attention from the matter he had in hand. He had to guard and protect the city of Acre ; to keep watch on the movements of the besiegers ; to send out small parties to attack them unawares, and harass them night and day without a moment's respite. He displayed the greatest confidence in God throughout, looking to Him alone for support, and cheerfully busied himself in providing for the wants of his soldiers, and loading with gifts the various *fakîrs*, doctors of law, heads of religious communities, *'ulema*, and men of letters who came to visit him. The news (of the coming of the Germans) had made a great impression on me, but when I went into the Sultan's tent and saw his serenity and resolution I breathed more freely, and felt convinced that under him Islâm and its supporters would win a glorious triumph.

CHAPTER LXXXII.

SHIPS ARRIVE FROM EGYPT.

DURING the second ten days of the month of Sh'abân (middle of September), Behâ ed-Dîn Karakûsh, at that time governor of Acre, and Hossâm ed-Dîn Lulu, the chamberlain and commander of the fleet, wrote to the Sultan informing him that there were barely sufficient provisions in the city to last till the 15th of Sh'abân. They added that they had kept this from the knowledge of the garrison, lest they should become despondent. But the Sultan had already sent to Cairo, ordering them to fit out three ships and dispatch them to Acre, laden with victuals, provisions, and corn, and all that a besieged city would stand in need of; these supplies were to be sufficient to last the besieged throughout the winter. The three vessels sailed from Egypt, put out to sea, and reached Acre on the evening preceding the 15th of Sh'abân. When they arrived there was not enough food in the city for the following day. The enemy's fleet came out to attack them whilst the Moslem army was drawn up on the beach, calling aloud upon God, the indivisible and Almighty. The soldiers bared their heads whilst they supplicated God, beseeching Him to save the ships and allow them to enter the harbour. The Sultan stood on the beach, like a parent robbed of a child, witnessing the struggle, and imploring the help of his Lord, and the tempest of anxiety in his heart was beyond words. The fight raged round the Egyptian ships, which were attacked on all sides; but, thanks to the protection of God, there was a strong breeze, and they entered the harbour safe and sound in the midst of the furious shouts of the one side and the acclamations of the other. The garrison received them with great joy, and began to unload their cargoes; and it was a very happy night in the city. It was in the afternoon of Monday, the 14th of Sh'abân, that the ships arrived.

CHAPTER LXXXIII.

THE FRANKS BESIEGE THE FLY-TOWER.

ON the 22nd of Sh'abân the enemy fitted out a great number of boats to lay siege to the Fly-Tower,[1] which is

---

[1] *The Tower of Flies* is shown on Marino Sanuto's map of Acre, at the end of the western mole in the harbour, S. of the city.

CIVITAS ACON SIVE PTOLOMAYDA.

ACRE AS IT WAS WHEN LOST (A.D. 1291).
FROM THE PLAN GIVEN BY
MARINO SANUTO.

built on a rock at the entrance to the harbour, and is surrounded on all sides by the sea. It protects the harbour; every vessel (coming in) that gets past the tower is safe from attack by an enemy. The besiegers were anxious to get possession of it in order to make themselves masters of the port, when they could effectually close it against (Moslem) vessels, and prevent provisions entering the city. With this view they fixed turrets on the top of the masts of their ships and filled them with faggots, intending to sail close up to the Fly-Tower, and, as soon as they came alongside, to set the wooden towers on fire, and hurl them on to the terrace of the Fly-Tower; they would then take possession of it after they had killed the garrison. One boat was filled with combustibles to throw on the tower as soon as it should have caught fire. The besiegers filled another ship with wood and similar materials, with a view of sending it into the midst of the Moslem vessels in the harbour, and then setting it on fire, so as to burn them and the provisions with which they were laden. A third ship was covered in with a roof (*Kabu*) to protect the soldiers, who were drawn up underneath, against arrows and projectiles hurled from the engines of war. These men, as soon as they had set (the tower) on fire were, according to their instructions, to withdraw under the roof, so as to be sheltered from our missiles. They dispatched the aforesaid (the first) vessel towards the tower, in great hopes, for the wind was favourable. Then they set fire to the fire-ship which was to go among the Moslem vessels, and also to the tower that was to consume the defenders of the Fly-Tower; they were throwing some more naphtha on it, when, by the grace of God, the wind changed and upset their plans. They then tried to extinguish the flames on the ship they had set on fire, but in vain, and all the godless crew

14—2

perished. The fire-ship dispatched against the Moslem vessels had caught fire ; but our comrades leapt on board and took possession of it. The crew of the ship that had been roofed in hesitated, were seized with fear and attempted to turn about ; a dispute ensued on the subject, and in the scuffle and confusion the ship capsized ; as no one could get out from underneath the roof, every one on board perished. These events were unmistakable signs of the will of God, and great wonders upholding God's religion; and it was a day of testimony.

CHAPTER LXXXIV.

JUNCTION BETWEEN THE GERMANS AND THE ENEMY'S ARMY.

WE will now continue our narrative of the king of the Germans. He halted in Tripoli to allow his troops time to rest and recover their strength, and sent on to Acre to announce that he would soon join the besiegers. They did not receive this intelligence with great joy, now that the marquis, Lord of Tyre, had become the king's chief counsellor and confidential adviser ; for King Geoffrey,[1] who, thanks to his army, was supreme in the districts on the coast, and whose decision was always final in their councils, saw very clearly that the German's arrival would deprive him of his authority. During the last ten days of the month of Sh'abân he (Frederick, duke of Swabia, chief of the German army) had some ships fitted out, and collected others from all parts, for he saw that unless they

---

[1] Beha ed-Dîn always makes the mistake of writing 'Geoffrey' for 'Guy.'

went by sea they would most certainly be lost, as our men held all the passes through which he would have to march. Then, having embarked with all his men, horses, and supplies, he set out to join the Frankish army. Hardly had he started before a furious wind sprang up, and his fleet was almost swallowed up in the waves that broke over them in all directions. Three cargo-vessels were lost, and the remainder returned to port to await a more favourable wind. After the lapse of a few days they put out once more with a favourable breeze, and succeeded in making Tyre. The marquis and the king remained there, sending all that remained of their troops to join the army that was encamped before Acre. On the 6th of Ramaḍân (October 7), the king of the Germans[1] embarked alone with a few followers, and arrived in the camp of the Franks the same day towards sunset. We were informed of what took place by the spies, and people who were allowed to visit the camp. His arrival produced a great effect both on besiegers and besieged. Being anxious to signalize his presence by some feat of arms, he made a speech to the Franks a few days after his arrival, reproaching them for having remained still so long, and representing how much better it would be to meet the Moslems in the open field. When they showed him the dangers of such a course, he declared they must absolutely make a sortie and attack the Moslem advanced guard, 'just to test it,' he said, 'to try its strength and see what they can do.' Thereupon he rode out to attack the guard, and the greater number of the Franks followed him. They crossed the plain lying between the hill they occupied and that of el-'Aiâdîya, where the advanced guard was drawn up. The different

---

[1] Frederick of Suabia was not king of the Germans, but brother of the Emperor Henry VI.

divisions of our army occupied this position in turn, and
that day it was the turn of the Sultan's *halka.* When they
saw the enemy advancing, they waited facing them, and
made them taste death in the conflict. As soon as the
Sultan heard what was taking place, he mounted his horse
and rode to the hill of Kîsân, followed by a great number
of Moslems. When the enemy saw this movement, they
withdrew, having had several men killed and a great
number wounded, and they returned to their camp about
sunset. Night separated the combatants. We had two
killed and a great many wounded. But the enemy of
God was baffled. After this, the king of the Germans
turned his attention to attacking the city, and took care
that the blockade was maintained very strictly. He had
some extraordinary engines made, of a most peculiar construction, the terrible aspect of which made the garrison
fear for the safety of the city. Amongst these new
inventions was a great machine, covered with iron plates
and mounted on wheels, that would accommodate a great
number of soldiers. It was furnished with a huge head
with a strong iron neck which was to butt against the walls.
It was called a *ram.* It required a great many men to
move it, and was to strike the walls with great force and
such impetus that they would give way before it. Another
of their machines was in the form of a roof, made to cover
a number of men ; it had an elongated head like the
share of a plough. The first of these machines would
destroy a tower by its mere weight, the other by its
combined weight and pointed form. This one was called
a *cat.* As to the mantelets and huge ladders they made,
they could not be counted. They also had a great ship,
which carried a tower provided with a drawbridge, which,
when they came close up to a wall, could be let down by
some peculiar mechanism, thus forming a way by means

of which soldiers could be introduced into the place
attacked. They intended to bring this machine alongside
the Fly-Tower and get possession thereof.

CHAPTER LXXXV.

THE RAM AND OTHER MACHINES OF WAR ARE BURNT.

WHEN the enemy had completed these machines, they
began to bring them up to the city, which they intended
to attack on all sides at once. The garrison displayed
undiminished resolution; as they were fighting in God's
cause, they determined to make a desperate resistance.
On Monday, the 3rd of Ramadân of the above year
(October 4) the Syrian troops, splendidly equipped, well
disciplined, and excellently armed, came into the camp
under the leadership of el-Melek ez-Zâher, the Sultan's son,
and Prince of Aleppo. This prince was accompanied by
Sâbek ed-Dîn, Lord of Sheizer, and Mejed ed-Dîn, Lord
of B'albek. The Sultan, although his health was not good,
and he was suffering from an attack of bilious fever,
mounted his horse and went out to meet them. This day
was like a feast-day in more respects than one. The
enemy marched close up to the city in great multitudes;
the inhabitants, the garrison, and the Moslem leaders most
renowned for the wisdom of their counsel, allowed them to
draw near; then—when they had plunged the claws of
their cupidity into the city, dragged their engines of war
right up to the walls, and lowered a number of men into
the ditches—then, and not till then, they hurled down
upon them bolts from their arbalists, stones from their
mangonels, arrows from their bows, and various combustibles; then they sallied out in a body, throwing open

the gates, prepared to lay down their lives for God. They rushed upon the enemy from all sides, and fell upon the people in the ditches unawares. God filled the hearts of our enemies with terror, they fled pell-mell to the protection of their camp, for they had lost a great number of killed and wounded, and many of those who had gone down into the ditches had lost their lives. The Moslems, seeing that the besiegers had given themselves up to panic and flight, ran up to their ram and succeeded in setting it on fire by throwing naphtha and flaming brands on it. Then there rose mighty shouts of the *takbîr* and the *tahlîl.* The conflagration of the *ram* raged so fiercely that it spread to the *cat*, which was burnt to the ground. The Moslems attached chains to the ram, furnished at the ends with iron hooks, and dragged it, all flaming as it was, right into the city. It was built of enormou beams. They threw water over it, and in a few days it became quite cool. I have been told that the iron used in the construction of this machine weighed one hundred Syrian quintals, each quintal weighing one hundred *ratl*.[1] One Syrian *ratl* is equal to four and a half Baghdad *ratl*. The head of the machine was brought to the Sultan and laid before him. I saw it and moved it myself; it was in form like the great axle of a mill-stone. I should think this machine would have destroyed anything it was brought to bear against. This was a glorious day for Islâm. The enemy, baulked of their expectations, dragged back all the machines that were left, and made no further movement. The Sultan was filled with joy at the coming of his son, el-Melek ez-Zâher, for he regarded his presence as the certain forerunner of good fortune. Indeed, this was the second time that el-Melek's arrival had coincided with the winning of a battle. On Wednesday, the 15th of Rama-

[1] The ordinary *ratl* weighs twelve ounces (Troy weight).

ḍân, our comrades sallied out (of the harbour) of the city
with several galleys and made an unexpected attack on
the ship that had been got ready to storm and take the
Fly-Tower. They threw bottles full of naphtha into it,
the ship caught fire, and the flames rose to a great height.
This occurrence grieved the king of the Germans very
much, and caused him the greatest vexation. On Thursday, the 16th, a carrier-pigeon brought us a letter from
Aleppo, in which was enclosed another from Hamah. In
the letter we were informed that the prince, Lord of
Antioch, had gone out at the head of his troops on an expedition against the Moslem villages that lay nearest to
his city. The officers and troops in the service of el-Melek
ez-Zâher were watching his movements, and had laid
several ambushes, which were unknown to the enemy until
they fell into them and were put to the sword ; they had
killed seventy-five (of the Christians) and taken a number
of prisoners. The prince himself had taken refuge in a
place called Shîha, from whence he had escaped to his own
city. During the second ten days of this month two ships
that were coming to the enemy, laden with men, women,
and children, and a great quantity of corn and sheep, went
aground in a storm of wind. They both fell into the
hands of the Moslems. The enemy had just seized one of
our ships that was bringing men and money to Acre, but
the taking of these two ships counteracted the bad impression produced on our men by the loss of our vessel, and
amply compensated for the mischance. From that time
we used continually to receive news from the spies and
people whom the enemy allowed in the camp, and we were
informed by them that the besiegers intended to come out
and fight a pitched battle with the Moslem army. The
Sultan was ill just then, suffering from a bilious fever ; he
therefore thought it best to move his army back as far as

the hills of Shefr'am.[1] He repaired thither himself on the
19th of Ramaḍân and took up his position on the summit
of the hill, and the troops encamped on the tops of the
tells to avoid the mud and prepare for settling into winter
quarters. The same day Zein ed-Dîn Yûsuf, son of Zein
ed-Dîn ('Ali), and Lord of Arbela, being very ill from two
successive fevers, asked leave to return to his own country.
Not obtaining this, he solicited and received permission to
go to Nazareth. There he spent several days nursing himself; but his illness grew worse and worse, and he died on
the night preceding Tuesday, the 28th of Ramaḍân
(October 29, 1190). His brother, Mozaffer ed-Dîn Kûkbûri,
was present when he died. Everyone deplored the prince's
fate, dying so young and so far from home. The Sultan
granted Mozaffer ed-Dîn the government of Arbela, and
received in exchange Ḥarrân, Edessa, Someïsât, el-
Muezzer, and the districts dependent on those cities; but
he gave him also the city of Sheherzûr. Having confirmed
these arrangements by oath, he summoned el-Melek el-
Mozaffer Taḳi ed-Dîn 'Omar, son of his brother Shahanshah (Prince of Princes), to take the position Mozaffer
ed-Dîn had occupied, and to fill the vacancy that his
departure would occasion. Mozaffer ed-Dîn remained in
the camp until Taḳi ed-Dîn arrived. On the 3rd of
Shawâl (November 3) Taḳi ed-Dîn came, bringing with
him Mo'ezz ed-Dîn.

[1] *Shefr'am*, now *Shefa 'Amr*, on the road to Nazareth, 10 miles
S.E. of Acre.

CHAPTER LXXXVI.

ADVENTURE OF MO'EZZ ED-DÎN.

MO'EZZ ED-DÎN, surnamed Sinjâr Shah (King of Sinjâr), was the son of Seif ed-Dîn Ghâzi, son of Maudûd and grandson of Zenghi. At the time of which we are speaking, he was prince of Jezîrat Ibn 'Omar. We have already recorded the date of his arrival to take part in the Holy War. Fatigued, tired-out, and overdone by the length of his stay, he several times sent messengers and letters to the Sultan, begging permission to return home. The Sultan declined granting him leave on the ground that though he was constantly receiving messengers from the Franks, who were now anxious to obtain terms of peace, he could not diminish his forces before he knew for certain whether there would be war or peace. The prince, nevertheless, continued to press his request for leave, and on the day of the breaking of the fast in the year 586 (November 1, 1190), he appeared at dawn at the entrance of the Sultan's tent, and demanded admittance. The Sultan declined to receive him on account of an illness from which he was suffering, and which had upset his health ; but Mo'ezz ed-Dîn persisted in his demand, until at last he was suffered to enter. He presented himself respectfully before the Sultan, and earnestly requested leave to depart. The Sultan answered him by pointing out once more the reasons of his refusal, adding : 'At a time such as this it is my duty to collect troops rather than to dismiss them.' The prince then knelt to kiss his hand in the manner of a man who is taking farewell, and left the tent at once. He went straight back to his troops, and commanded them to

abandon their cooking-pots and the food they contained,
and to strike their tents and follow him.   When the Sultan
was informed of the foolhardy step he had taken, he gave
orders that a letter should be written to the runaway prince
in the following terms : ' On several occasions you craved
my protection and told me the fear you entertained of
several members of your family, who, you said, were prepared to attack your person and take the city out of your
hands.   I granted your petition, and gave you both shelter
and support.   Since then you have laid hands on the goods
of your subjects ; you have spilt their blood, and brought
disgrace upon them.   Several times I sent to you, warning
you to desist from such a course, but you paid no heed to
my commands.   Afterwards, when this war arose—on the
results of which the future of our religion so largely depends
—you came here with the army, on my invitation, as you
yourself know, and as all the people know.   After remaining here some time, you grew restless, made a commotion,
and took your departure full of discontent, without waiting
to see the result of our war against the enemy.   Now, you
may do as you will ; look out for another protector, and
defend yourself as best you can against those who may
attack you.   I shall concern myself no further on your
account.'   A courier was dispatched with this letter on a
dromedary, and overtook the runaway close to Tiberias.
The prince acquainted himself with the contents of the
missive, but took no heed of their import, and continued
on his way.   El-Melek el-Mozaffer Taki ed-Dîn, who had
been summoned to replace Mozaffer ed-Dîn, whose departure we recorded above, met the prince on a hill called
the 'Akaba of Fîk,[1] and seeing how he was hastening along,
and that for some reason or other he seemed not best

---

[1] The *'Akabah* (or ' Ascent ') *of Fîk* was the road to the heights
E. of the Sea of Galilee.

pleased, he asked him what was the matter. The prince told him what had occurred, complaining that the Sultan had given him neither a robe of honour nor permission to depart. From this el-Melek el-Mozaffer saw at once that the prince had come away without the Sultan's leave, and even against his commands. He therefore said to him : 'The best thing you can do is to return to your duty in the camp, and wait until the Sultan will listen to you. You are but a young man, and have not reflected on the consequences of your action.' The prince replied : 'I cannot go back ;' whereupon Taki ed-Dîn said : 'Go back, or I shall make you ; there will be no peace of mind if you go off in this fashion.' The prince persisted in his determination, and answered el-Mozaffer very rudely ; whereupon the latter said : 'Back you go, willing or not.' Now, Taki ed-Dîn was a very resolute character, ready for any emergency, and afraid of no man. Therefore the prince returned with him, knowing full well that, unless he did so of his own accord, he would be stopped and taken by force. When they approached the camp, el-Melek el-'Âdel went out to meet Taki ed-Dîn, to show him honour, and, as we were in his train, we saw that Taki ed-Dîn had brought Mo'ezz ed-Dîn with him. The two princes (el-'Âdel and Taki ed-Dîn) repaired to the Sultan's tent, and obtained pardon for el-Mo'ezz. That prince was so fearful for his safety, that he sought and obtained leave to pitch his tent close to Taki ed-Dîn, remaining in that position until the time of his departure.

CHAPTER LXXXVII.

'IMÂD ED-DÎN REQUESTS LEAVE TO DEPART.

'IMÂD ED-DÎN, uncle of the above young prince, made
continual applications for permission to return home, complaining of the severity of the winter, for which he had
been able to make no preparations. The Sultan assigned
as an objection that negotiations for peace were pending
with the enemy, and that, if matters turned out as he
expected, he had decided, with the advice of his council,
that 'Imâd ed-Dîn ought to be present at the ratification
of the treaty. The prince then demanded winter tents,
but did not succeed in getting them; the money he
petitioned for was also refused. Messages were continually sent backwards and forwards on this subject between
the Sultan and the prince, the Sultan always finding good
reasons to justify his position. I myself took a part in
these negotiations. 'Imâd ed-Dîn's determination to depart
was so firmly fixed that it baffles description; whilst the
Sultan's resolution was equally strong to detain the prince
until the result of the negotiations with the Franks should
be known. This being the state of things, 'Imâd ed-Dîn
went so far as to send a formal request to the Sultan,
written in his own hand, asking permission to depart. A
certain bitterness was noticeable under the courteous terms
of this letter. The Sultan wrote the following words on
the back of the petition with his own royal hand : 'I should
like to know what advantage it would be to you to lose
the support of a man like me.' After 'Imâd ed-Dîn had
received this answer, he refrained from making any further
applications.

CHAPTER LXXXVIII.

THE ENEMY LEAVE THEIR CAMP AND GO AS FAR AS THE SPRING HEAD.

WE were constantly kept informed as to the enemy; they were suffering severely from scarcity of food, for famine prevailed throughout their territories, and had now invaded their camp. The scarcity reached such a height that at Antioch the price of a sack of corn rose to ninety-six Tyrian dinars. But this only strengthened the obstinate resolution of the besiegers. Nevertheless, the uncertainty of their position and their sufferings from want of food, which grew worse from day to day, caused a great many to desert to us, so as to escape the pangs of hunger. The rest, encouraged by an idea that the Sultan's illness kept him to his bed, left camp with their horse and foot, well supplied with provisions and materials for encamping. This was on Monday, the 11th of Shawâl (November 11, 1190). They made for the wells sunk by the Moslems below Tell 'Ajjûl, when they were encamped on the hill. They carried with them a supply of barley sufficient for four days. When the Sultan was informed that they had sallied forth, he ordered the advanced guard to retreat before them as far as Tell Kîsân. At this time they were drawn up on the hill of el-'Aiâdîya. The enemy halted close to the wells[1] about four o'clock that day, and passed the night there. Throughout the night our advanced guard maintained a strict watch round their encampment. At dawn the next morning the Sultan received news from the guard that the enemy was preparing to mount; but he

---

[1] There are still wells at *Tell Keisân.*

had already given orders, early in the night, for the baggage to withdraw to Nazareth and to el-Ḳeimûn.[1] The baggage was sent back, but our troops did not stir from their position, and I was amongst those who remained with the Sultan. He then drew up his army in order of battle, arranging them by right wing, left wing, and centre; after which he mounted his charger, and, at the call of the herald (*Shâwîsh*) they mounted. The army proceeded to march as far as a *tell* in the hills of el-Kharrûba, where we halted. The right wing marched on until its right flank rested on the mountain; then the left wing began moving and advanced until its extreme left reached the river,[2] close to the seashore. The leaders of the right wing were el-Melek el-Afḍal, Lord of Damascus, the Sultan's son; el-Melek ez-Zâher, Lord of Aleppo, another of the Sultan's sons; el-Melek ez-Zâfer, Lord of Boṣra, the Sultan's son; 'Alâ ed-Dîn Khorrem Shah, son of 'Izz ed-Dîn, Lord of Mosul; and his brother, el-Melek el-'Âdel,[3] who occupied the extreme right of this wing. Then came Hossâm ed-Dîn Ibn Lajîn; and next Ḳâimâz en-Nejmi, the eunuch; 'Izz ed-Dîn Jordîk (who had been one of Nûr ed-Dîn's memlûks); Hossâm ed-Dîn Bishâra, Lord of Bâniâs; Bedr ed-Dîn Dolderim, Lord of Tell-Bâsher; and a number of other emirs. The left wing was commanded by 'Imâd ed-Dîn Zenghi, Lord of Sinjâr; and his nephew, Mo'ezz ed-Dîn, Lord of Jezîrat Ibn 'Omar; and the extreme left was under the command of his nephew, el-Melek el-Mozaffer Taḳi ed-Dîn. 'Imâd ed-Dîn Zenghi,

[1] *El-Keimûn* (Jokneam of O.T., called Caimont by the Franks) was below Carmel by the Kishon, 18 miles S. of Acre.

[2] Apparently the south branch of the Belus at '*Ayûn el-Bass*, in front of the Franks and on their left flank.

[3] El-Melek el-'Âdel Nûr ed-Dîn Arslân Shah, the emir named above, was son of 'Izz ed-Dîn Mas'ûd, and, consequently, brother of 'Alâ ed-Dîn Khorrem Shah.

who was too ill to be at his post, had gone back with
the baggage; but his troops remained with the army.
On the left wing might be seen Seif ed-Dîn 'Ali Ibn
Ahmed el-Meshṭûb at the head of the troops (furnished
by the Kurdish tribes) of Mihrâni and Hekkâr; with him
were Khoshterîn, and several other Kurdish emirs. The
Sultan's *ḥalka* (or guard) occupied the centre. By the
Sultan's orders, each body of troops detached a company
of marksmen to join the advanced guard and surround
the enemy. He concealed several battalions behind the
hills, hoping they would be able to find an opportunity of
surprising the Franks. The enemy's troops continued to
advance, though they were entirely surrounded by our
marksmen; they followed the east bank of the river until
they came to the spring head.[1] There they wheeled, and
crossing to the west bank, came to a halt on rising ground,
where they pitched their tents. Their camp stretched
lengthwise from the hill to the river bank. During this
day's march they had had a great many wounded, and lost
a considerable number of killed. Whenever one of their
men was wounded, they took him up and carried him with
them, and they buried their dead as they marched, so that
we might not know the extent of their losses. They came to
a halt in the afternoon of Tuesday. Our troops then quitted
them, and returned to take up advantageous positions for
purposes of resistance and defence. The Sultan gave
orders for the left wing to face the enemy with their flank
resting on the sea-shore, whilst the right wing was drawn up
facing the river, their extreme right resting on the east

---

[1] *Râs el-Mâ* ('the spring head'), now *'Ayûn el-Bass* ('springs of
the swamp'), immediately E. of Tell Kurdâneh, 6 miles S. of Acre.
According to De Vinsauf, Geoffrey, brother of King Guy, made this
expedition in order to meet a convoy landed at Haifa, which he brought
back safely to Acre, forcing the bridge mentioned below.

bank.[1]   Meanwhile, our marksmen harassed the enemy with
an uninterrupted shower of arrows.   The whole night was
passed in this manner.   The Sultan, attended by us of his
suite, went to the top of Mount Kharrûba, and took up his
quarters in a small tent ; his attendants camped all round
in tents as small as his, and in full view of the enemy.
News of the enemy came in every hour until morning
broke; and the next day, being Wednesday, the 13th of
Shawâl (November 13, 1190), he was informed that they
were preparing to mount.   He lost no time, therefore, in
getting into the saddle, drew up his troops, and advanced
to the hills of el-Kharrûba that lay nearest the enemy,
whence he could observe all their movements.   Although
he was suffering from illness, and his body was very weak,
his heart was as resolute as ever.   He then sent an order
to his troops to attack, to hem the enemy in closely, and to
charge them from all sides ; the reserves were ordered to
keep close at hand—not too near, and not too far off—
to support those who were engaged.   This state of things
lasted until noon, when the enemy prepared to leave the
west bank of the river,[2] and cross to the other side to
return to their camp ; they were thereupon smartly attacked
on all sides, except in the direction of the river.   A fierce
fight ensued, in which they suffered heavy losses, burying
their dead, and carrying off their wounded, as is their
custom.   The standard of the Franks, on a staff as tall as

[1] The Moslem position thus extended N.E. and S.W., S. of the
Franks and N. of the Kishon, their base being at Shefa 'Amr — a
retreat of three miles from their former line near Tell Keisân.   The
right flank was near *'Ayûn el-Bass.*

[2] The Franks marched along the plain E. of the *Nahr N'amein,* or
S. affluent of the Belus River, towards *Tell Kurdâneh.*   Beha ed-Dîn
does not mention the convoy, but the Moslem left must have been
broken, and the attack now made was from the E. and N., to prevent
the retreat of the Franks by the D'aûk bridge.

a minaret, was set up on a cart drawn by mules ; it had a white ground with red spots ; the top of the (staff) was surmounted by a cross. The Franks defended it zealously, even at the cost of their lives. Their foot-soldiers formed an outer ring like a wall to cover their cavalry, and they used their arbalists and bows with such skill that no one could get near, or single out their horsemen. Meanwhile, the Moslems never ceased beating their drums, sounding their trumpets, and proclaiming with a loud voice the unity and power of God. The Sultan continually reinforced the detachments of marksmen from the reserves and the troops he had with him, so that at last he was left with but very few. The enemy continued to advance until past mid-day, when they reached the head of D'aûk bridge.[1] Their troops were then parched with thirst, worn out with fatigue, and riddled with wounds, and, moreover, they had suffered terribly from the heat. The Moslems exhibited the greatest valour this day, and the soldiers of the *halka* (the guard) particularly distinguished themselves. This body had had a great many men wounded ; amongst the number was 'Aiâz[2] et-Tawîl (the long man), who had displayed the greatest bravery in the fight ; Seif ed-Dîn Yâzkôj had received several wounds ; there were a great number of wounded among the memlûks and in the *halka*. Our men continued to press the enemy closely until past mid-day, when they reached D'aûk bridge and crossed it, cutting it down as soon as they had gone over, to prevent the Moslems following them. The Sultan withdrew once more to the hill (*tell*) of el-Kharrûba, which was guarded by a detachment of troops, and reports were constantly brought in to him of the movements of the enemy. During the night

---

[1] This bridge, N. of *D'aûk*, crossed the E. affluent of the Belus (now *Wadi Halzûn*), 3½ miles S.E. of Acre.

[2] Some editions have *Kâbâr et-Tawîl*.

he decided to attack the remainder of the enemy. He therefore wrote to the people in the city informing them of his plan, and commanding them to make a sortie on their side as soon as he should begin the attack. As he received no reply to his letter, he abandoned the idea. On Thursday morning, the 14th, as soon as the Sultan heard that the enemy were preparing to move, he mounted his horse, and drew up his battalions in their appointed order, commanding that no one should commence fighting until the signal was given. He feared an unexpected attack from the enemy's troops, who had advanced close to his camp. He posted his battalions on the east bank of the river that they might be in readiness to advance on the enemy, and pursue them to their camp. Amongst the leaders of the Franks on this expedition were Count Henry and the marquis. The son of the king of the Germans had remained in the camp with a strong body of troops. As soon as the enemy reached their camp, the battalions which had been left behind, and were fresh and eager for the fight, sallied out, and attacked the Moslem advanced guard. In the combat that ensued the enemy suffered heavily in killed and wounded. The Moslems lost five men, and the Franks lost a man of high rank amongst them. He rode a great charger, covered with a hammer-cloth of chain-mail that reached down to its hoofs, and he was apparelled in most extraordinary fashion. When the fight (*literally*, the war) was finished, his countrymen sent to ask his body at the Sultan's hands. The body was given to them ; but the head, which they were anxious to have as well, could not be found. The Sultan returned to his camp, and ordered the baggage forward from the place to which it had been sent. Both sides took up their respective positions once more. 'Imâd ed-Dîn also returned, having got rid of his fever. The Sultan was still very ill, and his recovery was hindered by his vexation at the escape of the Franks who had made the sortie. He had not been able to take an active part in the encounters, and all the while I myself witnessed the tears of vexation he shed. I was present, too, when he sent out his sons, one after another, to take part in the battle, and engage in the fight. I was there when someone said in his presence that the air of the plain of Acre had been made unhealthy by the great number of dead left by either side on the field. When he heard these words, he quoted the following verse, applying it to himself, ' Kill me and Mâlek ; kill Mâlek with me.'[1] By this he meant that he would be content to die, provided the enemies of God perished with him. This reply created a deep impression throughout the Moslem army.

CHAPTER LXXXIX.

FIGHT AT THE AMBUSH.

ON the 22nd of the month of Shawâl the Sultan, being minded to lay an ambush for the enemy, chose from his army a number of well-armed, brave, and resolute soldiers, who were all good horsemen. He ordered them to repair by night to the foot of a *tell* that lies to the north of

---

[1] In the battle of the Camel, which took place in the year 36 of the Hejra, between the followers of Khalif 'Ali and those of 'Aisha, Muhammad's widow, Mâlek el-Ashter, one of 'Ali's most devoted friends, attacked 'Abd Allah Ibn ez-Zobeir, and wounded him in the head. The wounded man clutched at his adversary, and fell to the ground with him. They struggled together for some time, and Ibn ez-Zobeir called out to his soldiers, in the words of an old poet, to kill Mâlek at any cost, even if they had to kill him at the same time. The combatants were separated by their respective friends. — Ibn el-Athîr's ' Kamel,' vol. iii., p. 206.

Acre, not far from the enemy's camp, and there to conceal
themselves.   This was the position El Melek el-'Âdel had
held in the fight that bears his name.   A few of their
number were instructed to show themselves to the enemy
and to advance in the direction of their camp ; then, as
soon as they had drawn them out, they were to take to
flight and rejoin their comrades.   During the night these
men repaired to the *tell* and hid themselves.   On the
following day, which was Saturday, the 23rd of the same
month (November 23), as soon as the sun had risen, a few
of their number, mounted on good horses, made their way
towards the camp, discharging arrows at the Franks.   The
enemy, provoked by this unceasing shower of darts, came
out to avenge themselves to the number of two hundred
knights, armed at all points, mounted on horses splendidly
caparisoned.   There was not a single foot-soldier among
them.   They advanced towards their assailants, expecting
to make short work of such a small company.   When our
men saw them advancing they began to retreat towards
the ambush, fighting as they went.   As soon as the Franks
had reached the spot, the soldiers who were in ambush
raised a mighty shout and rushed upon them, like lions
springing on their prey.   The Franks at first stood firm
and fought bravely, then they turned their backs and
began to retreat ; but the Moslems, having them in their
power, attacked them so furiously that they stretched
several of them dead upon the ground, took a great
number of prisoners, and obtained possession of their
horses and arms.   When the news of this success reached
the Moslem army, cries of the *tahlîl* and the *takbîr* (*There
is but one God ! God is almighty !*) rose on every side.
The Sultan mounted and went to meet the brave men
who had fought for the faith.   I was on duty at that time
and went with him.   We went as far as the hill (*tell*) of

Kîsân,[1] where we met the foremost of the band, and the Sultan halted there to await the others. Everyone congratulated these brave warriors, and thanked them for their successful enterprise. The Sultan reviewed the prisoners, and ascertained their rank and position. Amongst them was the leader of the body of troops that the French king had sent out to the assistance of the besiegers; the king's treasurer was also among the prisoners. The Sultan returned to the camp filled with joy, and ordered the prisoners to be brought before him. He also commanded the herald to proclaim that all those who had taken captives should bring them in person before him. He received all who had high rank amongst their countrymen, and who were held in good esteem by them, with every mark of respect, and clad them in robes of honour. He gave a furred robe of the first class to the leader of the King of France's troops; and on all the others, without exception, he bestowed a Jerkh fur, for they were suffering greatly from the cold, which was at that time very severe. He ordered a banquet to be spread before them, of which they all partook, and commanded a tent to be pitched for them close to his own. He constantly showed them marks of great kindness, and sometimes invited their leader to his table. By his orders they were supplied with horses to carry them to Damascus, and they were treated with the greatest respect. They received permission to write to their friends, and to send to the (besiegers') camp for their clothes and any other things they might need. They availed themselves of this privilege, and departed for Damascus.

[1] *Tell Kîsân* is 1½ miles E. of D'aûk, and 5½ miles S.E. of Acre.

CHAPTER XC.

THE RETURN OF THE ARMY AFTER THE HOLY WAR.

WINTER had now come on, and the sea was tossed by
storms ; it was therefore certain that the enemy would not
engage in a pitched battle ; we knew also that the heavy
rains would prevent their making any progress in the
siege of the city. Therefore the Sultan permitted his
troops to return to their respective countries, to rest
and give their horses time to recover before the season
arrived to recommence fighting. The first of the chiefs
to depart was 'Imâd ed-Dîn Zenghi, Lord of Sinjâr, with
whose impatience to obtain leave we have already
acquainted the reader. He set out on the 15th of the
month of Shawâl (November 15, 1190). He was followed
on the same day by his nephew Sinjâr Shah, Lord of
Jezîrat Ibn 'Omar. They had both received from the
Sultan more marks of favour, such as robes of honour,
rich presents, and curiosities, than that prince had ever
bestowed on any other chief. 'Alâ ed-Dîn, son of the
Lord of Mosul, set out on the 1st of the month of
Zu el-Ḳ'ada (November 30) laden with honours, precious
gifts, and rare and curious things. El-Melek el-Mozaffer
Taḳi ed-Dîn and el-Melek ez-Zâher postponed their departure until the following year, 587 of the Hejira
(1191 A.D.) ; the latter set out on the 9th of Moḥarrem
(February 6), and el-Melek el-Mozaffer started from the
camp on the 3rd of Ṣafer (March 2). There then remained
with the Sultan but a very few emirs and his especial *halka*
(guard). In the month of Zu el-Ḳ'ada, the previous year,
the Sultan had received a visit from Zulf Endaz.[1] He

---

[1] Some copies read *Zulfetdar*.

treated him with great honour, and gave him entertainment suitable to his rank; the day he arrived he had a splendid banquet set before him, and conversed with him in the most friendly fashion. The object of this man's visit was to obtain a decree for his reinstatement in property he had formerly held in the provinces of Nisiba and Khabûr, and of which he had been wrongfully deprived. The Sultan signed an order for their restoration, clad him with a robe of honour, and treated him with every mark of good-will. Zulf Endaz left us filled with joy and full of gratitude for the Sultan's goodness.

CHAPTER XCI.

THE SULTAN RELIEVES THE GARRISON OF THE CITY.

THE sea had now become very tempestuous, and the besiegers, being thereby prevented from employing their ships against the city, beached all that were left of their galleys. The Sultan then devoted his attention to introducing a fresh garrison into Acre, and stocking the city with provisions and supplies, with money and stores of war. He also took measures for the relief of the officers, who were worn out by their long imprisonment in the city, and made loud complaints of their sufferings and fatigue, for they had been obliged to watch night after night, and had fought night and day without cessation. He appointed Emîr Seif ed-Dîn 'Ali el-Meshtûb head of the new garrison; and that officer entered the city on the 16th of Moharrem in the year 587 (February 13, 1191). On the same day the retiring commandant, Emîr Hossâm ed-Dîn Abu el-Heija, with his comrades and all the other officers, left the castle, as Seif ed-Dîn was entering the city at the head of a large body of officers and men.　By the Sultan's orders every man who went into the city had to take with him a year's provisions.　El-Melek el-'Âdel repaired to Haifa[1] with his troops; this place is on the seashore, and he sent ships thence to Acre laden with supplies.　He remained there to enlist volunteers for the garrison at Acre, and to guard the victuals and supplies destined for that place from any attack by the enemy.　Seven ships laden with corn, provisions and money, which had been fitted out a long time since in Egypt by the Sultan's orders, had gone to Acre on the 2nd of the month of Zu el-Hijja in the previous year (December 31).　One of these ships had struck on a rock close to the harbour, and the whole of the garrison had gone down to the seashore to endeavour to save her cargo.　The enemy took advantage of this opportunity to make a sharp assault on the city from the land side.　They came close up to the walls, and began scaling them with a single ladder.　The people of the city ran up at once and killed a number of their men, forcing them to give up their enterprise and retreat.　The ships we have just mentioned were so tossed by the wind and waves that they struck one upon another, and were all lost, with the cargoes they had brought, and, it is said, not less than sixty men.　These ships contained a great quantity of corn that would have been sufficient to provision the city for a whole year.　This disaster was a great blow to the spirits of the Moslems, and a bitter vexation to the Sultan.　This was the first omen of the coming fall of the city.　On the night preceding Sunday, the 7th of Zu el-Hijja (January 5, 1191) a large part of the wall of the city fell on the outworks and destroyed them also for some distance; this was the second omen of the fall of the

---

[1] On the south of the bay of Acre, 9 miles from that city.

city. Encouraged by this accident, the enemy poured
towards the breach in great multitudes ; but the garrison,
full of courage, resisted them most effectually, standing in
the breach like a living rampart. All the masons, artificers
and workmen in the city were collected together at once,
and whilst they laboured to close the breach and rebuild
the wall, they were protected against the enemy by a body
of archers and mangonel-men. In the course of a few
nights the work was completed, and the wall was better
built than it had been in the first instance.

CHAPTER XCII.

SEVERAL SHIPS BELONGING TO THE ENEMY ARE CAPTURED.

A GREAT number of deserters had come over to us, driven
by want of food to leave the Frank camp. These men
said to the Sultan : ' If you will supply us with ships and
smaller craft, we will protect you against the enemy by
sea, and we will share our booty in equal parts with the
Moslems.' The Sultan gave them a bark (*barkûs*) a small
kind of vessel, in which they embarked ; they then fell in
with some merchantmen, whose cargoes consisted chiefly
of ingots of silver and silversmiths' work for the enemy's
camp. They boarded these ships and succeeded in
capturing them after a sharp fight. On the 13th of
Zu el-Hijja (January 11, 1191) of the aforesaid year, they
brought the rich booty and the prisoners they had taken
to the Sultan. I was present when they were admitted,
and remarked amongst the articles they had brought a
table of silver, on which was (a casket inlaid with ?) the
same metal. The Sultan left them the whole, reserving

nothing for himself. The Moslems rejoiced to see how God had inflicted a defeat on the enemy by means of their own men.

CHAPTER XCIII.

DEATH OF THE SON OF THE KING OF THE GERMANS.

THE winter season, which was attended with incessant rain and frequent changes of temperature, made the plain exceedingly unhealthy and caused heavy mortality amongst the Franks. In addition to this, scarcity of food grew greater every day, and the sea, on which they depended for supplies of provisions from all parts, was now impassable. Every day from one to two hundred people died in the camp ; the number of deaths was even greater if some reports speak true. The son of the king of the Germans fell grievously sick, and this, combined with an internal complaint from which he was suffering, carried him off. He died on the 22nd of Zu el-Hijja, 586 (January 20, 1191). The Franks mourned greatly for him, and lighted for themselves great fires in all directions, to the number of two or three in each tent. This gave the whole camp the appearance of being on fire. The joy displayed by the Moslems, when they heard of the prince's death, was as great as the grief evinced by the Franks. The enemy also lost another of their leaders, named Count Bâliaṭ.[1] Count Henry also fell sick, and at one time lay at death's door. On the 24th of the same month we captured two of their barks, whose crews numbered more

---

[1] Schultens considers *Baliât* to stand for ' Thibault.' The Oxford MS. reads *Baniât*. It is perhaps possible that *Kundbaliat* may stand for ' Canterbury ': for Baldwin, Archbishop of Canterbury, fought as a soldier at Acre, and died about this time in the camp.

than fifty men, and on the 25th we took a large bark, which, amongst other things, contained a surcoat (or robe) covered with pearl embroidery, belonging to the wardrobe of the king (of the Germans ?). I heard that his nephew, his sister's son, was on board this bark, and was taken prisoner.

CHAPTER XCIV.

ASAD ED-DÎN'S EXPEDITION.

THE name of the Asad ed-Dîn, who is the subject of this chapter, was Shîrkûh ; he was son of Nâṣr ed-Dîn Muhammad, and grandson of Asad ed-Dîn Shîrkûh senior. He held the principality of Emesa. The Sultan had given him instructions to keep strict watch over the Franks in Tripoli, and to provide for the safety of the Moslems who dwelt in that part of the country. He received information that the people of Tripoli had sent all their droves (horses, oxen, and baggage-animals) to grass in the plain close to the city ; he therefore laid his plans, and set out with his troops to carry these animals off. He left the city quite unknown to the enemy, fell on their droves, and took four hundred horses and one hundred oxen. About forty of these horses died, but the remainder were brought back in good condition. He returned home without having lost a single man. The Sultan received his letter announcing his success on the 4th of Ṣafer, 587 (March 3, 1191). The previous night one of the enemy's ships had been driven ashore by the wind, and our people, seeing its plight, went down and took prisoners the whole of the crew, which was a large one.

CHAPTER XCV.

OTHER EVENTS IN THIS YEAR.

ON the night preceding the first day of the month Rabi'a I. (March 29), the Moslems in Acre made a sortie, killed a great number of the besiegers, and carried off about a dozen women from their camp. On the 3rd of the same month, the advanced guard, which was that day composed of troops from the Sultan's *halka*, was furiously attacked by a strong body of the enemy. The besiegers had several men killed, one of whom was said to be of high rank. The Moslems lost only one man, named Ḳarâḳûsh, a servant in the Sultan's service, who had distinguished himself by his valour on more than one occasion. The Sultan was informed that a detachment of the enemy's army frequently took advantage of our distance from their camp to leave their quarters and disperse over the plain ; on the 9th of the month, therefore, he himself selected a considerable number of men from the ranks of the Moslem army, whom he put under the command of his brother, el-Melek el-'Âdel, with instructions to take up his position in ambush behind a *tell,* close to the scene of the action that bears that prince's name. The Sultan concealed himself also behind Tell el-'Aiâdîya, taking with him several of the princes of his family—to wit, el-Melek el-Mozaffer Taḳi ed-Dîn, Nâṣr ed-Dîn Muhammad (Taḳi ed-Dîn's son), el-Melek el-Afḍal (the Sultan's son), and the young princes (his) sons—to wit, el-Melek el-Ashref Muhammad, el-Melek el-Mo'azzem Tûrân-Shah, and el-Melek es-Ṣâleh Ism'aîl. Amongst the men of the turban (doctors of law) that accompanied him were el-Ḳâḍi el-Fâḍel and the officers of the Chancery ; I myself was of the party. A few of our warriors, mounted

on good horses, advanced towards the enemy and discharged a flight of arrows at them, so as to entice them
out into the plain ; but they would not leave their camp,
having probably received information from some traitor of
the real object of this manœuvre. Nevertheless, this day
did not pass without furnishing us with some cause for
rejoicing ; for forty-five Franks, who had been taken prisoner at Beirût, were brought in to the Sultan. On this
occasion I witnessed the great tenderness of his heart,
beyond anything ever seen. Amongst the prisoners was a
very aged man who had lost all his teeth, and who could
hardly move at all. The Sultan asked him through his
interpreter why, being so old, he had come to this country,
and how far off his home lay. He replied : ' My home is
several months' journey away ; I only came to this country
to make a pilgrimage to the Church of the Resurrection '
(el-Komâma). The Sultan was so touched by this answer
that he restored the old man to liberty, and supplied him
with a horse to carry him to the enemy's camp. The
Sultan's younger sons asked his permission to kill these
prisoners, which he forbade them to do. As they had
made their request through me, I begged him to tell me
the reason of his refusal, and he replied : ' They shall not
become accustomed in their youth to the shedding of
blood and laugh at it, for they as yet know no difference
between a Moslem and an infidel.' Observe the prince's
humanity, his wisdom and moderation ! El-Melek el 'Âdel,
having given up all hope of enticing the enemy out into the
plain, returned to the camp that same evening.

CHAPTER XCVI.

ARRIVAL OF MOSLEM TROOPS AND OF THE KING OF FRANCE.

THE sea now became navigable once more, the weather cleared, and the time drew near for the arrival of reinforcements to both armies, to enable them to carry on the war. The first to join us was 'Alem ed-Dîn Suleimân Ibn Jender, an emir in el-Melek ez-Zâher's service. He was an old man, and enjoyed a wide-spread fame, having made his mark by the wisdom of his counsels and the bravery he had displayed on many a field. The Sultan thought very highly of this chief, who was one of his old companions in arms. The next to arrive was Mejed ed-Dîn, son of 'Izz ed-Dîn Ferrûkh Shah, and Lord of B'albek. Other bodies of Moslem troops came in one after another from different parts of the country. The enemy, on their side, took every opportunity of informing our advanced guard and the people who visited their camp that they were expecting the King of France to arrive very shortly. This monarch held very high rank amongst the Christians ; he commanded the respect of their most powerful princes ; all the besiegers' forces would have to put themselves under his orders as soon as he arrived, and his authority would be universally acknowledged. This king arrived at last with six ships laden with provisions and as many horses as he had considered it necessary to bring. He was accompanied by his principal officers. His arrival took place on Saturday, the 23rd of Rabi'a I., of the above year (April 20, A.D. 1191).

CHAPTER XCVII.

A STRANGE OCCURRENCE OF GOOD OMEN.

THE king had brought with him a large white falcon (*lit.*, kite), of enormous size and a rare species; I had never seen one so beautiful. The king set great store by the bird, and was very fond of it. This falcon one day escaped from his hand and took flight, and instead of returning at his master's repeated calls, flew off, and perched on the wall of Acre. Our people took it and sent it to the Sultan. The flight of the bird to the Moslems gave rise to great rejoicing, and its capture seemed to them to augur well. The Franks offered a thousand dinârs as the price of its ransom, but we did not even send them an answer. After this arrived Count (Philip) of Flanders, a prince of high rank among them, and of great renown. It was he who laid siege to Ḥamah and Ḥârim the year (we were defeated) at Ramla. On the 12th of Rabi'a II., we were informed by letter from Antioch that a body of deserters from the Franks, who had been put in possession of several barks, with the view of despoiling the Christians by sea, had landed in the island of Cyprus on a certain feast-day. A great number of the inhabitants were in the church, which was close to the sea-shore. The pirates took part in their service, and then threw themselves upon the congregation, taking them all prisoners—the women as well as the men—and dragging the priest also along with them. They put them on board their boats and carried them to Laodicea. They had taken great store of treasure and twenty-seven women. They say that each of the men engaged in the adventure received four thousand pieces of silver, current money, as his share of the plunder. A

16

short time after this, on the 17th of the month Rabi'a II.,
Bedr ed-Dîn, *shihna* (or governor) of Damascus, came into
the camp. Our men fell upon the flock of sheep belonging
to the enemy, and carried off twenty of them ; their horse
and foot came out after them, but did not recover any of
their property.

CHAPTER XCVIII.

ACCOUNT OF THE KING OF ENGLAND.

THE king of England was very powerful, very brave, and
full of resolution. He had distinguished himself in many
a battle, and displayed the greatest boldness in all his
campaigns. As regards his kingdom and rank, he was
inferior to the king of France, but he outstripped him in
wealth, in valour, and in fame as a soldier. It was reported
of him that on his arrival in Cyprus he made up his mind
not to proceed any further until he had taken the island
and reduced it to submission. He therefore disembarked
and commenced hostilities, whilst the prince of the island
collected a great number of people together to oppose the
invader, and made a desperate defence of his dominions.[1]
The king of England then asked help from the Franks at
Acre, and King Geoffrey (*sic*)[2] sent him his brother at the
head of a hundred and sixty knights. Meanwhile, the
Franks remained under the walls of Acre, awaiting the
result of the war between the two parties. On the last day
of the month Rabi'a II. we received a letter from Beirût
informing us of the capture of five transports belonging to

[1] King Richard I. defeated Isaac Comnenos (who called himself
Emperor of Cyprus, and who was a nephew of Theodore, wife of
Baldwin III.) on May 6, 1191.

[2] De Vinsauf says that King Guy himself came to assist in the
conquest of Cyprus.

the king of England's fleet, laden with men and women, provisions and wood, machines of war and other things, besides about forty horses. This was a great piece of good fortune for the Moslems, and the cause of much rejoicing. On the 4th of Jomada I. the enemy attacked the city and put seven mangonels in position. Letters came in from Acre beseeching us in the most urgent manner to send them help, and begging us to so occupy the enemy that they should be forced to discontinue the assault. The Sultan therefore informed his troops that he had decided to advance closer to the enemy, and to invest their camp more completely. The following day, in pursuance of this determination, he drew up his troops in their appointed order and sent out spies to ascertain the enemy's exact position, and to see if they had posted men in hiding in their trenches. They returned with the information that the trenches were quite empty. Upon this he set out with a few of his friends and memlûks in the direction of the enemy's trenches, and climbed a hill called Tell el-Foḍûl,[1] that lay close to their camp, and from the top of which he could see all that was going on there. He could plainly distinguish which mangonels were at work and which were lying idle. He then returned to our camp. I had attended him (on this ride). The next morning some thieves brought him a child, three months old, that they had stolen from its mother.

---

[1] One of the hillocks in the plain E. of Acre.

CHAPTER XCIX.

ACCOUNT OF THE CHILD.[1]

THE Moslems kept a number of thieves whose business it was to carry off people from the enemy's camp. On one of their nightly expeditions they seized a little nursling of three months, and brought it to the Sultan's tent, the rule being that they should bring all they had taken to the prince, who gave it back at once into their hands. When the child's mother found that her child had disappeared, she spent the whole night in weeping and lamentations, and in seeking assistance. When the princes of the Franks heard what had happened, they said to the woman : ' The Sultan is very compassionate ; we will give you permission to leave the camp and repair to him, to ask for your child ; he is certain to give it back to you.' She thereupon left the camp and went up to the (Moslem) advanced guard, to whom she told her story. They brought her to the Sultan, who was on horseback and attended by his suite, of whom I was one. She threw herself on her face upon the ground and began weeping and lamenting. When the Sultan heard the cause of her grief he was affected even to tears, and commanded the child to be brought. When he was told that it had been sold in the market, he commanded that the purchaser should be reimbursed the price he had paid, and the child taken away from him. He remained where he was until the child was brought, and then gave it back to the poor mother, who pressed it to her breast whilst the tears ran down her cheeks. It was such an affecting sight that all who wit-

---

[1] Our author has already given us this account on p. 41.

nessed it were moved to tears. Then, by the Sultan's command, she and her child were put on a mare and taken back to the enemy's camp. Here is another instance of the tenderness he felt for the whole of the human race. Great God, who madest him merciful, grant him an ample share of Thy mercy out of Thy greatness and loving-kindness! Even his enemies bore witness to his kindness and tenderness of heart, as the following verse testifies :

> ' For goodness even rivals prize,
> And who the just man's right denies ?'

Zâher ed-Dîn Ibn el-Bolenkeri, one of the chief emirs of Mosul, came to the camp this same day. He had left the service of the princes of that city and wished to enter the Sultan's army. Very soon after Salâh ed-Dîn's return to the camp he heard that the enemy had renewed their assault on Acre. He therefore set out on horseback for the city, but found that the fight was over before he came up, for night intervening had separated the combatants.

CHAPTER C.

THE SULTAN REMOVES TO THE HILL OF EL-'AYÂDÎYA.

ON the morning of Tuesday, the 9th of the month Jomada I. (June 4), the Sultan heard that the Franks had set up their mangonels and were pressing the city very hard ; he therefore commanded the herald (Jâwîsh) to call (to arms). He then mounted his horse, and advanced towards el-Kharrûba at the head of his infantry and cavalry, the latter having lost as little time as he in getting into their saddles. Then he reinforced the advanced guard by a detachment of troops that he sent forward. As the

besiegers would not come out of their camp, but continued
their assault on the city, he rushed on their camp, which
was thus completely hemmed in, and fought a hand to
hand combat.   The attack was continued till past mid-day,
when the enemy, abandoning their hope of carrying the
city, suspended operations in that direction and returned
to their camp.   The Sultan sought shelter from the sun in
a small tent that was pitched for him close at hand, and,
after saying the mid-day prayer, he rested there for the
space of an hour.   He had previously sent reinforcements
to the advanced guard, and ordered his troops back to the
camp to get a little rest.   I was then on duty.   Whilst we
were recovering from our fatigue, a messenger came in
from the advanced guard to report that as soon as the enemy
saw that the Sultan had withdrawn, they had recommenced
their assault of the city even more furiously than before.
The Sultan dispatched an order recalling his troops,
bidding them advance, regiment by regiment, to the
quarter on which the enemy had collected their forces,
and remain there under arms for the night.   He remained
on the spot himself to share their toils.   Towards the end
of the day, which was Tuesday, I took my departure from
his tent and returned to the camp, my turn of duty being
over.   The Sultan spent the night with his troops, who remained drawn up in order of battle.   During the night one
detachment was posted close to the enemy's trenches, to
keep them from leaving their camp.   On the following
morning, which was Wednesday, the 10th of the month
(June 5), the Sultan removed to a position facing the
enemy, on Tell el-'Ayâdîya, and took up his quarters in
a little tent that had been pitched as a shelter for him.
Throughout the day he maintained a steady and uninterrupted attack on the besiegers, so as to keep their
hands full, and prevent their acting against the city, and

he went incessantly from rank to rank, urging them to fight bravely in God's cause, and assuring them of ultimate success. When the enemy saw the fury of his attack, they grew apprehensive for the safety of their camp ; and, to prevent its being carried by assault, they suspended hostilities against the city, and provided for the defence of the trenches and tents. Upon this the Sultan returned to the camp he had established on Tell el-'Ayâdîya, leaving detachments behind to keep watch over the enemy's trenches, and report to him from hour to hour whatever might happen.

CHAPTER CI.

THE CITY IS REDUCED TO THE DIREST STRAITS.

WE had already been informed of the energy with which the enemy carried on the assault and endeavoured to fill up the ditches. They even threw the bodies of their dead horses into the moat, and went so far as to cast their own dead in. All these things came to our knowledge by means of letters, which we constantly received from our co-religionists in the city. These people had been divided into four sections : the first used to go down into the moat and cut to pieces the bodies of the animals that had been thrown in, in order that they might thus be the more easily carried away ; the second division carried off the pieces and cast them into the sea ; the third maintained a constant discharge upon the enemy to protect the two first sections and enable them to perform their tasks ; the fourth worked the mangonels and provided for the defence of the walls. The garrison were so worn out with exertion and fatigue that they sent incessant complaints to the Sultan. Indeed, they suffered more than any other body of troops has ever done, and no amount of courage was of any avail. Nevertheless they bore up with considerable patience, and *God is with the patient.* Meanwhile the Sultan never ceased attacking the enemy. He fought them continually night and day, either in person, or by means of his officers and sons, with the view of distracting their attention and preventing them from prosecuting the siege. But the besiegers' mangonels were brought to bear on 'Ain el-Baḳar ;[1] stones from these engines fell on the city night and day, and the damage sustained by the (great) tower[2] was plainly visible. Whenever the enemy were making preparations to renew their assault on the city, the Sultan pressed right up to their trenches on the other side. At last one of the Franks came out of their camp and looked about for someone to speak to. The Sultan was informed of this, and made answer : ' Tell them, if they have anything to ask, to send us one of their men ; we have nothing, for our part, to ask at their hands, and nothing whatever to do with them.' The two sides were still engaged in fighting when the king of England arrived.

CHAPTER CII.

ARRIVAL OF THE KING OF ENGLAND.

THE king of England arrived in the Frank camp on Saturday, the 13th of the month Jomada I. (June 8, 1191), after having conquered the island of Cyprus, and having succeeded against its lord. The news of his coming spread great terror. He brought five-and-twenty galleys with him,

---

[1] *'Ain el-Baḳar* means 'the ox-pool.' It was probably inside the city.

[2] The ' Cursed Tower' at the N.E. corner of the outer wall of Acre.

filled with men, arms and stores. The Franks were filled with so great a joy at his arrival that they lit huge and terrible fires that night in their camp—a sure sign of the important support he had brought them. Their leaders had oftentimes boasted to us that he would come, and held his arrival as a menace over our heads; and now, according to the people who frequented their camp, they expected, the very moment he landed, to see him fulfil their dearest wish of pushing forward with the siege of the city. This prince, indeed, was justly distinguished for his good judgment and wide experience, for his extreme daring and insatiable ambition. Therefore, when the Moslems heard of his arrival, they were filled with terror and alarm. The Sultan, nevertheless, received the news undisturbed, for he counted upon God's favour and protection, and manifested the purity of his motives in warring against the Franks.

CHAPTER CIII.

A MOSLEM VESSEL SUNK—THIRD SIGN OF THE APPROACHING FALL OF THE CITY.

ON the 16th a great ship, bringing engines of war, arms, provisions, and a large body of troops from Beirût, was approaching the city. She had been equipped by the Sultan's orders at Beirût, and had sailed from that place with a great number of soldiers on board, and instructions to run the blockade and make the harbour of Acre. The soldiers on board numbered six hundred and fifty. The king of England fell in with this vessel,[1] and sent his

---

[1] According to De Vinsauf this ship was captured while the English were on the way from Tyre to Acre, which would be before June 8. The month is not named in this chapter.

galleys to attack her.   They surrounded her, I have been
told, to the number of forty, and a desperate encounter
ensued.   Providence ordained that the wind should fall.
The.enemy lost a number of men in this fight.   The crew
of our vessel were overmatched by the superior force of the
enemy, and seeing that there was no chance of anything
but defeat, the captain, Y'aḳûb, a native of Aleppo, and a
brave and experienced soldier, said, 'By God! we will die
with honour, nor shall they get anything from this ship!'
and he stove in the sides of his ship; everything on board
—men, engines of war, provisions, etc., all sank into the
waves, and nothing fell into the hands of the enemy.   The
Moslems were overwhelmed by the news of this catastrophe, but the Sultan heard the tidings with perfect resignation to God's will and with exemplary calm, and *God
wastes not the hire of those who do well* (Kurân ix. 121).

CHAPTER CIV.

A HUGE MOVING TOWER IS SET ON FIRE.

THE enemy had built an enormous tower, four stories
high; the first story was constructed of wood, the second
of lead, the third of iron, and the fourth of copper.   It
stood higher than the wall of the city, and· held men at
arms.   They had brought this tower up to within about
five cubits of the ramparts, as far as we could judge from
our position; then the besieged began to throw naphtha
on it, and continued to do so without ceasing night and
day, until, by God's grace, the engine was set on fire.
This success compensated for the loss of the ship from
Beirût, which occurred the same day.

CHAPTER CV.

VARIOUS OCCURRENCES.

ON Friday, the 19th of this month, the enemy made a
vigorous assault on the city, and attacked it at close
quarters ; but the garrison had previously arranged with
the Sultan to beat a drum when the enemy attacked
them, and they now beat it. The Sultan's drum replied,
and the army got to horse and rushed down on the camp,
attacking the enemy in the rear. A number of Moslems
leapt into the trenches, rushed into the tents, and carried
off the cooking-pots and what was in them. Part of the
booty taken in the camp was brought to the Sultan and
laid before him in my presence. They feasted their
swords (with the blood of the infidels) until the enemy
became aware that their camp had been invaded. They
then desisted from their attack on the city and faced
about to give battle to our army. A new battle began
in this quarter, which raged till noon, when both sides
returned to their respective camps, equally worn out by
fatigue and the heat. On Monday the 23rd the drum
sounded the alarm once more from the city, and the
Sultan's answered it as before. In the combat that
ensued the enemy bent all their fury on the city, thinking
we should not dare to attack them in their camp ; but the
Moslem troops promptly undeceived them. They made
their way once more right into the tents and carried off
great spoil. The besiegers were roused by the alarm-calls
and came back to oppose our men, great numbers of whom
they found within the trenches and walls of the camp. A
desperate encounter followed, in which two Moslems

were killed and many wounded.   A very remarkable thing
occurred this day.   An old man, a native of Mazanderân,
and a person of some consequence, had arrived this very
morning to take part in the Holy War, and, finding that a
fight was going on, he obtained the Sultan's leave to join
the men engaged ; he made a furious charge against the
enemy and fell a martyr at once.   When the Franks found
that the Moslems had penetrated within their trenches and
walls, they were filled with fury, their cavalry sprang to
horse, and, accompanied by the foot-soldiers, rushed from
their trenches and charged the Moslems like one man.
Our troops stood firm, and did not stir from their position ;
then both sides engaged in a desperate fight.   When the
enemy saw the calm bravery displayed by the Moslems,
they took advantage of an interval to obtain the Sultan's
permission to send him an envoy.   This messenger went
first to el-Melek el-'Âdel, and got him and el-Melek
el-Afdel to accompany him to the prince.   He then
delivered his message, which was to express the king
of England's desire for an interview with the Sultan.
The Sultan, without a moment's hesitation, made answer
in the following terms : ' It is not customary for kings to
meet, unless they have previously laid the foundations of
a treaty ; for after they have spoken together and given
one another the tokens of mutual confidence that are
natural in such circumstances, it is not seemly for them to
make war upon one another.   It is therefore absolutely
essential that the preliminaries should be arranged first of
all, and that a trustworthy interpreter should act as our
intermediary to explain to each of us what the other says.
As soon as the preliminaries are settled, the interview,
please God, shall take place.'   On Saturday, the 28th of
the month, the enemy's cavalry and infantry sallied out of
the camp and attacked that division of our army which

was encamped on the shore to the north of the city. As soon as the Sultan was informed of this movement, he sprang into the saddle, his troops followed him, and a fight ensued between the two armies. Bedawin and Kurds were killed on our side, whilst the enemy suffered great loss. One prisoner in full armour, on horseback, was brought before the Sultan. The battle raged till night fell and separated the combatants. On Sunday, the 29th, a strong party of the enemy's foot advanced along the bank of the Nahr el-Ḥalu, where they fell in with a detachment of our advanced guard. A smart encounter ensued, in which the enemy took a Moslem prisoner, put him to death, and burned his body. The Moslems on their side did the same with a Frank prisoner. I myself saw the light of the two piles that were burning at the same time. We constantly received news from the people in the city ; they besought us to occupy the enemy's attention, and complained of being obliged to fight both night and day. They told us they were utterly exhausted, being forced to be on the walls without any rest, to oppose the attacks of the enemy, which had been incessant since the arrival of the king of England. After this that prince fell sick of an illness of which he nearly died ; the king of France also was suffering from a wound, but this only increased the arrogance and obstinacy of the besiegers.

The sister of the king of England had two servants who were secretly Moslems, whom she had taken into her service in Sicily ; her husband had been king of that island,[1] and on his death her brother, passing through Sicily, took her with him and escorted her to the army. Her two servants fled to the Moslem army. The Sultan

---

[1] Joan, sister of Richard I., married William of Sicily in 1177. He died in 1190. Sicily contained a large Moslem population under its Norman Kings.

gave them a most kindly welcome, and loaded them with marks of his favour.

CHAPTER CVI.

THE MARQUIS (CONRAD OF MONTFERRAT) TAKES FLIGHT TO TYRE.

THE marquis was afraid that if he remained (where he was) he would be seized, and his city given to the ex-king, who had been taken prisoner by the Sultan, to compensate him for the captivity he had suffered whilst upholding the Messiah's religion with his sword. Feeling sure that this was the course things would take, he fled to Tyre on Monday, the 30th Jomada I. Priests were sent to bring him back, but he would not listen to them, and set out by ship for that city. His departure was a great loss to the Franks, for he was distinguished for his good judgment, experience, and valour.

CHAPTER CVII.

ARRIVAL OF THE LATEST CONTINGENTS FOR THE MOSLEM ARMY.

ON the 30th of the month Jomada I. the contingent from Sinjar reached the camp, under Mojâhed ed-Dîn Berenkash, a religious and well-informed man, very zealous for the war. The Sultan went out to meet him and do him honour ; he received him in his own tent and loaded him with tokens of esteem, after which he assigned him a position in the left wing of the army. The arrival of this chief gave him the greatest satisfaction. After this there came in a strong detachment from the Egyptian army under

A'lem ed-Dîn Korji Seîf ed-Dîn Sonḳor, the *dewâdâr*
(Secretary of State), and a number of others of high rank.
Then came 'Alâ ed-Dîn, prince of Mosul, at the head of
the troops from that city. The Sultan bade him welcome
at el-Kharrûba, and received him with the greatest honour.
This contingent remained at that place until the following
morning, which was the 2nd of Jomada II. ; their leader
then paraded his troops in front of the enemy, and the
Sultan reviewed them. 'Alâ ed-Dîn was lodged first of all
in the Sultan's tent ; Salâh ed-Dîn sent him the most
magnificent presents, and furnished him with most sump-
tuous appointments suited to the rank of so great a prince.
He then gave him a position in the right wing of the
army. On the 3rd of the same month a second detachment came in from Egypt. The Franks were at this time
so much concerned at the increasing gravity of the king
of England's illness that they even discontinued for a
while their attacks on the city. This was a mercy decreed
by God, for the besieged garrison were in a most exhausted
condition and reduced to their last gasp, as the mangonels
had beaten down the walls to no higher than a man's
height. Meanwhile the Arab thieves (in the Sultan's pay)
used to steal into the besiegers' camp and carry off their
goods. They used even to make prisoners without striking
a blow, and this was the method they used : they would
enter a man's tent whilst he was asleep, and having placed
a dagger at his throat, would wake him up and make him
understand by signs that if he said a word they would dispatch him at once ; then they would carry him out of the
camp and bring him to our army. The prisoner did not
dare to open his mouth. This they succeeded in doing on
several occasions. When the contingents from all parts
had come in, one by one, the Moslem army was brought
up to its full strength.

CHAPTER CVIII.

THE FRANKS SEND AN AMBASSADOR TO THE SULTAN.

I RELATED above that an ambassador had been sent by
the king of England to solicit an interview with the Sultan,
and that the Sultan had excused himself. Some time
afterwards the same messenger arrived bringing the very
same message. He first had an interview with el-Melek
el-'Âdel, and that prince communicated his message to the
Sultan. It was decided that the king should have permission to come out (of his camp), and that the meeting
should take place on the plain, surrounded by the armies,
and that an interpreter should accompany the two
sovereigns. The messenger returned with the answer, and
it was some days before he came to the camp again, on
account of the illness from which (his master) was suffering.
After this a report spread about that the (Frank) princes
had presented themselves in a body (before the king), and
expressed strong disapproval of his proposed interview, on
the ground that it would imperil the Christian cause.
Nevertheless, very soon afterwards the same messenger
came (to us) once more, with the following message : ' Do
not believe the reports that have been spread as to the
cause of my enforced delay : I am answerable to myself
alone for what I may do : I am master of my own
actions, and no one has any authority over me. But,
during the last few days, I have been prevented from doing
anything at all by sickness ; that alone has caused the
delay. It is the custom of kings, when they happen to be
near one another, to send each other mutual presents and
gifts. Now I have in my possession a gift worthy of

PLAIN OF ACRE & VICINITY.

PALESTINE EXPLORATION FUND.

SCALE OF MILES

Stanford's Geog. Estab't. London.

the Sultan's acceptance, and I ask permission to send it to him.' El-Melek el-'Âdel replied as follows: ' He may send this present provided he will accept a gift of equal value from us.' The messenger agreed to this condition, and added : ' Our present might be of falcons from beyond the sea, but just now they are weak, and it would be a good thing if you could send us a few birds and fowls ; we would give them to our falcons, and they would revive, so that we could bring them to you.' El-Melek el-'Âdel, who knew full well what tone to take with them, replied jokingly : ' I suppose the king wants some fowls and chickens for his own use, and this is the means he adopts to procure them.' The conversation went on for some time, and at last the messenger asked : ' What do you want at our hands ? Have you anything to say ? Speak, so that we may know what it is.' El-Melek made answer : ' It was not we who made advances to you : you came to us; if you have anything to say, it is for you to speak and tell us your views; we are prepared to listen.' The interview then came to an end, and we had no further communications until the 6th of Jomada II., when the king of England's ambassador came to visit the Sultan, bringing with him a Moghrabi Moslem, whom they had kept in captivity for a long time. The Sultan, to whom this man was given as a present, received him with the utmost kindness and with many tokens of goodwill. The envoy received a robe of honour and returned to his master. The object of these frequent visits from the ambassador was to ascertain the state of our spirits, and to learn whether we were inclined to resist or give way ; we, on our side, were induced to receive the enemy's messages by the very same motive that prompted them.

CHAPTER CIX.

THE BESIEGERS MAKE A FURIOUS ATTACK ON THE CITY, AND REDUCE IT TO THE LAST EXTREMITY.

THE enemy continued their assaults on the city, and played on the walls incessantly with their mangonels, until all the stonework and structure of the walls was ruined. The people of the city were worn out by fatigue and long watching, for there was but a handful of them, and it was only with difficulty that they were able to bear up against the multitude of their adversaries and the continuous work. Numbers of them passed several nights in succession without closing their eyes, taking no rest night or day, whilst the besiegers, who hemmed them in, were in great force, and could relieve each other in their attack on the city. The garrison had been obliged to divide their reduced numbers, so as to provide for the protection of the walls and ditches, to work the mangonels, and to furnish crews for the ships and galleys. When the enemy were informed of this melancholy state of affairs, and of the extent to which the fortifications had suffered, they began to assault the city on all sides; their battalions relieved each other without interruption, fresh men advancing to the fight whilst the others rested. On the 7th of the month they renewed the attack with the greatest fury, bringing all their forces, both infantry and cavalry, to bear on the walls of the city. They took the precaution of manning the walls that protected their trenches, and they kept troops there night and day. As soon as the Sultan knew what was going forward (he was informed of the state of things both by the report of eye-witnesses and by the

rolling of the drum, the signal agreed upon between the
garrison and himself), he mounted his horse, and, followed
by his army, rushed down upon the enemy. A desperate
encounter took place that day between the two armies ;
the Sultan, as restless as a mother weeping for her lost
child, darted hither and thither, and rode from battalion
to battalion, urging on his men to fight for God. I have
been told that el-Melek el-'Âdel charged the enemy in
person twice that day. The Sultan, with his eyes full of
tears, went from battalion to battalion, crying : ' *On for
Islâm !*' The more he gazed towards the city and saw the
ordeal the inhabitants were passing through, and their
terrible sufferings, the more often he charged with renewed
vigour and encouraged his troops to fight. That day
he took absolutely nothing to eat, and drank nothing
but a few cupfuls of a (certain) drink which his physician
advised him to take. I was not present at this battle,
being confined to my tent at el-'Aîadîya by an attack
of sickness, but I watched all that was going on from
that place. When night fell the Sultan returned to the
camp, after the last evening prayer. He was worn out
with fatigue, and a prey to melancholy and vexation. He
slept, but his sleep was not quiet. At daybreak he
ordered the drum to beat. At this summons the troops
came in from all sides and formed into squadrons, ready
to return to the work of the previous day. That same day
we received a letter from the city containing the following
statement : ' We are so utterly reduced and exhausted
that we have no choice but to surrender the city. If
to-morrow, the 8th, you do not effect anything for our
rescue, we shall offer to capitulate, and make no condition
but that we receive our lives.' This was the most distressing
news the Moslems could receive. The blow struck them to
the heart, for all the forces of the coast, of Jerusalem,

Damascus, Aleppo, and Egypt, and the other Moslem countries, had been collected together at Acre. Moreover the city was held by the most renowned emirs in the army, the bravest champions of Islâm, such as Seif ed-Dîn 'Ali el-Meshṭûb and Behâ ed-Dîn Ḳarâḳûsh, who had commanded the citadel from the very commencement of the siege. The Sultan, struck by a blow the like of which he had never before experienced, suffered so terribly that fears were entertained for his health. Nevertheless, he prayed to God without ceasing, and besought His aid, showing the most wonderful calmness and resignation, coupled with a determination to carry on the Holy War, and *God does not waste the hire of those who do well* (Kurân ix. 121).

Thinking that it would be best to storm the enemy's camp and force his way in, he summoned all his troops to arms; his warriors sprang to the saddle; the cavalry came together as well as the infantry; but this day our plan did not succeed. In truth the enemy's foot presented a front like a solid wall; behind the shelter of their ramparts they defended themselves with their arms, their arbalists and arrows. Some (of our men) forced their way across the trenches, but their opponents fought fiercely, and they could not dislodge them from their positions. One of the Moslems, who had leapt the trenches, reported that he had seen a man, a Frank of enormous stature, who, all alone on the top of the parapet, was holding the Moslems at bay by his own unaided strength; his comrades stood on either side and handed him stones, which he hurled at our men as they advanced to the scarp. ' This man,' said he, ' had been struck by more than fifty arrows and stones, but nothing distracted him from his work. He kept on fighting and driving back the men who were coming on, until at last he was burnt alive by

a bottle of naphtha, hurled at him by one of our pyrotechnists.' One very intelligent old man, belonging to the
mercenaries, was amongst those who forced their way into
the enemy's trenches that day. ' Behind their rampart,'
he told me, ' was a woman, wrapped in a green *mellita*
(a kind of mantle), who kept on shooting arrows from a
wooden bow, with which she wounded several of our men.
She was at last overpowered by numbers ; we killed her,
and brought the bow she had been using to the Sultan,
who was greatly astonished.' The battle raged throughout
the day and was only terminated by the fall of night.

CHAPTER CX.

THE CITY IS REDUCED TO THE LAST EXTREMITY, AND THE GARRISON OPEN NEGOTIATIONS WITH THE FRANKS.

THE desperate assault to which the enemy had subjected
the city, and the enormous multitude of troops that attacked
it on every side with constant relief from their comrades,
had so undermined the strength of the garrison by the
loss of horse and foot-soldiers, that the courage of the
besieged sank to the lowest ebb. They saw immediate
death before them : they felt that they could not make a
lengthened resistance now that the enemy had established
themselves in the ditches, and occupied the outer wall.
They had undermined it, and filled the hollow with combustibles, to which they had set fire, and thus destroyed
the curtain of the outwork.[1] The enemy had then forced
their way through the gap, but with a loss of more than a
hundred and fifty men in killed and prisoners. Amongst

---

[1] Acre was defended by double walls on the E,

the number were six officers, one of whom cried out : ' Do
not kill me, and I will make the Franks withdraw ;' but a
Kurd, who was close by, rushed on him, and slew him.
The five others met the same fate. The following day the
Franks cried out (to our people) to save the lives of the six
officers, promising in return to spare the lives of all the
garrison; but they replied that it was too late. This
occasioned the besiegers great grief, and for three days
they made no further attack on the city. We also heard
that Seif ed-Dîn el-Meshṭûb went in person to see the
French king, the leader of the besiegers, to offer to capitulate, and that he addressed him as follows : ' We have
taken cities from you, and even when we carried them by
storm, we have been accustomed to grant terms to the
vanquished, and we have had them taken to the places in
which they wished to take refuge, treating them with all
kindness. We, then, will surrender the city to you if you
will grant us terms.' To which the king made answer :
' Those you took were our servants and slaves ; you
are likewise our slaves. I will see what I shall do.' We
were informed that el-Meshṭûb then took a haughty tone,
and made a long speech, saying, amongst other things :
' We will rather kill ourselves than surrender the city, and
not one of us shall die before fifty of your greatest have
fallen.' Then he withdrew, and returned to the city with
the news he brought. Some of the besieged were so terrified
by the king's answer that they seized a vessel, and sailed
during the night of the 8th to 9th, and came out to join
the Moslem army. The most important of these men were
Ibn el-Jâwali, 'Izz ed-Dîn Arsel, and Sonḳor el-Washâḳi.
The two latter, on their arrival in the camp, feared the
Sultan's wrath, and hid themselves so effectually that
they could not be found. However, they succeeded in
taking Ibn el-Jâwali, and he was put into prison (*Zered-*

khana).[1] On the following day the Sultan mounted his horse, intending to take the enemy unawares, and commanded his men to take spades and other tools to fill up the trenches; but the troops did not support him—they disappointed his expectations, and retreated. They cried out to him: 'You will destroy all Islâm, and there is no good in that!' That same day three envoys arrived from the king of England, and asked the Sultan for some fruit and snow. They added that, on the following day, the chief of the Hospitallers was coming to discuss the feasibility of a peace. The Sultan, instead of being angry, gave them an honourable reception, and allowed them to walk about in the market-place that had been established close to the camp. They departed the same evening, and returned to their quarters. The same day the Sultan commanded Sârem ed-Dîn Kâimâz en-Nejmi to charge the enemy's trenches at the head of his men. Several emirs of the Kurds, amongst whom was el-Jenâh, the brother of el-Meshtûb, joined Kâimâz with the men under their command. As soon as they reached the walls before the trenches, Kâimâz planted his standard in the earth, and defended it for a great part of the day. In the thick of the fight, 'Izz ed-Dîn Jurdîk (en-Nûri) came up with his troops; they all dismounted, and took an active part in the engagement. On Friday, the 10th of the month Jomada II. (July 5), the enemy remained quietly in their camp, and the Moslem army was drawn up in a circle round them. Our brave fellows spent the night on horseback, and fully armed, hoping that their comrades in Acre would second them by attacking some part of the enemy's camp, and that they might force their

---

[1] According to el-Makrîzi, the man who was committed to the State prison of *Zered-khâna*, 'the storehouse of breastplates,' did not remain there long; he was soon either killed or set at liberty.—S. de Sacy's *Chrestomathie Arabe*, 2nd edition, vol. ii., p. 179.

way in from both sides, giving one another mutual support.
This was the plan they had formed, and were determined
to carry out at whatever cost ; but it was absolutely impossible for the besieged to effect a sortie that night, for
one of their servants had deserted to the enemy, and
betrayed the garrison's design. The Franks therefore
maintained a strict watch over the city, and guarded, with
unrelaxed attention, against every movement of the garrison.
On this same Friday, three envoys from the Frank camp
had an interview with el-Melek el-'Âdel, but returned, after
an hour's talk, without having settled anything. The close
of day found the whole Moslem army drawn up on the
plain under arms ; in this manner they passed the night.
On Saturday, the entire force of the Franks began to
make ready for battle, and the great commotion going on
in every part of their camp led us to believe that they meant
to take the field against us. Whilst the troops were getting
into line, about forty men were seen coming out of the
gate from which a flag was flying, and they called out to a
party of memlûks: 'Send out to us el-'Âdel ez-Zebedâni,
the Sultan's freedman, and Governor of Sidon !' When
this man went up to them, they entered into a discussion
on the subject of the evacuation of Acre by the garrison ;
but they were so exacting in their demands that the
Saturday passed without anything being concluded.

CHAPTER CXI.

WE RECEIVE LETTERS FROM THE CITY.

ON Sunday, the 12th of the month, letters came, saying :
' We have sworn to die together; we will fight until we fall,
and will not yield the city while there is breath in our

bodies. You, on your side, must do all you can to occupy the enemy and prevent their attacking us. Since we are resolved, be sure that you do not humble yourselves before the enemy, or show yourselves fainthearted. Our minds are made up.' The man who swam out to us with these letters told us that the Franks attributed the great noise they had heard during the night to the introduction of a strong body of troops into Acre, and believed them to be still in the city. ' Therefore,' said the man, ' a Frank came out below the wall and called to one of the men on the top, saying : " I beseech you, by the truth of your religion, to tell me how many men were thrown into the city last night," that is to say, on the night preceding the Saturday. For there had been a great noise during the night, which had roused both the armies without any apparent cause. The man who was questioned replied that they were a thousand horse-soldiers.' ' Nay,' answered the Frank, ' not so many as that, I saw them myself; they were clad in green.'[1] The arrival of the contingents (from the different Moslem districts) that had come in one after another enabled us to divert the enemy's attention from their attack on the city—which was now on the point of falling —for the space of several days. Breaches had been made in many places in the walls, but the besieged had built a wall behind them, from the top of which they maintained a brave struggle. On Tuesday, the 14th of the month, Sâbek ed-Dîn, Prince of Sheizer, came into the camp, and on Wednesday, the 15th, Bedr ed-Dîn Dolderim also arrived, at the head of a large body of Turkomans, that he had hired with money furnished by the Sultan. On Thursday, the 16th, Asad ed-Dîn Shîrkûh arrived. The

---

[1] Beha ed-Dîn quotes Frank evidence to show that the dead Martyrs of Islâm (whose colour is green) were fighting for the garrison. The mysterious noise appears to have been an earthquake.

Franks remained immovable; they would neither make peace nor accept the capitulation of the garrison, except on the condition that all the prisoners in the hands of the Moslems should be set at liberty, and that all the cities of the districts on the coast should be given up to them. A proposal was made to surrender the city and all it contained, with the exception of the inhabitants, but this they rejected. The cross of the crucifixion was then offered to them, in addition to the former terms, but they persisted in their demands, and showed the greatest arrogance. Thus all the subtlety of our diplomacy was thrown away upon them; they used all their skill (in these negotiations); but *God also was skilful, for God is the best of the skilful* (Kurân iii. 47).

CHAPTER CXII.

TREATY CONCLUDED BY THE BESIEGED, BY WHICH THEIR LIVES ARE PRESERVED.

ON Friday, the 17th of Jomada II., the man swam out from the city with letters. These informed us that the garrison were reduced to the last extremity, and were too weak to defend the breach, which was now very large; they saw Death himself looming before them, and feared that everyone would be put to the sword if the city were carried by storm. They had therefore concluded a treaty of peace, by which the city with all that it contained—its engines of war, stores and ships—was to be surrendered to the Franks, who were to receive, in addition, two hundred thousand gold pieces (dinârs), and five hundred prisoners not of rank, together with one hundred of the principal captives to be named by the Franks; the besieged had also promised to give up the cross of the crucifixion. As soon as these conditions were accepted the Moslems were to leave the city in safety, taking their money and personal property with them, and their wives and children were to be allowed to accompany them. The Franks had, moreover, stipulated for the payment of four thousand gold-pieces to the marquis, because this treaty had been brought about through his mediation.

CHAPTER CXIII.

THE ENEMY TAKES POSSESSION OF ACRE.

WHEN the Sultan had learnt the contents of the letters from the city, he expressed the greatest displeasure. The news made the profoundest impression upon him, and he summoned his councillors together, to inform them of it, and consult with them upon the course to be adopted. They were divided in opinion, and he did not adopt either of the plans they suggested. Full of anxiety, he determined to send the man back to the city that night, with a letter declaring his formal disapproval of a treaty containing such conditions. He was still in this state (of anxiety), when, all of a sudden, the Moslems saw the banners of the infidels floating from the walls of the city, with crosses and the distinctive pennons (of their leaders), whilst fires were lighted on the ramparts. This was on Friday, the 17th of Jomada II., in the year 587 (July 12, 1191 A.D.), in the middle of the day. The Franks with one accord raised a mighty shout, whilst the Moslems were overwhelmed by this dreadful blow, and the hearts of the believers in one God overflowed with grief. The people thought then of the word of wisdom, 'We come forth from God, and to Him we must return,' and they made the camp ring with their vociferations, groans, and lamentations. The grief of each heart was according to its belief, and every man was afflicted by this evil according to the measure of his faith and zeal. And it burst upon them that the treaty between the people of the city and the Franks was upheld. The marquis entered the city with the king's standards, and planted them that very Friday in the place of the banners of Islâm ; he planted one on the castle, one on the minaret of the mosque, a third on the Templars' Tower, and a fourth on the Slaughter-Tower.[1] The Moslems were all ordered to one particular quarter of the city. At that time I happened to be on duty in the Sultan's tent, and, seeing him struck down with grief like a mother who has lost her child, I offered him all the consolations that are usual in such a case, begging him to think of the future fate of the (other) cities of the coast, and of Jerusalem itself, and to turn his attention to delivering the Moslem captives in Acre. This was during the night preceding Saturday, the 18th of the month. He finally decided to leave the place where he was encamped, since there was no longer any reason for hemming in the enemy; he therefore dispatched the baggage by night to the position he had previously occupied at Shefr'am. He himself remained where he was with a small body of horse, to keep a watch on the enemy's movements and over the fate of the inhabitants. All that night, until morning dawned, our troops were moving off ; but the Sultan still nourished the hope that, by the grace of God, the Franks, rendered incautious by their success, would come out and attack him. Then he would have an

---

[1] The castle was on the N. wall of Acre, near the centre. The mosque was the Church of St. John, near the centre of the city. The Templars' fortress was by the sea, on the S.W. of the city. The Tower of Slaughter is probably the 'Bloody Tower' at the N.E. corner of the inner wall.

opportunity for rushing down upon them and avenging
all the wrong they had done him, leaving it in God's
hands to decide to whom He should give the victory.
The Franks, however, made no movement, they were
occupied in taking possession of Acre, and in establishing
themselves in the city. He remained in the same place until
daybreak on the 19th, when he removed to the baggage
(that is, to Shefr'am). That day three (Franks) came out
(of the city), accompanied by Akûsh, the chamberlain, a
very well-informed man, who came to speak on behalf of
his colleague Behâ ed-Dîn Karâkûsh. They came for
instructions regarding the money and prisoners which had
been stipulated for in the treaty of peace. They were
honourably received, and stayed the night, and on the 21st
of the month they departed for Damascus, still on business relating to the prisoners. The Sultan also sent an
ambassador to the Franks, to obtain information as to
late occurrences, and also to ascertain what period of time
would be allowed him to carry out the terms of the treaty,
which was to be the basis of the truce.

CHAPTER CXIV.

AN ENCOUNTER TAKES PLACE DURING THE INTERVAL.

ON the last day of the aforesaid month the Franks came
out, and, following the sea-shore to the north of the city,
spread out in a long line, with their horse and foot drawn
up in order of battle. The Sultan was informed of this
manœuvre by the advanced guard, and, ordering the drum
to be sounded, he mounted his horse, and sent considerable
reinforcements to the guard in front. He himself remained
behind, to give the Moslem troops time to mount and

assemble. The reinforcements had not reached the advanced guard before they became engaged in a furious encounter with the enemy. As soon as they received the reinforcements, they charged straight ahead, forced the division of the enemy that was in front of them back, and threw the cavalry into confusion ; the cavalry then abandoned the infantry and took to flight. The runaways thought that there must be troops in ambush in rear of the advanced guard; they therefore rushed headlong back to their camp, whilst our guard fell on their foot, killed about fifty men, and followed the others in hot pursuit right up to their trenches. That same day the envoys of the Franks, who had gone to Damascus to inquire into the condition of the Christian prisoners there, took away with with them four of the chief men. During the evening the men arrived who had been commissioned by the Sultan to prepare a statement of the Moslem prisoners detained in Acre. The two sides kept on sending messengers to one another until the ninth day of the following month.

CHAPTER CXV.

ARRIVAL OF IBN BÂRÎK (FROM ACRE).

THAT same day Hossâm ed-Dîn Hosein Ibn Bârîk el-Mehrâni came out (from Acre) with two of the king of England's officers. He announced that the king of France had taken his departure for Tyre, and that they had come to discuss the matter of the prisoners, and to see the cross of the crucifixion, if it happened to be in the Moslem camp, or to know if it had been sent to Baghdad. It was shown to them, and when they saw it they displayed the most profound reverence, prostrating themselves on the ground till their faces were covered with dust, and humiliating themselves in adoration. They informed us that the princes of the Franks had accepted the proposal made by the Sultan, which was that he should deliver into their hands what was stipulated by the treaty, at three periods[1] of a month each. After this the Sultan despatched a messenger to Tyre with magnificent presents, and great store of perfumes and beautiful apparel, as an offering to the king of the French. On the morning of the 10th of Rejeb, Ibn Bârîk and his companions returned to the English king, and the Sultan, with his personal friends and the troops of his guard (*halka*), betook himself to the *tell* close to Shefr'am. The rest of the troops established themselves as best they could in a spot which was only divided by the valley from the Sultan's previous camping-ground. Messengers went constantly to and fro between the two armies, engaged in trying to lay the foundations of a permanent treaty of peace. This continued until we had procured the sum of money and number of prisoners we had undertaken to give up to the Franks at the expiration of the first period, in accordance with their demands ; viz.: that we should give them the cross of the crucifixion, one hundred thousand pieces of gold (*dinârs*), and sixteen hundred prisoners. Commissioners employed by the Franks to examine the instalment we had in readiness for them, reported that we had fulfilled the conditions imposed except with regard to the prisoners whom they had specially named, and who had not all been brought together. They therefore let the negotiations drag on till the first period had expired. On that day, which was the 18th of Rejeb, they sent to demand what was due to them, and the Sultan returned the following answer : 'You must

---

[1] Our author here uses the word *term*, *torûm* in the plural, evidently the French word *terme*, which was employed in the treaty of peace.

choose either one of two things : either send our comrades
back to us and accept the instalment due for this period,
and we will give you hostages for the performance of the
conditions imposed for the periods still to come ; or receive
the instalment we are sending you to-day, and send us
hostages to be retained until our comrades who are now
your prisoners are returned to us.' The envoys replied :
' We will do neither ; send us the instalment that is now
due, and accept our solemn oath that your comrades shall
be sent back.' The Sultan rejected this proposal, for he
knew that if he were to give them the money, the cross,
and the prisoners whilst our men were still detained by
the Franks, there would be no guarantee whatever against
an act of treachery on the part of the enemy, which would
strike a great blow at Islâm.

CHAPTER CXVI.

MASSACRE OF THE MOSLEMS IN ACRE—MAY GOD HAVE MERCY UPON THEM !

WHEN the king of England saw that the Sultan was
making some delay in the fulfilment of the above-mentioned
conditions, he acted treacherously with regard to the
Moslem prisoners. He had promised to spare their lives
if they surrendered the city, adding that if the Sultan sent
him what had been agreed upon, he would give them their
liberty,. with permission to take their wives and children
with them and to carry away all their moveable property ;
if the Sultan did not fulfil the conditions, they were to
become slaves. The king broke the solemn promises he had
made them, openly showed the intentions he had hitherto
concealed, and carried out what he had purposed to do as

soon as he had received the money and the Frank prisoners. That is what the people of his nation said afterwards.[1] About four o'clock in the afternoon of Tuesday, the 27th of Rejeb, he rode out with the whole of the Frank army—infantry, cavalry, and Turcopoles (that is, light-armed soldiers)—and advanced as far as the wells at the foot of Tell el-'A'yâḍîya, to which place he had already sent forward his tents. As soon as the Franks reached the middle of the plain between this *tell* and that of Kîsân, which was occupied by the Sultan's advanced guard, they brought out the Moslem prisoners, whom God had pre-ordained to martyrdom that day, to the number of more than three thousand, all tied together with ropes. The Franks rushed upon them all at once and slaughtered them in cold blood with sword and lance. The advanced guard had previously informed the Sultan that the enemy had got to horse, and he sent them some reinforcements, but they did not arrive until the massacre had been accomplished. As soon as the Moslems saw what they were doing to the prisoners, they rushed down on the Franks, and a certain number were killed and wounded on both sides in the action that took place, and lasted until night separated the combatants. The following morning our people went out to see what had happened, and found all the Moslems who had been martyred for their faith stretched on the ground ; they were able to recognise some of them. This was a terrible grief to them. The enemy had only spared the prisoers of note and such as were strong enough to labour. Various motives have been assigned for this massacre. According to some, the prisoners were killed to avenge the deaths of

[1] De Vinsauf says (iv. 4) that the prisoners were killed to avenge those slain by Moslems during the siege, and at the expiration of the term granted for giving up the cross and the Christian prisoners.

those slain previously by the Moslems; others say that the
king of England, having made up his mind to try and
take Ascalon, did not think it prudent to leave so many
prisoners behind in Acre. God knows what his reason
really was.

CHAPTER CXVII.

THE ENEMY MARCH UPON ASCALON, ALONG THE SHORE OF THE WESTERN SEA.

ON the 29th of Rejeb the Franks all mounted their horses,
and packed the tents they had struck on the backs of their
beasts of burden; then they crossed the river and encamped on the west bank, close to the road leading to
Ascalon. Whilst this division showed their intention to
march along the sea-shore, the king of England sent
the rest of his men back to Acre, where he had repaired
the breaches and made the fortifications strong again.
The army that had set out on this fresh expedition included a great number of notable men, and was led by the
king of England in person. At daybreak on the 1st of
Sh'abân the enemy lit their fires, as was always their
custom when they were breaking up their camp. The
Sultan was informed by the advanced guard that the
Franks were preparing to move, and he at once ordered
that the baggage should be loaded up while the people
waited; and the people did so. Many of the people and
of the merchants from the markets lost quantities of their
goods and merchandize on this occasion, for they had not
enough horses and beasts of burden to carry all they
possessed. Any one man could carry enough for his
needs for a month, but each of these merchants had such
quantities of wares that he would have been obliged

to make several journeys to move them all. On this occasion it was impossible for anyone to remain behind, on account of the proximity of the Franks, who, now that they were occupying Acre, were very strong. It was quite light by the time the enemy's army began their march. They marched in several separate divisions, each capable of providing for its own defence, and followed the line of the sea-shore. The Sultan sent reinforcements to the advanced guard, and despatched a large part of his troops against the enemy. A desperate encounter took place, and el-Melek el-Afḍal, the Sultan's son, sent back to tell his father that he had cut off one division of the enemy in such a way as to prevent its receiving any support from the others, and that his men had attacked it so smartly that it had been obliged to retire in the direction of the camp. ' If we had been in full force,' he added, ' we should have taken them all prisoners.' The Sultan forthwith sent out a strong detachment of his troops, going with them himself as far as the sands. On our way (for I was with him) we met el-Melek el-'Âdel, the Sultan's brother, and learnt from him that the division in question had managed to effect a junction with the one ahead of it, and that the chief part of the enemy's forces had crossed the Ḥaifa river,[1] and then halted to allow the rear divisions to come up. He added that it was useless to follow them up, and that we should only tire the men and lose our arrows to no purpose. When the Sultan had convinced himself of the correctness of this view, he desisted from the pursuit, and sent a detachment back to the baggage-train to help the stragglers to join those in front, and to protect them against marauders and attacks by the enemy. He himself set out for

[1] The Kishon, N. of Haifa.

el-Ķeimûn,[1] where he arrived the same day, as evening began to close in. The outer part of his tent only was set up for him, a long piece of cloth being hung all round it to form a wall. He then sent to summon his principal officers, and gave them to eat, after which he consulted them as to what should be done. As I was on duty, I was present at this meeting.

Second halt.—At this council it was decided that the army should march the following morning. A line of troops had already been posted round the Franks to keep watch over their movements during the night. Early in the morning of the 2nd of Sh'abân the Sultan sent the baggage forward, remaining where he was until he received information of the enemy's movements. As none came in, he set out, as soon as it was fully light, to follow the baggage, and made a halt for some time at a village called es-Sabbâghîn,[2] in the hope of receiving information regarding the Franks. Suleimân Ibn Jender was now occupying the ground on which the Sultan had halted on the previous day, and had left Emir Jordîk encamped close to the enemy. A number of troops, who came in one after another, spent the night there. As the Sultan received no intelligence of any kind, he set out and overtook the baggage at a place called 'Ayûn el-Asawîr.[3] On our arrival there we noticed several tents, and when he learnt that they belonged to el-Melek el-'Âdel, he went up to them and spent an hour with that prince; after that he repaired to his own tent. There was absolutely no bread

---

[1] *Tell Keimûn* (ancient *Jokneam*) called Caymont by the Franks, E. of Carmel, 12 miles S.E. of Haifa.

[2] Now *Subbarîn*, 8 miles S.W. from Tell Keimûn, on Carmel, overlooking the plain of Sharon.

[3] Springs at *Tell el-Asawîr*, 6 miles S. of Subbarîn, on the E. edge of the plain of Sharon.

at all in this halting-place, and provisions rose to such a price that one piece of silver was paid for a quarter of a measure of barley, and two pieces of silver for a pound of biscuit. The Sultan remained there till mid-day, when he mounted his horse and rode on to el-Mellâha,[1] where the enemy would be obliged to make their next halt after leaving Ḥaifa. He went on in advance to ascertain if the ground would lend itself to a pitched battle, and rode all over the lands of Cæsarea right up to the spot where the woods began. He returned to the camp very tired, shortly after the hour of evening prayer. I asked him if he had received any news of the enemy, and he replied : ' I have heard that up to this evening, the 2nd of Sh'abân, they have not left Ḥaifa ; we will wait here till we get news, and then determine what it will be best to do.' He spent the night on Tell ez-Zelzela,[2] and remained there during the morning in the hope of receiving intelligence of the enemy's movements.

The herald (*Jâwish*) then proclaimed that there was to be a review, and the troops mounted and formed in order of battle. The morning was far advanced before the Sultan took any rest, having first breakfasted and received some of his emirs. He consulted them as to what he should do, and then went to the celebration of mid-day prayer; after that he held a reception in his tent until the hour of evening prayer, and made compensation to such as had lost their horses and other property ; these sums varied from one hundred gold pieces to one hundred and fifty, sometimes more, sometimes less. I have never seen anyone do things so liberally, and seem so pleased in

---

[1] Apparently *Khurbet Mâlhah*, 11 miles S. of Haifa, near the shore, 2½ miles S. of Dustrey (District), where the first halt was made by King Richard's army after leaving Haifa. Salâh ed-Dîn would have thus ridden 35 miles on this day.

[2] *Tell ez-Zelzela* (' Earthquake Hill ') was apparently Tell el-Asawîr.

being able to make presents. As evening drew in that day they decided to dispatch the baggage forthwith to Mejdel Yâba.[1]

Third halt.—The Sultan remained where he was with a small body of light cavalry, and did not set out till the following morning, the 4th of the month. He mounted and rode to the source of the river that flows down to Cæsarea,[2] where he made a halt. Here we had to pay four pieces of silver for a *ratl* (pound of twelve ounces) of biscuit, and two pieces and a half for a quarter of a measure of barley; bread could not be obtained at any price. The Sultan went to his tent and took a light meal, then, after mid-day, having said his prayer, he mounted and rode out along the road that the enemy would have to follow, to search for a suitable site for a pitched battle. He did not return until after the hour of the *'asr* (afternoon prayer). After that he held an audience for an hour, took a little rest, and mounted his horse once more. He gave the order for resuming our march, and had his tent struck, and when evening fell the tents of the whole army had been struck.

Fourth halt.—The army marched towards a hill that lay behind the hill we had just left. Whilst we were there they brought two Franks to the Sultan who had been made prisoners by the advanced guard. He had them beheaded on the spot, and the soldiers cut their bodies to pieces to satisfy their thirst for revenge. He spent the night in this place and remained there throughout the morning of the following day, for he had not yet received any intelligence as to the march of the enemy. As the want of provisions and forage was very keenly felt by the troops, he sent

---

[1] *Mejdel Yâba* is 28 miles S. of Tell el-Asawîr, and 12 miles E.N.E. of Jaffa.

[2] The Crocodile River (*Nahr ez-Zerka*), N. of Cæsarea.

an order to the baggage to come up that night. Then, at his usual time, he rode out in the direction of the enemy, and covering Cæsarea. He returned to the camp about noon. We had just heard that the enemy had not yet left el-Mellâha. Two other Frank prisoners were brought before the Sultan, who had been captured on the flanks of the enemy's army. They were put to death in the most cruel manner, for the Sultan was terribly wroth at the massacre of the prisoners from Acre. He then took a moment's rest, and gave audience after the midday prayer. I was in his presence when they brought in a Frank knight, evidently a person of consequence, whose dress indicated the high rank that he held among the enemy. An interpreter was called that we might question him concerning them, and we asked him what was the price of provisions with them. He replied that, on the day they first left Acre, a man could satisfy his hunger for six groats (*Kerâtîs*), but that prices had gone on rising until the same quantity now cost eight groats. He was then asked why the army remained such a long time in each halting-place, and he replied that it was because they were awaiting the arrival of the fleet, which was to bring men and supplies. When he was questioned as to the loss they had sustained in killed and wounded on the day they set out, he replied that it had been great. When asked what number of horses had been killed that day, he made answer, ' About four hundred.' The Sultan then commanded that his head should be cut off, but forbade his body to be mutilated. The prisoner asked what the Sultan had said, and it was explained to him, whereupon he changed colour and said : ' But I will give you one of the captives in Acre.' The Sultan replied : 'God's mercy, but it must be an emir.' ' I cannot get an emir set at liberty,' answered the Frank. The interest shown in him by all present, and his fine figure, all spoke in his favour. And, indeed, I never saw a man so well made, with such elegant hands and feet, and such a distinguished bearing. The Sultan therefore postponed the execution of his commands, had him put in chains, and reproached him with the treachery of his fellow-countrymen and the massacre of the prisoners. He acknowledged that it was an abominable act, but said that it was the king alone who had decreed and commanded it to be done. After the *'asr*, the Sultan rode out according to his custom, and on his return ordered that the prisoner should be put to death. Two other prisoners were then brought in before him, whom he likewise ordered to be put to death. He spent the night in this place, and at daybreak the next morning heard that the Franks were marching on Cæsarea, and that their vanguard was near the city; he therefore thought it best to withdraw from the enemy's road and take up another position.

Fifth halt.—He removed with his troops to a place close to the *tell* we had been occupying, and, after having the tents pitched, set out to examine the district through which the enemy would have to pass, hoping to find a suitable site for a pitched battle. He returned towards mid-day, and called his brother el-Melek el-'Âdel, and 'Alem ed-Dîn Suleimân Ibn Jender, to consult them as to what was to be done. He then snatched a few moments' rest, and when the call to the *zohr* (mid-day) prayer was cried, he attended its celebration. After this he mounted and set out in quest of news of the enemy. Two Franks who were brought before him were put to death by his orders; and two others, brought in shortly afterwards, suffered the same fate. Towards the close of the day he had two others killed, who were brought before him later on. On returning from his ride, he was present at the celebration of the *maghrib*[1] prayer, and then held an audience according to his custom. Afterwards he summoned his brother el-Melek el-'Âdel, and sending everyone else away, remained closeted with him in conversation until a very late hour. On the following day, the herald announced that there would be a review, but of the guard (*halka*) only. The Sultan rode out in the direction of the enemy, and halted on (one) of the *tells* rising above Cæsarea, which city the enemy had entered on Friday, the 6th of Sh'abân. He showed himself there during the morning, then halted and gave his officers a repast. He then got into the saddle again and visited his brother; after the mid-day prayer he rested for a short while and then held an audience. At this audience they brought in fourteen Frank prisoners, and a woman of the same race, who was the daughter of the knight mentioned before. She had a Moslem woman with her whom she kept a prisoner. The Sultan ordered the Moslem woman to be set at liberty, and sent the others to prison. They had been brought from Beirût, where they had been taken with a number of others in a ship. They were all put to death on Saturday, the 7th of Sh'abân. The Sultan maintained his position, keeping constant watch for an opportunity of attacking the enemy's forces on the march.

Sixth halt.—On the morning of the 8th the Sultan rode out according to his custom, and on his return received news from his brother that the enemy were preparing to move. The battalions[2] had maintained their several positions round Cæsarea during the night. He then ordered food, and the people ate. After this a second messenger came in to announce that the enemy had commenced their

---

[1] See p. 21.

[2] We use the words 'battalions' and 'squadrons' indiscriminately to translate *atlâb* in the plural.

march, whereupon the Sultan ordered his drum to beat, and
mounted at the head of his cavalry. He then set out, and
I accompanied him close up to the army of the Franks,
when he formed his troops in line round the enemy, and
gave the signal for battle. The marksmen were posted
in front, and the arrows shot by both sides fell thick as
rain. The enemy had already formed in order of battle ;
the infantry, drawn up in front of the cavalry, stood firm
as a wall, and every foot-soldier wore a vest of thick felt[1]
and a coat of mail so dense and strong that our arrows
made no impression on them. They shot at us with
their great arbalists, wounding the Moslem horses and
their riders. I saw some (of the Frank foot-soldiers)
with from one to ten arrows sticking in them, and still
advancing at their ordinary pace without leaving the
ranks. Their infantry was divided into two divisions, one
of which was posted in front of the cavalry ; the other
was not called upon to fight, and took its ease as it
advanced along the shore. When the division that was
engaged was fatigued and the men were exhausted by
their wounds, it was relieved by the other division, and
went off to rest. The cavalry was in the centre, and did
not quit its position except when it was ordered to
charge. It was drawn up in three divisions. In the
first, which formed the van-guard, rode Geoffrey (*sic*)
the ex-king, followed by all the troops of the sea-coast
countries which had remained faithful to him ; the kings
of England and France[2] rode in the centre, and the
sons of the Lady of Tiberias[3] were in the rear-guard with
a detachment (of Hospitallers). In the centre of their
army was a cart, on which was fixed a tower as high as

---

[1] See p. 367. This was called the gambison or pourpoint.

[2] The King of France was not with the army.

[3] The wife of Raymond of Tripoli, who held the castle of Tiberias.

a minaret, and from this floated the standard of the people. This was the disposition of their forces, according to my own observation, and to information given me by some of the Frank prisoners and the merchants who frequented their camp. Their troops continued to advance in the order we have just described, all the while maintaining a steady fight.[1] The Moslems discharged arrows at them from all sides to annoy them, and force them to charge ; but in this they were unsuccessful. These men exercised wonderful self-control ; they went on their way without any hurry, whilst their ships followed their line of march along the coast, and in this manner they reached their halting - place.[2] They never made long marches, because they were obliged to spare the foot-soldiers, for those of them who were not engaged in fighting used to carry the baggage and tents, as they had so few beasts of burden. One cannot help admiring the patience displayed by these people, who bore the most wearing fatigue without having any participation in the management of affairs, or deriving any personal advantage. They fixed their camp on the bank of the river furthest from Cæsarea.

Seventh halt.—At daybreak, on the 9th, the Sultan was informed that the enemy was already in the saddle, and ready to march. He therefore mounted his horse, drew up his squadrons, and sent his marksmen to the front. Whilst he was marching to the attack, the marksmen surrounded they enem on all sides, and kept up a constant discharge of arrows, but without making any impression on them. The three divisions in which the army was drawn up, as we have described above, commenced their

[1] Literally, while the market of war was well thronged.
[2] This camp was on the *Nahr el-Mefjir*, 3 miles S. of Cæsarea, called the 'Dead River' by De Vinsauf.

march, and if one of them proved unable to resist us, the
nearest division came up to its support. They assisted one
another mutually, whilst the Moslems surrounded them on
three sides, and attacked them with the greatest energy.
The Sultan busied himself in bringing his battalions
forward, and I saw him ride between the marksmen of
the two armies, with the enemy's arrows flying over
his head, attended only by two youths who were each
leading a horse. He hurried from one squadron to another,
encouraging them to advance, and commanding them to
press on and come to close quarters with the enemy. With
the roll of the drums and the bray of the trumpets were
mingled cries of the *tahlîl* and the *takbîr* (*There is but
one God! God is great!*). But the enemy stood firm
without moving or turning aside. The Moslems charged
the Franks several times, but they had a number of men
and horses wounded by missiles from the arbalists, and
by the arrows discharged against them by the infantry.
We kept on surrounding them, attacking them and charging
them, until they reached a river called *Nahr el-Kasab*,[1]
where they pitched their camp. This was at mid-day,
and the heat was overpowering. Our troops drew off and
discontinued the attack, knowing that they could not hope
to gain any advantage over the enemy when they were
once encamped. That day Islâm lost one of its bravest
champions, a man named Aiâz, surnamed el-Tawîl, 'the
long man,' one of the Sultan's memlûks. He had been
fighting, and had killed several of the bravest of the
enemy's horsemen, who had left the ranks and engaged

---

[1] This stream, now called *Nahr Iskanderûneh*, is 5 miles S. of the
Dead River, and is called by De Vinsauf the 'Salt River'; it is
marshy and reedy. The Franks reached it on September 2, and
remained there till after the 5th, which agrees with the present account
of the Nahr el-Kasab or 'reedy river.'

in single combat in the space between the two armies. Aiâz had had several encounters of this sort with them, and after awhile the Franks avoided him. But he kept on measuring his strength with them until at last his horse fell under him, and he testified (for the faith) on the field of battle. The Moslems were terribly grieved at his death. He was buried on a *tell* above el-Birka,[1] which is a place where the waters of a great many streams flow together. The Sultan ordered his baggage to halt in el-Birka, and when the hour of the *'asr* had passed, he had a meal served for his men, and gave them an hour's rest. He then set out along the Nahr el-Kasab, and halted again somewhat higher up the river, watering there whilst the enemy watered lower down at a very little distance from the place where we were.[2] At this halting-place the price of a quart of barley had risen to four dirhems (pieces of silver), but we found plenty of bread at half a dirhem a pound. The Sultan remained there, waiting until the Franks should resume their march, and he could attack them again ; but as they spent the night in their camp, we also remained where we were.

CHAPTER CXVIII.

A FIGHT TAKES PLACE.

A DIVISION of the Moslem army which had been detached to watch the enemy's movements fell in with a body of

---

[1] *El-Birka* is the 'pool' or swamp in the lower part of the Nahr el-Kasab. On the sand-hills immediately S.W. is the ruined monument called *Mejâhed Sheikhah*, 'the place where chiefs fought in the Holy War.' This is possibly the site of the tomb of Aiâz.

[2] Salâh ed-Dîn's camp was some 10 miles E. of that of Richard near the head of the Nahr el-Kasab.

our adversaries that had also come out to reconnoitre.
As soon as our men could get near the Franks they
rushed on them and attacked them furiously. The enemy
lost a considerable number in the encounter, but as they
were reinforced by another body of Franks, who had seen
what was going on and had run up to their support, they
held their ground and kept on fighting. The Moslems lost
two men[1] and took three prisoners, whom they brought to
the Sultan. When questioned by him, these men stated that
the king of England had been informed by two Bedawîn,
who had visited him at Acre, that the Moslem army
was very small, and that it was their information which
had induced him to take the field. They added : ' Yester-
day evening—they referred to the evening of Monday—
when he saw the Moslems fight so obstinately, and observed
the number of their squadrons (taking also into consideration
that he had nearly a thousand wounded, and that several
of our men had been killed), he was obliged to remain
to-day encamped in the same place to rest his troops.
Then, when he thought of the battle which had just been
fought, and the host of Moslems he had to fight, he sent
for the Bedawîn and had them beheaded.' During all that
day, which was Tuesday, the 10th of Sh'abân (September 3,
1191) we maintained our position, because the enemy had
not left theirs.

Eighth halt.—Towards noon that same day the Sultan
made up his mind to march out in front of the enemy.
Our men moved off to the roll of the drum, and made
their way into the wood of Arsûf, with orders to halt at a
tell in its midst, close to a village called Deir er-Râheb.[2]

---

[1] Our author takes pleasure in minimising the losses of the Moslems.

[2] *Deir er-Râheb*, ' Monk's monastery,' is probably the present *Deir
Asfîn*, a ruin in the woodland region S. of the Nahr Iskanderûneh,
7 miles E. of the camp at Nahr el-Fâlik.

Night surprised them, and the troops lost their way among the thickets, so the Sultan was obliged to remain there till Wednesday morning, the 11th of the month, to reassemble them. He then rode out to look for an advantageous site for a battle. He remained all that day in the position he had taken up, and was informed that the enemy had remained on the banks of the Nahr el-Kaṣab, to await the reinforcements that were to be sent them from Acre, in eight great ships. The Moslem outposts picketed round the Frank army kept us well supplied with intelligence, and had an encounter with the enemy's foragers in which several were killed on both sides.

CHAPTER CXIX.

THE ENEMY SENDS TO COMMUNICATE WITH US THAT SAME DAY.

THE enemy informed our advanced guard that they wished to communicate with us, and begged that some one might be sent to confer with them. Therefore 'Alem ed-Dîn Suleimân Ibn Jender, who was in charge of the guard that day, sent a man out to know what they had to say. He learnt that they wished to confer with el-Melek el-'Âdel. With the Sultan's permission, that prince went out to the advanced guard and passed the night with them, having an interview with the envoys. Their proposal, in brief, was as follows : 'The war between us has been maintained for a long time, and a number of brave warriors have fallen on both sides. We ourselves only came out to help the Franks of the coast districts ; make peace with them, and let the two armies return each to its own country.' During the morning of Thursday, the 12th of the month,[1] the Sultan sent a letter to his brother, saying : ' Try to protract the negotiations with the Franks and keep them where they are until we receive the Turkoman reinforcements we are expecting.' Indeed, at that moment they were very close at hand.

CHAPTER CXX.

EL-MELEK EL-'ÂDEL'S INTERVIEW WITH THE KING OF ENGLAND.

WHEN the king of England learnt that el-Melek el-'Âdel had come to the outposts, he sent to him to ask for an interview. El-'Âdel consented, and the two princes met, each attended by a magnificent cortège. The son of Honferi,[2] a man of high rank in the countries on the coast, acted as their interpreter. I had an opportunity of seeing this young man on the day when peace was concluded ; he was, in truth, a fine young fellow, but his beard was shaved after the manner of his nation. The King of England opened the conversation by expressing his desire for the conclusion of peace, and el-'Âdel replied : ' If you wish to obtain peace and desire me to act as your agent with the Sultan, you must tell me the conditions you have in view.' ' The basis of the treaty,' said the king, ' must be this: You must return all our territory to us and withdraw into your own country.' El-'Âdel replied with scorn, and a discussion ensued, which resulted in their each withdrawing to his own camp. When the Sultan saw that the enemy was on the move, he dispatched his baggage, but remained

[1] The Franks were still halting at the Salt River on September 5.
[2] Humphrey of Toron, one of the chief barons of the kingdom of Jerusalem.

where he was himself to draw up his troops in order of battle. The small baggage had already started, and was on the point of overtaking the heavy, when the Sultan sent an order for its return ; but as night had now closed in, the people were in great confusion all that night. The Sultan then sent for his brother to know what had passed between him and the king, and had a private conversation with him. This was on the night preceding Friday, the 13th of the month. The enemy resumed their march and encamped in another place called *el-Birka*,[1] from which they could see the sea. During the morning of Friday the Sultan went out to get news of the Franks. On his ride they brought him two men who had been taken prisoners by the advanced guard, and he ordered their heads to be struck off. When he had ascertained that the enemy would not leave their camp that day, he dismounted, and had a talk with his brother on the unwillingness of the Franks to move, and discussed the measures that should be taken. He spent the night in the same halting-place.

CHAPTER CXXI.

THE BATTLE OF ARSÛF, WHICH WAS A BLOW TO ALL MOSLEM HEARTS.

ON Saturday, the 14th of Sh'abân (September 7, 1191), the Sultan was informed that the enemy were marching on Arsûf. He mounted forthwith, and drew up his troops in order of battle, being resolved to come to close quarters

[1] *Birket Ramadân*, here intended, is a swampy lake, drained by a cutting in the rocks, on the course of the *Nahr el-Fâlik*, or ' River of the cleft,' called *Rochetaillie* by De Vinsauf. It is 9 miles S. of the Salt River, and was reached by the Franks on September 6—a Friday. Arsûf was a fortress on the shore five miles further S.

19

with the enemy that day. The marksmen drawn from each battalion went out in advance, and rained a shower of arrows on the enemy, who were approaching the thickets and gardens of Arsûf. The Moslem troops harassed them on every side, some advancing, led by the Sultan in person, others remaining in position to cover them in case of retreat. They charged the enemy furiously ; the fire of war burst from the marksmen, and killed and wounded. The enemy were obliged to hurry forward to try and reach the place where they were to halt and encamp, and they then found that they were in a most galling position, and that we had them at our mercy. The Sultan rode from the right wing to the left, urging his men to fight for the Faith. I several times saw him, attended by only two pages, who were each leading a horse ; I met his brother also with no greater a following, and they could both see the enemy's arrows falling to right and left of them. The enemy's progress was forced to become slower and slower, and the Moslems were flattering themselves that it would prove an easy victory, when the first ranks of the enemy's foot reached the wood and the gardens of Arsûf. Then the enemy's cavalry formed in one body, and, knowing that nothing but a supreme effort could save them, they resolved to charge. I myself saw their knights gathered together in the midst of a protecting circle of infantry ; they put their lances in rest, uttered a mighty war-cry, and the ranks of infantry parted to allow them to pass; then they rushed out, and charged in all directions.[1] One division hurled

---

[1] The charge was begun by the Hospitallers in rear, and gradually involved all the cavalry. According to De Vinsauf (IV., 9-25), Richard had 100,000 men in five divisions. The Templars led the van ; the Angevins and Bretons came next ; then King Guy's forces and those of Poitou ; then the Normans and English round the standard on its truck ; and lastly the Hospitallers. A flanking party on the left (east) was led by Henry of Champagne.

itself on our right wing, another on our left, and a third on our centre, throwing our whole force into confusion. I was in the centre, and when that body fled in the wildest disorder, it occurred to me that I might take refuge in the left wing, which was the nearest to me. But when I came up with it, I found that it, too, was struck with panic, and had taken to its heels even quicker than ·the other. Then I turned to the right wing ; but when I reached it, I found it in still greater confusion than the left. I then turned to the position occupied, according to custom, by the Sultan's squadron, which was always a rallying-point for the others. I there found only seventeen men ; but the standards were still flying, and the drum continued to beat. When the Sultan saw the dire discomfiture of the Moslems, he returned to his squadron, and found but very few men. He stopped here, and, perceiving that the whole neighbourhood was filled with fugitives, he ordered the drums to beat without ceasing, and had all whom he saw escaping brought to him. But, in truth, he could not stop the people in their flight ; when the enemy charged, they gave way, and when he drew rein for fear of an ambush, they also came to a stand, and did battle with him. During the second charge, they fought even while they fled, and halted as soon as their pursuers stopped ; and in the third, in which the enemy reached the top of the hillocks and rising ground that happened to be in his way, they fled once more, but, seeing him draw up, they also came to a stand. All those who saw that the Sultan's squadron was still at its post, and who heard the drum beating, were ashamed to go on, and, dreading the consequences if they continued their flight, they came up, and joined that body of troops. A number of soldiers had now rallied in the centre, and the enemy, who had reached the top of the hillocks (*tells*),

halted, and turned to face their ranks. The Sultan, for
his part, occupied the centre of his squadron, and displayed
such energy in rallying the fugitives that he finally succeeded in collecting the whole of his army together again.
The enemy, fearing that some ambush was concealed
in the woods, retired towards their halting-place, and
the Sultan regained some rising ground close to the edge
of the wood, and there drew up his troops; having no tent
to take shelter in, he stood in the shadow of a piece of
cloth. I stood beside him, endeavouring to console him;
but he would not listen to me—he was so overwhelmed by
the events of the day: however, he took a little food that
we offered him. He remained in this position, awaiting
the return of the horses that had been taken to water at
some considerable distance, and while we were thus drawn
up, he had the wounded brought to him to comfort them,
and to see that their wounds were dressed. He gave his
own horses to those who had lost theirs. There were a
great number of killed and wounded this day on both sides.
Amongst the leaders who stood firm, the chief were el-Melek
el-'Âdel, Kâimâz en-Nejmi the eunuch, and el-Melek el-
Afḍal, the Sultan's son. El-Afḍal charged so furiously
that a tumour he had in the face burst, and his face was
drenched with blood; but he suffered it with remarkable
patience. The squadron from Mosul displayed the greatest
bravery, and won the Sultan's thanks for its leader, 'Alâ
ed-Dîn. Our people sought for their comrades, and found
many a one who had died a martyr on the battle-field.
The bodies of persons of note were found, especially that
of Mûsek, the grand emir (of the Kurds), a chief renowned
for his bravery; that of Kâimâz el-'Âdeli, who was also
celebrated; and that of Lîghûsh, a brave officer, whose
death was a cause of great grief to the Sultan. We had a
large number of men and horses wounded, and the enemy

on their side had a great many casualties. We took only
one prisoner, who was brought to the Sultan, and beheaded
by his command. We also captured four horses from them.
The Sultan then ordered the baggage forward (to the river)
el-'Aûja,[1] and I obtained his permission to follow it, and
to precede him to the place he had appointed for our encampment. I left him seated, waiting until all his troops
were collected, and till intelligence came in regarding the
enemy, who were encamped close to Arsûf.

Ninth halt.—I set out after the mid-day prayer, and
when I reached the crossing, saw the baggage-train drawn
up on the further bank of the 'Auja in a beautiful spot
covered with grass. The Sultan reached the camp towards
the close of the same day, and whilst the soldiers were
crowding together at the head of the bridge,[2] he took up
a position on a hill commanding the river; then, instead
of coming to the camp, he sent his herald to proclaim that
the troops were to cross the river again and come to the
place where he was standing. God alone knows the depth
of grief which filled his heart after this battle; our men
were all wounded, some in their bodies, some in their spirits.
On (Sunday) the 15th of Sh'abân, the Sultan ordered
the drum to be beaten, and mounted his horse; then,
followed by the whole army, he retraced his steps of the
previous day, and advanced towards the enemy. When
he drew near Arsûf, he drew up his squadrons in order
of battle, hoping to draw the Franks from their position,
and to get an opportunity of attacking them. But they
made no movement that day, being worn out with fatigue

---

[1] The *'Aûja* flows into the sea N. of Jaffa; the camp (near Mejdel
Yâba) was 10 miles S.E. from the battlefield.

[2] This bridge (*Jisr el-Abâbneh*) was S. of the camping ground,
which was near Mejdel Yâba. The Moslems appear to have been
flying beyond the camp.

and suffering severely from their wounds.[1] He stood facing them until evening came on, when he withdrew to the camping-place of the previous night. The next morning, the 16th day of the month, he again ordered the drum to be beaten, and rode out at the head of his troops in the direction of the enemy. On his way he heard that they were on the march to Jaffa; he then advanced close to them, drew up his troops in order of battle, and sent his marksmen forward. The Moslem army completely surrounded the enemy, and discharged such a shower of arrows that one could hardly see the sky, for they were attacking them with all the fury of hatred. The Sultan hoped by this means to provoke them to charge, that his men might have an opportunity of attacking them, leaving it in God's hands to give the victory to whom He would. But the Franks would not charge; they restrained themselves, keeping always behind the infantry, and continued to advance in their usual order of march. Proceeding in this manner, they came to the 'Aûja, on the upper banks of which river we were encamped, while they took up a position further down the stream. Some of their troops crossed to the west bank,[2] the others remaining on the east. When our men saw that they were preparing to encamp, they withdrew, and the Sultan returned to the baggage, and when he reached his tent took food. They then brought him four Franks and a woman, who had been taken prisoner by the Arabs, and he ordered them to be kept in strict confinement. He spent the remainder of the day writing to the provinces, commanding them to dispatch the contingents still to come. They brought him information

---

[1] Sunday, September 8, 1191, was the feast of the Nativity of the Virgin. The Franks, according to De Vinsauf, were giving thanks for their victory in the Church of Arsûf.

[2] The *'Aûja* runs nearly N. and S. in the central part of its course.

(that same day) that the enemy had lost great numbers
of their horses in the action at Arsûf, for the Arabs who
had gone over the battle-field had counted more than
a hundred chargers. He then dispatched the loads to
Ramla, and I preceded them on their march to that place.
He himself spent the night in the place where we had
been encamped.

Tenth halt.—On the 17th of the month, as soon as he
had said the morning prayer, he set out for Ramla[1] with
the light baggage. Two Franks were brought to him,
whom he ordered to be beheaded. A messenger sent back
by the advanced guard brought him news that the Franks
were marching from Jaffa; he then advanced as far as
Ramla, where two more Franks were brought before him.
When these prisoners were questioned as to the enemy's
movements, they stated that their countrymen would probably remain in Jaffa for some days, for they intended
to put the city into a good state of defence, and furnish
it with plentiful supplies of men and provisions. He therefore called the members of his council together, and asked
their opinion whether it would be better to destroy the
city of Ascalon, or to leave it as it was. They decided
unanimously that a division of the army under el-Melek
el-'Âdel should remain behind, to keep a strict watch over
the enemy's movements, and make constant reports thereon
to the Sultan, whilst the Sultan himself should set out
for Ascalon, and destroy it before it fell into the hands
of the Franks. For the enemy, as soon as they had
massacred the garrison, would probably make that city
the basis of their operations in an attack on Jerusalem,
and thus cut off all communication with Egypt. The
Sultan wished to prevent this, and, knowing that it would

[1] *Ramleh* is 12 miles from Mejdel Yâba, where the camp of Salâh
ed-Dîn was fixed.

be impossible for the Moslems to hold the city, with the remembrance of Acre and the fate of its garrison fresh in their minds, and being convinced, moreover, that his soldiers would be afraid to shut themselves up in the city, he declared that he intended to embody all the forces at his disposal in the army under his command, and then concentrate his attention on the defence of Jerusalem. It was therefore decreed that Ascalon should be destroyed. So, as soon as night began to fall, he dispatched all the heavy baggage and commanded his son, el-Melek el-Afdal, to set forth at midnight and follow it. He himself started on the Wednesday morning, and I went with him.

Eleventh halt.—About mid-day on Wednesday, the 18th of Sh'abân, the Sultan reached Yebna,[1] where he gave his people time to rest, and then marched into the territory of the city of Ascalon. His tent had already been pitched at some distance from the city, and he spent the night there, though he slept very little, for the thought of being obliged to destroy the city filled his mind. I had left him after midnight, but at daybreak he summoned me to him again, and began to discuss his plans with me. He then sent for his son, el-Melek el-Afdal, to consult him on the subject, and they talked together for a long while. He said to me, whilst I was on duty in his tent: 'I take God to witness I would rather lose all my children than cast down a single stone from the walls, but God wills it; it is necessary for the Moslem cause, therefore I am obliged to carry it through.' He sought counsel with God, and God made him see that it was necessary to destroy the city since the Moslems were unable to protect it. He therefore sent for 'Alem ed-Dîn Ḳaiṣar, the governor, one of his chief memlûks, and a man of good

---

[1] *Yebnah* (ancient *Jamnia*), called Ibelin by the Franks, was 9 miles S.W. of Ramleh, and 12 miles S. of Jaffa, near the shore.

judgment, who commanded that all the workmen in the
town should be gathered together. I myself saw (that
officer) walking up and down the market-place, and going
from tent to tent to hire workmen. He assigned a certain
portion of the ramparts to each group of labourers; the
task of destroying a curtain and tower was also given to
each emir and company of soldiers. When these people
entered the city there arose a great sound of mourning and
lamentation, for it was pleasant to look upon and delightful
to the senses; its walls were strong, its buildings beautiful,
and it occupied a most charming situation. The inhabitants
were overwhelmed by the news that their city was to be
destroyed, and that they would have to give up their
homes; they uttered loud lamentations, and began at
once to sell everything they could not carry away with
them, giving for one piece of silver what was really worth
ten, and even selling ten hens for one dirhem. Great
distress reigned in the city; the inhabitants repaired to
the camp with their wives and children to sell their household goods. Some of them set out for Egypt, some for
Syria; numbers were obliged to depart on foot, having no
money with which to hire beasts to carry them. This was
a horrible time during which terrible things occurred.
The Sultan, assisted by his son el-Melek el-Afdal,
spent his time in getting workmen together and encouraging them to work well, for he was very apprehensive
that if the Franks heard what he was doing, they would
come up and prevent him from carrying out his intention.
The troops, worn out by fatigue, both of mind and body,
spent that night in their tents. The same night a messenger came from el-Melek el-'Âdel, informing the Sultan
that that prince had had an interview on the subject of
peace with ambassadors from the Franks, and that he
had also conversed on the same subject with the son of

Honferi, who had come to visit him, and asked him to surrender to the Franks all the cities of the districts on the coast. The Sultan—whose troops were worn out and weary of such constant fighting and warfare, besides being broken down by neediness—felt inclined to accept this proposal, and wrote to el-'Âdel to enter into negotiations on the subject, granting him full powers to make such terms as should seem best to him. On the 20th of Sh'abân the Sultan busied himself from early morning in urging forward the work of demolition, and putting more workmen on the walls. As an encouragement to them he gave them all the corn that had been stored there, and which he saw it would be impossible to carry away ; moreover, time pressed, and he feared an attack from the Franks. By his orders they set fire to all the houses and other buildings in the city, and the inhabitants were obliged to sacrifice whatever property they had still remaining, as they had no means of taking it away. We constantly received intelligence of the enemy's movements ; they were now very hard at work repairing (the fortifications of) Jaffa. We were informed by a letter from el-Melek el-'Âdel that the enemy did not know we were engaged in demolishing the city (of Ascalon). ' We are delaying matters as much as we can with these people,' the prince added, ' and we will prolong the negotiations to give you time to destroy the city.' By the Sultan's orders all the towers were filled with wood, and then set on fire. On the morning of the 21st he left the camp on horseback to urge the labourers on in their work; he kept them well occupied in their task of destruction, and visited them periodically to see that they were at work; he was therefore very soon so ill that for two days he was unable either to ride or take any food. Every moment news of the enemy came in with tidings of encounters with them—sometimes successful, sometimes disastrous—for there were continual engagements in the short space between them and our advanced guard. (Meanwhile) he kept pressing forward the demolition of the city, and brought the camp closer to the walls, which enabled the servants, the camel and ass-drivers, and all the other camp-followers to take part in the work. Therefore the walls were soon partially demolished, although they were most solidly built, being from nine to ten cubits thick—the thickness varying with the position. One of the stonemasons informed the Sultan in· my hearing that (the wall of) one of the towers which he was then undermining was as thick as a lance is long. Demolition and fire laid the city low during the whole of the month of Sh'abân. Towards the end of the month a letter came from Jurdik, saying that the enemy had begun to make expeditions from Jaffa, and to overrun the neighbouring districts. This news inspired the Sultan with the hope of being able to punish the invaders. He resolved to advance upon them and take them by surprise, leaving the miners at Ascalon with a body of cavalry to prótect them ; but he afterwards thought it best to postpone his departure until after they had burnt down the 'Hospitallers' Tower,' a building that commandod the sea, and was as strong as a castle. I had been in the tower, and gone all over it ; it was so solidly built that the workmen's picks made no impression on it whatever, and they were obliged to set it on fire to make the stones more friable before the labourers attacked it with their tools. On the 1st of Ramadan the Sultan gave this task into the hands of his son el-Melek el-Afdal and his officers. I watched them carrying up the wood to set the tower on fire. It burnt for two days and nights. The Sultan did not ride out that day, in order to spare himself, and I, too, was seized with an indisposition that prevented my attending him throughout the day. In spite of the important matters he had on his mind, he sent three times during the day to inquire how I was.

CHAPTER CXXII.

THE SULTAN SETS OUT FOR RAMLA.

THE Sultan started at midnight on the 2nd of Ramaḍân, in order to avoid the heat of the day, and spare himself as much as possible. He reached Yebna towards mid-day, and dismounted, to rest in his brother (el-'Âdel's) tent, and also to obtain information regarding the enemy from him. He remained there an hour, and then rode off to his own tent, where he spent the night. On the following day, the 3rd, he set out very early for Ramla, arriving at that place about noon. There he took up his position with the heavy baggage in a way that showed he intended to remain for some time. He then drew up his troops in order of battle, by right wing, left wing, and centre; after which he gave the people a meal, and then rested for a short while. Between the afternoon and the four o'clock prayer he visited Lydda,[1] and, observing that the church in that place was a very fine building, he ordered that it should be destroyed, as well as the castle of Ramla. That same day several troops of workmen began the work of demolition. All the straw and corn stored in the Government granaries here was given up to the people. The inhabitants were obliged to emigrate to other centres of population, and very few people remained in the place. The labourers worked until the evening, when the

---

[1] Salâh ed-Dîn destroyed all the castles on the plain, or near the foot of the hills, according to De Vinsauf.

Sultan returned to his tent. The following day, the 4th of Ramaḍân, he set the people to work again in both places, and left them under the direction of superintendents, who were instructed to make them push on with the task in hand. He visited the works every evening, and had a meal served after the *maghreb* prayer; then, when everyone had broken their fast,[1] they returned each one to his own tent. The idea of visiting Jerusalem then occurred to the Sultan, and he set out secretly with a small following to ascertain the condition of the city, charging his brother el-Melek el-'Âdel to take his place at the head of the army, and to press forward with the work of destruction. He started at night-fall for Beit-Nûba,[2] where he halted until the following day. As soon as morning-prayer had been said, he set out for the Holy City (el-Ḳuds) which he reached on the 5th of the month. The remainder of the day he spent in examining the condition of the city—its fortifications and garrison, the state of its supplies, the efficiency of its war-stores, etc. That same day the servants of Ḳâimâz the eunuch brought him two Christians they had stopped, with letters from the governor (*Wâli*) to the Sultan. These letters, written but a few days before, stated the needs of the city as to corn, military stores, and garrison. The Sultan read them, and ordered all concerned to be beheaded. He carried on his examination of the city until the 8th of the month, on which day he took his departure at noon, leaving orders that the fortifications should be repaired; he spent the night at Beit-Nûba, and started in the morning to return to the army. That same day M'oin ed-Dîn Ḳaiṣar Shah, Lord of Malaṭia, son of Ḳilîj Arslân, came to beg the Sultan's support against his father and brothers,

---

[1] Being Ramaḍân, the fast was only broken at sunset.

[2] See p. 11.

who were trying to take the city from him.   El-Melek
el-'Âdel went out from Lydda to welcome him, and gave
him the most honourable reception.   They pitched our
visitor's tent close to Lydda.   That same day the enemy's
foragers scattered over the plain, and were attacked by our
advanced guard.   As soon as the enemy were informed of
this, they sent a detachment of cavalry to their support,
which was likewise attacked by the guard.   One of the
prisoners stated that the king of England had ridden out
with this detachment, and that a Moslem was about to
pierce him with his lance, when a Frank threw himself in
between, and received the blow, which caused his death ;
he himself (the king) was wounded.[1]   That, at least, is
what we were told, but God alone knows the truth.   On
the 9th of Ramadân the Sultan rejoined the army, and
was received by all with great demonstrations of joy.
When Ḳilij Arslân's son came before him, he dismounted
to receive him, treated him with every mark of honour,
and welcomed him in his own tent.   He pressed forward
the work of demolition he had ordered with unrelaxed
energy.   Meanwhile, intelligence of the enemy came in
very frequently.   There had been several engagements
between the Franks and the advanced guard, and the
Arabs had stolen numbers of their horses and mules.

CHAPTER CXXIII.

ARRIVAL OF AN AMBASSADOR FROM THE MARQUIS.

In the meantime an ambassador was sent by the marquis
to state that he would make peace with the Moslems on

---

[1] King Richard was hawking when he fell into this ambush.—De
Vinsauf, v. 31.

condition that they gave up to him the cities of Sidon and Beirût. Under those circumstances he undertook to make an open rupture with the Franks, to lay siege to Acre, and take it from them, provided that the Sultan would ratify the proposed conditions beforehand. The Sultan sent el-'Adl en-Nejeb (the courier), who bore a reply accepting the marquis's proposals. He was very anxious to make the marquis break with the Franks, for he was a man greatly to be feared, and accursed. The marquis, on his side, saw that the Franks intended to deprive him of the city of Tyre; he had therefore shut himself up in that place, which was strongly fortified. El-'Âdel set forth on the 12th of Ramaḍân, accompanied by an ambassador from the Sultan; the offer made by the marquis was to be accepted on condition that he should first openly declare war against the Franks by making an attack on Acre, and that, as soon as that city was taken, he should release the (Moslem) prisoners detained there, as well as those in captivity in Tyre; then, and not till then, would the Sultan give him the two cities he had asked for. During the evening of the same day the ambassador, sent by the king of England to confer with el-Melek el-'Âdel concerning the treaty of peace, was brought before that prince. On the 13th of Ramaḍân the Sultan thought it necessary to withdraw to the neighbouring hills with his troops, so as to send the baggage-animals out to collect forage: for Ramla, where we were quartered, was too close to the Franks for us to risk sending them out, lest they should be carried off. He therefore left that place and took up a position on a hill adjoining that of en-Natrûn,[1] taking with him the heavy baggage and the whole of the troops, excepting, of course, the advanced guard. This manœuvre was carried out after the demolition of Ramla and Lydda. As soon as

[1] See p. 32.

he had taken up his position, he went all round en-Naṭrûn —a castle celebrated for its strength and massiveness— and forthwith gave an order for its demolition, on which they set to work at once. Messages were frequently sent between el-Melek el-'Âdel and the king of England. The king's ambassadors declared that their master had the greatest confidence in el-Melek el-'Âdel, and trusted him implicitly in the matter of arranging the terms of peace. After this ten persons chosen by the Franks brought him such satisfactory messages, that he at once communicated them in writing to the Sultan. This occurred on the 17th of the month. Among the news they brought was intelligence of the death of the king of France, which had taken place at Antioch in consequence of an illness with which he had been seized. They also informed us that the king of England had returned to Acre, having obtained certain intelligence that the marquis had entered into correspondence with the Sultan, broken all his promises to the king, and undertaken to advance upon Acre. The king, therefore, had hastened back to that city, to break off these negotiations, and get back the marquis's allegiance to the cause. After this the Sultan rode out to the advanced guard, and, meeting his brother at Lydda, questioned him on the news he had received. In the evening, about the hour of the *'asr* prayer, he returned to the camp, and two Franks were brought before him who had fallen into the hands of the advanced guard. These men confirmed the news of the death of the king of France, and the departure of the king of England for Acre.[1]

---

[1] The king of France, who was ill, had left Palestine on August 1. Richard's visit to Acre was with the intention of coming to terms with the French, who supported the claims of Conrad of Montferrat as king of Jerusalem. Philip died in 1223 A.D.

CHAPTER CXXIV.

EL-MELEK EL-'ÂDEL VISITS JERUSALEM.

As it seemed necessary to make an inspection of the Holy City and the state of its fortifications, el-Melek el-'Âdel was commanded to repair to that place. This was on the 29th of the month ; he had just left the advanced guard, having heard that the leaders of the Franks had withdrawn from our neighbourhood, and he started on his journey immediately. That same day a letter was received from el-Melek el-Mozaffer Taki ed-Dîn, announcing the death of Kizil, son of Aildekez, and king of Persia ; his own people had attacked and assassinated him. It was said that the murder had been committed at the instigation of his wife, who had joined the faction of Sultan Toghrîl. This occurrence, which took place during the first third of the month of Sh'abân that year, gave rise to great disturbances in the different provinces of Persia. El-'Âdel returned from Jerusalem on the 21st of Ramadân. The same day a letter arrived from the August and Prophetic Court (that is to say, from the Khalif's Chancery) referring to el-Melek el-Mozaffer's expedition against Khelât, and expressing the greatest interest in Bektimor. They interceded also on behalf of Hasan Ibn-Kafjâk, kept prisoner at Arbela by Mozaffer ed-Dîn, son of Zein ed-Dîn, and begged the Sultan to give orders that he should be set at liberty. They likewise requested that el-Kâdi el-Fâdel might be sent to the Khalif's Court to settle various questions and make divers arrangements. This letter was sent to el-Kâdi el-Fâdel for his information, with instructions that he should write to Taki ed-Dîn.

CHAPTER CXXV.

INTELLIGENCE RECEIVED FROM THE OUTPOST STATIONED
BEFORE ACRE—ACCOUNT OF THE DOINGS OF SOME
ARAB THIEVES WHO USED TO GET INTO THE ENEMY'S
CAMP.

ON the 22nd of the month of Ramadân some of our
thieves brought the Sultan a mare and mule that they
had carried off from the enemy's camp, into which they
had made their way. The Sultan had hired three hundred
Arab brigands, who used to get into the enemy's camp
and steal their money and horses; they also carried off
living men. They proceeded as follows: one of them
would enter the tent of some Frank whilst he was asleep,
and awake him by planting his dagger at his throat.
When the sleeping man saw the robber armed with the
dagger, he did not dare to say a word, and would suffer
them to carry him out of bounds of the camp. A few of
them who had called out had had their throats cut on the
spot; others, finding themselves in the same circumstances,
had not said a word, preferring captivity to death. This
state of things continued until peace was concluded. The
same day a messenger came in from the advanced guard
with the news that a body of troops had left Acre and
marched out on the plain; the guard had attacked them and
taken twenty of them prisoners; these prisoners had confirmed the report of the king of England's return to Acre,
and stated that he was ill; the garrison of Acre, they added,
was very weak, provisions were getting scarce, and there
was no money. That same day a large fleet, said to have
come from Acre, and bringing the king of England,[1]

[1] King Richard brought French and other forces to Jaffa, which
meantime was being rebuilt.

anchored alongside the enemy's camp, and disembarked a great number of troops, who, according to one report, were to garrison Ascalon ; according to another, were to be led against Jerusalem. On the 24th of the month the prisoners we noticed above arrived from ez-Zîb,[1] and their presence in the camp was a source of great joy to the Moslems. The same day an ambassador arrived who had been despatched by Ḳizil shortly before his death ; whilst another came on behalf of his nephew, Ainâj. During the evening a messenger came from the king of England bringing a horse as a present from that prince to el-Melek el-'Âdel, in return for the gifts he had received at his hands. We also received tidings that day of the death of Ḥossâm ed-Dîn (Muhammad Ibn 'Omar Ibn) Lajîn, son of one of the Sultan's sisters ; he had died at Damascus in consequence of an illness that had attacked him very suddenly. The Sultan was much grieved at this loss. That same day he received a dispatch from Sâma (the commanding officer), saying that the prince (of Antioch) had made an inroad into the districts of Jebela and Laodicea, that his troops had been routed and he himself obliged to seek shelter in his city after having lost a great number of men, and utterly failed in his undertaking.

CHAPTER CXXVI.

EL-MELEK EL-'ÂDEL SENDS A MESSAGE TO THE KING OF ENGLAND.

ON the 26th of Ramaḍân el-Melek el-'Âdel, who was then on duty in command of the advanced guard, was invited by the king of England to send a messenger to him. El-Melek sent him es-Sanî'a Ibn en-Naḥḥâl, a fine young

---

[1] The Biblical Achzib, 8½ miles N. of Acre.

fellow, who acted as his secretary. The interview took place at Yazûr,[1] whither the prince had gone with a large detachment of the infantry, which was then scattered over the plain. They spent a considerable time talking of the peace, and the king uttered these words : ' I will keep the promise I have given to my friend and brother,' referring by these terms to el-Melek el-'Âdel : he then sent the same messenger back to him with the proposals he had to make to us. He also wrote and forwarded by the same messenger a letter for the Sultan, couched in the following terms : ' You are to greet him, and say that both the Moslems and the Franks are reduced to the last extremity ; their cities are destroyed, and the resources of both sides in men and stores brought to nought. And since right has been done in this matter, we need speak only of Jerusalem, of the cross, and of the land in question. As to Jerusalem, we are fully resolved never to give it up, even though we had but one man left ; touching the land, you must restore it to us as far as the other side of Jordan ; and lastly, as regards the cross—to you it is nothing but a piece of wood, but it is very precious in our eyes, and if the Sultan will graciously give it into our hands, we will make peace and breathe again after continual weariness.' When the Sultan had read the contents of this letter, he called his councillors together to consult them on the answer that should be made. Afterwards he wrote thus : ' Jerusalem belongs to us just as much as to you, and is more precious in our eyes than in yours, for it was the place of our Prophet's journey, and the place where the angels gathered. Therefore, do not imagine that we shall give the city up to you, or that we shall suffer ourselves to be persuaded in the matter. As regards the land, it belonged originally to us, and you came to attack us ; if you succeeded in getting

¹ See p. 32.

possession of it, it was only because you came unexpectedly
and on account of the weakness of the Moslems who then
held it ; as long as the war lasts God will not suffer you to
raise one single stone upon another in this country. Lastly,
as concerns the cross, its possession is a great advantage to
us, and we cannot give it up except we could thereby gain
some advantage to Islâm.' This was the answer that the
messenger took back to the king of England.

CHAPTER CXXVII.

SHÌRKÙH IBN BAKHEL, THE KURD, MAKES HIS ESCAPE FROM ACRE, WHERE HE WAS KEPT A PRISONER.

DURING the last days of the month of Ramadân, Shîrkûh
Ibn Bakhel, one of the emirs imprisoned in Acre, came
into the camp. He had been successful in concealing a
cord under his pillow, and emir Hasan Ibn Bârîk had
hidden another in the privy. They had made arrangements to escape together, and got out of the window of
the privy and let themselves down from the top of the
first wall by means of their ropes. Shìrkûh climbed over
the outer wall and succeeded in getting clear without
accident; but Ibn Bârîk, who was following him, had the
misfortune to fall, the cord giving way under his weight.
Shîrkûh found him, stunned by his fall, and spoke to him,
but could get no answer; he then shook him, in the
hope of reviving him and taking him with him, but all his
efforts were in vain. Then, seeing that if he stayed with
his comrade they would both be taken, he left him, and,
in spite of his fetters, ran till he came to the hill of el-
'Aiâdîya. The sun was just beginning to rise, so he hid
himself there, and remained concealed until the day was

well advanced. By that time he had managed to break off his fetters; so he set out once more and succeeded, under the protection of God, in reaching our camp. He presented himself before the Sultan, and informed him, amongst other things, that emir Seif ed-Dîn el-Meshtûb was being kept in very close confinement, and that he had undertaken to pay a heavy ransom in horses, mules, and precious things of all kinds. He said also that the king of England had been to Acre and taken away with him all that belonged to him—servants, memlûks and portable property, leaving nothing whatever behind. He added that the farmers (Fellahîn) on the mountains were supplying him with provisions. He also stated that Toghrîl, one of the Sultan's chief memlûks and his sword-bearer, had made his escape before him.

CHAPTER CXXVIII.

EL-MELEK EL-'ÂDEL SENDS ME ON A MISSION TO THE SULTAN, ATTENDED BY SEVERAL EMIRS.

On the 29th of Ramadân el-Melek el-'Âdel sent to summon me, with 'Alem ed-Dîn Suleimân Ibn-Jender, Sâbek ed-Dîn Lord of Sheizer, 'Izz ed-Dîn Ibn el-Mokaddem, and Hossâm ed-Dîn Bishâra. He informed us of the proposition made by the king of England to his messenger, which was as follows : that el-Melek el-'Âdel should marry the prince's sister, whom he had brought with him from Sicily, on his way to Palestine, after the death of her husband, king of that island ; she was to live in Jerusalem,[1] and her brother would give up to him those

---

[1] The English chroniclers say nothing of this extraordinary pro-posal. It was not regarded as serious by either side, if indeed it was ever proposed. See pp. 325, 326.

cities of the Sâhel (coast) which belonged to him, to wit,
Acre, Jaffa and Ascalon and their dependencies ; the
Sultan, on his side, was to grant el-Melek el-'Âdel all the
cities he possessed in the Sâhel, and proclaim him king of
those districts. El-'Âdel was to retain all the cities and
fiefs he then held ; the cross of the crucifixion was to be
given back to the Franks ; the villages and strongholds
belonging to the Templars and Hospitallers were to be
theirs. All the Moslem and Frank prisoners were to
be set at liberty, and the king of England was to take
ship and return to his own country. The king suggested
that matters could be very well settled in this way. When
el-'Âdel knew this, he acted on it, and he summoned us,
and instructed us to lay the message he had received before
the Sultan. I was to act as spokesman of the embassy
and inform the Sultan of the interview with the king. If
he approved of the arrangement, and thought it would be
advantageous to the Moslems, I was to take my colleagues
to witness that the Sultan had given his consent and appro-
bation ; and if he rejected the proposal, now that the
negotiations for peace had assumed a definite shape, I was
in like manner to call upon them to bear witness to his
refusal. We presented ourselves before the Sultan, and I
spoke, setting forth all that had taken place at our interview ; then I read (el-Melek el-'Âdel's) letter in the presence
of my above-named colleagues. He consented to the proposals on the spot, for he knew very well that the king of
England would not carry them out, and that it was nothing
but trickery and mocking on his part. He gave his formal
consent at my request, saying 'Yes' three several times, and
calling all who were present to witness his promise. When
we had obtained his consent, we returned to el-Melek el-
'Âdel, and informed him of what had taken place. My
colleagues stated that I had several times warned the

Sultan that I should call witnesses to his assent, and that
he had not hesitated to give his entire approval.   The
proposals, therefore, could be accepted with his full consent.

CHAPTER CXXIX.

A MESSENGER TAKES EL-'ÂDEL'S ANSWER TO THE KING OF ENGLAND'S PROPOSAL.

ON the 2nd Shawâl (October 24) Ibn en-Nahhâl was sent
to the enemy's camp on the part of the Sultan and el-
Melek el-'Âdel.   As soon as the king heard of his arrival
he sent to tell him that the princess had been greatly
enraged when she heard of the projected marriage, and
that she had formally refused her consent, declaring she
would never give herself to a Moslem.   Her brother added :
' If el-Melek el-'Âdel will consent to become a Christian,
we will celebrate the marriage.'   By this means he left a
door open for further negotiations.   When el-'Âdel received
this message, he wrote to his brother informing him of the
position of affairs.   On the 5th of Shawâl we heard that
the Moslem fleet had captured several ships from the
Christians, one of which was known as being (covered over)
and carried more than five hundred men.   They were all
killed, with the exception of four important personages.
This news gave us the greatest pleasure, and was proclaimed to the sound of music.   On the 6th of Shawâl the
Sultan called his chief emirs and councillors together to
consult on the measures to be adopted in case the enemy
should take the field ; for repeated messages had arrived,
stating that the Franks had arranged to come out and
attack the Moslem army.   They thought it best to main-

tain their position and begin by sending away the heavy
baggage, which would leave them prepared to meet the
Franks in case of an attack on their part. During the
evening of the same day two deserters from the Franks
came in to the camp and informed us that the enemy intended to come out, to the number of more than ten
thousand horse; but they did not know what direction the
army was to take. According to a Moslem prisoner, who
had managed to make his escape, they were going to march
first upon Ramla, and decide upon their further movements when there. When the Sultan had satisfied himself
of the truth of this information, he commanded the herald
to proclaim that the troops were to take their light arms
and set out with the standards, for he had made up his
mind to maintain his position in face of the enemy if they
came out; then, on the 7th of the month, he advanced,
and encamped south of Ramla church,[1] where he spent the
night.

CHAPTER CXXX.

THE FRANKS COME OUT FROM JAFFA.

IN the morning of the 8th of Shawâl our troops formed in
order of battle, and el-Melek el-'Âdel, who had been appointed to the command of the advanced guard, went
forward to join that body, with all the volunteers who
offered to go with him. Amongst them was a body of
men who had come from Asia Minor (*er-Rûm*) with a view
of taking part in the Holy War. As soon as el-Melek's
detachment approached the enemy's camp the Sultan's
memlûks, relying on their courage, their excellent horses,

[2] The church of St. Mary, Ramleh, now a mosque.

and their being so used to fighting the Franks, rushed forward and discharged a flight of arrows at the enemy. The volunteers from Asia Minor, led astray by the rashness of the memlûks, followed their example. The Franks, angry and irritated by the close attack, rode from within the camp and charged on them like one man, uttering a mighty shout. Those only of our men escaped who were borne out of danger by their horses, or who were predestined to save their lives by the swiftness of their own limbs. The enemy took a great number prisoner, and on their side had three men killed. The Franks then removed their tents to Yâzûr, and the Sultan that night was at their halting-place till dawn.

CHAPTER CXXXI.

DEATH OF EL-MELEK EL-MOZAFFER TAKI ED-DÎN.

ON the 11th of the month the Sultan set out in the direction of the enemy, and, after having examined their position, returned to charge me to tell el-Melek el-'Âdel that he wished to see him, together with 'Alem ed-Dîn Suleimân Ibn Jender, Sâbek ed-Dîn Ibn ed-Dâya, and 'Izz ed-Dîn Ibn el-Mokaddem. When they came into his presence he ordered a servant to send everyone away excepting those emirs and myself, and to cause everyone to withdraw from the vicinity of his tent. He then drew a letter from his cloak, the seal being broken; when he read it, we saw the tears flow down his cheeks. Then he gave way to his grief and wept and lamented until we wept also, though we knew not why. When he told us that this letter was to inform him of the death of el-Melek el-Mozaffer, we all began once more to groan and weep. I then spoke to

him, and bade him remember Almighty God, and submit
to what had been determined and preordained. He
replied : ' I ask pardon of God '; *we are His, and to Him
we return* (Kurân ii. 151). 'We must keep this news
secret, lest the enemy learn it whilst they are close upon
us.' He then ordered a meal to be served for all who were
present, and after partaking of it we withdrew. Taḳi ed-
Dîn had died on his return from Khelât to Miâfârekîn.
His body was taken to that city, and later on was trans-
ferred to a mausoleum within a college, now very well
known, that was founded in his honour, close to Ḥamah.
I myself have visited his tomb. His death took place on
Friday, the 19th of Ramaḍân, 587 (October 10, 1191).

CHAPTER CXXXII.

A DESPATCH ARRIVES FROM BAGHDAD.

ON the 12th of Shawâl the Sultan received a letter from
his officers at Damascus, enclosing a despatch from
Baghdad, sent from the August and Prophetic Court. It
contained .observations on three several matters : first, it
expressed disapprobation of the conduct of el-Melek
el-Mozaffer (Taḳi ed-Dîn) in marching against Bektimor,
disavowing his action so strongly that it was formally
stated the Khalif's Divân would not salute that prince ;
secondly, it disapproved of the conduct of Mozaffer
ed-Dîn, son of Zein ed-Dîn, in keeping Ḥasan Ibn Ḳafjâḳ
in captivity, and commanded that the prisoner should be
put in possession of el-Kerkhâni.[1] This is what had

---

[1] Behâ ed-Dîn's Kerkhâni, or Kerkhîni, is probably identical with
the Kerkhîni of the author of the ' Merâsed el-Ittilâ,' and of Ibn el-
Athîr (' Kamel,' vol. xii. of Tornberg's edition). It lies E. of the Tigris,
and is apparently *Kïrkuk*, the chief town of the Shehrizor Sanjak, and
an important Turkish military station.

happened with regard to Ibn Ḳafjâḳ: he had marched
against the city of Urumiah[1] with Sultan Toghrîl, who had
visited him with the view of obtaining assistance after his
flight from Persia. He had first assisted the Sultan, and
given him his sister in marriage, and then, in the hope of
being made that prince's atabeg (guardian), and governor
of the country as such, he had marched upon Urumiah, and
was reported to have put all its male population to the
sword, and carried off its women and children into
slavery. He used to make his headquarters in the stronghold of el-Kerkhâni, and from thence he issued forth to
way-lay caravans and ravage the country round. Sultan
Toghrîl, seeing that Ibn Ḳafjâḳ was growing formidable,
left him, and returned to his own country, whilst his former
protector continued his depredations. Mozaffer ed-Dîn,
Lord of Arbela, succeeded in gaining the man's confidence,
enticed him into his city, treated him as a confidential
friend, and then made him prisoner. When Ibn Ḳafjâḳ
found that Mozaffer ed-Dîn had seized his dominions, he
wrote to inform the Khalif's Divân, hoping to earn the
Khalif's goodwill and favour by imploring his intervention.
In the third place, the despatch commanded that el-Ḳâdi
el-Fâdel should be sent to Baghdad as an ambassador to
settle the preliminaries of certain agreements, and to be
informed by the Divân on certain points. The Sultan
sent an answer in the following terms : ' In the first place,
we gave no instructions in the matter of which you complain. The prince crossed the river with a view of raising
troops for the Holy War, and returning forthwith ; but as
circumstances obliged him to remain some time, we sent,
commanding him to return ; in the second place, you had
been informed as to Ibn Ḳafjâḳ's character and his depredations, and instructions had been sent to Mozaffer

[1] *Urumiah*, W. of Lake Urumiah in Kurdistan.

ed-Dîn to take him with him into Syria, where he was to assign him a fief, in order that his whole energies might be absorbed in the Holy War ; in the third place, el-Kâdi el-Fâdel cannot possibly go to you ; he is almost always an invalid, and is not strong enough to undertake the journey to Irâk.' This was the purport of his answer.

CHAPTER CXXXIII.

THE LORD OF SIDON COMES ON AN EMBASSY FROM THE MARQUIS.

ON the 13th of Shawâl we were informed that the Lord of Sidon[1] had arrived as an ambassador from the marquis, Lord of Tyre. We had already had frequent discussions with him, which resulted in his declaring that they wished to break with the Franks, and join us against them. The cause of this defection was a quarrel that had arisen between the marquis and the other princes of the Franks, concerning a marriage which he had contracted with the wife of King Geoffrey's[2] brother. This marriage was

---

[1] This was Renaud, Lord of Sidon, who, after having escaped from the defeat at Tiberias, and then played upon Salâh ed-Dîn's credulity in the matter of surrendering the castle of Shakîf (see above, pp. 150-153), had been made prisoner by the Sultan, and sent to Damascus. Having subsequently recovered his freedom, he joined the faction of Conrad, Marquis of Montferrat.

[2] Isabel, second wife of Conrad of Montferrat, and daughter of King Amaury of Jerusalem, by Maria, grandniece of the Emperor Manuel Comnenos, of Constantinople, was related to the first wife of Conrad—also a Greek princess. The marriage was thus within prohibited degrees ; and, in addition, Humphrey of Toron, stepson of Renaud of Chatillon, and first husband of Isabel, was still alive, and the question of the divorce was controverted. These were the causes of scandal. But Beha ed-Dîn is wrong, not only as to the king's name (Geoffrey for Guy), but as to the relationship. Isabel was half-sister of King Guy's wife, not wife of his brother.

declared a scandal on religious grounds, and was the cause
of great dissensions. The marquis, apprehensive for his
personal safety, took advantage of night to escape to Sidon,
taking his wife with him. He then addressed himself to
the Sultan, and endeavoured to obtain the support of that
prince. The marquis's rupture with the Franks was a good
thing for the Moslems, for the enemy lost in him their
most energetic leader, their most experienced warrior, and
their cleverest counsellor. When the Sultan was informed
of the arrival of his ambassador, he commanded that he
should have a most magnificent reception. A tent was
pitched for him within a canvas enclosure, furnished with
cushions and carpets fit for kings and great men. By the
Sultan's orders, he was invited to dismount where the
baggage was drawn up, so that he might rest a little before
the interview.

CHAPTER CXXXIV.

AMBUSH WHERE AIYÂZ EL-MEHRÂNI TESTIFIES (FOR THE FAITH).

ON the 16th of Shawâl the Sultan ordered his bodyguard
to conceal themselves in the hollows of the valleys round,
and to take command of a number of Arabs. As soon as
they had taken up their position, the Arabs, according to
their custom, began to keep watch on the enemy, who used
to come out to forage and get wood near their encampment, so as to seize the best opportunity of attacking
them. When the foraging-party of the enemy came up,
the Arabs began to shoot furiously at it. They defended
themselves, and the enemy, hearing their cries of alarm,
sent out a detachment of cavalry to charge the Arabs
who gave way, and retreated in the direction of the am-

buscade. The enemy followed them, thinking that they could soon overtake them, when all of a sudden the Moslem foot and horse rushed from their hiding-place, with a mighty shout. It was now the turn of the Franks to retreat, and they fled back towards their camp. Their countrymen, as soon as they heard the Moslems had charged, sent a large body of troops to the scene of the action. The fight began anew ; the fight became serious, and both sides suffered heavy losses. The enemy had a number of men wounded ; we also took several prisoners and a quantity of horses. Thanks to the measures taken by the Sultan, this action terminated (fortunately for us) : he foresaw what would happen, and had commanded Akhar Aslem, Seif ed-Dîn Yâzkoj, and several other officers on whom he could rely, to take up a position in rear of, and supporting the Moslems. 'If you see the troops in ambush are getting the worst of it,' he said, 'show yourselves.' When the emirs saw the superior strength of the enemy's forces, they ordered their foot and horse forward. As soon as the Franks saw the Moslem battalions bearing down on them, they turned back, and made for their camp, our men rushing after them in hot pursuit. The fight was over a little before mid-day. I attended the Sultan that morning when he rode out to get news of the battle, and we met the first of the soldiers who were returning from it. They proved to be the whole of the Arabs, who had left the field before the action was finished, bringing with them five horses they had taken. Meanwhile, the scouts and messengers had kept us constantly informed of what was going on : the enemy had upwards of sixty men killed ; a certain number of the Moslems had been wounded, and Aiâz el-Mehrâni, a warrior renowned for his valour, had fallen on the field, covered with wounds ; a young man in el-Gheidi's service, named Jâwali, had met with the same fate ; they had taken prisoner two important knights of the Franks, and two deserters came over from them, bringing their horses and arms. The Sultan returned to his tent, and gave the horses to those who had lost their own, and ordered that the greatest care should be taken of the wounded. Towards the end of the day, el-Melek el-'Âdel received a message from the king of England, complaining of the ambush, and begging for an interview with him.

CHAPTER CXXXV.

EL-MELEK'S INTERVIEW WITH THE KING OF ENGLAND.

ON the 18th of Shawâl, el-Melek el-'Âdel joined the advanced guard, where a large tent was erected to receive him. He had brought with him all sorts of dainties and delicacies, various kinds of drinks, and beautiful gifts and presents fit for one prince to offer to another. When he made presents of this kind, no one could outdo him in magnificence. When the king of England came to visit him in his tent, he met with the most honourable reception at his hands ; then the king took him to his quarters, and had a repast served, consisting of such dishes peculiar to his country as he thought would be most agreeable to his palate. El-'Âdel partook of them, and the king and his suite ate of the dishes provided by el-'Âdel. Their interview lasted during the greater part of the day, and they parted from one another with mutual assurances of perfect goodwill and sincere affection.

CHAPTER CXXXVI.

THE KING OF ENGLAND'S MESSAGE TO THE SULTAN.

THAT same day the king of England asked el-Melek el-'Âdel to procure an interview for him with the Sultan. When a message was brought to Ṣalaḥ ed-Dîn upon the subject, he consulted his advisers as to the answer that he should make. None of the various opinions expressed coincided with that held by the Sultan, who couched his reply in the following terms : ' It would be a disgrace for kings to strive with one another after they had met. Let the question at issue between them be arranged first. Only after matters have been settled would it be fitting for them to have an interview, and talk over serious business. Besides, I do not understand your tongue any more than you understand mine ; therefore we should require an interpreter whom we could both trust to act as our go-between. As soon as some definite arrangement has been concluded, we will have an interview and lay the foundation for a sincere friendship between the two nations.' The king of England much admired this reply, and saw that he could only accomplish the object he had in view by conforming to the wishes of the Sultan.

CHAPTER CXXXVII.

THE LORD OF SIDON IS RECEIVED BY THE SULTAN.

ON the 19th of Shawâl the Sultan held a reception, and ordered the Lord of Sidon to be brought before him that he might converse with him, and be informed of the

21

object of his mission. I was present when the ambassador and his suite were introduced. The Sultan accorded him a most honourable reception, addressed a few words to his followers, and then ordered a magnificent banquet to be served for them. After this he remained alone with them. They asked the Sultan to conclude a treaty with the marquis, Lord of Tyre ; several influential leaders among the Franks had lately joined his faction, such as the Lord of Sidon, and other well-known chiefs. We have already given an account of his affairs. The Sultan replied that he was very willing to conclude peace with him, but only on condition that he should openly and actively oppose the Franks from beyond the seas. He would be induced to take this step by the fears he entertained, and by their attitude towards him in the matter of his marriage. The Sultan promised to accept this treaty, but only on conditions calculated to sow disunion among the Franks, and ensure that the efforts of one faction would neutralize those of the other.

CHAPTER CXXXVIII.

AN AMBASSADOR ARRIVES FROM THE KING OF ENGLAND.

IN the evening of that same day, the son of Honferi, one of the greatest among princes and princes' sons of the Franks, came to the Sultan's camp with a message from the king of England. In his suite was a man said to be a hundred and twenty years old. The king's message ran as follows : ' I like your sincerity, and desire your friendship. You said that you would give your brother all the districts on the sea-coast, and I am anxious that you should judge between him and me in the division of the land. But we

must absolutely have part of the city of Jerusalem (el-
Ḳuds esh-Sherîf). It is my wish that you should divide
(the land) in such a way that your brother shall be acquitted
of all blame by the Moslems, and that I shall incur no
reproach from the Franks.' The Sultan answered this
message at once with promises of compliance, and immediately dismissed the ambassador, whose message had
made a profound impression upon him. Directly they had
departed, he sent after the deputation to speak to them
on the subject of the prisoners, a business to be settled
separately. They replied that, if peace were made, it would
embrace all; if not, there could be no question of the
prisoners. The Sultan's object was to prevent the conclusion of the peace. At the close of the audience, when
the envoys had withdrawn, the Sultan turned to me, and
said : ' If we make peace with those people, there is
nothing to protect us against their treachery. If I were
to die, it might be difficult to get an army together such as
this, and (meanwhile) the enemy would have waxed strong.
The best thing to do is to persevere in the Holy War until
we have either driven them all from the coast, or we ourselves die in the attempt.' That was his own opinion, but
he was over-persuaded to conclude peace.

CHAPTER CXXXIX.

A COUNCIL IS HELD AS TO WHETHER IT WILL BE BETTER
TO TREAT WITH THE KING OF ENGLAND OR THE
MARQUIS.

ON the 11th of Shawâl,[1] the Sultan had summoned his
emirs and councillors of state to lay before them the
marquis's proposals, which he was much inclined to accept.

[1] The narrative reverts from 19th to 11th Shawâl (November 4).

It was a question of allowing him to take possession of
Sidon, on condition that he would openly break with the
Franks, and join us in actively opposing them. The Sultan
then set forth the proposals made by the king of England
as the basis of a treaty. He asked for a certain number
of towns in the coast-districts, which he specified by name,
while he gave up the hill-country to the Moslems, or else
that the towns should be held half and half by either side;
in either case, the Christians were to be allowed to have
priests in the monasteries and churches of the Holy City.
The king gave us the choice of these two proposals, and
the council was to consider which should be adopted. He
then submitted to the emirs the conditions of the treaty of
peace desired by the king, and the terms of the treaty the
marquis was desirous of concluding, inviting them to give
their opinions on the subject, and to consider which were
to be preferred—the king's proposals or those of the marquis. He also charged them to determine which of the
two proposals suggested by the king should be chosen.
The council declared that, if peace were to be made, an
arrangement should be concluded with the king : for an
honest alliance between Moslems and the Franks (of Syria)
could hardly be counted on, and they must expect to be
betrayed by them. The meeting then broke up, and the
subject of the peace was continually discussed. Messengers
kept on passing to and fro until the preliminaries of the
treaty were finally arranged. The principal condition was
that the king should offer his sister in marriage to el-Melek
el-'Âdel, on condition that the pair should be put in possession of all the cities of the coast-districts held by either
Moslems or Christians ; the latter were to be given to the
princess in the name of her brother the king, the former to
be granted to el-'Âdel in the Sultan's name. In his last
message (to el-'Âdel), the king expressed himself as follows

on this point: 'All the Christians cry out against me
for thinking of marrying my sister to a Moslem without
having obtained permission from the pope, who is the head
of our religion. I am therefore sending an ambassador to
him, and I shall have an answer in six months. If he gives
his consent, the arrangement will be carried out ; if not, I
will give you my brother's daughter to wife, for which we
should not require the pope's permission.' In the meantime hostilities were kept up, for a state of war seemed to
have become a necessity. The Lord of Sidon rode out
sometimes with el-'Âdel, and they would go up a hill to
survey the disposition of the forces of the Franks. Whenever the enemy saw them together, they made fresh efforts
to get the peace signed, for they were in the greatest dread
lest the marquis should conclude a peace with the Moslems,
and thus rend asunder the chief bond of strength of the
Franks. Things remained in this condition until the 15th
of Shawâl.

CHAPTER CXL.

THE SULTAN ENCAMPS ON TELL EL-JEZER.

ON the following Friday the Sultan rose with the intention
of removing the camp. He called his councillors together,
and asked them what reply should be made to the proposals
of the enemy ; he submitted to the meeting the various
propositions that had been made, and informed them fully
as to the motives which governed the Franks in their
offers. He then introduced the envoys from the Franks
who had come from abroad, the son of Honferi acting as
their interpreter. He arranged with them that two commissioners should accompany them on their return—one to
represent himself, the other to represent el-Melek el-'Âdel,
who was the person most interested in this business. The

message from the Franks stated, among other things, that if the pope approved of the matrimonial alliance, the arrangement would be carried out; 'if not, we will give the daughter of the king's brother to el-Melek el-'Âdel in marriage. She is a virgin, and although, according to our religion, the pope's consent is necessary for the marriage of a king's daughter who is a widow, such is not the case with an unmarried princess; the family may dispose of the maiden's hand as they please.'[1] To this answer was made as follows : ' If the marriage is permissible, let the arrangement we have made be carried out, for we will not break our engagements ; if, however, it is impossible, you need not select another woman for us.' This statement brought the meeting to an end. The envoys then repaired to el-Melek el-'Âdel's tents to await the ambassador the Sultan was to send to the king, who was engaged in preparing for his mission. Some time afterwards a messenger came from the advanced guard, bringing news that a large body of foot had left the city, and scattered over the plain without any apparent hostile intentions. The Sultan had gone to Tell Jezer,[2] and everyone packed up and followed him. The hour of noon had hardly passed before the army was established in its new camp. As soon as the Franks heard that the Sultan had changed his position, they beat a retreat. After making a halt on this hill, the Sultan set out in the direction of Jerusalem, and the Franks began to march back to their own territory.[3] Wintry weather now set in, and rain fell in torrents; the Sultan

---

[1] A second marriage would require an indulgence. King Richard had no grown-up nieces in 1192.

[2] Gezer. See p. 76.

[3] The retreat from Beit Nûba began early in January, 1192. Richard was then busy rebuilding Ascalon, which he reached January 20, and he then went to Acre. Beha ed-Dîn does not describe the rebuilding of Ascalon.

therefore set out for the Holy City, and dismissed his
troops. We spent the winter in Jerusalem. The enemy
retired into their own territory, the king of England
returning to Acre, where he remained some time, having
left a garrison in Jaffa. He sent us a message at this time,
saying : ' I am anxious to have an interview with el-Melek
el-'Âdel to discuss a matter that would be equally advantageous for both sides, for I hear that the Sultan has entrusted the business of negotiating peace to *my brother*,
el-Melek el-'Âdel.' But it was thought that el-'Âdel ought
to go and collect the troops we were then keeping in
the Ghôr, Kaukab, and other places in that part of the
country, and that therefore he should send to the king,
saying : ' We have had a great many interviews without
any good result to either side. It is useless for us to meet
if the conference you now propose is to be like its pre-
decessors, and unless you show me that there is a likelihood
of a speedy settlement of the question.' It was also arranged
that el-'Âdel should conclude peace if he found it possible
to do so, and if not, that he should prolong the negotiations so as to allow our provincial contingents time to join
the army. El-Melek el-'Âdel then desired that a document
should be drawn up and delivered to him, stating the
utmost limits of the concessions he would be empowered
to make in order to come to a final settlement. The
provisions of this document required that the different
cities and districts should be divided equally, and held
half-and-half by either side; that if the king insisted on
the possession of Beirût, a condition should be made that
the citadel was to be demolished, and not rebuilt, and the
same for el-Ḳeimûn (or el-Ḳâiûn) if they wished to build
on the rocks (*W'ara*) ; that the cross of the crucifixion
should be restored to them ; that they should have their
own priests in the *Komâma* (Church of the Resurrection) ;

and that they should be allowed to make pilgrimages thither, but unarmed. We were induced to make such concessions by the state of our troops, worn out by the fatigues of continual war, harassed by want of money, and pining at their long absence from their homes, although there were some among them who followed the Sultan without thinking of asking for leave of absence.

CHAPTER CXLI.

DEPARTURE OF EL-MELEK EL-'ÂDEL.

EL-'ÂDEL set out from Jerusalem in the afternoon of Friday, the 4th of Rabi'a I., 588 (March 20, 1192). On his way he wrote to us from Kîsân, saying that (the son of) Honferi and Abu Bekr, the chamberlain, had come to meet him with a message from the king of England. The king sent to say : 'We consent to the division of the country. Each side shall keep what they now hold, and if one side has more than the half that is their just share, they shall give the other side a proper concession. The Holy City to belong to us, but the Ṣakhra shall be reserved for you.' Such were the contents of the letter. The Sultan laid it before his emirs, and one of them, Abu el-Heija, declared that it was a very satisfactory proposal. This opinion seemed to the others to coincide exactly with el-Melek el-'Âdel's, and they thought the arrangement would be a good one. An answer in this sense was dispatched to el-'Âdel. On the 11th of Rabi'a I., Abu Bekr, the chamberlain, one of el-Melek el-'Âdel's suite, came to inform us that the king of England had left Acre for Jaffa,[1] and that

---

[1] King Richard went to Acre to see the Marquis of Montferrat, who met him at Casale Imbert. The king returned to Ascalon on Tuesday before Easter. The advice of the Templars and Hospitallers was that Ascalon should be rebuilt before Jerusalem was attacked.

el-Melek el-'Âdel saw no necessity for any further interviews with the king unless there were any fresh condition
to be discussed. The chamberlain added that he himself
had had several interviews with the king, with the result
that that prince had relinquished some of his demands,
and consented that the Ṣakhra should be given up to us,
that the citadel should remain in our hands, and that the
rest should be equally divided (between the Franks and
the Moslems); that any Frank specially mentioned should
not reside there, and, finally, that the villages in the districts
belonging to the Holy City, as well as the whole of the
city itself, should be equally divided. On the 16th of the
month Rabi'a I., el-Melek el-'Âdel arrived on his return
from the Ghôr, and was received by the Sultan, to whom
he gave all the information we have set forth above.
Towards the close of the same day, a messenger came in
to say that the Franks had attacked the camp of some
Arabs near ed-Dârûn,[1] and had carried off several men, as
well as about a thousand of their sheep. The Sultan was
much annoyed at this news, and sent a detachment of
troops against the marauders, but they did not succeed in
coming up with them.

CHAPTER CXLII.

DEPARTURE OF THE MARQUIS'S AMBASSADOR.

YÛSUF, the Lord of Sidon's page, had come, on behalf of
the marquis, to negotiate a treaty of peace, and the Sultan
had given his consent, but only on the following con-

---

[1] *Dârûn*, or *Darum* (see p. 117), was the only fortress in the plains
not destroyed by Salâh ed-Dîn. It was taken by King Richard after four
days, according to De Vinsauf.

ditions : After the ratification of the treaty, the marquis
was to break with his countrymen and make open war
upon them ; he was to be allowed to retain all the land he
might capture from the Franks by his own unaided efforts,
while all we ourselves might take was, in like manner, to
belong to us ; the people of any city we might take by a
combination of our forces were to be given to the marquis,
while we were to have the Moslem prisoners and the
treasure that happened to be in the captured cities ; the
marquis was to set at liberty all the Moslem prisoners in
his dominions ; if the king of England were to grant him
the government of the country, by any arrangement that
might be made between them, peace was to be maintained
on the terms of the treaty concluded between us and the
king of England, the city of Ascalon and the districts beyond not being included ; the plains were to belong to the
marquis, and what we then occupied to be ours, and that
which lay between to be halved.[1]   The envoy took his
departure as soon as he had received a statement of these
conditions.   On Monday, the 28th of Rabi'a I., Asad
ed-Dîn, son of Muhammad, and grandson of the (great)
Shîrkûh, came into the camp with an escort of light
cavalry, having pushed on in advance of the contingent he
was bringing.

CHAPTER CXLIII.

SEIF ED-DÎN EL-MESHTÛB RECOVERS HIS FREEDOM.

IT was on Thursday, the 1st of Jomada II., that this emir
arrived in the Holy City. The Sultan, who happened to
be with his brother, el-Melek el-'Âdel, and caught sight of
el-Meshtûb quite unexpectedly, was greatly delighted to

---

[1] The country in the low hills was the debateable land.

see him, and rose up to embrace him. He then had the
room cleared, and entered into conversation with him,
talking of what the enemy was doing, and of their opinion
of the peace, in the course of which he learnt that the king
of England said nothing on the subject. That same day
the Sultan sent a dispatch to his son, el-Melek el-Afdal,
bidding him cross the Euphrates and take possession of
the provinces occupied by el-Melek el-Mansûr, son of el-
Melek el-Mozaffer (Taki ed-Dîn). That prince, fearing
the Sultan on his own account, had declared himself in
open rebellion; but he trusted in el-Melek el-'Âdel, and
besought him to intercede on his behalf. This made a
very bad impression on the Sultan's mind; he was greatly
incensed at such proceedings among members of his own
family, for he had never suspected any of his family, nor
had he required proof of their fealty. This was the reason
why the king of England put off the conclusion of peace,
for the discord that had broken out (in the Sultan's family)
seemed likely to give him a distaste for the war, and would
force him to accept whatever conditions he himself might
choose to impose. The Sultan therefore commanded el-
Melek el-Afdal to enter the country (of the rebellious
prince), and wrote to el-Melek ez-Zâher, Prince of Aleppo,
to go, if necessary, to the assistance of his brother (el-
Afdal), and to lend him a strong detachment of troops.
El-Afdal took his departure laden with honours, and on
his arrival in Aleppo received the most cordial welcome at
the hands of his brother, ez-Zâher. He set a splendid
banquet before him, and made him presents of great value.

CHAPTER CXLIV.

RETURN OF THE AMBASSADOR FROM (THE LORD OF) TYRE.

ON the 6th of Rabi'a II., 588 (April 21, 1192), the ambassador Yûsuf returned to resume negotiations on behalf of the marquis. ' An arrangement,' he said, ' is on the point of being concluded between him (the marquis) and the Franks ; if this comes off shortly, the Franks will take ship for their own country ; therefore, if you delay any longer, you may look upon all the negotiations on the subject of peace as though they had never taken place.' The Sultan was very anxious with regard to what was going on in the East, and was apprehensive lest (el-Melek el-Mansûr), son of Taki ed-Dîn, should make an alliance with Bektimor, which would have precluded all possibility. of carrying on the Holy War. This made him desirous of closing with the marquis's proposals, for he thought that a treaty with him would be an advantage. He therefore ordered an agreement to be drawn up, embodying the conditions set forth above, which answer he delivered to the envoy Yûsuf, who took his departure on the 9th of the same month.

CHAPTER CXLV.

ASSASSINATION OF THE MARQUIS.

ON the 16th of the month Rabi'a II. (May 1, 1192) we received a dispatch from our envoy accredited to the marquis, announcing that that prince had just been assassinated, and his soul hurled by God into hell-fire. It

came about in the following manner :[1] On Tuesday, the
13th of the month, he had dined with the bishop, and left
his house with a very small escort. Two of his servants
then rushed on him, and kept on stabbing him with their
daggers until life left the body. They were at once
arrested and questioned, when they declared they had been
suborned by the king of England. Two of the marquis's
officers then assumed the command in chief, and provided
for the protection of the citadel, until information of the
occurrence could reach the Christian princes. Matters
were then arranged, and order was restored in the city.

CHAPTER CXLVI.

CONCLUSION OF THE BUSINESS OF EL-MELEK EL-MANSÛR,[2] AND WHAT HAPPENED TO HIM.

WHEN this prince was informed of the Sultan's displeasure,
he sent a messenger to el-Melek el-'Âdel, beseeching him
to speak in his favour, and to ask that he should receive
either the cities of Ḥarrân, Edessa, and Someisât, or, failing that, the cities of Hamah, Manbej, Salemîya,[3] and
Ma'arra, and also that he should be appointed guardian to

---

[1] The bishop of Beauvais, grandson of Louis VI. of France, was
then in Tyre. According to De Vinsauf (v. 6-31), the murderers
acknowledged that they were Assassins, acting by order of the Sheikh
of the Mountain. Ernoul (289, 290) says that Conrad had previously
pillaged a ship belonging to this sect at Tyre. The French suspected
King Richard. A letter from the Sheikh, absolving him, and said to
be written in 1193 to the duke of Austria, is believed to be a forgery.
—Röhricht, *Regesta Reg. Hierosol.*, No. 715.

[2] Muhammad el-Melek el-Mansûr Nâsr ed-Dîn was the grandson of
Shahanshah, the elder brother of Salaḥ ed-Dîn. He died in 1221.

[3] *Salamîya* is placed by Abu el-Feda two days from Hamah, in the
desert to the east.

his younger brothers. El-'Âdel made several applications to the Sultan (in support of these requests), but obtained no concession from him. The Sultan gave way at last to the representations of all his emirs, who constantly interceded on the prince's behalf, and he felt ashamed of his obstinacy; then, yielding to his natural generosity, he swore to fulfil a deed by which he made over to el-Mansûr the cities of Harrân, Edessa, and Someisât. This deed provided that the young prince should be put in possession of the places he had solicited as soon as he should cross the Euphrates (and leave Syria); he was to have the wardship of his brothers, and to give up (to the Sultan) all he then held (in Syria). El-Melek el-'Âdel undertook to be responsible for the due performance of the appointed conditions, and asked the Sultan to append his sign-manual (to the deed). The Sultan refused, and he insisted. Then the Sultan tore the document into little pieces. This occurred on the 29th of Rabi'a II., and put an end to the negotiations. The business had been arranged through my intervention. The Sultan was incensed at the thought that one of his children's children (that is to say, his great nephew) should have dared to make such a demand.

CHAPTER CXLVII.

ARRIVAL OF THE GREEK AMBASSADOR.

ON the 1st of Jomada I. an ambassador came from Constantinople the Great, and was received with the greatest honour. On the 3rd of the month he was introduced into the presence, and delivered his message. He asked, among other things, that the cross of the crucifixion should be given to him; secondly, that the Church of the

Resurrection and all the other churches in the Holy City should be made over to priests of his party; thirdly, that an alliance, offensive and defensive, should be concluded between the two peoples. He also asked the Sultan's co-operation in an expedition against the island of Cyprus. He stayed with us for two days, and took his departure, accompanied by Ibn el-Bezzâz the Egyptian, who had been appointed our ambassador. A negative answer was returned to every one of his demands. It is said that the King of the Georgians offered two hundred thousand gold pieces [*dînârs*] to obtain possession of the cross, and that his proposal was refused.

CHAPTER CXLVIII.

EL-MELEK EL-'ÂDEL AND THE COUNTRY BEYOND THE EUPHRATES.

AFTER el-Melek el-Afḍal had set out for that country, el-Melek el-'Âdel suceeeded in softening the Sultan's heart and obtaining pardon for the son of Taḳî ed-Dîn. This he effected only after numerous interviews on the subject. Then the Sultan instructed me to go and ascertain the opinion of the emirs in el-Afḍal's service upon the matter in hand. That prince called them all into his presence, and I informed the meeting of the motive with which the Sultan had sent me to them. Emir Ḥossâm ed-Dîn Abu el-Heija then spoke, and made answer in the following terms: 'We are the servants and slaves of the Sultan. It may be that the young man, being afraid, will form an alliance with another. It would be quite impossible for us to carry on two wars at the same time, one against Moslems, and the other against the infidels; if the

Sultan wishes us to fight the Moslems, he must let us make peace with the infidels ; then we will cross the Euphrates and fight, but it must be under his leadership. If, on the other hand, he wishes us to keep on the Holy War, let him pardon the Moslems and grant them peace.' All present applauded this answer. The Sultan then relented, ordered a fresh deed to be drawn up, which he confirmed by oath and sent to the son of Takî ed-Dîn, appending his sign-manual to the document. El-'Âdel then asked of the Sultan those provinces (of Syria) which had still remained in the possession of Takî ed-Dîn's son after his assertion of independence. Negotiations, in which I acted as go-between, then opened between the two sides as to what the Sultan should receive in return for the provinces he was to give up. It was finally arranged that he (el-Melek el-'Âdel) should receive the provinces he asked for, and should make over (to the Sultan) his possessions in Syria near the Euphrates. The castles of el-Kerak, esh-Shôbek, and es-Salt, the district of el-Belkâ,[1] and the appanages held by the prince in Egypt were to be excepted, but he was to give up el-Jîza[2] to the Sultan. He was, besides, to furnish the Sultan with sixteen thousand sacks of corn annually, to be sent from es-Salt and the Belkâ to Jerusalem ; the crops of the current year he was to retain, except those in the districts beyond the Euphrates, which were to belong to the Sultan. Salâh ed-Dîn signed this agreement, and on the 8th of the month Jomada I. (el-'Âdel) set out to conclude the business with Takî ed-Dîn's son, and to set that prince's mind at rest.

---

[1] The *Belka*, or 'empty land,' was the country beyond Jordan, in Gilead and Moab. *Es-Salt* (the *Saltus Hieraticus*) is the capital of Gilead, S. of the River Jabbok.

[2] *Gizeh*, S. of Cairo.

CHAPTER CXLIX.

THE FRANKS SEIZE ED-DÂRÛN.

THE Franks—may God confound them !—seeing that the Sultan had sent his troops away, went up and attacked ed-Dârûn, in the hope of taking it. The governor of this place was 'Alem ed-Dîn Ḳaiṣar, and it was then held by his lieutenants. On the 9th of Jomada I. (May 24, 1192) the enemy's infantry and cavalry began to storm the place smartly. Sappers belonging to Aleppo and attached to the outpost on guard before Acre had been suborned by the king of England, and they now succeeded in driving a mine under the fortress and setting it on fire. Upon this the garrison asked for an armistice to allow them time to communicate with the Sultan, but the enemy disregarded them, and attacked the place furiously until they carried it by storm. Those of the garrison whom God had pre-ordained to martyrdom there met their death, the rest were made prisoners. *God's bidding is a decreed decree !* (Kurân xxxiii. 38.)

CHAPTER CL.

THE FRANKS MARCH UPON MEJDEL YÂBA.

AFTER having taken the necessary steps and established a garrison of picked men in ed-Dàrûn, the Franks marched off and halted at a place called el-Ḥesi,[1] close to the mountains of el-Khalîl (Hebron). They arrived there on the 14th. They spent the day there, and then, having

---

[1] *Tell el-Hesi*, the ancient *Lachish*, is 14 miles S.E. of Ascalon, and 24 miles N.E. of Darum, at the foot of the Hebron hills.

made their preparations, they marched in the direction of a stronghold called Mejdel Yâba.[1]   They made their appearance before that place lightly-armed, for they had left their tents at el-Ḥesi.   The garrison left by the Sultan in Mejdel Yâba came out and engaged the enemy, and in the furious fight that followed they killed a count of great renown among the Franks.   The Moslems lost only one man ; he had dismounted to pick up his lance, and was trying to remount his horse, which was very restive, when the Franks swooped down on him and killed him.   The enemy then returned to their camp, which they reached the same evening, having failed to execute their design— God be praised !

CHAPTER CLI.

SKIRMISH IN (ON THE OUTSKIRTS OF) TYRE.

ON the 16th of Jomada I. we received a dispatch from Emir Ḥossâm ed-Dîn Bishâra, informing us that the garrison left in Tyre, and consisting of one hundred horsemen, had been reinforced by about fifty men from Acre, after which they had made an incursion into Moslem territory in search of booty.   The detachment of troops left to guard that part of the country had fallen upon the invaders and killed fifteen of them, without losing a single one of their number.   The enemy's plans had been frustrated, and they had been obliged to retreat.

[1] *Mejdel Yâba* is 40 miles N. of Tell el-Hesi.   The stronghold may be the castle of Mirabel, at Râs el-'Ain, 2 miles W. of the village, which, however, had been dismantled by Salâh ed-Dîn.

CHAPTER CLII.

ARRIVAL OF MOSLEM TROOPS TO TAKE PART IN THE HOLY WAR.

SEEING that the enemy's troops had begun to over-run the open country, the Sultan sent out on all sides to summon his own soldiers back. The first of the leaders to arrive was Bedr ed-Din Dolderim, who brought with him a great number of Turkomans. The Sultan went out to meet him, and received him with every mark of honour. Then, on the 17th of the month of Jomada I., 'Izz ed-Din Ibn el-Mokaddem came in, with a fine army and well-appointed engines of war, whereat the Sultan was greatly pleased. The enemy left el-Hesi, and encamped at the place where the road divides, leading in one direction to Ascalon, in the other to Beit-Jibrin,[1] and several strong-holds belonging to the Moslems. When the Sultan was informed of this, he gave an order for the army to advance in the direction of the Franks. Abu el-Heija (nick-named) the Fat, Bedr ed-Din Dolderim and Ibn el-Mokaddem, set out one after another at the head of their troops; but the prince himself, who was suffering from illness, remained behind in Jerusalem. As soon as the confounded enemy perceived that the Moslem army was advancing, they retreated as speedily as they could without striking a blow. Letters from our emirs subsequently informed us that the Franks were marching upon Ascalon.

[1] *Beit Jibrin* is 11 miles N.E. of Tell el-Hesi. It was fortified by King Fulk in 1134 A.D.

CHAPTER CLIII.

THE ENEMY MAKES PREPARATIONS TO ADVANCE AGAINST JERUSALEM.

ON Saturday, the 23rd of Jomada I., a courier came from the army, bringing news that the enemy had come out with their cavalry, infantry, and a large number of followers, and had encamped on Tell es-Ṣâfia.[1] The Sultan immediately despatched a messenger to the Moslem army, warning them to keep a good look out, and summoning the emirs forthwith to Jerusalem to hold a council of war, and decide what was to be done. On the 26th of Jomada I. the Franks left Tell es-Ṣâfia, and took up their position to the north of en-Naṭrûn. A body of Moslem Arabs, who had been on a pillaging expedition in the neighbourhood of Jaffa, had halted for the night to divide the spoil, when they were attacked by the enemy's troops whom they did not know to be on the march. They were all taken prisoners, excepting six men, who ran to carry the news to the Sultan. According to the reports of our spies and watchmen, the enemy were waiting at en-Naṭrûn for provisions and engines of war, which they would need during the siege. As soon as they had received all that was necessary, they were to advance upon Jerusalem. On Wednesday an envoy arrived from the Franks, accompanied by a former servant of el-Meshṭûb's, whom they had kept with them; he came on a mission with regard to Ḳarâḳûsh and the peace.

[1] *Tell es-Ṣâfi* is 7½ miles N.W. of Beit Jibrîn, and was the Blanche Guarde of the Franks, built by King Fulk in 1144, but dismantled by Salâḥ ed-Dîn. *En-Natrûn* is 11 miles to the N.E. from Tell es-Sâfi, on the Jerusalem road. See p. 32.

CHAPTER CLIV.

THE ENEMY HALTS AT BEIT-NÛBA.

ON Wednesday, the 27th of Rabi'a I.,[1] the Franks left en-Natrûn, and moved their camp to Beit-Nûba, (a village) in the plain, a day's journey from the Holy City. On receiving this news, the Sultan called his emirs together, and took counsel with them as to what should be done. It was decided that each emir should be entrusted with the defence of a certain portion of the walls; and that the Sultan should command the rest of the troops, who were to be lightly armed, in their engagements with the enemy. Each division of the garrison, knowing the part of the walls it was to defend, was to hold itself in readiness to receive the enemy. In case of need these troops were to make sorties, but otherwise they were to remain at their posts. Proclamations containing instructions were dispatched to all the emirs. The road from Jaffa to the enemy's camp was constantly crowded with convoys of provisions for the Franks, and the Sultan commanded the advanced guard to take every opportunity of attacking them. Bedr ed-Dîn Dolderim, who was (at that time) on duty at the head of the advanced guard, posted a goodly number of picked men in ambush on either side of this road. A detachment of the enemy's cavalry, acting as escort to a convoy of provisions, charged the men in ambush, thinking they had to do with a small body of Moslems only. A desperate conflict ensued, in which the enemy was worsted, having thirty men killed and a number taken prisoner. The

---

[1] The story goes back to April 13.

latter were taken to Jerusalem, and entered the city on the
19th of Jomada I., where their arrival created a profound
sensation. This blow disconcerted the enemy, whilst it
gave fresh courage to the advanced guard, inspiring them
even to charge the whole Frank army, and to take up
a position close to the enemy's camp. As the convoys
continued to come in, a detachment of our men, with
a strong force of Arabs, was sent out to lay an ambush.
A convoy, escorted by a large body of soldiers, came
along, and the Arabs advanced to stop it. They were
attacked by the cavalry of the escort, and gave way,
retreating towards the spot where the Moslems were
concealed. The latter, who were Turks, rushed from
their ambush and hurled themselves on the enemy, killing
several men, and making a number of prisoners. They
themselves had a good number wounded. This encounter
took place on the 3rd of Jomada II.

CHAPTER CLV.

THE CARAVAN FROM EGYPT IS CAPTURED.

THE Sultan had commanded the Egyptian army to begin
its march, and to keep a constant look-out as soon as
it neared the enemy. These troops halted at Bilbeis
for several days, until the convoys were collected. The
whole train then set out for Syria, never suspecting
that Arab miscreants were keeping the enemy informed
of its movements. When (the king of England) received
certain information that the caravan was close at hand,
he commanded his army to keep a good look-out and
to hold itself in readiness, while a thousand horsemen
set out, each of whom took a foot-soldier in front of

him. In this way it (the army) came to Tell es-Sâfia,
where it spent the night; and he proceeded to es-Saña,
where he ordered a good number (of foot-soldiers) to
be taken on the horses of the cavalry, and advanced
as far as the water east of el-Hesi.[1] The Sultan, who
had received intelligence of the enemy's movements,
sent to warn the caravan. Those who were sent on
this service were Akher Aslem, Altonba el-'Adli, and
other eminent officers. They had instructions to take
the caravan through the desert, and to avoid the neighbourhood of the Franks, for an encounter was to be
dreaded above all things. They brought the caravan
by the road which they had just followed, thinking
that there was nothing to fear, as they had performed
the journey in safety. They were also anxious to take
the shortest road. When they came to the water called
el-Khuweilfa,[2] everyone was allowed to disperse in order
to water the beasts. The enemy, who were then posted
at the spring head of el-Hesi, were informed of this
by the Arabs. They lost not a moment in setting out,
and surprised the caravan a little before dawn. Felek
ed-Dîn, el-Melek el-'Âdel's own brother, who was in
command of the Egyptian troops, had been advised by
Emir Aslem to set out during the night, and gain the
top of the mountains by a quick march; but he had not
followed the suggestion, fearing lest the caravan should
get scattered in a night-march. He had given orders

---

[1] King Richard brought supplies from Ascalon. According to De
Vinsauf, he himself slept at Galatia (*Jelediyeh*), 6 miles W. of Tell es-
Sâfi. There is a stream at Tell el-Hesi, which is 12 miles S.W. of
Tell es-Sâfi.

[2] *El-Khuweilfah*, called the 'Round Cistern' by De Vinsauf (v. 4),
has round masonry wells like those at Beersheba. It lies at the foot
of the Hebron hills, 11 miles N. of Beersheba, and 14 miles S.E. of
Tell el-Hesi.

that no one was to start until the following morning. We were told that when this was reported to the king of England he did not believe it ; but he mounted, and set out with the Arabs and a small escort. When he came up to the caravan, he disguised himself as an Arab, and went all round it. When he saw that quiet reigned in their camp, and that everyone was fast asleep, he returned, and ordered his troops into the saddle. At daybreak he took the great caravan unawares, falling on it with his infantry and cavalry. Those among them (Egyptian troops) who passed for brave men were glad to owe their lives to the swiftness of their horses. All the people fled towards the caravan, closely pursued by the enemy, who, when they saw the caravan, turned back to attack it from their fight with the escort. This caravan had originally been divided into three parts, the first of which, under the escort of a detachment of Arabs and el-Melek el-'Âdel's troops, had taken the road by el-Kerak ; the second, also escorted by Arabs, had taken the road leading through the desert ; the third was the one seized by the enemy. Camels, bales, everything belonging to the travellers, and the travellers themselves, were carried off by the enemy. This was a most disgraceful event ; it was long since Islâm had sustained so serious a disaster. There were (nevertheless) several chiefs of great renown — such as Khoshtekîn el-Jerâji, Felek ed-Dîn, and the sons of el-Jâweli — with the Egyptian army on this occasion. According to one report we received the enemy had about one hundred horsemen killed ; according to another account they lost only ten men. No one of importance on the Moslem side was killed, excepting Yûsuf, the chamberlain, and the younger son of el-Jâweli. A baggage train belonging to the Sultan, in the charge of Aibek el-'Azîzi, was so bravely defended by that officer, that it escaped the general disaster. This advanced him very greatly in the prince's favour. The people were scattered in the desert, throwing away all the valuables they had, and he was fortunate who managed to escape with his life. The enemy collected all they could find—horses, mules, camels, property of all sorts, and everything that had any value—and forced the camel-drivers, the muleteers and grooms, to go with their respective beasts. The king set out to rejoin his army, laden with spoil ; he halted at el-Khuweilfa to take water, and then made his way to el-Hesi. I have been told by one of those he took prisoner that that night a report was spread amongst the Franks that the Sultan's army was advancing, and that they thereupon took to flight, abandoning their booty ; but as soon as they found it was a false alarm, they returned to their spoils. However, during their absence, a number of the Moslem prisoners had succeeded in making their escape, the man in question being among the number. I asked him what number of camels and horses he thought the enemy had taken, and he replied : ' About three thousand camels, and about the same number of horses. As to the prisoners, there were five hundred of them.' This disastrous occurrence took place on the morning of Tuesday, the 11th of Jomada II. In the evening of that day I was seated in the Sultan's tent, when one of the young memlûks attached to the stables came in, and informed him of what had just happened. Never was the Sultan more grieved or rendered more anxious. I tried to calm and comfort him, but he would hardly listen to me. This is what occurred. Akher Aslem had advised that the caravan should be taken up to the top of the hills; but his advice was not taken. He himself went up into the mountains with his colleagues, and was there at the time the caravan was surprised. The enemy did not suspect his being there, and not a single one of them appeared in the place where he was. The Frank cavalry pursued the Moslems in their headlong flight, while their foot-soldiers were engaged in collecting the property our men had abandoned. The Master of the Horse, seeing the cavalry of the Franks at a distance from their foot, came down with the horsemen he had with him, and fell on the foot-soldiers unawares, killing several of them, and carrying off some of the baggage animals. The mule ridden by the messenger himself (who brought the news to the Sultan) was part of the booty. The enemy then marched back to the camping-place (of the main body of their army), which they reached on Friday, the 16th of Jomada II., a day of great rejoicing among them. After that they moved their tents back again to the plain of Beit-Nûba, and then came to the serious determination of marching on Jerusalem. Their spirits were raised by having taken such store of treasure, such numbers of camels and other baggage animals, as to enable them to transport their various supplies. They posted a detachment of troops close to Lydda, to protect the road by which their convoys were to travel, and they sent Count Henry to bring in all the soldiers then in Tyre, Tripoli, and Acre. When the Sultan saw that they were preparing to march upon Jerusalem, he apportioned the defence of the walls among his emirs, and bade them get everything ready to withstand a siege. He also took care to pollute all the water near the Holy City, to stop up the springs, destroy the cisterns, and fill up the wells ; and this he did so energetically and with such thoroughness that in all the neighbourhood there was not left a drop of water fit to drink. One must bear in mind that it is no use to sink wells for drinking-water anywhere near Jerusalem, for this great

mountain is of the hardest rock. The Sultan also sent
to all the provinces, commanding that troops should be
forwarded to him.

CHAPTER CLVI.

RECALL OF EL-MELEK EL-AFDAL.

WHEN el-Melek el-Afdal received the Sultan's commands
to return (see Chapter CXLIII.), he had just reached
Aleppo. He started at once, heart-broken and inwardly
vexed at the message, and came to Damascus. There he
stayed, indulging his feelings of discontent by not returning
to duty. The news with regard to the Franks having now
become very serious, the Sultan sent a messenger to
summon him. El-Afdal could delay no longer, and set
out with the troops he had brought with him from the
East (the districts round the Euphrates), reaching
(Jerusalem) on Thursday, the 19th of Jomada II. The
Sultan went out to meet him, and dismounted at el-
'Azerîya[1] to receive him, and to gratify his wounded
feelings by this mark of honour. El-Afdal then took up
his position on the ridges near Jerusalem to watch the
enemy, having under his command the Sultan's son, el-
Melek ez-Zafer, and Kotb ed-Dîn.

CHAPTER CLVII.

THE ENEMY WITHDRAW INTO THEIR OWN TERRITORY;
CAUSE OF THEIR RETREAT.

ON the night preceding Thursday, the 19th of Jomada II.,
the Sultan summoned his emirs to him. Abu el-Heija

[1] *El-'Azerîyeh,* ' Place of the Lazar-house,' is Bethany, on Olivet,
one mile E. of Jerusalem.

the Fat, who could hardly move, and was obliged to sit in a chair in the Sultan's tent, came to the council, as did also el-Meshtûb, the officers who had formerly served under Asad ed-Dîn (Shîrkûh), and all the other leaders. The Sultan then commanded me to address them, encouraging them to continue the Holy War, and I spoke to them such words as God suffered me to call to mind on that subject. I said among other things : ' When the Prophet—pray God for him !—was suffering great tribulation, his comrades swore to fight for him to the death. That is an example which it behoves us, above all others, to imitate. Then let us meet together at the Sakhra and swear to stand by one another to the death. Perhaps the sincerity of our purpose will obtain for us the boon of seeing the enemy driven back.' All who were present applauded my suggestion, and promised to put it into practice. The Sultan remained for some time without speaking, in the attitude of a man who is reflecting, and everyone respected his silence[1] ; then he spoke in the following terms : ' Praise be to God and a blessing on His Messenger ! You to-day are the army and the support of Islâm. Remember that the blood of the Moslems, their treasures and their children, are under your protection, and that there are none besides yourselves among Moslems who can stand up against this enemy. If you give way— which may God forbid !—they will roll up this land *like the rolling up of a scroll* (Kurân xxi. 104), and you will be answerable, for it was you who undertook to defend it ; you have received money from the public treasury, and on you alone depends the safety of Moslems throughout the land. I wish you well.' Seif ed-Dîn el-Meshtûb then spoke, saying : ' My lord, we are your servants and slaves.

---

[1] *Lit.,* ' and the people were as still as if a bird was on their heads.'

You have been gracious to us, and made us great, and
mighty, and rich; we have nothing but our necks, and
they are in your hands. By God! not one among us will
turn back from helping you till we die.' All who were
present gave utterance to the same sentiment, and their
oath reassured the Sultan's mind and solaced his heart.
He then ordered the usual meal to be served, after which
the officers withdrew. The close of that Thursday saw
everyone hard at work and preparations in full swing. In
the evening we went to the Sultan's tent as usual on duty,
and sat up with him part of the night, but he was not as
cheerful as usual. We said the night prayer together,
which was the signal for everyone to withdraw, and I was
leaving with the rest, when he called me back. I remained
standing before him, and he asked me if I had heard
the latest news. I replied that I had not. He then
said : ' I have had a communication from Abu el-Heija
'the Fat' to-day, reporting that many of the memlûks
had come to him, and that we had been censured for our
decision respecting the siege, and proposing to shut ourselves up in the city. They said that no advantage could
result from such a course, and that if we shut ourselves up
in the citadel we should meet the same fate as the garrison
of Acre, whilst in the meantime all the Moslem land would
fall into the hands of the enemy; that it would be better
to risk a pitched battle; then, if God grants us the
victory, we should be masters of all they now hold; that
if not, we should lose the Holy City, but we should save
the army; and that our forces used to be able to protect
Islâm without having possession of the Holy City.' Now
the Sultan had an affection for Jerusalem that almost sur-
passes imagination; this message therefore was a great
grief to him. I spent the whole night with him, and it
was one of those that we spent in the path of God. The

message which had been sent to him contained the following passage : ' If you wish us to remain in the Holy City,
you must stay with us, or else leave some member of your
family in command ; for the Kurds will not obey the
Turks, and the Turks in like manner will never obey the
Kurds.' It was therefore determined that the Sultan
should leave his (great-nephew), Mejed ed-Dîn, son of
Ferrûkh-Shah, and Lord of B'albek, in Jerusalem. He
had at first proposed to shut himself up in the city, but
was obliged to give up this idea on account of the great
danger that the cause of Islâm would thereby run.   I
found him still watching at dawn ; it gave me great concern to see him, and I begged him to take an hour's rest. I
had hardly left him before I heard the *muezzin* calling
to prayer, and I had barely time to wash, for day was
already beginning to break. As I used sometimes to say
the morning prayer with the Sultan, I repaired once more
to him, and found him washing again. When we had
performed the prayer together, I said : ' I have an idea ;
have I permission to tell you what is in my mind ?' He
gave me leave.   ' Your Highness,' I said, ' is weighed
down with anxiety, your soul is overburdened with care,
you can hardly bear up. Earthly means are useless ; you
can only turn to God Almighty. To-day is Friday, the
most blessed day in the week, the day when prayer is
most heard, and we are here in the most blessed of places.
Let the Sultan perform ablution, and then distribute alms
in secret, so that no one knows from whence they come ;
then say a prayer of two *rek'a* between the *azân* and the
ikâma, beseeching your Lord under your breath, and con-
fiding all your anxieties, confessing your own inability to
carry out what you have undertaken. It may be that God
will take compassion on you and will grant your prayer.'
Now the Sultan held a sincere belief in all the doctrines of

the faith, and practised absolute submission to all the precepts of God's law. I then left his presence. Afterwards,
at the time of prayer in the mosque, I prayed at his side
in the Aḳṣa, and he said two *rek'a,* and bowed himself,
praying in a low voice; his tears rolled down on to his
prayer-carpet. Then the congregation withdrew. During
the evening of the same day we were on duty with him as
usual, and behold! he received a dispatch from Jurdîk,
who was at that time in command of the advanced guard.
It contained the following words: 'The whole of the
enemy's forces came out on horseback and took up their
position on the top of the *tell,* after which they returned
to their camp. We have sent out spies to ascertain what
is going on.' On the Saturday morning another despatch
arrived, which ran as follows: 'Our spy has returned, and
brings intelligence that discord is rife among the enemy;
one party is anxious to push on to the Holy City,
the others wish to return to their own territory. The
French insist upon advancing on Jerusalem[1]: "We left
our own country," they say, "only for the sake of the
Holy City, and we will not return until we have taken it."
To this the king of England replies: "All the springs in
the neighbourhood of the city have been polluted, so that
there is not a drop of water to be had; where, then, shall
we find water?" They said: "We will drink the stream
of Teḳû'a,[2] which is about a parasang from Jerusalem."
"How could we water there?" said he. "We will divide
the army into two sections," they replied; "one will ride

---

[1] According to De Vinsauf, Richard alone was anxious to reach
Jerusalem, and the French were not.

[2] *Teḳû'a* (Tekoah of the Old Testament) is 10 miles S. of Jerusalem.
The water intended was perhaps that of the aqueduct, which has its
head W. of Teḳû'a, and which may have been available near Beth-
lehem.

out to the watering-place, while the other will remain close up to the city to carry on the siege, and we will go to water once each day." To this the English king made answer: "As soon as one division of the army has gone to the watering-place with their beasts, the garrison will sally out from the city and attack the troops that remain, and destroy all Christendom." They finally determined to elect three hundred from among the chief men, who in their turn were to elect twelve, who were to choose out three of their number to finally decide the question. They spent the night awaiting the decision of the three.[1]

On the morning of the following day, the 21st of Jomada II., they broke up their camp in consequence of the decision that was given, by which they had undertaken to abide. They took the road to Ramla, that is to say, retreated in the direction whence they had come ; but their troops, armed from head to foot, occupied the position until the whole of the baggage had been removed. When the Sultan heard from several different quarters that the enemy had returned to Ramla, he rode out at the head of his troops, and everyone gave way to the greatest rejoicing. Still, as he knew the enemy had secured a number of camels and other baggage-animals, he grew apprehensive for Egypt, for the king of England had been plainly inclined to invade that country on several former occasions.

[1] The Franks retreated from Beit Nûba on July 6, 1192, by advice of a council consisting of five Frenchmen, five Templars, five Hospitallers, and five nobles of the kingdom of Jerusalem. The policy recommended was an attack on Egypt, as Salâh ed-Dîn feared.

CHAPTER CLVIII.

COUNT HENRY SENDS AN AMBASSADOR.

THE Sultan, relieved from anxiety by the enemy's retreat, ordered to be brought before him the ambassador of Count Henry, who sent saying, 'The king of England has given me all the land on the coast, and it is now in my hands. Now give me back my other lands, and I will make peace with you and be as one of your children.' These words put the Sultan into such a rage, that he meditated using violence to the ambassador. He commanded him to rise. But he said, 'Wait and listen to this : the Count is anxious to know how much of the country that is now in your hands you will give him ?' The Sultan replied by reprimanding the ambassador, and commanded that he should be led away. On the 23rd of Jomada II. he sent for him, and addressed him as follows : 'All negotiations between us must be restricted to Tyre and Acre, and must proceed on the basis of the conditions accepted by the marquis.' After this Hâji Yûsuf Ṣâhib el-Meshtûb came from the Frank camp ; he stated that he had been sent by the king of England as well as by Count Henry, and that the king, when the council had left, had addressed him as follows : 'Tell your lord you and I can go on no longer, and the best thing for us to do is to put an end to the shedding of blood. But do not think it is because I am weak ; it is for our common good. Act as mediator between the Sultan and me, and do not be deceived by the manœuvre of withdrawing my camp ; the ram backs for butting.' The king had sent two men with the Hâji (Pilgrim) who listened to el-Meshtûb's words.

The ostensible object of this embassy was to negotiate

23

for the liberty of Behâ ed-Dîn Ḳarâḳûsh, but the real motive underlying this was the arrangement of a treaty of peace. The Hâji informed us that the Franks had left Ramla on their way to Jaffa, and that they were too exhausted to undertake any enterprise whatever. El-Meshṭûb had been summoned from Nâblus to hear this message, and the following was the answer : 'We will make peace with Count Henry as Lord of Acre,[1] since that city has been granted to him ; but, as to the rest of the land, he must let us (make our arrangements) with the king of England.' The Sultan had stationed a detachment of troops close to Acre, to prevent the enemy from making incursions on the country round. But on the 22nd of the month a body of men left the city to over-run the neighbouring districts. This manœuvre did not escape the watchfulness of the Moslems ; they planted ambushes in several places, and succeeded in killing and taking prisoner a goodly number of the marauders.

CHAPTER CLIX.

THE FRANKS SEND THEIR AMBASSADOR ONCE MORE TO NEGOTIATE A PEACE.

ON Friday, the 26th of the month, the ambassador from the Franks returned, conducted by Hâji Yûsuf, who was charged with the message in presence of their Lord, and it

---

[1] Acre was part of the royal domain. The rest of the lands, in the fiefs of Cæsarea, Jaffa, and Ascalon, conquered by King Richard, were, to a great extent, the property of the Templars and Hospitallers, who only obeyed the Pope. Henry of Champagne had married Isabel, heiress of the kingdom, on the death of the marquis, and was acknowledged king of Jerusalem in place of Guy of Lusignan, by French, English, and Syrians alike.

was ' The king of England says, I am anxious to deserve
your friendship and goodwill ; I have no desire to be a
Pharaoh to rule over this land, and I do not suppose you
wish to be so either. It is not right for you to allow all
the Moslems to perish, nor for me to suffer all our Franks
to be killed. Now, there is Count Henry, my sister's son,[1]
whom I have put in possession of all these districts ; I
commend him and all his troops to you. If you invite
him to accompany you on an expedition to the East, he
will be willing.' The king said further : ' On many occasions monks who have been turned out have petitioned
you for churches, and you have never shown yourself
niggardly, and now I beg you to give me a church. I
promise to renounce all that was unpleasing to you in my
former negotiations with el-Melek el-'Âdel, and to relinquish
all idea of it. Will you not, then, give me a barren spot,
and the ruin of its shrine ?'[2] After this message had been
delivered, the Sultan summoned his councillors together
and asked them what reply should be sent. They one
and all advised him to be compliant and to conclude peace,
for the Moslems were worn out with fatigue and anxiety,
as well as overwhelmed with the burden of their needs.
It was therefore determined that an answer should be sent
in the following terms : ' Since you trust us with such
trust, and as one good turn deserves another, the Sultan will
treat your sister's son like one of his own sons, of which
you shall shortly receive proof. He grants you the largest
of all the churches — the Church of the Resurrection
(*Ḳomâma*), and he will share the rest of the country with

---

[1] Henry of Champagne was the son of the eldest daughter of
Louis VII. of France by Eleanor of Guienne, mother of Richard I.,
through her second marriage with Henry II. of England. He was
thus the son of Richard's half-sister, and nephew of Philip of France.

[2] King Richard meant the ruined site of Calvary.

you ; the cities of the coast-districts, which you now hold, shall remain in your possession ; the strongholds we occupy in the hill country shall continue in our hands, and the country lying between the mountains and the coast-districts shall be shared equally between us ; Ascalon and the places beyond that city shall be demolished, and belong neither to you nor to us. If you are desirous of a grant of some of its villages you shall have them. What has been most bitter has been the decision as to Ascalon.' On the 28th of the month, which was the day after his arrival, the ambassador took his departure, perfectly satisfied. After he had returned, we heard that the Franks were marching towards Ascalon, on their way to Egypt. We also received an ambassador from Ḳoṭb ed-Dîn, son of Ḳilîj-Arslân, who brought the following message from his master : ' The pope is marching on Constantinople at the head of an immense multitude ; God Almighty alone knows how many they may be '—here the ambassador added that he had killed twelve horsemen on his way—' send me some one,' the prince continued, ' to whom I may give up my kingdom, for I am not strong enough to defend it.' The Sultan did not believe the statements of this message, and did not trouble himself about it.

CHAPTER CLX.

THE FRANK AMBASSADOR RETURNS FOR THE THIRD TIME.

ON the 29th of the month Hâji Yûsuf Ṣâhib el-Meshṭûb came to us, accompanied by Geoffrey, the ambassador from the king of England,[1] and said : ' The king thanks the

---

[1] This Geoffrey was perhaps the brother of King Guy.

Sultan for his kindness, and says : " I beg your permission
to lodge twenty of my soldiers in the citadel at Jerusalem,
and that the Christians and Franks dwelling in that city
may not suffer any ill-treatment. As to the rest of the
land, the plains and lowlands will be ours; the hill-country
will be yours." ' The ambassador informed us that, of his
own accord and of good will to us, the king had given up
all claim to the Holy City, excepting only the right of
pilgrimage thither, but that he had said it was not on
account of his being weak. The ambassador spent all
Monday with us, which was the last day of the month.
We further learnt from him that everyone (in the Frank
camp) was anxious for peace, and that the king was absolutely obliged to return to his own country. On this occasion he had brought the Sultan a present, consisting of
a couple of falcons. The Sultan called all his emirs
together to consult them as to the answer that should
be sent to this message. They decided to inform the
ambassador that they could grant the king no rights in
Jerusalem excepting that of pilgrimage. Then, when the
ambassador demanded that pilgrims should not be subject
to any tax, they made it clear that they agreed with
him on that point. As regards Ascalon and the places
beyond, he was told that they must absolutely be demolished ;[1] and when he observed that the king had spent
large sums of money upon repairing the fortifications, el-
Meshtûb said to the Sultan : ' Let him have the corn-lands
and villages as an indemnity for his losses,' to which the
Sultan gave his consent; but he demanded that ed-Dârûn
and other places should be demolished, the territory belonging to the cities destroyed to be shared equally between
the two sides. As touching the other cities and their
dependencies, they agreed to assign all those between Jaffa

[1] Ascalon having been rebuilt by King Richard.

and Tyre to the Franks, adding: ' In every instance, when we cannot agree as to the possession of a village, we will divide it in half.' This was the answer sent to the king's message. The ambassador took his departure on Tuesday, the 1st of the month of Rejeb, taking Hâji Yûsuf with him. He had made a request that someone should be sent with him, to swear to the ratification of the treaty of peace, as soon as its preliminaries were settled; but the Sultan refused, saying that he would send someone as soon as the treaty was definitely concluded. He loaded the ambassador with rich presents for the Franks in return for those they had sent him, for no one could outstrip him in the matter of presents; his heart was so large, and his generosity so great.

CHAPTER CLXI.

THE AMBASSADOR RETURNS.

At a late hour of the night preceding the 3rd of Rejeb, Hâji Yûsuf and the king's ambassador returned. The former was received that night, and gave the Sultan his news, and on the morning of Thursday, the 3rd, the ambassador was introduced into the Sultan's presence. He delivered to the Sultan this message : ' The king begs you to allow him to keep those three places[1] as they are, and not to demolish them ; of what importance can they be in the eyes of so powerful a prince? The king is forced to persist in his request by the obstinacy of the Franks, who refuse to consent to their being given up. He has abandoned all claim to Jerusalem, and will not insist on keeping either monks or priests there, except only in the Church of the Resurrection. Therefore, if you

---

[1] The three places were Ascalon, Dârûn, and Gaza.

will give him the cities in question, peace can be made on every point. The Franks will keep all they now possess from Dârûn to Antioch, and you will retain all that is in your hands ; in this way everything can be settled, and the king will be enabled to depart. If peace is not concluded, the Franks will not suffer him to go, and he could not withstand them.' See the cunning of this accursed man ! To obtain his own ends, he would employ first force, and then smooth-speaking ; and, although he knew he was obliged to depart, he maintained the same line of conduct. God alone could protect the Moslems against his wiles ; we never had among our enemies a man more crafty or bolder than he. When the Sultan received this message, he summoned his emirs and councillors together to discuss the answer that he should make, and this was what they finally decided : ' As regards the people of Antioch, we are already engaged in negotiations with them direct concerning that city. Our ambassadors are now there, and if they return with a satisfactory answer, we shall include that place in the peace ; otherwise, it will not be included. Touching the cities the king wishes to possess, it is not a matter of great moment to us, but the Moslems will never consent to give them up. As regards the fortifications of Ascalon, let the king accept Lydda, a city in the plain, to indemnify him for the expenses he has been at.' The ambassador was dismissed on the morning of Friday, the 4th of Rejeb. On the following day, the Sultan's son, el-Melek ez-Zâher, prince of Aleppo, came to visit his father. The Sultan was very fond of him, and showed a marked preference for this son, for he saw in him all the signs of a man favoured by fortune, and gifted with great talents, together with a great capacity for administering affairs. He therefore went out to meet him, and met him near el-'Azerîa, for the young prince was coming up from the valley of the Jordan. When he saw him, he dismounted to do him honour, took him into his arms, and kissed his forehead ; then he assigned him the house of the Hospitallers[1] for his lodging. On the 7th of the month Hâji Yûsuf came back alone, and informed us that the king had said to him : 'We cannot possibly allow a single stone to be thrown down from the fortifications of Ascalon ; we cannot suffer such a thing to be said of us in this country. As to the boundaries of the country, they are well defined, and admit of no debate.' In consequence of this information, the Sultan set preparations on foot for an expedition against the enemy to convince them by this energetic step that he was determined to continue the struggle.

CHAPTER CLXII.

THE SULTAN'S EXPEDITION.

THE Sultan was informed that the Franks had taken the field and were marching on Beirût ; on the 10th of Rejeb he therefore left Jerusalem, and made a halt at a place called el-Jîb.[2] On the morning of the following day, the 11th of the month, el-Melek el-'Âdel arrived in the Holy City from the country near the Euphrates. He visited the Sakhra, and offered prayer there, after which he set out to rejoin the Sultan. That Prince had already left el-Jîb, and was then at Beit-Nûba, from which place he had sent to Jerusalem to summon his troops. I rejoined the Sultan at Beit Nûba, for I had not been with him the evening he made preparations for his departure. On Sunday, the 13th of Rejeb, he set out for Ramla, and came to a halt a

---

[1] The *Muristân*, or Hospital of St. John.
[2] *El-Jîb* (Gibeon) is 5½ miles N.W. of Jerusalem.

little before mid-day on the Tells between that city and
Lydda; there he spent the remainder of the day. The
next morning, very early, the light armed troops rode to
Yâzûr and Beit-Jibrîn, threatening Jaffa, and then returned
to the previous halting-place, where he had spent the rest
of the day. He called a meeting of his councillors, and
with their unanimous advice, resolved to lay siege to Jaffa.

CHAPTER CLXIII.

SIEGE OF JAFFA.

DURING the morning of Tuesday, the 15th of Rejeb, the
Sultan started on his march for Jaffa, and encamped there
a little before noon the same day. His army was drawn
up in three divisions, the right and left wings resting on
the sea; the Sultan himself was in the centre. The right
wing was commanded by el-Melek ez-Zâher, the left by
el-Melek el-'Âdel; the rest of the troops were placed
between the two wings. On the 16th of the month the
army began to attack the city, which they thought would
fall an easy prey. The Sultan drew up his troops in order
of battle, and ordered the mangonels to be brought forward,
and to be set up in position facing the weakest part of the
walls, which happened to be on the side of the east gate;
he then sent his miners forward to effect a breach in the
wall. Then a great clamour was raised, and mighty
shouts; a smart attack was begun, and the miners commenced a mine to the north of the east gate towards
an angle of the curtain. This portion of the wall had
been destroyed by the Moslems in the former siege, but
the Franks had rebuilt it. The miners took possession of
the mine they had sunk, and everyone thought the city

would be taken that very day. The king of England had
just left Acre and was going to Beirût, and it was the news
of his movements that had induced the Sultan to lay siege
to Jaffa. An obstinate struggle was maintained until the
end of the day, the enemy displaying a hardy valour and
a determined resistance that discouraged the besiegers.
Meanwhile, the miners were just finishing their mine,
when the besieged found means to destroy it in several
places ; and the miners were obliged to make what haste
they could in escaping. When the Moslem troops saw
that it would be a matter of difficulty to capture the city,
and that the attacking forces would have to be greatly
increased before they could hope for success, they began
to relax their efforts. Then the Sultan formed a resolution worthy of himself, and commanded that the mine
should be carried through the rest of the curtain from
the tower to the gate, and that the mangonels should
be brought to bear on that part of the wall that was
already undermined. A third of the night had gone
before he returned to the camp, which was on a *tell*
facing the city, and at a little distance from it. By the
following morning two mangonels had been set up, and
during the day they succeeded in mounting a third. The
Sultan rose, determined to storm the city ; but he observed
great want of energy in the ranks, for they thought the
mangonels that were being set up could not possibly
produce any effect for several days to come. The Sultan,
seeing his men irresolute and but little disposed to support him, was obliged to drive them forward and force
them to fight. The siege waxed hot and the garrison
suffered greatly. As soon as our men saw that the city
must fall they one and all lost every other feeling but a
longing to get possession of it. The besiegers, however,
had many wounded, both by arrows and by the missiles

shot from the arbalists.· When the besieged saw the situation in which they were placed, they sent two ambassadors
to the Sultan to negotiate for peace. One of the ambassadors was a (native) Christian, the other a Frank. He
consented to receive the surrender of the city on the same
terms, and with a stipulation for the same contribution, as
had been imposed on the Holy City. They accepted these
conditions, but asked for an armistice until Saturday, the
19th of Rejeb,[1] saying, if they had not received succours
by that time, they would carry out the terms of the treaty.
The Sultan refused to wait and the ambassador took his
departure. The besieged made a second attempt to obtain
a respite, but with the same result. When the Moslems
saw the envoys going backwards and forwards, they lost
the eagerness that had inspired them, and fought half-
heartedly, growing more listless than usual. But at this
juncture the miners finished their mine, and were commanded by the Sultan to fill it with combustibles; these
were set on fire, with the result that half the curtain was
brought down. The enemy had found out beforehand
where the fire would break out, and they had collected a
great heap of wood behind that point, to which they set
fire the moment the wall gave way, thus precluding any
attempt to effect an entrance through the breach. The
Sultan conducted the attack on the besieged with the
greatest conceivable energy ; but what fine soldiers they
were ! how brave and how courageous ! In spite of all
they had suffered, they did not barricade the gate, but
came out to fight incessantly. Our men maintained a
desperate struggle with them, till night intervened and put
an end to the fighting. It was useless to light fires in the
mines that had been sunk under the walls that were still
standing, for we could not take the place that day. The

[1] King Richard landed on August 1, just at the expiry of this truce.

Sultan was very much vexed, and, torn by conflicting thoughts, he regretted not having accepted the conditional surrender. He spent that night in the camp, and determined to increase the number of mangonels to five; these were playing on the curtain, now weakened by the mines, by fire, and by the operations on their side.

CHAPTER CLXIV.

CAPTURE OF JAFFA; EVENTS IN THAT CITY.

BY the morning of Friday, the 18th of Rejeb, the mangonels had been set up, and a great quantity of stones collected (to be hurled from these engines); these had to be brought from the ravines and other places at some distance, for there was no stone anywhere near the city. They were brought into play on that part of the wall that had been undermined; the Sultan himself, as well as his son el-Melek ez-Zâher, took an active part in the attack, whilst el-Melek el-'Âdel, at the head of the troops of the left wing, attacked the city on the opposite side. El-'Âdel was ill at the time. Then a mighty shout was raised, the drums sounded, the trumpets blared, the mangonels hurled their stones, and the enemy saw nothing but disaster threatening them on every side. The miners were actively engaged in setting fire to the mines, and the day had hardly reached its second hour, when the wall fell with a fall like the end of all things. At the cry, heard by all the people, that the curtain had fallen, there was none, however small his faith, who did not fly to the assault, and the heart of every one of the enemy trembled. They rushed on; none flinched; all were determined; all were consumed with longing for the most glorious and noble of

deaths. A cloud of dust and smoke arose from the fallen
wall, that darkened the heavens and hid the light of day,
and none dared to enter the breach and face the fire.
But when the cloud dispersed, and disclosed the wall of
halberds and lances replacing the one that had just fallen,
and closing the breach so effectually that even the eye
could not penetrate within, then indeed we beheld a
terrifying sight—the spectacle of the enemy's unwavering
constancy, as they stood undaunted, unflinching, self-
controlled in every movement. I myself saw two men
standing on the path of the rampart driving back those
who were trying to climb through the breach. One was
knocked down by a stone from a mangonel, and fell backward inside ; his comrade took his place at once, regard-
less that he was exposing himself to the same fate, which
overtook him in the twinkling of an eye, and so that none
but the quickest sight could have distinguished one from
the other. When the enemy saw how it must end, they
sent two ambassadors to the Sultàn to ask for their lives.
He made answer : ' Knight shall be exchanged for
(Moslem) horseman, Turkopole for light-armed soldier,
foot-soldier for foot-soldier. The old people shall pay the
ransom paid by those at Jerusalem.' When the envoys
saw that the fight in the breach was raging hotter than
the fiercest furnace, they asked the Sultan to put a stop to
it, in order that they might return to the city. ' I cannot
prevent the Moslems from continuing the fight,' he said.
' Return to your own people, and tell them to retreat into
the citadel and surrender the city to the Moslems, for
nothing will prevent them from making their way in.'
The envoys returned with this answer, and the enemy
withdrew into the citadel of Jaffa, losing some on the way,
who were killed by mistake. Our men made their way
into the city, sword in hand, and took a great quantity of

spoil; stores of fine stuffs, abundance of corn, furniture, and even the remains of the booty taken from the caravan from Egypt—all fell into their hands. The armistice was accepted on the conditions laid down by the Sultan. During the afternoon of Friday—always an auspicious day —the Sultan received a letter from Kâimâz en-Najmi, who was stationed close to Acre to protect the adjoining districts from the sorties of the garrison; this officer stated that the news of the siege of Jaffa had caused the King of England to abandon his project of going to Beirût, and that he had decided to come to the aid of the besieged city. On receipt of this news the Sultan resolved to bring matters to a speedy conclusion by insisting on the surrender of the citadel by men who could hope for no relief, for the fall of the place seemed imminent. Moreover, it was a long time since our troops had taken any booty, or won any advantage over the enemy; they were therefore most eager to take the place by storm. I was amongst the number who pointed out the necessity of forcing the enemy to evacuate the citadel, in order that we might occupy that fortress before the enemy received reinforcements. This also was the Sultan's wish; but his troops, worn out by fatigue, by their wounds, by the heat and the smoke from the fire, could hardly move, and were but little disposed to carry out his commands. Still, he never ceased urging them on till a late hour of the night; then, seeing that they were really too weary to do anything more, he mounted and rode off to his tent, which had been pitched close to the baggage. Those of his officers who were on duty joined him there, and I afterwards went to lie down in my tent, but I could not sleep, my mind was so oppressed with dread. At daybreak we heard the sound of the Frank trumpets, and heard that succours had come in to them. The Sultan sent for me at once, and said:

' The succours have come, it is true, by sea, but there is a strong enough force of Moslem troops on the beach to prevent their landing. This is what we must do : Go and find el-Melek ez-Zâher, and tell him to take up a position in front of the south-east gate (of the city) ; you must make your way into the citadel with a few picked men, and bring out the garrison ; you will take possession of the treasures and arms that are there, making an inventory of them, which you will write with your own hand ; this document you will send to el-Melek ez-Zâher, who will be outside the city, and will forward it to me.' He then gave me 'Izz ed-Dîn Jurdîk, 'Alem ed-Dîn Ḳaiṣar, and Derbâs el-Mehrâni, as colleagues to help me in this undertaking. I set out forthwith, taking Shems ed-Dîn, the treasurer, with me. When I reached the position occupied by el-Melek ez-Zâher, I found him with the advanced guard on a *tell* near the sea. He was sleeping in his coat of mail (*yelba*), wrapped in his wadded tunic,[1] and armed at all points for the fight. May God not leave unrewarded the good deeds of all these warriors who toiled in the cause of Islâm ! I awoke him, and he got up, still half asleep, and mounted his horse. We rode together to the place where he was to take up his position by the Sultan's instructions, and on the way he made me explain to him the object of my mission. After that I entered the city of Jaffa with my men ; we made our way to the citadel and delivered the order to the Franks to evacuate the place. They made answer that they would obey, and began to make their preparations for departure.

---

[1] Our author calls this sort of protective garment by the Persian name *kazâghend*. Geoffrey de Vinsauf tells us that the *gazegans* was a *lorica consuta*. See the collection by Gale and Fells, vol. ii., p. 407. Also M. de Wailly's *Villehardouin*, notes, p. 40. On p. 39 of that work the same garment is called *gambotson*. Henry de Valenciennes writes *gazygan*.

CHAPTER CLXV.

HOW THE CITADEL REMAINED IN THE ENEMY'S HANDS.

JUST as they were on the point of going, 'Izz ed-Dîn remarked that we ought not to allow them to depart until we had withdrawn the people from the city; otherwise, they would probably rush on the Franks, and take all they had. In truth, our troops were eager to pillage the city. Jordîk then set out to beat our men off; but as they were no longer under control, and were scattered about in different places, he was unable to get them all away. Still, in spite of my remonstrances, he kept on struggling with their obstinacy until at last it was broad daylight. Seeing how time was going, I said to him : ' The succours will get in, and the best thing we can do is to effect the evacuation of the citadel at once ; that was the Sultan's chief object.' When he saw why I was so impatient, he gave in to what I wanted. We took up our position at the gate of the citadel next to that where el-Melek ez-Zâher was stationed, and we got forty-nine men, with their horses and wives, to leave the fortress, and go. But at this juncture, those who were left took courage, and hardened their hearts to oppose us. Those who had gone out had thought that there were only a few ships come to their relief, and that these would not be able to give them any assistance. They did not know that the king of England was there with all his men ; and as they saw the hour of noon approach without any attempt being made to land, they feared that their comrades on the ships dared not venture, and that they themselves would therefore be taken and put to death. That is the reason why some of them left the citadel.

But when the rescuing fleet drew nearer, and they could see that it consisted of five-and-thirty vessels, those who were left behind took new heart of grace, and, by unmistakable signs, made it very evident that they meant to renew hostilities. One of them came out to tell me that they had changed their minds; they donned their cuirasses once more, and seized their shields, and were now manning the walls that had only just been rebuilt, and which were standing unfinished without battlements or parapets. Seeing the turn things were taking, I left the hillock on which I had taken my position, and which was quite close to the gate of the citadel, and went to 'Izz ed-Dîn Jurdîk, who was posted further down the hill with the men under his command. I put this officer on his guard, telling him that the besieged had changed their minds. A few moments afterwards I was outside the city talking to el-Melek ez-Zâher, when the besieged mounted, and sallied out of the citadel ; they charged down in a body on our men, and drove them out of the city. The fugitives crowded together so closely in the gateway that some of them only narrowly escaped with their lives. A great number of camp followers had stopped in some of the churches—what they were doing there is not known; the Franks rushed in and killed some of them, taking others prisoners. El-Melek ez-Zâher had sent me to inform his father of what was going forward, and as soon as the Sultan heard the news, he commanded the herald to sound the call to arms. The drums beat the charge, our soldiers ran up from all sides to take part in the fight, rushed into the city, and drove the enemy back into the citadel. When the besieged found some delay was taking place in landing the succours, they thought death was inevitable; so they sent their patriarch and the chatelain, with any number to guard them, to bear their excuses to the Sultan, and beg that a truce might be

24

granted them on the same terms as before. These envoys
were obliged to make their way through the hottest of the
fight in order to reach our camp. The delay in the dis-
embarkation of the succours was occasioned by the appearance of the city; Moslem standards were floating in every
quarter, and they were afraid that the citadel had already
been taken. The noise of the waves, the yells of the combatants, and the shouts of the *tahlil* and the *takbîr* (*There
is but one God! God is great!*), prevented those on board
from hearing their own countrymen's calls. A furious
attack was made on the garrison, and when they saw that
in spite of the strength of the rescuing fleet, they hesitated
to effect a landing, they felt convinced that those on board
believed the citadel to be already taken. The fleet consisted of more than fifty vessels, among which were fifteen
swift galleys, the king being on board of one of the galleys.
At this point one of the besieged committed himself into
the keeping of the Messiah, and jumped from the citadel
on to the pier; he came down unhurt, for it was sandy.
He then ran to the edge of the water, and got into a galley
which put out for him; this put him on board the king's
galley, and to him the man explained how things stood.
As soon as the king heard that the citadel was still holding
out, he made all speed for the shore, and his galley—which
was painted red, its deck being covered with a red awning,
and flying a red flag—was the first to land the men on
board. In less than an hour all the galleys had landed
their men under my very eyes. They then charged the
Moslems, scattering them in all directions, and driving
them out of the harbour. As I was on horseback, I started
off at a gallop to tell the Sultan. I found him engaged
with the two envoys, pen in hand, just about to write,
giving them grace. I whispered to him what had happened;
then, without writing anything, he turned to them, and

began to talk to divert their attention. A few moments afterwards some of the Moslems came up, flying before the enemy; he at once called to his troops to mount, had the envoys arrested, and ordered the baggage and the supplies to be transported to Yâzûr. The troops set out on their march, abandoning an enormous number of bales in which was packed the booty taken at Jaffa, and which they had no means of carrying away. The heavy baggage was sent off, and the Sultan remained where he was, spending the night there with a detachment of light cavalry. The king of England came right up to the position the Sultan had occupied during the attack on the city; and, as the garrison had come out by his orders to join him, he found himself at the head of a large body of troops. Many of our memlûks were with them, and he had several interviews with them.

CHAPTER CLXVI.

FRESH NEGOTIATIONS CONCERNING PEACE.

ABU BEKR, the chamberlain in el-Melek el-'Âdel's service, then received an invitation to visit (the king). Aibek, a follower of el-Melek el-'Aziz, Sonkor, one of el-Meshtûb's followers, and several others were with him. He found several memlûks of high rank,[1] who were treated with great cordiality by the king, and whom he often summoned to his presence. He found also several of our emirs there, such as Bedr ed-Dîn Dolderim, and others. When all had met together in his presence, he spoke half seriously and half in joke, and, among other things, he said: 'This Sultan is mighty, and there is none greater or mightier than him in this land of Islâm. Why, then,

---

[1] Beha ed-Dîn omits to say that they were prisoners.

did he make off at my first appearance? By God! I
was not even armed or ready to fight; I am still wearing
only the shoes I wore on board. Why, then, did you
retreat?' And again he said: 'Great and good God! I
should have thought he could not have taken Jaffa in two
months, and yet he made himself master of it in two
days!' He then turned to Abu Bekr, and addressed him
as follows: 'Greet the Sultan from me, and tell him that I
beseech him, in God's name, to grant me the peace I ask
at his hands; this state of things must be put a stop to;
my own country beyond the seas is being ruined. There
is no advantage either to you or me in suffering the present
condition of things to continue.' The envoys then took
their leave, and Abu Bekr came before the Sultan to
inform him of what the king had said. This was on the
evening of Saturday, the 19th of Rejeb. Then, when the
Sultan had taken the advice of his council of state, he
commanded that an answer should be written to the king,
couched in the following terms: 'You began by asking for
peace on certain terms, and at that time the question of
Jaffa and Ascalon formed the main point at issue; Jaffa
now is in ruins; you can have the country from Tyre to
Cæsarea.' Abu Bekr took this answer back to the king,
and returned accompanied by an envoy from the Franks,
who came to the Sultan to say: 'The king sends you this
answer: Among the Franks it is customary for a man to
whom a city has been granted to become the ally and
servant of the giver; if, therefore, you give me these two
cities, Jaffa and Ascalon, the troops I leave there will be
always at your service, and, if you have any need of me, I
will hasten to come to you and be at your service, and you
know that I can serve you.' To this the Sultan returned
the following answer: 'Since you trust with such trust in
me, I propose that we share the two cities. Jaffa and

what is beyond it shall be yours, whilst Ascalon and what
is beyond it shall be mine.' The two envoys returned, and
the Sultan went to join the baggage at Yâzûr, where the
camp had been pitched. He then resolved to demolish
that place as well as Beit-Dajan,[1] and left his miners there
for that purpose under the protection of the advanced
guard. He came to Ramla on Sunday, the 20th of Rejeb,
and there received a visit from the Frank ambassador,
who came in company with Abu Bekr, the chamberlain.
By the Sultan's orders the ambassador was received with
great honour. He was charged to deliver the king's thanks
for the concession of Jaffa, and to renew his request for
the possession of Ascalon. He added that, if peace were
concluded within six days, the king would have no occasion to spend the winter in Syria, and would return to his
own country. Without a moment's hesitation the Sultan
returned the following answer : ' It is absolutely impossible
for us to give up Ascalon, and in any case the king will be
obliged to spend the winter here. He knows full well that,
if he departs, all the country he has conquered will fall
into our hands without fail ; that will most certainly
happen, please God, even if he remains. If he can
manage to spend the winter here, far from his people, and
two months' journey from his native land, whilst he is still
in the vigour of his youth and at an age that is usually
devoted to pleasure, how much easier is it for me to remain
here not only during the winter, but during the summer
also ? I am in the heart of my own country, surrounded
by my household and by my children, and able to get all I
want. Moreover, I am an old man now, I have no longer
any desire for the pleasures of this world; I have had my
fill of them, and have renounced them for ever. The

---

[1] *Beit Dejan* is 6 miles S.E. of Jaffa, *Yâzûr* 3½.

soldiers who serve me in the winter are succeeded by
others in the summer.   And, above all, I believe that I am
furthering God's cause in acting as I do.   I will not cease
therefrom until God grants victory to whom He will.'
After having received this answer, the ambassador asked
and obtained permission to visit el-Melek el-'Âdel.   He
travelled to his tent, which was in rear, because he was ill,
at a place called Mâr Samwîl,[1] and the envoy had many
persons with him.   Soon after this the Sultan received
intelligence that an army of the enemy had set out from
Acre in order to succour the city of Jaffa ; he therefore
called his councillors together, and, with their unanimous
advice, determined to oppose the enemy, and whilst the
rest withdrew with the baggage to the mountains, the light-
armed troops were to march against the Franks, and to
avail themselves of any opportunity that might offer,
otherwise they were to return ; this would be better than
to give the Franks time to collect their forces, when our
men would have to retreat towards the mountains, looking
as if they fled, whereas now they would appear to be the
attacking party.   It was on the evening of Monday, the 21st
of Rejeb, that the Sultan issued the order for the baggage to
be transported to the mountains.   On the following morning he set out with a small escort for the 'Auja, and had
come to a halt on the banks of that river when intelligence
was brought him that the enemy's forces had entered
Cæsarea.   This put a stop to any idea of surprising that
army ; but he learnt that the king of England was
stationed outside Jaffa with a very small body of men, his
camp consisting of nothing but a few tents ; he therefore
determined to seize this opportunity of surprising that
camp, and thus realizing, at any rate, part of his plan.   In

---

[1] *Nebi Samwîl* (Montjoie of the Franks) is 4½ miles N.W. of
Jerusalem.

pursuit of this design, he set out as soon as night began
to close in; preceded by a few Arabs, who acted as
guides, he marched all through the night, and reached the
vicinity of the camp early in the morning. When he saw
that it consisted of only about a dozen tents, he entertained
a strong hope of capturing it as it stood, and charged
headlong down on the enemy. But the Franks displayed
such hardihood in the face of death that our troops lost
heart at their sturdy resistance, and were obliged to draw
off, and to content themselves with completely surrounding
the camp, though at some little distance. By the will of
God I was not present at this fight, being kept behind
with the baggage by an attack of illness from which I was
suffering; but I learnt from a man who was there that,
according to the largest computation, they had but seventeen horsemen, while, according to the lowest reckoning,
they numbered but nine; their infantry was under a
thousand; other accounts say three hundred; and others,
again, give a larger number. The Sultan was greatly
chagrined at what had happened, and went from squadron
to squadron making them the most liberal promises if they
would return to the charge ; but no one responded to his
appeal excepting his son, el-Melek ez-Zâher, who was preparing to rush on to the enemy when he was held back by
his father. I have been told that on this occasion el-
Meshtûb's brother, el-Jenâh, said to the Sultan : ' Send for
your servants who beat the people on the day we took
Jaffa, and who took away the booty from them.' It must
be noted that the terms granted on the surrender of Jaffa
had been a cause of great annoyance throughout the army,
for it had deprived them of the opportunity of pillage.
When the Sultan saw the temper of his men, he realized
that he could not remain in face of this handful of Franks
and do nothing, for that would have been a grievous blow

to his reputation. I have been assured by men who were there, that on that day the king of England, lance in hand, rode along the whole length of our army from right to left, and not one of our soldiers left the ranks to attack him. The Sultan was wroth thereat, and left the battle-field in anger for Yâzûr, where he came to a halt on Wednesday, the 23rd of Rejeb. Our troops spent the night where they were, acting as advanced guard. On Thursday morning the Sultan rode on and took up his position at en-Natrûn, summoning the army to come to him there. Towards the close of the day, which was Thursday, the 24th of Rejeb, we advanced to that place and spent the night encamped there. The following day he set out to visit his brother, el-Melek el-'Âdel, who was still ill ; then he repaired to Jerusalem, and celebrated Friday prayer in that city. He also inspected the various works in hand there, and gave instructions as to the way in which they were to be carried out. After that he took his departure from the city and returned to the camp at en-Natrûn, where he spent the night.

CHAPTER CLXVII.

(NEW) FORCES ARRIVE.

THE first of the chiefs to arrive was 'Alâ ed-Dîn, son of the Atabeg, Lord of Mosul, who joined us about noon on Saturday, the 26th of Rejeb. The Sultan rode out a considerable way to meet him, welcomed him with every mark of honour, and brought him back to his own tent, where he had made splendid preparations for his reception. After the prince had received a handsome present, he withdrew to his tent. That same day the king (of England's)

ambassador, accompanied by Abu Bekr, the chamberlain,
set out on his return to Jaffa, bearing a letter with which
el-Melek el-'Âdel had entrusted him for the king. Very
soon afterwards Abu Bekr returned, and presented himself
before the Sultan, saying : 'The king would not suffer me
to enter Jaffa, but came out of the city to see me, and
these are the words he used : " How long am I to go on
making advances to the Sultan that he will not accept ? I
was anxious above all things to be able to return to my
own country, but now the winter is here, and the rain
has begun. I have therefore decided to remain here, so
that question no longer remains to be decided between
us." ' On Thursday, the 9th of Sh'abân, the Egyptian
troops came in, and the Sultan set out from en-Natrûn to
meet them ; they followed (his son), el-Melek el-Moweîyed
Mas'ûd. With them were Mejed ed-Dîn Helderi, Seif
ed-Dîn Yâzkoj, and all the Asadîyeh (those who had been
Asad ed-Dîn Shîrkûh's memlûks). They arrived in
splendid array, the flags and banners flying; it was a day
of rejoicing. The Sultan received them, in the first place,
in his own tent, and spread a banquet before them, after
which he sent them to the positions appointed for them.

CHAPTER CLXVIII.

ARRIVAL OF EL-MELEK EL MANSÛR, SON OF TAKI ED-DÎN.

THIS prince had taken possession of the cities that had
been promised to him, and on Saturday, the 11th of
Sh'abân, he came to Mâr Samwîl, where el-Melek el-'Âdel
was at the time, and dismounted to visit him. The same
day el-'Âdel wrote to the Sultan, informing him of the

arrival of his kinsman, and begging him to be lenient to the youth, and to give him an honourable reception. El-Melek ez-Zâher, on his side, as soon as he heard of el-Melek el-Mansûr's arrival, obtained permission to go out and meet him, and to visit el-'Âdel to make inquiries concerning his health. He found el-Mansûr encamped at Beit Nûba; he dismounted in front of his tent, expressing the greatest joy at their meeting. This occurred on the Sunday. He made him come with him, and, attended by light troops, they came to the Sultan's tent, where I was on duty at the time. When the Sultan saw el-Mansûr, he advanced to meet him and folded him in his arms. Tears came into his eyes, and all who were present wept in sympathy. He then put the young prince completely at his ease by addressing him in the most kindly tones, asking him how he had fared on his journey. After this he gave him permission to withdraw, and sent him to spend the night in the tent of his own son, el-Melek ez-Zâher. The next morning, Monday (el-Mansûr) returned to his troops, who received him with colours flying. The fine appearance of these men gave the Sultan the greatest pleasure, and that same day — Monday, the 13th of Sh'abân—he assigned them a position near to Ramla, close to the vanguard of our army.

CHAPTER CLXIX.

THE SULTAN GOES TO RAMLA.

WHEN the troops had all come in, the Sultan called his emirs together and addressed them as follows: 'The King of England is very ill, and it is certain that the French will embark very shortly and return to their own country.

Now that they have exhausted all their resources, the enemy are weighed down by the mighty hand of God. I am therefore of opinion that we ought to march against Jaffa and take that city by surprise, if we can get a favourable opportunity ; if not, we will march by night and fall upon Ascalon ; and then, if our courage does not fail us, we will carry our purpose through.' The plan was approved by the council. He therefore gave an order to 'Izz ed-Dîn Jordîk, and Jemâl ed-Dîn Farej, and several other emirs, to march upon Jaffa during the night of Thursday, the 16th of Sh'abân. There they were to take up their position as though they were acting as an advanced guard, and to send out spies to ascertain the effective force of the garrison in infantry and cavalry. Meanwhile the king constantly sent messengers to the Sultan for fruit and snow, for all the while he was ill he had a great longing for pears and peaches. The Sultan always sent him some, hoping by means of these frequent messages to obtain the information of which he stood in need. In this way he managed to ascertain that there were three hundred knights in the city, according to the highest computation, or two hundred reckoning them at the lowest numbers reported ; he also learnt that Count Henry was using every endeavour to persuade the French to remain with the king, but that they were one and all determined to cross the seas. He heard, moreover, that they were neglecting the walls of the city, centring all their attention on getting the fortifications of the citadel into good order, and the king of England had expressed a wish to see Abu Bekr the chamberlain, with whom he had become very intimate. As soon as he had received trustworthy confirmation of this news, he marched on the Thursday morning to Ramla, and encamped in that place about noon the same day. He then received the following message from the detach-

ment of troops sent forward to over-run the country:
' We made an expedition against Jaffa, and they sent only
about three hundred knights against us, the greater part of
whom were riding on mules.' The Sultan sent them an
order to remain where they were. Very shortly after this
Abu Bekr the chamberlain came to the camp, bringing
with him a messenger from the king, sent to thank the
Sultan for his kindness in sending him fruits and snow.
Abu Bekr related that on one occasion, when he happened
to be alone with the king, he had said to him : ' Beg *my
brother* el-Melek el-'Âdel to consider what means can be
used to induce the Sultan to make peace, and ask him to
request that the city of Ascalon may be given to me. I
will take my departure, leaving him here, and with a very
small force he will get the remainder of their territory out
of the hands of the Franks. My only object is to retain
the position I hold amongst the Franks. If the Sultan
will not forego his pretensions to Ascalon, then let (el-
'Âdel) procure me an indemnity for the sums I have laid
out in repairing its fortifications.' When the Sultan received this message, he sent the chamberlain and the
messenger to el-Melek el-'Âdel, and he privately instructed
a confidential servant to go to el-'Âdel and tell him : ' If
they will give up Ascalon, conclude the treaty of peace, for
our troops are worn out by the length of the campaign,
and have spent all their resources.' It was on Friday, the
17th of Sh'abân, that they departed.

CHAPTER CLXX.

THE KING AGREES TO GIVE UP ASCALON.

AFTER sunset on the evening of Friday, the 17th of
Sh'abân, a letter came from Bedr ed-Dîn Dolderim, who

was then with the advanced guard, saying : ' Five men—
one of whom, called Huât,[1] is of high rank in the king's
service—have come to us from the city, and have expressed
a desire for an interview with us. Shall we hear what they
have to say, or not ?' The Sultan sent them permission,
and at the hour of the last night prayer Bedr ed-Dîn himself came to the camp to inform us that the king agreed to
give up Ascalon, that he surrendered his claim to compensation on that score, and that he had a most hearty desire
for peace. The Sultan ordered this message to be repeated
to him, and then sent a plenipotentiary to the king to take
his hand on this matter. He was to say : ' Now that the
Sultan has collected all his forces together, I cannot take
back any message to him, until I have obtained an assurance
from you that you will keep your word.' Bedr ed-Dîn
took his leave after receiving these instructions, and wrote
an account of what was going forward to el-Melek el-'Âdel.
On Saturday, the 18th of Sh'abân, we received the following dispatch from Bedr ed-Dîn : ' I have received the king's
promise (*literally*, hand) through the plenipotentiary; the
boundaries of our respective territories are to be those
established in the former agreement with el-Melek el-'Âdel.'
The Sultan's ministers (*literally*, diwân), when summoned
to a council, decided that the city of Jaffa and its dependencies should be made over to the king, with the exception of Ramla, Lydda, Yebna, and Mejdel Yâba; Cæsarea
also, with its dependencies, was to be his, as well as Arsûf,
Haifa, and Acre and their dependencies, with the exception
of Nazareth and Seffûrieh. This decision was recorded in
writing. The Sultan sent a letter in answer to Bedr ed-
Dîn's dispatch, and Torontai set out to carry it to the
emir in company with the king's ambassador. That envoy

---

[1] Perhaps *Huât* is for ' Howard.'

arrived in the afternoon of Saturday to conclude the peace
with Bedr ed-Dîn, and he said to the ambassador : ' These
are the boundaries fixed to your territory. If you accept
peace on the terms, well and good. I will give you my
hand upon our promises. Let the king send a man (to
the Sultan) empowered to swear (in his name), and let
this be done the day after to-morrow. Otherwise, we shall
believe you are only temporizing to gain time, and we
shall break off all negotiations.' After they had come to
an agreement as to the terms, they set out together on the
Sunday morning. The hour of the last prayer on that
Sunday, the 18th of Sh'abân, had gone by, when they came
to the Sultan to announce that Torontai and the king's
ambassador had returned. Only Torontai received permission to come into the Sultan's presence. He stated
that, when the king was informed of the tenor of the
written resolution of the council, he called out that he had
never given up the compensation (he claimed), whereupon
the men who had been sent to Dolderim declared to the
king that he had given it up without a doubt. ' If I did,'
the king had said, ' I will not break my word. Tell the
Sultan from me that it is well; that I accept the treaty,
but trust myself to his generosity, and know that, if he
does anything further in my favour, it is to his kindness
I shall owe the boon.' Torontai went that night to bring
the king's ambassadors, who waited until the Monday
morning before they were admitted to the Sultan's presence.
They then stated what had been agreed upon by their
prince, after which they withdrew to their own tents. The
Sultan held a council at which a final decision was taken
and the preliminaries of the arrangement settled. Emir
Bedr ed-Dîn Dolderim then set out for el-Melek el-'Âdel's
tent, taking the king's ambassadors with him, with the
intention of asking that Ramla might be granted in addi-

tion. He returned after the last evening prayer on Monday, and a convention was then drawn up, by the terms of which peace was to be made for three years, commencing from the date of the document, that is to say, from Wednesday the 22nd of Sh'abân, 588 (September 2, 1192), and Ramla and Lydda were to be made over to the Franks. El-'Âdel was then dispatched with the following instructions: ' If you can induce (the king) to be contented with only one of those cities, or to agree to share them equally (with us), do so, and do not enter upon the question of the possession of the hill-country.' The Sultan thought it desirable to make peace, because his troops had suffered a great deal, and all their funds were exhausted ; he knew also that they were very anxious to return to their homes, and did not forget the unwillingness they had shown before Jaffa, when he had ordered them to advance to the attack, and they had refused to move. Reflecting, therefore, that if he came to need them, he might find they had gone off, he felt obliged to give them sufficient time to rest, and to forget the state to which they were now reduced. He was also anxious to set about the re-organizing of the country, and to furnish the Holy City with all the war-stores he could command, and to obtain time to put her defences in good order. One of the clauses of the treaty provided that Ascalon should be demolished, and that our soldiers should co-operate with theirs in razing the walls ; for they were afraid that, if we received the city as it stood, we should neglect to demolish its defences. El-'Âdel set out to negotiate on this basis, and demanded that all Moslem countries should be included in the treaty ; the Franks, on their side, obtained a promise that the Lord of Antioch and Tripoli should be included in the truce, besides the treaty of peace which we had made with him. These preliminaries arranged, the ambassadors took their departure, having received an intimation that they would have to make up their minds either for peace or for war. For we were afraid that these negotiations were like the former ones—nothing but a means employed by the king to gain time ; and by this time we were well acquainted with his methods. That same day an ambassador came from Seif ed-Dîn Bektimor, Lord of Khelât, with a message that his master put himself at the Sultan's disposal, offered his support, and promised to send him troops. An ambassador also came from the Georgians, with instructions relative to the places of pilgrimage maintained by that people in Jerusalem, which they were anxious to keep in good order. They complained that they had been dispossessed, and begged the Sultan to have compassion on them, and order that the places in question might be restored to those in charge of them. The Lord of Erzerûm also sent in his submission to the Sultan, with offers of service.

CHAPTER CLXXI.

PEACE IS CONCLUDED.

ON el-'Âdel's arrival (at Jaffa) they made him halt at a tent outside the city. The king was informed of his coming, and, although he was very ill, he had him brought before him with the others. When el-'Âdel put into his hands the draft, he said : ' I am not strong enough to read it ; but I solemnly declare that I will make peace, and here is my hand.' The ambassadors then met together with Count Henry and the son of Bârezân (Balian II. of Ibelin), and the other members of the council, and informed them of the provisions of the treaty. All the conditions were accepted, even that regarding the

equal division of Ramla and Lydda, and it was decided
that it should be confirmed by oath on the Wednesday
morning. For the Franks said they were unable to swear
to it on the spot, because they had eaten (that day), and
it was their custom never to take an oath except fasting.
El-'Âdel sent a courier to the Sultan with the news. On
Wednesday, the 22nd of the month Sh'abân, the members
of the embassy were summoned into the king's presence,
and he gave them his hand, while they, on their side,
pledged themselves to him; he excused himself from
taking an oath, saying that kings never did so,[1] and the
Sultan accepted this declaration. All who were present
then took the oath with Count Henry, son of the king's
sister, who was to succeed him in the Sâhel, and with
Bâliân, son of Bârezân, Lord of Tiberias. The Hospitallers, Templars, and all the leaders of the Franks gave
in their adhesion. In the evening of that same day the
Sultan's envoys set out to return to their master, and
arrived in the camp about the time of the last evening
prayer, accompanied by the son of Honferi, the son of
Bârezân, and several other chiefs. The Frank envoys
were received with great honour, and were lodged in a
tent pitched for that purpose, and befitting their rank.
El-'Âdel then presented himself before the Sultan, and
informed him of all that had taken place. On the morning
of the following day, the 23rd of Sh'abân, the king's
ambassador was introduced to the Sultan, and, taking his
royal hand, declared that he accepted peace on the proposed conditions. He and his colleagues then asked that
an oath to observe the treaty should be taken by el-Melek
el-'Âdel, el Melek el-Afdal, el Melek ez-Zâher, 'Ali Ibn
Ahmed el-Meshtûb, Bedr ed-Dîn Dolderim, el Melek

---

[1] St. Louis was in like manner excused from an oath when taken
prisoner in Egypt.

el-Manṣûr, and all the other leaders, such as Ibn el-Moḳaddem and the Prince of Sheizer, whose dominions bordered on those of the Franks. The Sultan promised to send a commissioner with them to the last-named leaders to receive their oath. He also swore (peace) with the Lord of Antioch and Tripoli, stipulating, however, that his oath should be null and void unless that prince would give a like pledge to the Moslems, otherwise he should not be included in the treaty. He then ordered a proclamation to be made in the camp and in the market-places, to announce that peace was made throughout the land, that free passage was to be allowed to Christians through Moslem territory, and that the Moslems were at liberty to go into the dominions of the Christians. It was also proclaimed that the Hajj road (to Mekka) was now open from Syria, and he resolved himself to make the pilgrimage. I was present at the council when he so decided. After this he ordered a hundred miners to be sent to Ascalon to demolish the walls of the city ; he put them under the command of an emir of high rank, who received instructions to see that the Franks were withdrawn. A detachment of Franks was to accompany the miners, and to remain on the spot until the fortifications had been entirely destroyed, for the Christians were afraid that the Moslems would leave the place standing. It was a day of rejoicing ; God alone knows the boundless joy of both peoples. It was known, however, that the Sultan had not made peace altogether of his own free will. With regard to this, he said to me in one of our conversations : 'I am afraid of making peace, and I do not know what may happen to me. The enemy will increase their forces, and then they will come out of the lands we are leaving in their possession, and recapture those we have taken from them. You will see that each one of them will make a fortress on some hill-top; I cannot draw back, but the Moslems will be destroyed by this agreement.' So he spoke, and what he said afterwards came to pass[1]; but he saw that at that juncture it would be advantageous to make peace, for the troops had lost heart and were abetting one another in disobedience. God saw that peace must be for our good, because the Sultan's death occurred shortly after the ratification of the treaty; had he died in the midst of the struggle he had carried on, Islâm would have been in the greatest danger. It was therefore by the special providence of God, and in accordance with his usual felicity, that the Sultan was enabled to conclude the peace himself.

CHAPTER CLXXII.

DEMOLITION OF ASCALON.

ON the 25th of the month Sh'abân the Sultan commanded Alem ed-Dîn Kaiṣar to set out for Ascalon with a body of miners and masons to demolish that city. It had been agreed that the king should send people from Jaffa to accompany this officer, to watch the progress of the work of demolition and to see to the evacuation of the place by the Franks who were there. The following day they prepared to set to work immediately on their arrival; but the garrison prevented them, saying that the king owed them arrears of pay, and that they would not leave the city until the money was in their hands. 'Let him pay us,' they said, 'and we will leave the city; or, if you like, pay us yourselves.' But an officer came,

---

[1] From about 1218 A.D. onwards the Franks erected several new castles. In 1229 the Emperor Frederic II. entered Jerusalem as king.

bearing a commission from the king to force them to
evacuate the place. It was the 27th of Sh'abân when the
work was begun, and it was carried on without any interruption. He (the king) had written to his people to take
their share in the work of demolition, and the razing of a
certain portion of the walls was assigned to each side.
'When you have demolished it,' the order ran, 'you will
have leave to depart.' On the 29th of the month the
Sultan set out for en-Naṭrûn, and the two armies mingled
one with another. A company of Moslems repaired to
Jaffa to buy goods in that city, and a number of Franks
(*literally* of the enemy) went up to Jerusalem to perform
the pilgrimage. The Sultan opened the way for them
(*literally* the door) ; he even sent guards with them to
protect them on their way, and to accompany them on
their return to Jaffa. These pilgrimages became very frequent, and were promoted by the Sultan, because he knew
that the Franks would make haste to depart home as soon
as they had visited the holy places, whereby the Moslems
would be delivered from their presence, which was always
a source of danger. The king (of England) was much
vexed to see so great a number of pilgrims ; he sent to ask
the Sultan to put what hindrance he could in their way,
only allowing those to pass who presented some symbol to
be agreed upon or a passport issued in his name.[1] The
Franks were very indignant at this, and it only made them
the more eager to perform the pilgrimage. Day after day
crowds of people came in—chiefs, people of lower rank,
and princes in disguise. The Sultan then began to give
honourable entertainment to such of the pilgrims as he

---

[1] Richard sent to Salâh ed-Dîn, asking him not to allow any pilgrim
to go to Jerusalem without a passport from himself, and he took care
not to give a passport to any Frenchmen, to punish them for having
refused to assist him at Jaffa.—Geoffrey de Vinsauf.

chose; he received them at table, and entered into familiar conversation with them, taking care to let them know that he should thereby incur the reproaches of the king. He used then to give them permission to continue their pilgrimage, declaring he took no notice of the prohibition he had received. He sent the following message to the king to excuse himself on this score : ' There are men here who have come from afar to visit the holy places, and our law forbids us to hinder them.' Very soon after this the king's illness became so serious that a report was circulated of his death. He nevertheless set out for Acre on the night preceding the 29th of the month, accompanied by Count Henry and all the rest of the enemy, leaving only the sick and old in Jaffa.

CHAPTER CLXXIII.

RETURN OF THE MOSLEM ARMIES TO THEIR HOMES.

As soon as this business was settled and the treaty concluded, the Sultan gave his troops permission to depart. The first of the contingents to set out was that from Arbela ; they started on their march on the 1st of the month of Ramaḍân. The following day saw the departure of the contingent furnished by the cities of Mosul, Sinjâr, and Ḥiṣn Keifa. The Sultan had announced his pilgrimage (to Mekka), and he now turned all his thoughts to carrying out what he had undertaken. It was I who had suggested the idea to him the day that peace was concluded. My words made a deep impression on him ; he issued an order that everyone in the army who decided to undertake the pilgrimage was to have his name put down, being anxious to ascertain by that means the number of people likely to accompany us. Lists were drawn up of

everything that would be required for the journey—to wit,
utensils, clothing, provisions, and other things. These
documents were sent into the country in order that everything that was necessary might be prepared. After the
Sultan had dismissed his troops, and had heard that the
enemy had set out preparatory to their return home, he
determined to repair to Jerusalem to make every arrangement for the work of its restoration, and to examine its
condition, as well as to make preparations for his pilgrimage. He set out from en-Naṭrûn on Sunday, the 4th of
Ramaḍân, and went first to Mâr Ṣamwîl to visit el-Melek
el-'Âdel. But that prince was no longer there ; he had
just returned to Jerusalem, and I was with him, having
been sent with a message from the Sultan, together with
Bedr ed-Dîn Dolderim and el-'Âdel. For some time el-
Melek el-'Âdel had been obliged to live apart from his
brother on account of his illness, but he was now quite
convalescent. When we informed the prince that the
Sultan was (going) to Mâr Ṣamwîl to visit him, he made a
great effort of will, and came with us to meet the Sultan,
whom we met just as we reached Mâr Ṣamwîl, and before
he had dismounted. El-'Âdel went forward to him, got
down from his horse, kissed the ground, and then re-
mounted. The Sultan told him to come near, and asked
him about his health. They then rode together to
Jerusalem, where they arrived towards the end of the same
day.

CHAPTER CLXXIV.

ARRIVAL OF AN AMBASSADOR FROM BAGHDAD.

ON Friday, the 23rd of the month Ramaḍân, el Melek
el-'Âdel received the Sultan's permission to go to el-Kerak
after having assisted at the public prayer that day. He

was to inspect that fortress, and then make the best of
his way to the country to the east (of the Euphrates),
where he was to take upon him the government which had
been entrusted to him by the Sultan. He had just bidden
his brother farewell, and was encamped at el-'Azerîya, when
he was informed that an ambassador from Baghdad had
come to see him. He therefore sent a courier to the
Sultan to inform him of this, saying he was going to receive
the ambassador with a view of ascertaining the object of
his mission. On Saturday, the 24th, he came to visit the
Sultan, and told him that the ambassador came from
Ibn en-Nâfedh, who had been made assistant of the Vizier
of Baghdad. He came to deliver a letter from his master
to el-'Âdel, begging him to use his influence with the
Sultan and persuade him to show respect to the Khalif,
and urging him to act as mediator between the Sultan
and the Khalif's Divân. The same messenger brought a
reprimand to the Sultan for having delayed to send envoys
to the threshold of the Khalifate, and was instructed to
require him to send el-Kadi el-Fâdel to the Khalif's Divân,
to conclude certain negotiations of the Sultan with the
Divân which hitherto had led to nothing. (On this
occasion) the Divân made the most splendid promises
to el-Melek el-'Âdel, that in case he should be successful
the service he would thereby render to the Divân would
thenceforward give him the greatest influence, with other
considerations of a like nature. When el-'Âdel spoke to
the Sultan on the subject, he showed no disposition to
send an ambassador to receive the orders of the Divân, or
to suffer it to appear that the Khalif's interference had any
influence with him at all. The discussion was interrupted
and resumed more than once ; they had several conversations, more or less lengthy, on the subject, until at last
the Sultan decided to dispatch ed-Diâ esh-Sheherzûri

(to Baghdad).[1] As soon as el-'Âdel had arranged this
business, he returned to his camp at el-'Azariya, and made
known the Sultan's answer,—that he had consented to send
an ambassador to the Khalif's Divân. On the (following)
Monday he set out for el Kerak, and on Tuesday, the
26th of Ramadân, ed-Dia started for Baghdad.

CHAPTER CLXXV.

EL-MELEK EZ-ZÂHER SETS OUT ON HIS RETURN TO HIS
OWN DOMINIONS, BUT THE SULTAN IS ANXIOUS ABOUT
HIM.

ON the morning of the 27th, el-Melek ez-Zâher—may his
glory increase!—set out, after going to the Sakhra to say
his prayers and implore the favour of God. He rode out
and I rode in attendance, when he turned to me, saying:
' I have just recollected something I must speak to the
Sultan about.' He sent forthwith to ask permission to
come into his father's presence, and as soon as the permission was granted took me with him into the audience-
chamber. Everyone else withdrew, after which the Sultan
addressed him as follows: ' I commend you to God
Almighty. He is the source of all good. Do the will of
God, for that is the way of peace. Beware of bloodshed ;
trust not in that, for spilt blood never sleeps. Seek to
gain the hearts of thy subjects, and watch over all their
interests, for thou art only appointed by God and by me
to look after their good ; endeavour to gain the hearts of
thy emirs, thy ministers, and thy nobles. I have become
great as I am because I have won the hearts of men by
gentleness and kindness. Never nourish ill-feeling against
any man, for death spares none. Be prudent in thy

[1] Diâ ed-Dîn esh-Sheherzûri (El-Kâsem Ibn Yahya) was appointed
Kâdî of Damascus about the year 572 (A.D. 1176-1177).

dealings with other men, for (God) will not pardon unless they forgive you ; but as to that which is between God and thyself, He will pardon the penitent, for He is gracious.' He added other injunctions, but this is all I could remember after we had left the Sultan's presence, for a great part of the night had gone and dawn had begun to appear before we left the audience-chamber. He finally gave us leave to withdraw, and rose from his seat to bid the prince farewell ; he dismissed him with a kiss on the cheek, and, placing his hand on his son's head, committed him to the care of God. The prince went to sleep in the wooden alcove belonging to the Sultan, and we remained with him until daybreak. Ez-Záher then started on his journey, and I rode with him some way before bidding him farewell ; he then continued on his road under God's protection. Very shortly afterwards el-Melek el-Afdal dispatched his baggage, but the business he was transacting with the Sultan through me detained him till the 4th of the month of Shawâl. He set out on his journey that evening, towards the middle of the night, after having suffered a reprimand from the Sultan. Instead of following the road through the valley of the Jordan, he started across country with a lightly-armed escort.

CHAPTER CLXXVI.

THE SULTAN LEAVES JERUSALEM.

THE Sultan was occupied during his stay in Jerusalem in granting fiefs, in dismissing his troops, and making preparations for his journey into Egypt. His intention as to the pilgrimage was interrupted, so the most important of profitable things was lost to him. He spent his time in this way until he heard for certain that the ship had sailed

on which the king of England had embarked, on his
return to his own country ; this was on the first day of the
month of Shawâl (October 10, 1192).   He then determined
to ride through the districts on the coast with a small
escort, with a view of inspecting the maritime fortresses,
and reaching Damascus by way of Bâniâs.   He proposed
to remain only a few days in that city, returning thence to
Jerusalem, preparatory to starting for Egypt.   He meant
to examine into the condition of that country, to make the
necessary arrangements for its government, and to take
various measures of public utility.   According to his command I was to remain in the Holy City until his return, to
superintend the erection of a hospital he had ordered to be
built, and to press forward the completion of a college, the
foundations of which he had laid.   He left Jerusalem on
Thursday, the 6th of Shawâl, and I rode with him to bid
him farewell, which I meant to do first at el-Bîra,[1] where
he halted for dinner ; he continued his journey to Nâblus,
and I went part of the way with him.   He halted for the
night, and then started for that city, where he arrived about
mid-day on Friday, the 7th of Shawâl.   A crowd of people
came out to meet him, to complain of el-Meshtûb and the
oppressive way in which he governed them.   He resolved
to inquire into the matter, and therefore remained at
Nâblus until the afternoon of Saturday, when he set out for
Sebastieh,[2] to examine into the state of that city.   He
then took the road to Kaukab, where he arrived on Monday, the 10th of the month.   He made an inspection of
the fortress, and ordered the necessary repairs.   Behâ ed-
Dîn Karâkûsh, who had recovered his freedom, came to
pay his respects to the Sultan on Tuesday, the 11th of
Shawâl.   His coming gave the Sultan the greatest pleasure,

[1] *Birch*, 8½ miles N. of Jerusalem.
[2] Samaria.

and, indeed, he had many titles to his prince's favour, and
had rendered great service to the cause of Islâm. He
obtained his sanction to go to Damascus to procure the
money necessary for his ransom, which was fixed, as I have
been told, but God knows, at two hundred thousand (gold
pieces ?). When the Sultan was at Beirût, he received a
visit from the prince, Lord of Antioch, who came to
salute him and to ask a favour. He gave him an honourable reception, and entertained him hospitably, granting him the territory of el-'Amk[1]—corn lands, the crop
bringing in an annual return of fifteen thousand gold
pieces (dinârs) annually. El-Meshtûb had been left at
Jerusalem with the other emirs who had remained there,
but the government of the city had not been entrusted to
him ; 'Izz ed-Din Jurdîk exercised authority as governor,
having been appointed by the Sultan on that Prince's
return to the city after the conclusion of peace. Before
appointing him to that post, the Sultan had employed me
to ascertain the opinion of el-Melek el-'Âdel, el-Melek el-
Afdal, and el-Melek ez-Zâher upon the subject. Jurdîk
was, moreover, elected as governor by the voice of all
religious and just men, because he was dependable in
character, and protected all honest men. One Friday, at
the Sakhra, in accordance with the Sultan's commands, I
installed Jurdîk in his office. After the conclusion of
public prayer I invested that emir with his new dignity,
urging him very specially to do his duty faithfully, and
acquainting him with the high esteem in which he was held
by the Sultan. He acquitted himself of the duties of his
position in the most praiseworthy manner. El-Meshtûb
remained in the city in company with the other emirs, and
died there on Sunday, the 23rd of Shawâl (November 1,

[1] See p. 38.

A.D. 1192). Prayers were said over his body in the
Mesjed el-Akṣa,[1] and he was buried in his own house.

CHAPTER CLXXVII.

THE SULTAN RETURNS TO DAMASCUS.

THE Sultan inspected all the strongholds he possessed in
the Sàḥel (Western Palestine), and ordered the necessary
repairs to be carried out ; he then turned his attention to
the condition of the troops composing their garrisons, and
filled each one of the fortresses with infantry and cavalry.
On the morning of Wednesday, the 26th of Shawâl, he
entered Damascus, and there he found el-Melek el-Afḍal,
el-Melek ez-Zâher, el-Melek ez-Zâfer, and his younger
children. He preferred this city as a place of abode to
any other. On the Thursday morning, the 27th of the
month, he held a public reception, to which everyone was
allowed to come and satisfy their thirst to see him. People
of all classes were admitted, and poets recited poems in his
praise : 'that he spread the wings of Justice over all, and
rained down boons on his people from the clouds of his
munificence and kindness.' For he held audiences at appointed times at which he gave ear to the complaints of
the oppressed. On Monday, the first day of the month
of Zu el-Ḳ'ada, el-Melek el-Afḍal gave a great dinner
to el-Melek ez-Zâher, who had come to Damascus on
hearing that the Sultan intended to stay in that city. He
had stayed there in the hope of having the pleasure of
seeing his father once more ; it seemed as though his noble
heart had a presentiment that his father's death was at
hand. In the course of the evening he returned several
times to bid him farewell. In the banquet that el-Afḍal

---

[1] The Haram enclosure.

gave his brother, he displayed a magnificence and good taste worthy of his fine character. He intended it as a token of gratitude for the splendid reception ez-Zâher had given him on his visit to Aleppo. The great officers of State, both civil and ecclesiastical (literally, the lords of this world and the sons of that which is hereafter), were present at this assembly. The Sultan also went, at el-Afdal's invitation, to gladden his heart. So at least I have been told.

CHAPTER CLXXVIII.

ARRIVAL OF EL-MELEK EL-'ÂDEL.

EL-MELEK EL-'ÂDEL had been to inspect the fortress of el-Kerak and to give orders for the improvements he considered necessary, after which he set out on his return to his dominions on the Euphrates, and on Wednesday, the 17th of the month of Zu el-Ḳ'ada, he entered the territory of Damascus. The Sultan went out to meet him, and remained hunting in the districts between Ghabâgheb[1] and el-Kisweh till he came, and they set out together for Damascus, and entered the city on the evening of Sunday, the 21st of the month. The Sultan stayed at Damascus, hunting in company with his brother and sons, amusing himself in the country of Damascus and in the haunts of the gazelle. It seemed to afford him the rest of mind that his continual fatigues—working by day and watching by night—had rendered absolutely necessary for him ; but he did not think that he was then bidding farewell to his children and the scenes of his pleasures in the chase. The pressure of business and the number of projects in hand prevented him from thinking of revisiting Egypt. I was still in Jerusalem when I received a letter summoning me

[1] This place is about 19 miles S. of Damascus.

to rejoin him.   Rain was falling in torrents, and the roads
were so deep in mud that I was nineteen days in accomplish-
ing the journey.   I set out from Jerusalem on Friday, the
23rd of Moharrem, 589, and did not reach Damascus till
Tuesday, the 12th of Safer, just as the first pilgrims were
nearing the city, which the Sultan had reached in the afternoon of Monday, the 11th of Safer, so my appearance was
delayed.   In the northern ante-chamber the emirs and
high functionaries were thronging round el-Melek el-Afdal,
awaiting audience of the Sultan.   But when he heard I
was there, he ordered that I should be admitted before all
the others to a private interview with him, and he rose
from his seat to greet me.   Never before had his face
expressed such satisfaction at the sight of me ; his eyes
filled with tears, and he folded me in his arms.   May God
have mercy upon him !

CHAPTER CLXXIX.

THE SULTAN GOES OUT TO MEET THE HÁJ.

ON Wednesday, the 13th of the month of Safer, he sent to
summon me, and when I went to him, asked me who was
in the antechamber.   I replied that el-Melek el-Afdal was
sitting there, waiting to be permitted to pay him his
respects, together with a crowd of emirs and people, who
had come for the same purpose ; but he sent Jemâl ed-Din
Ikbâl to inform them that he could not receive them.   The
next morning he sent for me again early, and I found him
sitting in a summer-house (Soffa) in the garden, surrounded
by his younger children.   He asked if there were anyone
waiting for him, and when he heard that some envoys had
come from the Franks, and were waiting to be admitted,
together with his emirs and chief officers, he commanded

that the ambassadors should be introduced into his presence. One of his young children, Emir Abu Bekr, of whom he was very fond, and with whom he was playing, happened to be there. As soon as he saw these men, with their shaven chins, their close-cropped hair and strange garments, he was frightened and began to cry. The Sultan made his excuses to the ambassadors, and dismissed them without hearing the message they had brought. He then said to me, speaking in his usual kindly way: ' It is a busy day.' Then he added : ' Bring us whatever you have ready.' They brought him rice cooked in milk and other light refreshments, and he ate of them, but without much appetite as it seemed to me. He had latterly omitted holding his receptions, and excused himself, saying it was a great trouble to him to move ; indeed, he was suffering from indigestion, lassitude, and weakness.[1] When we had finished our meal, he asked me if I had heard anything of the Ḥàj. I made answer : ' I met some of the travellers on the road ; if there were not so much mud they would have been here to-day ; but they will come in to-morrow.' He then said : ' We will go out, please God, to meet them ;' and he gave an order that their road should be cleared of the water, for it was very rainy that year and there were streams of water in the roads. After this I withdrew, noticing that he no longer had the good spirits I knew so well. On the Friday morning early he set out on horseback. I followed shortly with the pack animals, and came up just as he met the Ḥàj. Among the pilgrims were Sâbek ed-Din and Ḳarâla el-Yârûki, and the respect for these Sheikhs was very great. El-Melek el-Afdal then came out to join him, and took me aside to speak to me. At that moment I noticed that the Sultan was not wearing

---

[1] All symptoms of typhoid fever.

his *kazâghand*,[1] without which he never went riding. It was a magnificent sight that day, for the inhabitants of the city came out in crowds to meet and to look at the Sultan. I could not control myself any longer, and hastened up to him, telling him he had forgotten his *kazâghand*. He seemed like a man waking out of a dream, and asked for the garment, but the master of the wardrobe could not be found. It appeared to me very serious. I said to myself : ' The Sultan is asking for something he never used to be without, and he cannot get it !' This filled my heart with apprehension, and I considered it as a bad omen. I then turned to him and asked if there were not another way, less crowded with people, by which he could return to the city. He replied that there was, and turned into a path between the gardens, leading in the direction of el-Muneib'a.[2] We followed him, but I was heavy at heart, for I feared very much for his health. When we came to the castle, he entered by crossing the bridge as usual, but this was the last time he rode over it.

.

CHAPTER CLXXX.

THE SULTAN'S ILLNESS.

ON the Friday evening the Sultan suffered from extreme lassitude, and a little before midnight he had an attack of bilious fever, which was internal rather than external. On Saturday morning, the 16th of Safer, 589 (21st of February, A.D. 1193), he was in a very low state in consequence of the fever, although it was suppressed. I went to visit him

---

[1] See above, p. 367.

[2] El-Muneib'a means ' the little spring.' The place that bears this name lies in the Ghûta of Damascus.

with el-Kâdi el-Fâdel, and we entered his room at the same time as el-Melek el-Afdal, his son. We had a long conversation with him ; he complained at first of the bad night he had had, but after that he seemed to take pleasure in talking to us. This lasted till noon, when we withdrew, leaving our hearts with him. He told us to go and partake of the meal in attendance on el-Melek el-Afdal. El-Kâdi el-Fâdel was not accustomed to that, and he therefore returned (home) ; I, for my part, went into the great southern hall, and found the table laid, and el-Afdal seated in his father's place. As I could not endure this sight, I withdrew without sitting down to table ; and several others, seeing his son seated in his place, held it as an omen of ill, and shed tears at the sight. From that time the Sultan's illness grew more and more serious, and we never omitted visiting him both morning and evening. El-Kâdi el-Fâdel and I used to go into the sick-room several times a day, whenever a lull in the pain he suffered allowed him to receive our visits. It was in his head that he suffered most. One of the things from which we augured that his life would be taken was the absence of his chief physician, who knew his constitution better than anyone, having always attended him, both in the city and on his journeys. On the fourth day of his illness the other physicians thought it necessary to bleed him, and from that moment he grew seriously worse, and the humours of the body began to cease their flow. His condition was aggravated by the predominance of this dryness, and he was reduced to the last degree of weakness. On the sixth day we got him to sit up, propping him up at the back with a pillow ; we then brought him a cup of lukewarm water to drink, which was to act as an emollient after the medicine he had taken. He tasted it and found it too hot ; another cup was brought him which he thought too

26

cold, but still he did not get vexed or angry, but only
said : ' O God, perhaps there is no one who can make the
water of the right temperature !' El-Fâdel and I left him
with the tears streaming from our eyes, and he said to me :
' What a great soul the Moslems will lose ! By God, any
other man in his place would have thrown the cup at the
head of the man who brought it !' During the sixth,
seventh, and eighth days the illness increased, and then his
mind began to wander. On the ninth day he fell into a
stupor, and was unable to take the draught that was
brought to him. The whole city was in commotion, and
the merchants, being afraid, began to carry away their
goods out of the bazaars ; it is impossible to give any idea
of the sorrow and trouble with which one and all were
oppressed. Every evening el-Kâdi el-Fâdel and I used to
sit up for the first third of the night together, and then we
would go to the gate of the palace ; and if we found means,
we took a look at him and withdrew at once, and if not,
we still learned how he was. When we came out we used
to find the people waiting to gather from the expression of
our faces what was the Sultan's state. On the tenth day of
his illness they treated him twice with a clyster, which gave
him some relief. After that it gave the greatest delight to
all to hear that he had drunk some barley-water. That
night, as usual, we waited some hours, and then we went
to the palace, where we found Jemâl ed-Daula Ikbâl. On
our asking as to the health (of the Sultan), he went in and
sent us word from el-Melek el-Mo'azzem Turân Shah—
God increase his power!—that perspiration was visible in
both legs. We gave thanks to God for this news, and
begged him to feel the rest of the body, and to let us know
of any perspiration elsewhere. He did as we asked him
and came back to us, saying the perspiration was profuse.
We then departed with lightened hearts. On the follow-

ing day, which was Tuesday, the eleventh day of the illness and the 26th of the month of Ṣafer, we went to the gate to ask for news. They told us that the perspiration was so profuse that it had gone right through the mattress and the mats, and the moisture could be seen on the floor ; and as the dryness of the body had increased to such a degree, the doctors were astonished at his strength.

CHAPTER CLXXXI.

EL-AFDAL RECEIVES THE OATHS OF ALLEGIANCE.

WHEN el-Melek el-Afḍal saw his father's condition, and all men realized that there was no hope of his recovery, he made all haste to secure the oaths of allegiance of the people. He· held a reception for that purpose in the Reḍwân palace, so called because Reḍwân (one of the former princes of Aleppo) had resided there. He then summoned the Ḳâḍis and instructed them to draft a brief form of oath, promising fidelity to the Sultan as long as he lived, and after his death to el-Afḍal. The prince excused himself to the people on the ground that the Sultan's illness was most critical, and that one could not tell what might happen, and that it was necessary to provide for any event after the manner of princes. The first he called upon to swear was S'ad ed-Dîn Mas'ûd, brother of Bedr ed-Dîn Maudûd and *Shiḥna* (or governor of Damascus) ; he took the oath without any hesitation and quite uncon- ditionally. Nâsr ed-Dîn, governor of Ṣahyûn (near Laodicea), then came forward and took the oath, but made it a condition that the fortress he commanded should be his. Sâbek ed-Dîn, Lord of Sheizer, also swore, but not by the (triple) divorce ; 'for,' said he, 'I have never

26—2

taken an oath that contained such a condition.' Khosh-
terin Ḳosein (emir of the) Hakkâri (Kurds) swore next;
then came Nûsherawân ez-Zerzâri (another Kurdish emir),
who, however, made it a condition that he should be
granted a suitable fief. 'Alkân and Milkân (two other
Kurdish emirs) also took the required oath. A banquet
was then served of which the whole assembly partook, and
after the *'asr* (prayer) the ceremony of the taking of the
oath was resumed. Maimûn el-Ḳaṣri—God be merciful to
him !—and Shems ed-Dîn (Sonḳor) the elder swore, but
conditionally ; they exacted a promise that they should
never be called upon to draw sword against any of el-
Afḍal's brothers : ' In any other case,' said Maimûn, ' I
will answer with my head.' Sonḳor began by refusing to
take the oath ; afterwards he said : ' I will swear allegiance
to you in my capacity as governor of en-Naṭrûn, and on the
condition that that place shall remain mine.' Then Sâma
came forward and said : ' Why should I swear ? I have
no fief.' They then talked to him awhile, and he swore
as the others had done, but on condition of receiving an
adequate fief. Sonḳor, the Scarred (el-Meshṭûb), swore,
but conditionally upon his receiving the grant of a satisfactory fief. Aibek el-Afṭas—God have mercy on him !—
took the oath with the proviso that he should get what he
wanted, but he omitted the (triple) divorce clause. Ḥossâm
ed-Dîn Bishâra, the superior officer of all the above emirs,
also took the oath. None of the Egyptian emirs were
present at this ceremony, nor, indeed, had they been required. The others had only been required to take the
oath with a view of maintaining order, and possibly the
formula of their oath is not well known. The text of
the oath was as follows : ' *Clause* 1. From this moment
forth, with single aim and unflinching purpose, I vow my
allegiance to el-Melek en-Nâṣr (Ṣalâh ed-Dîn) as long as he

lives, and I will never relax my efforts to uphold his government, consecrating to his service my life and wealth, my sword and my men ; I will obey his commands and conform to his will. Afterwards I will keep the same faith with his son, el-Afḍal 'Ali, and the heirs of that prince. I take God to witness that I will obey him and uphold his government and land, consecrating to his service my life and wealth, my sword and my men ; I will observe his commands and prohibitions, and I swear that my private resolutions correspond with my oath. I call upon God to be witness of my words.'[1]

CHAPTER CLXXXII.

DEATH OF THE SULTAN—MAY GOD HAVE MERCY UPON HIM, AND SANCTIFY HIS SOUL !

THE eve of Wednesday, the 27th of Ṣafer, in the year 589, was the twelfth night of the illness. He grew worse, and his strength failed ; and from the first there was no hope. He remained sometimes with us, and sometimes wandering; but that night they sent for me, as well as el-Ḳâḍi el-Fâḍel and Ibn ez-Zeki,[2] and it was not the usual time for our being present. El-Melek el-Afḍal wished us to spend the night with him, but the ḳâḍi objected, because people used to wait for us on our return from the castle, and he feared that if we did not make our appearance, an alarm might spread through the

---

[1] Our author omits the second clause containing the penalties at·ached, and which must have run somewhat as follows : ' If I break my oath, I swear that by that fact alone my wives are divorced, my slaves set free, and I must go, barefoot, on the pilgrimage to Mecca,' etc.

[2] See p. 40.

city, and they might begin pillaging. He therefore thought
it best for us to leave. El-Afdal then decided to summon
Abu J'afer, *imâm* of the Kellâsa, and a man of known
rectitude, in order that he might be at hand in the castle
if God should call the sick man to Himself that night.
But he lived on, half attending to him, and half wandering,
while the confession of faith and of God Almighty was
repeated to him. The kâdi and I took our departure,
both ready to have laid down our lives for his. He
remained all night in the state of one going to God, and
Sheikh Abu J'afer read to him passages from the Kurân,
and reminded him of God Almighty. Since the ninth
day of the fever the Sultan had been wandering, and his
brain was clear only at intervals. The sheikh afterwards
assured us thus : ' I was reciting the Divine Word to him
—*He is the God than whom there is no other God; who
knows the unseen and the visible* (lix. 22), and I heard
him say—God have mercy on him—" *It is true!*" And
this at the time of his passing away, and it was a sign
of God's favour to him. God be thanked for that !' The
Sultan died after the hour of morning prayer, on Wednesday,
the 27th of Safer, in the year 589 (March 4, 1193 A.D.).
El-Kâdi el-Fâdel had hastened back to the castle before
dawn at the time of his passing away, and I went too,
but he was dead, and had entered into God's favour, and
the place of His goodness and grace. I was told that
while Sheikh Abu J'afer was reading from the Divine
Word—*There is no God but He! in Him do I trust*
(ix. 130), the sick man smiled, his face grew radiant,
and he went in peace to his Lord. Never since Islâm
and the Moslems lost the (four) first khalifs, never, from
that time, had the faith and the faithful suffered a blow
such as that they received on the day of the Sultan's
death. The castle, the city, the whole world, were thereby

plunged into grief, of which God alone could fathom the intensity. I had often heard people say they would lay down their own lives for that of someone very dear to them, but I thought it was only a manner of speaking, from which a good deal must be deducted in reality ; but I swear before God, and I am sure that had we been asked that day, ' Who will redeem the Sultan's life ?' there were several of us who would have replied by offering his own. El-Melek el-Afḍal then held a reception in the north hall, to receive the condolences of his officers ; but he placed a guard at the entrance to the castle, and only admitted emirs of high rank, and doctors of law (*literally*, ' men of the turban '). It was, indeed, a melancholy day ; everyone was so entirely given up to sorrow and anxiety, to tears and lamentations, that they thought of nothing else. No poet was admitted to the audience chamber to recite elegies ; no preacher appeared to exhort the people. The Sultan's children went out into the streets to excite the compassion of the public, and the sorrow of the piteous sight almost killed all who saw them. This went on till the mid-day prayer ; they were meanwhile busy in washing the body, and putting it in its shroud. We were obliged to borrow money to purchase everything necessary for the funeral, even down to things that cost but a halfpenny, such as the straw to be mixed with the clay (to make the bricks).[1] Ed-Dûl'ai, the jurist, was charged with the task of washing the body. They asked me to superintend this operation, but I was not strong enough to bear it. When mid-day prayer was over, the bier was brought forth, covered with a piece of striped cloth. El-Ḳâdi el-Fâḍel had provided this, and the garments necessary to cover the corpse, and he had been careful to select such as were proper and

---

[1] It is well-known that the tombs of people of high rank are lined with sun-baked bricks.

suitable. When the crowd saw the bier, they raised cries
of sorrow, and the air resounded with their wailings. They
·were so distracted by their grief, that instead of regular
prayer the people could only exclaim. The Ḳâḍi Mohi
ed-Dîn Ibn ez-Zeḳi was the first to say the regular prayer.
The body was then brought round to the palace in the
garden, where the Sultan had lived during his illness, and
it·was buried in the west *Soffa* (or summer-house). It
was a little before the hour of the *'asr* prayer when the
Sultan was committed to the grave. May God sanctify
his soul, and shed light upon his tomb! During the day
his son el - Melek ez - Zâfer went out into the city to
console the people, and to calm the minds of the inhabitants, but the people were too much taken up with weeping
to think of pillaging or making any disturbance. Everyone
was heartbroken. All eyes were filled with tears, and
there were very few who did not weep. After this everyone
went home with death in their very souls, and no one
appeared again (in the streets) throughout the night. We
alone went to visit and to recite passages from the Kurân
over the grave, and renewed our grief. El-Melek el-Afḍal
spent the whole of the day writing to his uncle (el-Melek
el-'Adel) and his brothers, informing them of the sad event,
and offering them his consolation. The next day he held
a public reception to receive the condolences of the people,
and threw open the gate of the city to the doctors of law
and the *'ulema*. Sermons were delivered, but no poet
recited any elegy, and shortly after mid-day the assembly
broke up. The people went to the tomb in crowds from
morning till night, reciting passages from the Kurân, and
imploring God's blessing on him. El-Melek el-Afḍal spent
the remainder of the day dictating dispatches to be sent
to his brothers and his uncle.

> ' So passed those years and men, and seem,
>   Both years and men, to be a dream.'

Behâ ed-Din Abu el-Mehâsan Yûsuf, ibn Râfi, ibn Temîm, kâdi, lawyer, imâm and grand kâdi, with the permission of the (khalif) Commander of the Faithful, adds : It was my plan to gather together information regarding el-Melek en-Nâsr (the prince strong to aid) Abu el-Mozaffer Yûsuf, son of Ayûb, and I have ended my collection at the day of his death—may God have mercy upon him! My object has been to earn the favour of God, and to urge men to pray for him, and to remember what is good.

INDEX.

THE END.

BILLING AND SONS, PRINTERS, GUILDFORD.

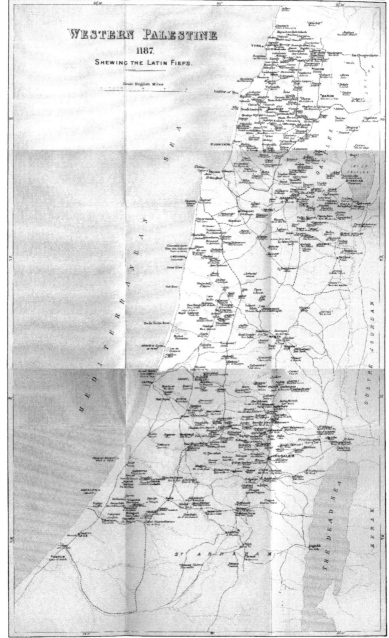

WESTERN PALESTINE

1187.

SHEWING THE LATIN FIEFS.

Scale English Miles

THE LIBRARY
OF THE

𝔓alestine 𝔓ilgrims' 𝔗ext 𝔖ociety.

*In 13 Volumes, with an Index, royal 8vo., bound in cloth, with numerous
Maps and Illustrations. Price for the complete set, £10 10s., to be
obtained only of Mr. George Armstrong, Acting Secretary, Palestine
Exploration Fund, 24, Hanover Square.*

THIS Society was established for the translation and publication, with explanatory notes,
of the various descriptions and accounts of Palestine and the Holy Places, and of the
topographical references in ancient and mediæval literature, from the earliest times to
the period of the Crusades or later. These accounts are written in Greek, Latin,
Arabic, old French, and old German, in the curious records of pilgrimages which
begin with the unknown Pilgrim of Bordeaux, and follow in almost unbroken line to
the present day. After twelve years of work, the programme originally laid down by
the founders has been substantially carried out.

The whole of the pilgrims' texts enumerated in the original prospectus have been
accounted for and issued to members. The price of the whole Library of thirteen
volumes, complete with index, is fixed at Ten Guineas.

Arrangements have therefore been made with the Committee of the Palestine
Exploration Fund for the winding up of the Society on the following terms and
conditions :—

(1) That any member who wishes to complete the Library of Pilgrims may do so,
provided he writes to Mr. George Armstrong, Acting Secretary of the
Palestine Exploration Fund, and paying the difference between his subscrip-
tion and Ten Guineas.

(2) At the end of 1895 the copies that remained were taken over by the
Palestine Exploration Fund.

(3) The stereos will be destroyed and no further copies will be printed. The
edition is, therefore, very small and it is believed that the value of the books
will rapidly go up.

The following is a brief account of the Library, now completed :—

VOLUME I.

a. "**THE CHURCHES OF CONSTANTINE AT JERUSALEM.**"
Pp. 1–38. With illustrations.

> This work contains translations by the Rev. J. H. Bernard, D.D., Fellow of Trinity College,
> Dublin, from Eusebius (Life of Constantine) and the Early Pilgrims. Major-General Sir Charles
> Wilson, K.C.B., D.C.L., has contributed a Preface. Professor Hayter Lewis, F.S.A., has written
> an Introduction and Explanatory Notes. A right understanding of the group of buildings erected
> by Constantine over the holy places is indispensable to the study of the subject. Professor Hayter
> Lewis furnishes a restoration which, if accepted, will be found to clear the ground and remove
> all the difficulties.

β. "**THE BORDEAUX PILGRIM.**" A.D. 333. Translated from the original
Latin by AUBREY STEWART, M.A., late Fellow of Trinity College, Cambridge, and
annotated by Sir C. WILSON. Pp. 1–68, with maps.

> This very interesting Itinerary is the earliest record of a pilgrimage extant. It shows, first of all,
> the route followed by the pilgrims from Gaul; next, it marks the later legends and traditions
> by the fact of their absence; thirdly, it lays down the sites of the sacred places as they were
> pointed out to the pilgrims of the fourth century. A map shows the route of the pilgrims across
> Macedonia and Asia Minor into Syria. Besides the notes there are appendices on the Pool of
> Bethesda, the site of Zion, &c.

(6491)

γ. "**THE PILGRIMAGE OF ST. SILVIA OF AQUITANIA.**" A.D. 385. Translated by the Rev. J. H. BERNARD. Annotated by Sir CHARLES WILSON. Pp. 1-150, with map and illustrations.

This document was discovered in 1883 by Signor Gamurrini, Librarian at Arezzo, in Tuscany. It is extremely doubtful whether the pilgrim really was Silvia, for reasons which the learned translator points out; but the narrative itself is undoubtedly that of the fourth century, and it is only second in interest to that of "The Bordeaux Pilgrim."

δ. "**THE LETTER OF PAULA AND EUSTOCHIUM TO MARCELLA.**" A.D. 361. Translated from the original Latin by AUBREY STEWART. Annotated by Sir CHARLES WILSON. Pp. 1-16.

ε. "**THE PILGRIMAGE OF THE HOLY PAULA, BY ST. JEROME.**" A.D. 382. Translated from the original Latin by AUBREY STEWART. Annotated by Sir CHARLES WILSON. Pp. 1-16, with map.

VOLUME II.

α. "**THE EPITOME OF ST. EUCHERIUS ABOUT CERTAIN HOLY PLACES,**" A.D. 440, and the "Breviary, or Short Description of Jerusalem." Translated from the original Latin by AUBREY STEWART. Annotated by Sir CHARLES WILSON. Pp. 1-23.

Eucherius was Bishop of Lyons, A.D. 434-450. The "Epitome" was probably written down from the description of travellers. The "Breviary" is a description of Jerusalem about the year 530.

β. "**THEODOSIUS.**" A.D. 530. Translated from the original Latin by the Rev. J. H. BERNARD, D.D., Fellow of Trinity College, Dublin. Annotated by Sir CHARLES WILSON. Pp. 1-20.

Nothing is known about the author of this tract. The date of his work is some time in the first half of the sixth century. He is one of the most interesting of our pilgrims.

γ. "**THE BUILDINGS OF JUSTINIAN BY PROCOPIUS.**" A.D. 560. Translated from the original Greek by AUBREY STEWART. Annotated by Sir CHARLES WILSON and Professor HAYTER LEWIS. Pp. 1-178, with maps and illustrations.

This most remarkable history of the buildings erected by Justinian has never before been translated into English. It is now presented with numerous architectural plans and drawings, and with notes by Hayter Lewis, F.S.A., late Professor of Architecture at University College.

δ. "**THE HOLY PLACES VISITED BY ANTONINUS MARTYR.**" A.D. 560-570. Translated from the original Latin by AUBREY STEWART. Annotated by Sir CHARLES WILSON. Pp. 1-44, with a map.

Like the Bordeaux Pilgrim, Antoninus has left behind him an Itinerary of an actual journey, with interesting particulars of the legends attached to the holy places.

VOLUME III.

α. "**THE PILGRIMAGE OF ARCULFUS.**" *Circa* A.D. 670. Translated from the original Latin and annotated by the Rev. JAMES ROSE MACPHERSON. Pp. 1-64, with illustrations.

The history of this work, which is mentioned by Bede, is very curious. Arculfus was Bishop of one of the French dioceses; he went on pilgrimage, and on his return got safely as far as Rome, where he took ship for the port nearest his home, probably Bordeaux. But a storm which arose drove the ship so far out of her course that it was cast away on the western coast of Scotland, and Arculfus found himself the guest of Adamnan, Abbot of the monastery in Iona. Here he related his adventures and described the holy places. Adamnan took down his descriptions and had them carefully rewritten and copied. The work includes a rough drawing of the Holy Sepulchre.

β. "**THE VENERABLE BEDE ON THE HOLY PLACES.**" Pp. 27.

This work was composed as a kind of compendium of previous writers on the same subject.

γ. "**THE HODŒPORICON OF ST. WILLIBALD.**" *Circa* A.D. 754. Translated from the original Latin by the Right Rev. the LORD BISHOP OF CLIFTON. Followed by the "**ITINERARY OF ST. WILLIBALD.**" Pp. 1-58, with two maps.

Willibald was the first English pilgrim to the Holy Land of whom any account has come down to us. He was the son of one Richard, *rex Anglorum*, but of which petty kingdom is not known. His mother, Winna, was a connection of Ina, King of Wessex. This Richard—St. Richard—was buried at Lucca, where his tomb was visible in 1645. Winna was also sister of Wynfrith, known as St. Boniface, Apostle of Germany.

δ. MUKADDASI, "DESCRIPTION of SYRIA, including PALESTINE."
A.D. 485. Translated from the Arabic and annotated by GUY LE STRANGE.
Pp. 1–116, with a map.

This is the first complete translation into English that has been made of this important Arabic
geography of the Holy Land.

ε. "THE ITINERARY OF BERNARD THE WISE." A.D. 870. Translated from the original Latin by the Rev. J. H. BERNARD. Pp. 1–14.

VOLUME IV.

α. NASIR-I-KHUSRAU, "DIARY OF A JOURNEY THROUGH SYRIA AND PALESTINE." Translated from the Persian and annotated by GUY LE STRANGE. Pp. 1–72, with maps.

This work may be taken as a companion to the Geography of Mukaddasi.

β. SAEWULF. A.D. 1103. Translated by the Right Rev. the LORD BISHOP OF CLIFTON. Illustrated by a facsimile of part of the MS. Pp. 1–55, with map and plans.

Of Saewulf himself nothing is known. The date of his pilgrimage is fixed with sufficient certainty
by internal evidence.

γ. "THE PILGRIMAGE OF THE ABBOT DANIEL." A.D. 1106–1107. Annotated by Sir CHARLES WILSON. Pp. 1–108, with illustrations.

The Abbot Daniel was a Russian Abbot. His work is written with great fulness of detail, and
throws abundant light upon the condition of the country very soon after its conquest by the
Crusaders. The narrative has been translated into French, Greek, and German. It now appears
for the first time in English, being translated from the latest and best French version, made by
Madame Sophie de Khitrowo for the Société de l'Orient Latin.

VOLUME V.

α. FETELLUS. A.D. 1130. Translated from the original Latin and annotated by the Rev. JAMES ROSE MACPHERSON, B.D. Pp. 1–58, with a map.

Fetellus was Archdeacon of Antioch about the year 1200. The translation is illustrated by a
contemporary plan of Jerusalem.

β. JOHN OF WURZBURG, A.D. 1160–1170, "DESCRIPTION OF THE HOLY LAND." Translated from the Original Latin by AUBREY STEWART. Annotated by Sir CHARLES WILSON. Pp. 1–72, with a map.

John was a priest at Würzburg, afterwards, according to some editors, Bishop of Würzburg.

γ. JOHANNES PHOCAS. A.D. 1185. Translated from the original Greek by AUBREY STEWART. Pp. 1–36.

Johannes was a native of Crete, the son of one Matthew, who afterwards became a monk. He
himself began by serving in the army under Emmanuel Comnenus. He married, had a son, and
then, imitating his father, assumed the monastic habit. He was already a monk when he made
this pilgrimage.

δ. THEODERICH, "DESCRIPTION OF THE HOLY PLACES." A.D. 1172. Translated from the original Latin by AUBREY STEWART. Pp. 1–86, with plan of Jerusalem.

Nothing certain is known about Theoderich. His description may be compared with that of
John of Würzburg.

ε. TWO LETTERS: ONE FROM SIR JOSEPH DE CANCY, KNIGHT HOSPITALLER TO KING EDWARD I; AND ONE FROM KING EDWARD I TO SIR JOSEPH. Communicated to the Palestine Pilgrims' Text Society by WILLIAM BASEVI SANDERS. Pp. 1–16.

These letters were published in the collection known as "Lettres des Rois et des Reines" of
Champollion Figeac. The Knight Hospitaller's letter is probably the only account of the fighting
in Palestine towards the close of the twelfth century, written by a soldier on the very field. Sir
Joseph was a war correspondent.

VOLUME VI.

α. ANONYMOUS PILGRIMS, I—VIII. Translated by AUBREY STEWART. Pp. 1–86.

These are tracts and journals by unknown authors of the eleventh and twelfth centuries. The
numbers I—VIII are those given by Tobler, whose text has been taken by the translator.

β. "**THE CITY OF JERUSALEM.**" Translated from the old French, with Notes by Lieut.-Colonel C. R. CONDER, R.E., Pp. 1–69.

The "Citez de Jherusalem" is a tract dating after Salah ed Din's conquest of the city, A.D. 1187. To this tract is added the "Account of Palestine" by Ernoul, about the year 1231. A map of Jerusalem and a map of Syria are included.

γ. "**GUIDE-BOOK TO PALESTINE.**" A.D. 1350. Translated from the original Latin by the Rev. J. H. BERNARD. Pp. 1–44.

This guide-book is preserved as a Latin MS. in the Library of Trinity College, Dublin.

δ. **JOHN POLONER, "DESCRIPTION OF THE HOLY LAND."** A.D. 1421. Translated from Tobler's Text by AUBREY STEWART. Pp. 52.

Nothing, except the name, of this pilgrim is known. His account is careful, and he was the first pilgrim who made a map of the country, but this has been lost.

VOLUMES VII—X.

FELIX FABRI, THE WANDERINGS OF. A.D. 1484. Translated from the original Latin by AUBREY STEWART, M.A. In four volumes (1,333 pp. in all), with map and plan.

These volumes consist entirely of the long account by Felix Fabri of his pilgrimage in the year 1484. Felix was a Friar of the Dominican Order, and of the Convent of Ulm. He made the journey to the Holy Land and back twice, and he wrote this account of his travels for the brethren of the convent. By this time the business of conducting pilgrims was as completely organised as it is at present.

We see in the pages of Felix how the pilgrim paid so much there and back; how he was entertained on the voyage; how he was escorted and guided on the pilgrimage; and how he came back again. The work is filled with information, with personal details, and with descriptions of manners and customs.

VOLUME XI.

α. **EXTRACTS FROM ARISTEAS ; HECATÆUS OF ABDERA;** ORIGEN'S TREATISE AGAINST CELSIUS; LECTURES OF ST. CYRIL; THE LIFE OF ST. SABA; DION CASSIUS; PASCHAL CHRONICLE; THE PATRIARCH SOPHRONIUS; THE CHRONICLE OF THEOPHANES; AND THE EUTYCHII ANNALES. Translated from the original by AUBREY STEWART, M.A. Pp. 1–70.

β. **JACQUES DE VITRY.** A.D. 1180. Part of the abbreviated history of Jerusalem. Translated from the original Latin by AUBREY STEWART, M.A.

VOLUME XII.

α. **BURCHARD OF MOUNT SION.** 1280 A.D. Translated from the original Latin by AUBREY STEWART. M.A., with geographical notes by Lieut.-Colonel CONDER, R.E., LL.D., &c. Pp. 1–111.

β. **PART XIV OF BOOK III OF MARINO SANUTO'S "SECRETS FOR TRUE CRUSADERS TO HELP THEM TO RECOVER THE HOLY LAND."** (Written in the year A.D. 1321.) Translated by AUBREY STEWART, M.A., with geographical notes by Lieut.-Colonel CONDER, R.E., LL.D. Pp. 1–73, with three maps.

γ. **LUDOLPH VON SUCHEM'S "DESCRIPTION OF THE HOLY LAND."** (Written in the year A.D. 1350.) Translated from the Latin by AUBREY STEWART, M.A. Pp. 1–142.

VOLUME XIII.

THE LIFE OF SALADIN. By BEHA ED DIN. A.D. 1145–1232. Compared with the original Arabic, and annotated by Lieut.-Colonel CONDER, LL.D., R.E., with a preface and notes by Major-General Sir CHARLES WILSON, K.C.B., F.R.S., R.E., &c. Pp. 1–420, with five maps.

The opportunity of obtaining this perfectly unique collection of books, which will always be indispensable to the student of the geography and the topography of the Holy Land and of Jerusalem, is offered in the first instance to Subscribers to the work of the Fund and the libraries of the United Kingdom and the Colonies. Complete sets are now ready.

753011

Printed in Great Britain by
Amazon.co.uk, Ltd.,
Marston Gate.